D0897879

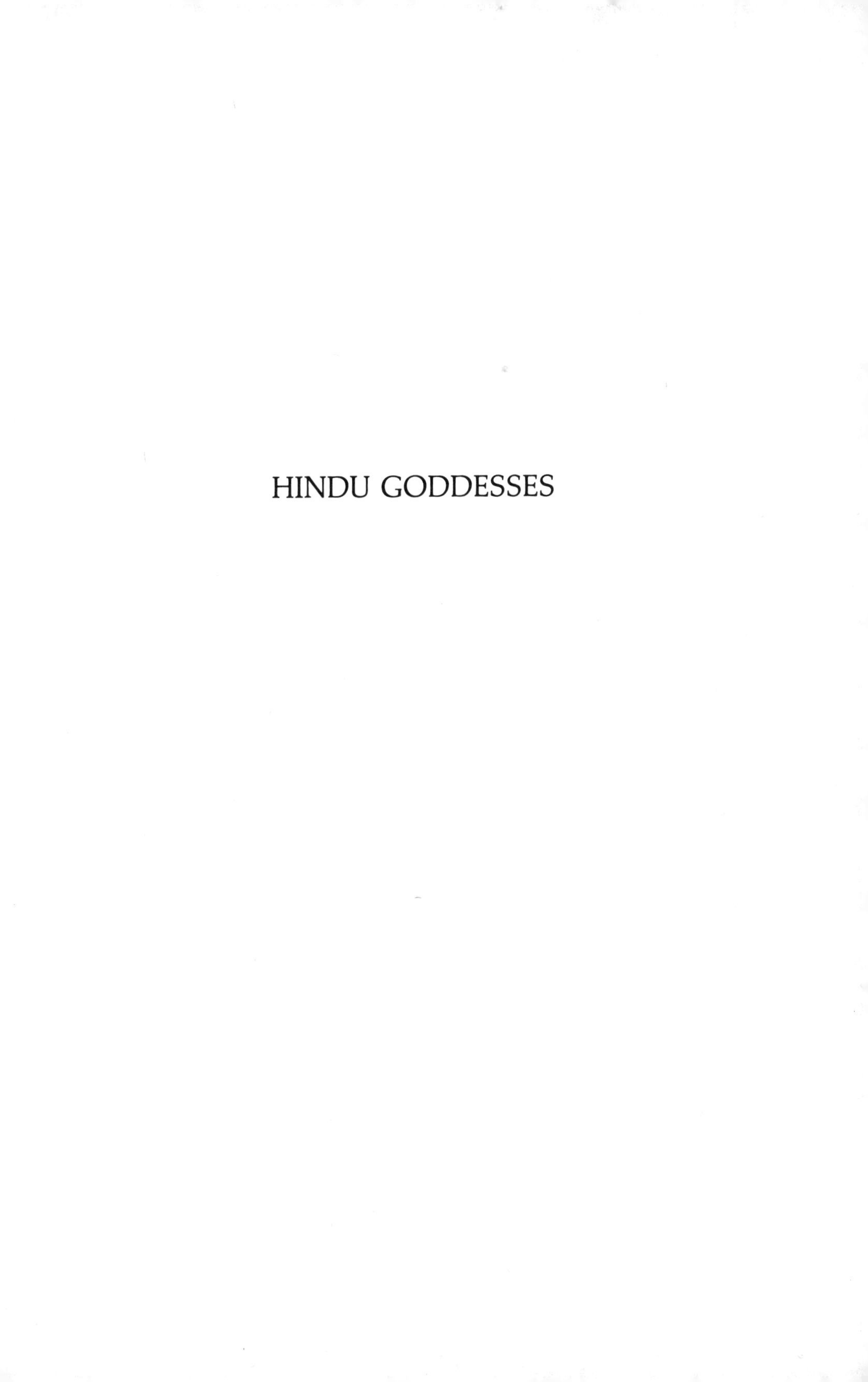

HINDU GODDESSES

HINDU GODDESSES

Visions of the Divine Feminine in the Hindu Religious Tradition

David Kinsley

University of California Press
Berkeley Los Angeles London

University of California Press
Berkeley and Los Angeles, California

University of California Press, Ltd.
London, England

Library of Congress Cataloging in Publication Data

Kinsley, David R.
Hindu goddesses.

Bibliography: p.
Includes index.
1. Goddesses, Hindu. I. Title.
BL1216.2.K56 1985 294.5'211 84-28000
ISBN 0-520-05393-1

1 2 3 4 5 6 7 8 9

Durgā. Contemporary. First published in *L'Art du Mithila* (Paris: Les Presses de la Connaissance/Editions sous le Vent, 1985). Reprinted by permission of Editions sous le Vent.

To Margaret Airey and Louise Crittenden

Contents

INTRODUCTION

One of the most striking characteristics of the ancient and multifaceted Hindu religious tradition is the importance of goddess worship. A considerable number of goddesses are known in the earliest Hindu scriptures, the Vedic hymns. In contemporary Hinduism the number and popularity of goddesses are remarkable. No other living religious tradition displays such an ancient, continuous, and diverse history of goddess worship. The Hindu tradition provides the richest source of mythology, theology, and worship available to students interested in goddesses.

Although there are several books on the history of goddesses in India,[1] there is still need for a survey of Hindu goddesses which not only describes their main appearances and roles but also interprets the significance of each goddess within Hinduism. Some studies have sought to apply this kind of approach to an individual goddess,[2] but to my knowledge there is no study that attempts to describe and interpret all of the central Hindu goddesses. My approach in this book is to provide portraits of the most important goddesses of the Hindu pantheon. I have tried to suggest some of the history of each goddess, to summarize her most important myths and roles, and to show how she illustrates important Hindu (or human) truths. Although common themes occur in the myths, iconography, and functions of several of the goddesses treated in this book, each portrait is intended to be complete and to be appreciated by itself. The book need not be read in its entirety by people interested in just one or two of the Hindu goddesses. My intention is to provide a sourcebook on Hindu goddesses for students of the Hindu tradition and for those interested in goddesses in general.

The book also seeks to be a sourcebook for the growing study of women and religion. In recent years, especially in North America, considerable interest has developed in this field. A whole new area of religious studies now focuses on the ways in which women are perceived in traditional religions and on the status of women within those religions. The importance of goddesses in these traditions is of particular interest to people studying this field. While this book does not attempt to rethink female self-perception in the West in light of Hindu goddesses,[3] I hope that it will make Hindu visions of the feminine accessible to those interested in such pursuits.

This book does not pretend to be exhaustive on the subject of goddesses in Hinduism. The number of goddesses in contemporary Hinduism alone is simply overwhelming. Nor does it pretend to be exhaustive of any of the particular goddesses who are included. Most of the ones I discuss have been known and widely worshiped for hundreds of years, some of them for thousands of years. Rather, this book seeks to represent the nature and diversity of goddess worship in Hinduism and to include all of the most important Hindu goddesses.

My primary sources have been literary and to some extent iconographical. I am aware that my views of the divine feminine in Hinduism may thus be slanted in the direction of the so-called great tradition, namely, the tradition that is high caste, educated, and predominantly male. In many cases, however, the only information that we have on some goddesses and on certain aspects of other goddesses, or the only information that we have from the past, is found in such sources. The chapter on village goddesses, which draws on the work of anthropologists and sociologists, suggests a quite different vision of the divine feminine from those visions underlying the great goddesses of the Hindu pantheon. Nevertheless, this book is out of necessity weighted toward the literary stream of the Hindu tradition, which tends to ignore or look with suspicion on popular worship, in which goddesses are widely revered.

This book does not try to present the material on goddesses in a historical or chronological way. Although I begin the book by discussing the evidence for goddess worship in Vedic literature and close the study with a treatment of village goddesses which suggests a look at the modern situation, the order in which I treat the most important Hindu goddesses is not meant to suggest a historical sequence. Only in very general terms is there a discernible historical progression. The earliest evidence of goddess worship in Hinduism is discussed first. The main sources here are Vedic texts. In these sources no goddesses of great popularity or prominence appear. This situation persists in the Hindu literary tradition till after the epic period. Sometime around the fifth or sixth century A.D., however, several goddesses suddenly appear in iconographic and literary sources in situations of great importance, which indicates an acceptance (or resurgence) of goddess worship in the Hindu tradition. All the individual goddesses that I discuss in the book (with the possible exception of Rādhā) are important from that period to the present: Śrī-Lakṣmī, Pārvatī, Sarasvatī, Sītā, Durgā, Kālī, the Mātṛkās, and such geographical goddesses as Gaṅgā. The central focus of the book is on these goddesses, and chapters treating them form the bulk of the work. The chapters on geographical goddesses, groups of goddesses, and village goddesses shift the focus of the book toward the present and rely more on the work of contemporary observers of Hinduism. Only in this limited way, then, might the book be seen to have a very general historical or developmental character.

My interest in Hindu goddesses dates to 1968, when I went to India to undertake doctoral research on the worship, mythology, and theology of Kṛṣṇa. During that year in India I was struck by the number of goddesses popular in Bengal, by my lack of knowledge about them, and also by the central role that Rādhā played in Bengal Vaiṣṇavism. My first systematic attempt to study a Hindu goddess focused on Kālī.[4] Despite her popularity in the Hindu tradition, very little scholarly research had been done on her. I have found a similar absence of research on other important and popular Hindu goddesses.

I doubt whether this state of affairs results from an inherent male chauvinism among scholars of Hinduism, because a similar gap has existed until recently with regard to most male deities of the Hindu pantheon as well. Perhaps the situation is simply a reflection of what scholars of Hinduism, both Western and Indian, have found interesting and worthy of study. Until recently what was called popular Hinduism did not seem worthy of scholarly attention. Vedic literature and the philosophic schools of the Hindu tradition, in particular, dominated the interests of students of the Hindu religious tradition. Perhaps it seemed to scholars that there was little connection between the philosophic systems of the Hindu tradition and the beliefs, myths, and rituals that occupy the lives of most Hindus. In some cases, I suppose, there is little in common. But it seems clear to me that in most cases popular Hinduism expresses central truths of the Hindu tradition.

The goddesses, who are usually associated with popular Hinduism, often illustrate important ideas of the Hindu tradition, ideas that underlie the great Hindu philosophic visions. Several goddesses, for example, are unambiguously identified with or called *prakṛti*, a central notion in most philosophic systems. *Prakṛti* denotes physical (as opposed to spiritual) reality. It is nature in all its complexity, orderliness, and intensity. The identification of a particular goddess with *prakṛti* is a commentary on her nature. At the same time, descriptions of her nature and behavior are a commentary on the Hindu understanding of physical reality.

Other goddesses express and explore the nature of devotion and the divine-human relationship. Rādā and Sītā, in particular, are important examples of devotional models in the Hindu tradition and suggest a significant feminine dimension to devotion as understood in Hinduism. Lakṣmī expresses Hindu thinking about kingship and the relationship of the ruler to the fertility of the world. The many goddesses associated with geographical features of the Indian subcontinent suggest Hindu thinking about the relationship between sacred space and spiritual liberation.

Most goddesses in their mythologies and natures also express Hindu thinking about sexual roles and relationships. Indeed, goddess mythology to a great extent is probably a means by which the Hindu tradition has thought about sexual roles and sexual identity. Many goddess myths seem to take particular delight in casting females in roles that appear contrary to the social roles of females as described in the *Dharma-śāstras*, the Hindu books on law and society. Several goddesses are cast in untraditional, "masculine" roles that express unconventional, perhaps even experimental, thinking about sexual roles.

Other goddesses, in their myths and personalities, express central tensions that characterize the Hindu tradition. The best example is the mythology of the goddess Pārvatī, in which the tension between dharma, the human tendency to uphold and refine the social and physical order, and *mokṣa*, the human longing to transcend all social and physical limitations, is explored in the relationship between Pārvatī and Śiva.

Although the truths underlying the goddesses may tend to be more world-affirming, more supportive of the emphasis in Hinduism on dharma, whereas the philosophic systems, especially Advaita Vedānta, tend to support the *mokṣa* thrust of the tradition, the great variety of goddesses allows one to find in their mythology and worship expressions of almost every important Hindu theme. In short, a study of Hindu goddesses is not so much a study of one aspect of the Hindu tradition as it is a study of the Hindu tradition itself.

Throughout this book I have tried to resist the theological assumption found in much scholarship on Hindu goddesses that all female deities in the Hindu tradition are different manifestations of an underlying feminine principle or an overarching great goddess. There are, indeed, certain Hindu texts, myths, and traditions that assert this position unambiguously. But to assume that every Hindu goddess in every situation is a manifestation of one great goddess prevents us from viewing such goddesses as Lakṣmī, Pārvatī, and Rādhā as deities containing individually coherent mythologies, theologies, and meanings of their own.

Hindu goddesses are very different from one another. Some have strong maternal natures, whereas others are completely devoid of maternal characteristics. Some have strong, independent natures and are great warriors; others are domestic in nature and closely identified with male deities. Some Hindu goddesses are associated with the wild, untamed fringes of civilization; others are the very embodiment of art and culture. Although the centrality of a great goddess is clear in some texts and although this goddess *does* tend to include within her many-faceted being most important Hindu goddesses,[5] her presence is not indicated in the majority of texts that speak of Hindu goddesses.

The case of the male gods of the Hindu pantheon is similar. Although some texts, philosophic systems, and traditions insist that all gods are actually manifestations of one god, or one ultimate reality, most texts, myths, cults, and traditions understand such deities as Śiva, Viṣṇu, Brahmā, Rāma, Kṛṣṇa, Skanda, Surya, and Gaṇeśa as individually significant gods whose coherent mythologies and theologies are quite unrelated to an overarching great god. Scholars have long recognized this and have written about the male deities as individual beings. Why should we not do the same thing for the many Hindu goddesses? I think that we should, and this is the approach that I have followed in this book.

1

GODDESSES IN VEDIC LITERATURE

The Hindu tradition affirms Vedic literature as the foundation, the sacred source, of Hinduism. This body of literature, which is exceedingly vast and varied, is held to be eternal and alone is classed as *śruti*, "that which is heard," or revelation.[1] It is therefore important to survey this literature even though goddesses do not play a central role in the religion that is central to these texts. Another important reason for looking at Vedic literature is that some scholars have argued that the great goddesses of later Hinduism are in fact the same beings mentioned in the *Vedas*, only with new names.[2]

The *Ṛg-veda*, the oldest and most important Vedic text for a study of goddesses, is a collection of mantras, or hymns, celebrating deities, divine presences, or powers. The hymns were sung by *ṛsis*, great sages who the Hindu tradition affirms did not compose the hymns but heard them directly and then transmitted them, probably in a cultic, sacrificial context. The beings who are celebrated in the hymns of the *ṛsis* are numerous and diverse. The Ṛg-vedic pantheon, moreover, seems highly unstructured, and it is difficult to reconstruct a coherent Indo-Aryan mythology on the basis of the *Ṛg-veda*, which is primarily interested not in describing the mythological deeds of the deities but in praising the gods in a ritual context—a ritual context that unfortunately is also difficult to deduce in any detail.

It is clear nevertheless, that a few deities dominated Ṛg-vedic religion. Agni, Soma, and Indra, all male deities, are praised repeatedly throughout the *Ṛg-veda* and are the most important gods if frequency of occurrence in the hymns is any measure of their significance. Such gods as Varuna, Mitra, Surya, Bṛhaspati, Viśvakarman, and Tvaṣṭṛ are also fairly significant male powers. Although many goddesses are mentioned in the *Ṛg-veda*, none is as central to the Ṛg-vedic vision of reality as Agni, Soma, or Indra, and only Uṣas among the goddesses could be considered on a par with the male deities of the second rank. We should therefore keep in mind while studying the goddesses in the *Ṛg-veda* that although there are many female deities they do not, either individually or collectively, represent the "center" of Ṛg-vedic religion. In most cases they are mentioned infrequently and must have played minor roles compared to the great male gods of the *Ṛg-veda*.

UṢAS

In the *Ṛg-veda* the goddess Uṣas is consistently associated with and often identified with the dawn. She reveals herself in the daily coming of light to the world. A young maiden, drawn in a hundred chariots (1.48), she brings forth light and is followed by the sun (Surya), who urges her onward (3.61). She is praised for driving away, or is petitioned to drive away, the oppressive darkness (7.78; 6.64; 10.172). She is asked to chase away evil demons, to send them far away (8.47.13). As the dawn, she is said to rouse all life, to set all things in motion, and to send people off to do their duties (1.48, 92). She sets the curled-up sleepers on their way to offer their sacrifices and thus renders service to the other gods (1.113). Uṣas gives strength and fame (1.44). She is that which impels life and is associated with the breath and life of all living creatures (1.48). She is associated with or moves with *ṛta*, cosmic, social, and moral order (3.61; 7.75). As the regularly recurring dawn she reveals and participates in cosmic order and is the foe of chaotic forces that threaten the world (1.113.12).

Uṣas is generally an auspicious goddess associated with light (6.64) and wealth. She is often likened to a cow. In *Ṛg-veda* 1.92 she is called the mother of cows and, like a cow that yields its udder for the benefit of people, so Uṣas bares her breasts to bring light for the benefit of humankind (3.58; 4.5). Although Uṣas is usually described as a young and beautiful maiden, she is also called the mother of the gods (1.113.12) and the Aśvins (3.39.3), a mother by her petitioners (7.81), she who tends all things like a good matron (1.48), and goddess of the hearth (6.64).

Uṣas observes all that people do, especially as she is associated with the light that uncovers everything from darkness and with *ṛta*, moral as well as cosmic order. She is said to be the eye of the gods (7.75). She is known as she who sees all, but she is rarely invoked to forgive human transgressions. It is more typical to invoke her to drive away or punish one's enemies. Finally, Uṣas is known as the goddess, reality, or presence that wears away youth (7.75). She is described as a skilled huntress who wastes away the lives of people (1.92). In accordance with the ways of *ṛta*, she wakes all living things but does not disturb the person who sleeps in death. As the recurring dawn, Uṣas is not only celebrated for bringing light from darkness. She is also petitioned to grant long life, as she is a constant reminder of people's limited time on earth (7.77). She is the mistress or marker of time.

PṚTHIVĪ

The goddess Pṛthivī is nearly always associated with the earth, the terrestrial sphere where human beings live. In the *Ṛg-veda*, furthermore, she is almost always coupled with Dyaus, the male deity associated with the sky. So interdependent are these two deities in the *Ṛg-veda* that Pṛthivī is rarely addressed alone but almost always as part of the dual compound *dyāvāpṛthivī*, sky-earth. Together they are said to kiss the center of the world (1.185.5). They sanctify each other in their complementary relationship (4.56.6). Together they are said to be the universal parents who created the world (1.159) and the gods (1.185). As might be expected, Dyaus is often called father and Pṛthivī mother. There is the implication that once upon a time the two were closely joined but were subsequently parted at Varuna's decree (6.70). They come together again when Dyaus fertilizes the earth (Pṛthivī) with rain, although in some cases it is said that together they provide abundant rain (4.56); it is not clear to what extent Pṛthivī should be exclusively associated with the earth alone and not the sky as well.

In addition to her maternal, productive characteristics Pṛthivī (usually along with Dyaus in the *Ṛg-veda*) is praised for her supportive nature. She is frequently called firm, she who upholds and supports all things (1.185). She encompasses all things (6.70), is broad and wide (1.185), and is motionless (1.185), although elsewhere she is said to move freely (5.84). Pṛthivī, with Dyaus, is often petitioned for wealth, riches, and power (6.70), and the waters they produce together are described as fat, full, nourishing, and fertile (1.22). They are also petitioned to protect people from danger, to expiate sin (1.185), and to bring happiness (10.63). Together they represent a wide, firm realm of abundance and safety, a realm pervaded by order (*ṛta*), which they strengthen and nourish (1.159). They are unwasting, inexhaustible, and rich in germs (6.70). In a funeral hymn the dead one is asked to go now to the lap of his mother earth, Pṛthivī, who is described as gracious and kind. She is asked not to press down too heavily upon the dead person but to cover him gently, as a mother covers her child with her skirt (10.18.10–12).

The most extended hymn in praise of Pṛthivī in Vedic literature is found in the *Atharva-veda* (12.1). The hymn is dedicated to Pṛthivī alone, and no mention is made of Dyaus. The mighty god Indra is her consort (1.6) and protects her from all danger (12.1.11, 18). Viṣṇu strides over her (12.1.10), and Parjanya, Prajāpati, and Viśvakarma all either protect her, provide for her, or are her consort. Agni is said to pervade her (12.1.19). Despite these associations with male deities, however, the hymn makes clear that Pṛthivī is a great deity in her own right. The hymn repeatedly emphasizes Pṛthivī's fertility. She is the source of all plants, especially crops, and also nourishes all creatures that live upon her. She is described as patient and strong (12.1.29), supporting the wicked and the good, the demons and the gods. She is frequently addressed as mother and is asked to pour forth milk as a mother does for a son. She is called a nurse to all living things (12.1.4), and her breasts are full of nectar. The singer of the hymn asks Pṛthivī to produce her breasts to him so that he might enjoy a long life. Pṛthivī is also said to manifest herself in the scent of women and men, to be the luck and light in men, and to be the splendid energy of maids (12.1.25).

In sum, Pṛthivī is a stable, fertile, benign presence in Vedic literature. She is addressed as a mother, and it is clear that those who praise her see her as a warm, nursing goddess who provides sustenance to all those who move upon her firm, broad expanse. The *Ṛg-veda* nearly always links her with the male god Dyaus, but in the *Atharva-veda* and later Vedic literature she emerges as an independent being.

ADITI

Although the goddess Aditi is mentioned nearly eighty times in the *Ṛg-veda*, it is difficult to gain a clear picture of her nature. She is usually mentioned along with other gods or goddesses, there is no one hymn addressed exclusively to her, and unlike many other Vedic deities she is not obviously associated with some natural phenomenon. Compared to Uṣas and Pṛthivī, her character seems ill defined. She is virtually featureless physically.

Perhaps the most outstanding attribute of Aditi is her motherhood. She is preeminently the mother of the Ādityas, a group of seven or eight gods which includes Mitra, Aryaman, Bhaga, Varuna, Dakṣa, and Aṁśa (2.27.1). Aditi is also said to be the mother of the great god Indra, the mother of kings (2.27), and the mother of the gods (1.113.19). Unlike Pṛthivī, however, whose motherhood is also central to her nature, Aditi does not have a male consort in the *Ṛg-veda*.

As a mothering presence, Aditi is often asked to guard the one who petitions her (1.106.7; 8.18.6) or to provide him or her with wealth, safety, and abundance (10.100; 1.94.15). Appropriate to her role as a mother, Aditi is sometimes associated with or identified as a cow. As a cow she provides nourishment, and as the cosmic cow her milk is identified with the redemptive, invigorating drink *soma* (1.153.3).

The name Aditi is derived from the root *dā* (to bind or fetter) and suggests another aspect of her character. As *a-diti*, she is the *un*bound, free one, and it is evident in the hymns to her that she is often called upon to free the petitioner from different hindrances, especially sin and sickness (2.27.14). In one hymn she is asked to free a petitioner who is tied up like a thief (8.67.14). In this role as the one who binds and loosens Aditi is similar in function to Varuna, who in fact is one of her sons. Aditi thus plays the role of guardian of *ṛta*, the cosmic-moral order. As such she is called a supporter of creatures (1.136). She supports creatures by providing or enforcing *ṛta*, those ordinances or rhythms that delineate order from chaos.

Aditi is also called widely expanded (5.46.6) and extensive, the mistress of wide stalls (8.67.12), and in this respect one is reminded of Pṛthivī. In fact, Aditi and Pṛthivī become virtually identified in the *Brāhmaṇas*.[3]

SARASVATĪ

The close association between natural phenomena and such Vedic goddesses as Uṣas and Pṛthivī is also seen in the goddess Sarasvatī, who is associated with a particular river. Although scholars have debated precisely which river she was identified with in Vedic times (the Sarasvatī River of that period has since disappeared), in the *Ṛg-veda* her most important characteristics are those of a particular mighty river. Indeed, at times it is not clear whether a goddess or a river is being praised; many references hail the Sarasvatī River as a mighty goddess.

Sarasvatī is called mighty and powerful. Her waves are said to break down mountains, and her flood waters are described as roaring (6.61.2, 8). She is said to surpass all waters in greatness, to be ever active, and to be great among the great. She is said to be inexhaustible, having her source in the celestial ocean (7.95.1–2; 5.43.11). She is clearly no mere river but a heaven-sent stream that blesses the earth. Indeed, she is said to pervade the triple creation of earth, atmosphere, and the celestial regions (6.61.11–12).

She is praised for the fertility she brings the earth. She is praised or petitioned for wealth, vitality, children, nourishment, and immortality, and as such she is called *subhaga* (bountiful). As a fecund, bountiful presence, she is called mother, the best of mothers (2.41.16). As a nourishing, maternal goddess, she is described in terms similar to Pṛthivī: she quickens life, is the source of vigor and strength, and provides good luck and material well-being to those whom she blesses. In one particular hymn she is called upon by unmarried men who yearn for sons. They ask to enjoy her breast that is swollen with streams and to receive from her food and progeny (7.96.4–6; 1.164.49). She is sometimes petitioned for protection and in this aspect is called a sheltering tree (7.95.5) and an iron fort (7.95.1), neither image being particularly fluvial.

Sarasvatī is also closely related to Vedic cult, both as a participant in or witness of the cult and as a guardian of the cult. She is invoked with and associated with the sacrificial goddesses Idā and Bhāratī and with the goddesses Mahī and Hotrā, who are associated with prayer (7.37.11; 10.65.13). She is said to destroy those who revile the gods and to be a slayer of Vṛtra, a demon of chaos.

Sarasvatī is described particularly as a purifying presence (1.3.10). Her waters cleanse poison from men (6.61.3). Along with rivers and floods in general, she cleanses her petitioners with holy oil and bears away defilements (10.17.10)

Anticipating her later nature as a goddess of inspiration, eloquence, and learning, the hymns of the *Ṛg-veda* also describe Sarasvatī as the inciter of all pleasant songs, all gracious thought, and every pious thought (1.3.10–12). In this vein she is similar to the Vedic goddess Vāc (speech), with whom she is consistently identified in the *Brāhmaṇas*.[4]

VĀC

Although the significance of sound and speech as the primordial stuff of creation is primarily a post-Ṛg-vedic concept, it is apparent even in the *Ṛg-veda* that sound, and especially ritual speech, is powerful, creative, and a mainstay of cosmic-ritual order. The goddess Vāc, whose name means "speech," reveals herself through speech and is typically characterized by the various attributes and uses of speech. She is speech, and the mysteries and miracles of speech express her peculiar, numinous nature. She is the presence that inspires the *ṛsis* and that makes a person a Brahman (10.125). She is truth, and she inspires truth by sustaining Soma, the personification of the exhilarating drink of vision and immortality (10.125). She is the mysterious presence that enables one to hear, see, grasp, and then express in words the true nature of things. She is the prompter of and the vehicle of expression for visionary perception, and as such she is intimately associated with the *ṛsis* and the rituals that express or capture the truths of their visions. In an important sense she is an essential part of the religious-poetic visionary experience of the *ṛsis* and of the sacrificial rituals that appropriate those visions.

Perhaps reflecting her role as the bestower of vision, Vāc is called a heavenly queen, the queen of the gods (8.89), she who streams with sweetness (5.73.3) and bestows vital powers (3.53.15). She is described as a courtly, elegant woman, bright and adorned with gold (1.167.3). She is, like most other Vedic goddesses, a benign, bounteous being. She not only bestows on people the special riches of language, she is praised in general terms for giving light and strength; one hymn says that she alone provides people with food. She is, then, more than a kind of artificial construct, a personified abstract. She is a pervasive, nourishing deity who stimulates organic growth as well as providing the blessings of language and vision. She is often invoked as a heavenly cow (4.1.16; 8.89) that gives sustenance to the gods and men. She is also called mother, as it is she who has given birth to things through naming them. Her benign nature is also celebrated for enabling people to see and recognize friends. Bearing her mark of intelligible, familiar speech, one friend may recognize and commune with another (10.71). Thus Vāc is a bounteous cow who provides, first, the lofty, discerning vision of the *ṛsi*; second, the ritual formulas of the priest; and third, the everyday language of people which enables them to establish themselves as a community of friends.

Vāc's character is richly developed in the *Brāhmaṇas* in a series of myths and images that associate her with creation and ritual. Vāc's indispensability in ritual and cult (in which spoken or chanted mantras are essential) is emphasized in myths that tell of how the gods stole her or seduced her away from the demons after the creation of the world and, having obtained her, instituted sacrificial rituals that sustain the creation and produce bounty, life, and immortality for the gods.[5] Without her the divine rituals would not have been possible. In her role as creator, Vāc is said to create the three *Vedas*,[6] and the three *Vedas* are in turn equated with the earth (*Ṛg-veda*), the air (*Yajur-veda*), and the sky (*Sama-veda*).[7] At another place she is said to have entered into the sap of plants and trees, thus pervading and enlivening all vegetation.[8] Prajāpati, the central deity in the *Brāhmaṇas*, is described as initiating creation by impregnating himself by comingling his mind and his speech.[9] Elsewhere it is said that Vāc, having been created by Prajāpati's mind, wished to become manifest, to multiply herself, to extend herself, and so it was that creation proceeded, impelled by Vāc's urge to create.[10]

Vāc plays a significant role in Vedic literature, not only in terms of being mentioned often but also from a theoretical point of view. Theologically it is suggested that she is coeternal with Prajāpati. Although the *Brāhmaṇas* are not consistent, sometimes stating that Vāc is created by Prajāpati, she does seem to have a theologically exalted position in these texts. There are also hints that it is through Vāc, or in pairing with her, that Prajāpati creates. This is different from the role of *śakti* in later Hindu philosophic schools, in which the male counterpart of *śakti* tends to be inactive. Prajāpati toils and desires the creation. Nevertheless, her role in the *Brāhmaṇas* is suggestive of the nature of *śakti* in later Hinduism. Her role vis-à-vis Prajāpati is also suggestive of the theory of *śabda-brahman* (the absolute in the form of sound) and the *sphoṭa* theory of creation (in which the world is created through sound).

NIRṚTI

The Vedic goddesses we have looked at so far are generally benign, protective deities to whom the hymnist typically appeals for wealth, strength, and general well-being. The goddess Nirṛti has no such benign qualities. She is not mentioned very often in the *Ṛg-veda*, but when she is, the concern of the hymn is to seek protection from her or to ask that she be driven away. The scattered references to her seem to equate her with death, ill luck, and destruction. There is just one hymn in the *Ṛg-veda*, 10.59, in which she is mentioned several times, but that hymn sums up very well Nirṛti's nature. After four verses in which renewed life, wealth, food, glorious deeds, youth, and continued long life are requested from the gods, the following refrain is invoked: "Let Nirṛti depart to distant places." Decay, need, anger, cowardice, old age, and death: these are the ways in which Nirṛti manifests herself. She thus represents a dark side to the Vedic vision of the divine feminine.

Later Vedic literature describes Nirṛti in far more detail and mentions her more frequently than does the *Ṛg-veda*. Appropriately, she is said to be dark, to dress in dark clothes, and to receive dark husks for her share of the sacrifice,[11] although once she is said to have golden locks.[12] She lives in the South, the direction of the kingdom of the dead,[13] is associated with pain,[14] and is repeatedly given offerings with the specific intention of keeping her away from the sacrificial rituals and from the affairs of people in general.

RĀTRĪ

The goddess Rātrī is almost always associated with the night. Indeed, she is the night, and as such she is the presence or power that is petitioned by people for comfort and security in the dark hours before the triumphant return of the dawn. Her physical appearance is rarely mentioned, although she is sometimes described as a beautiful maiden along with her sister, Uṣas, the dawn. She is called glorious and immortal and is praised for providing light in the darkness, bedecked as she is with countless stars. Generally she is pictured as a benign being. She is lauded for giving rest to all creatures.[15] She is praised for bestowing life-sustaining dew[16] and with Uṣas is said to provide and strengthen vital powers.[17] She is especially invoked to protect people from dangers peculiar to the night. Thus, she is petitioned to keep wolves away, to protect against thieves,[18] and to protect people from any creature that might do them harm in the night.[19]

Despite Rātrī's usually benign nature, some texts refer to her in negative terms or associate her with things inimical to people. In the *Ṛg-veda* she is chased away by Agni, the god of fire (10.3.1), and also by Uṣas (1.92.11). Rātrī is called barren (1.122.2) and gloomy (10.172.4) in comparison with her bright and bounteous sister, Uṣas. Occasionally she is associated with the very creatures or dangers of the night from which she is elsewhere asked to protect people.[20] Rātrī, then, is not only the guardian of the night, the protectress of people during the dark hours of their rest, but the night itself and those things, both benign and hostile, which inhabit the night.

The majority of references to Rātrī in the *Ṛg-veda* link her with Uṣas, who is said to be her sister. Usually they are said to be two lovely maidens, sometimes twins. Together they are called powerful mothers (1.142.7) and strengtheners of vital power (5.5.6). They are also called weavers of time and mothers of eternal law. In their alternating, cyclical, and endless appearances, they represent the stable, rhythmic patterns of the cosmos in which light and dark inevitably follow each other in an orderly, predictable manner. Together they illustrate the coherence of the created order: the ordered alternations of vigor and rest, light and dark, and the regular flow of time.

MINOR VEDIC GODDESSES

Several goddesses known to the *Ṛg-veda* are mentioned so infrequently that it is difficult to perceive what their distinctive natures might have been. Some of these minor goddesses seem to be synonymous with abundance. Puraṁdhi, Pārendi, Rākā, and Dhiṣaṇā, none of whom is mentioned more than about a dozen times in the *Ṛg-veda*, are all associated with bounty and riches. As is the case with most Vedic goddesses, their natures appear to be benign and their presences revealed through material well-being. Sinivālī is also a benign goddess but is specifically associated with progeny. She is described as mistress of the family, broad-hipped, and prolific. When she is invoked it is to grant the petitioner offspring (2.32; 10.184).

Another group of minor goddesses seems to be associated primarily with the sacrificial cult of the *Ṛg-veda*. When Iḷa, Bhāratī, Mahī, and Hotrā are mentioned, they are almost always being summoned to take their place on the sacrificial grass prior to a ritual. They are also almost invariably grouped with Sarasvatī. Iḷa (Iḍa in the *Brāhmaṇas*) seems to be associated with the sacrificial offering itself, specifically the cow from which many sacrificial objects were taken. She is called butter-handed and butter-footed, which is reminiscent of Agni's description as the presence or deity who actually takes the sacrifice and transmits it to the other gods. While it may be the case that these goddesses are some type of personification of certain aspects of the sacrificial ritual, they are mentioned so seldom, and almost always along with a list of many other deities, that such a conclusion seems only a guess, with the possible exception of Iḷa (Iḍa). Why these goddesses happen to be invoked with Sarasvatī is also not clear. There is no indication that they are associated with rivers, and Sarasvatī is not a particularly important goddess in the sacrificial ritual itself.

The most interesting references in the *Ṛg-veda* to the goddess Sūryā, the daughter of the sun god Surya (sometimes Savitṛ), concern her wedding. All the gods desire her, but her father wishes to give her to Soma; however, it is settled that the first to reach the sun will wed her. The twin gods, the Aśvins, win the race and the bride, and although Sūryā is said to be given to the god Pusan (6.58.4) and to be wooed by Soma (10.85.9), the other references to her in the *Ṛg-veda* almost always describe her as riding in the chariot of her twin husbands, the Aśvins, who after winning her are said to have attained all that they desired (8.8.10). Although it may be implied that Sūryā is fair and desirable, there is actually little description of her beyond the rather obscure picture of her in the *Ṛg-veda* (10.85) in which she seems to be likened to the sacrifice and is said to pervade the cosmos. Her husband in this hymn is Soma; the hymn may be describing the interdependence of Soma and the sacrifice (personified as Sūryā) in the metaphor of a marriage. The Aśvins in this hymn are the groomsmen of her father, which is unusual.

References to Dānu, Saraṇyū, and Saramā are so infrequent and so lacking in description that it is difficult to even speculate on what their distinctive natures might have been. Dānu is identified as the mother of the cosmic demon Vṛtra, who is defeated by the god Indra. She is compared to a cow (1.32.9), although her son, who is described as without hands and feet, is more reptilian in appearance. The word *dānu* is used elsewhere in reference to the waters of heaven; it may be that Dānu was associated with the formless, primordial waters that existed prior to creation, the waters in which Vṛtra hid and which he withheld from creation until they were freed by Indra's mighty deed.

Saraṇyū is the daughter of Tvaṣṭṛ and the sister of Viśvarūpa. She is said to marry the god Vivasvat (10.17.1) and to give birth to twins, Yama and Yamī (the progenitors of the human race). It has been suggested that her nature is essentially impetuous, for her name means "quick, speedy, nimble,"[21] but there are no references to this aspect of her nature in the *Ṛg-veda*. Saramā, whose name has a similar meaning, "the fleet one," is in later literature known as the mother of dogs, a heavenly bitch. But there is no indication of this aspect in the *Ṛg-veda*. In the *Ṛg-veda* her only significant action is to seek out the thieving Paṇis, who have stolen cows, and to act as Indra's messenger to the Paṇis in negotiating the return of the cows. Perhaps her ability to track and cross rivers hints at her later canine nature.

One hymn of the *Ṛg-veda* (10.146) refers to a goddess of the forest, Araṇyānī. From this one hymn we get a rather clear picture of the goddess. She is an elusive figure who vanishes from sight and avoids villages. She is more often heard than seen. She speaks through the sounds of the forest, or one may even hear her tinkling bells. She seems to make her presence known especially at evening, and those who spend the night in the forest sometimes think they hear her scream. She never kills unless provoked by some murderous enemy. She is sweetly scented, is mother of all forest things, and provides plenty of food without tilling.

This goddess is interesting for two reasons. First, she hints at an archaic type of goddess known as the mistress of animals, although there is no specific reference to her guarding animals or providing them for human hunters. Second, she sounds very much like the Yakṣīs of the later Indian tradition, those female beings who dwell in the forest, are worshiped away from the village, and who have, despite their generally benign qualities, certain uncanny characteristics. This late hymn of the *Ṛg-veda* may well be an early literary reference to a Yakṣī or to a goddess modeled on those indigenous creatures of the Indian forests.

Several important Vedic gods are said to have wives or consorts. None of these goddesses is mentioned very often in Vedic literature, but it is important to note their existence in light of subsequent Hindu mythology, in which many of the most important goddesses are consorts of well-known Hindu gods, and also in light of the later Hindu concept of *śakti*. The names of these early goddesses are usually formed simply by the addition of a feminine suffix to the god's name: for example, Indrāṇī, Varunāṇī, Agnāyī, and in later Vedic literature Rudrāṇī (the wife of Rudra). With the exception of Indrāṇī, these goddesses have no independent character of their own. They are mentioned so infrequently and are so lacking in descriptive detail that they appear to be mere minor appendages to their husbands, who are powerful beings in the Vedic pantheon. Indrāṇī is mentioned far more often than any other goddess of this type, but even so it is clear that she is greatly overshadowed by her husband, Indra. She is described as beautiful, and one hymn of the *Ṛg-veda* pictures her as jealous of rivals (10.86). She is also called by the name Śacī, which denotes power and suggests the later idea of *śakti*, the feminine, personified might of the gods of later Hindu mythology. Indeed, in another hymn (10.159) Indrāṇī-Śacī boasts of having won her husband by conquering him and brags that he is submissive to her will. In the same hymn, however, she goes on to petition the gods to rid her of rivals for Indra's favor, and elsewhere she is said to stay at home (3.53.6). Despite suggestions of the later *śakti* idea, then, Indrāṇī is actually a minor goddess of little power, despite her boasts to the contrary.

CONCLUSION

Several conclusions concerning goddesses in Vedic literature are clear. First, none of them rivals the great male gods in these texts. Indeed, Uṣas, the most popular goddess (in terms of the number of times she is mentioned and the number of hymns addressed specifically to her), is only a deity of the third rank. In short, male deities dominate the Vedic vision of the divine.

Second, there is evidence that some of the Vedic goddesses survive in the later Hindu tradition. Pṛthivī persists in later Hinduism and becomes associated with the god Viṣṇu. She is often called Bhūdevī (the goddess of the earth) and appears in myths primarily in the role of supplicant to the gods because of the burden of having to sustain a notoriously evil demon. Sarasvatī also continues to be known in the later tradition and becomes popular primarily as a goddess of learning, wisdom, and culture.[22] Although the goddess Vāc disappears, in later Hinduism Sarasvatī might be said to express Vāc's primary meaning as inspired speech, and the idea of the creation of the world through sound probably finds inspiration in the ideas about Vāc in Vedic literature. Similarly, the idea of *śakti,* though it is not developed in Vedic literature, is suggested in the various consorts of the male deities, especially in Śacī (Indrāṇī). Many of the Vedic goddesses, however, simply disappear in the later Hindu tradition. Uṣas and Aditi, for example, are rarely found in later texts.

Third, many of the most important goddesses of the later tradition are not found at all in Vedic literature or are simply mentioned by name in passing. Such important goddesses as Pārvatī, Durgā, Kālī, Rādhā, and Sītā are unknown in early Vedic literature. Śrī, though she appears in later Vedic literature, is not fully developed and does not occupy the central role that she does in the later tradition. Furthermore, none of the Vedic goddesses is clearly associated with battle or blood sacrifice, both of which are important associations in the myths and cults of several later Hindu goddesses.

Fourth, there is no one great goddess in the Vedic literature. Although some scholars have affirmed her existence in this literature,[23] she quite simply is nowhere mentioned. There is no evidence that the authors of the Vedic texts supposed that all the individual goddesses are manifestations of one great goddess. Since the Vedic texts do not assume a great god who manifests himself in individual gods, I fail to understand why such an assumption should be made for the female deities. It is as if the sexual identification of the goddesses is so overwhelmingly significant that one is justified in lumping them all together. But clearly the goddesses vary greatly and are as distinct from one another as the male gods are from one another.[24] The Mahādevī (great goddess) does not appear until the medieval period in Hinduism, and she is the product of a carefully articulated theology.[25] Although some goddesses *are* conflated with one another at certain times and places and in certain texts, even in Vedic literature,[26] this does not justify imposing on such examples a much later, systematic *śākta* theology.

2

ŚRĪ-LAKṢMĪ

The goddess Śrī, who is also commonly known by the name Lakṣmī, has been known in the Hindu tradition since pre-Buddhist times. She is one of the most popular goddesses in the Hindu pantheon. She has a considerable body of mythology and is widely worshiped by Hindus of all castes throughout India to this day. Since the late epic period (ca. A.D. 400) she has been particularly associated with the god Viṣṇu as his wife or consort. In this role she plays the part of a model Hindu wife, obediently serving her husband as lord. Throughout her history Śrī has been associated with prosperity, well-being, royal power, and illustriousness. In many respects she is the embodiment of these qualities, and it is commonly understood that when these qualities are evident, Śrī herself is present or reveals herself.

THE EARLY HISTORY OF ŚRĪ-LAKṢMĪ

The goddess Śrī-Lakṣmī does not appear in the earliest Vedic literature.[1] The term *śrī*, however, does occur quite often, and it is clear that the meanings of the term are related to the nature of the later goddess Śrī-Lakṣmī. As used in the Vedic hymns the term *śrī* suggests capability, power, and advantageous skills. As an external quality *śrī* suggests beauty, luster, glory, and high rank. The term is especially used in later Vedic literature to refer to the ruling power, dominion, and majesty of kings. As such it seems to be a distinct, disembodied power that is acquired by kings in various ways. It seems to be a power associated more with the office of the king than with the king himself. At one point *śrī* is identified with the cushion upon which the king sits. The idea is that the cushion or seat, *śrī*, ruling power, is temporarily possessed by the current owner of the seat.[2] *Śrī* also refers to riches, prosperity, and abundance in general. In that sense it is something that may be acquired or possessed by anyone. In short, *śrī* refers to most auspicious qualities and suggests general well-being in terms of physical health, material prosperity, bodily beauty, and ruling majesty.

In what may be the earliest myth that speaks of Śrī as a goddess, she is the personification or embodiment of auspicious, particularly royal, qualities.[3] She is born as a result of the austerities of Prajāpati. Seeing Śrī, the other gods covet her qualities and proceed to steal them from her. Ten qualities, or objects, are listed: food, royal power, universal sovereignty, noble rank, power, holy luster, kingdom, fortune, bounteousness, and beauty.[4] In Vedic literature, then, the goddess Śrī's origin seems to be the result of the personification of auspicious qualities, particularly those associated with royal power and riches.

The most detailed picture of Śrī-Lakṣmī in Vedic literature is found in the *Śrī-sūkta,* a hymn in praise of Śrī which is part of an appendix to the *Ṛg-veda* and which is probably pre-Buddhist in date.[5] This is surely one of the earliest hymns to Śrī and associates her with certain symbols and qualities that persist throughout her history in the Hindu tradition. Not surprisingly, and in conformity with the meanings of the term *śrī* in early Vedic literature, Śrī is invoked to bring fame and prosperity (verse 7). She is said to be bountiful and to give abundance (5). She is said to bestow on her worshiper gold (14), cattle, horses (1), and food (10). She is asked to banish her sister Alakṣmī, "misfortune" (5, 6, 8), who appears in such inauspicious forms as need, poverty, hunger, and thirst (8). Royal qualities are suggested when she is described as seated in the middle of a chariot, possessed of the best horses, and delighted by the sounds of elephants (3). In outward appearance she is glorious and richly ornamented. She is radiant as gold, illustrious like the moon, and wears a necklace of gold and silver (1). She is often said to shine like the sun (6, 13) and to be lustrous like fire (4).

An important feature of Śrī in this hymn is her association with fertility, a feature that was not significantly emphasized in earlier usages of the term *śrī* in Vedic literature. In the *Śri-sūkta* she is described as moist (13, 14), perceptible through odor (9), abundant in harvest, and dwelling in cow dung (9). Her son is said to be Kardama, which means mud, mire, or slime (11). Clearly, Śrī is associated with growth and the fecundity of moist, rich soil. Her presence is affirmed to be discernible in the mysterious potency of the earth. Although Śrī's association with agricultural fertility does not play a central role in her later literary history in Hinduism, this aspect of Śrī remains important to this day at the village level. Villagers, particularly women, are reported to worship Śrī in the form of cow dung on certain occasions, and this form of worship is actually enjoined in the *Nīlamata-purāṇa.*[6]

The hymn to Śrī also mentions two objects that come to be consistently associated with Srī throughout her history: the lotus and the elephant. She is seated on a lotus, is the color of a lotus (4), appears like a lotus (5), is covered with lotuses, and wears a garland of lotuses (14). Throughout her history, in fact, Śrī-Lakṣmī is often called Padmā and Kamalā, "lotus." The popularity of the lotus in Indian art and iconography, both Buddhist and Hindu, suggests a complex and multivalent meaning associated with the lotus.

As expressive of Śrī-Lakṣmī's nature two general meanings seem apparent. First, the lotus is a symbol of fertility and life which is rooted in and takes its strength from the primordial waters.[7] The lotus symbolizes vegetative growth that has distilled the life-giving power of the waters into embodied life.[8] The lotus, and the goddess Śrī-Lakṣmī by association, represents the fully developed blossoming of organic life. At the macrocosmic level the lotus might be taken as a symbol of the entire created world. The lotus growing from the navel of Viṣṇu marks the beginning of a new cosmic creation. The frequent use of the lotus in Tantric *maṇḍalas* also points to the lotus as a symbol of the entire created universe.[9] The lotus suggests a growing, expanding world imbued with vigorous fertile power. It is this power that is revealed in Śrī-Lakṣmī. She is the nectar (the *rasa*) of creation which lends to creation its distinctive flavor and beauty. Organic life, impelled as it is by this mysterious power, flowers richly and beautifully in the creative processes of the world.

The second meaning of the lotus in relation to Śrī-Lakṣmī refers to purity and spiritual power. Rooted in the mud but blossoming above the water, completely uncontaminated by the mud, the lotus represents spiritual perfection and authority. A common motif in Hindu and Buddhist iconography is the lotus seat. The gods and goddesses, the buddhas and bodhisattvas, typically sit or stand upon a lotus, which suggests their spiritual authority. To be seated upon or to be otherwise associated with the lotus suggests that the being in question—god, buddha, or human being—has transcended the limitations of the finite world (the mud of existence, as it were) and floats freely in a sphere of purity and spirituality. Śrī-Lakṣmī thus suggests more than the fertilizing powers of moist soil and the mysterious powers of growth. She suggests a perfection or state of refinement that transcends the material world. She is associated not only with royal authority but with spiritual authority as well and she combines royal and priestly powers in her presence.

One of the most popular and enduring representations of Śrī-Lakṣmī shows her flanked by two elephants in the so-called Gaja-Lakṣmī images. The elephants shower her with water from their trunks or empty pots of water over her.[10] The elephants seem to have two related meanings. First, they most likely represent fertilizing rains. An ancient Hindu tradition says that the first elephants had wings and flew about the sky. In fact, they were clouds and showered the earth with rain wherever they went. These sky elephants, however, were cursed by a sage when they landed on a tree under which he was meditating and broke his concentration. Stripped of their wings, they henceforth had to remain earthbound. But these earth elephants are still regarded as cousins of clouds, and their presence is supposed to attract their "white cousins," who bring fertilizing rains with them.[11] The flanking, showering elephants in images of Śrī-Lakṣmī reinforce one of the principal themes that we have already noted in her nature, her association with the fertility of crops and the sap of existence. Where Lakṣmī is, there elephants are, and where elephants are, there is produced the fertilizing potency of rain.

Second, elephants suggest royal authority. Kings in ancient India kept stables of elephants, which formed their heavy artillery in military campaigns. Kings often traveled on elephants in ceremonial processions, and in general elephants were considered an important indication of royal authority. Kings in ancient India were also believed to be responsible for rain and the fertility of the crops.[12] To ensure the kings' beneficial influence, it was probably important for them to keep several elephants for their power to bring fertilizing rains. In the king and the elephant, then, are brought together two central themes in the imagery of Śrī-Lakṣmī, royal authority and fertility.

Images of Śrī with elephants are probably meant to portray the act of royal consecration. The central ritual action of the Vedic royal-consecration ceremony, the Rājasūya, was the *abhiṣekha* ritual, in which the king was consecrated by having auspicious waters poured over him to bestow authority and vigor on him.[13] Insofar as the elephants in these images of Lakṣmī may be understood to be portraying the *abhiṣekha*, they bestow the qualities of fertility and royal authority on Lakṣmī, herself the source of these very qualities.[14] The elephants, furthermore, are often shown standing on lotuses,[15] the preeminent symbol of Lakṣmī. The elephants thus imbue Lakṣmī with those very qualities that she possesses to the highest degree, and she in turn infuses the elephants with the same qualities. A more highly charged image denoting the increase of royal authority, fertility, and vigor would be difficult to imagine.[16]

ŚRĪ-LAKṢMĪ IN LATER HINDUISM

In the course of her history Śrī-Lakṣmī has been associated with male deities, each of whom is significant in suggesting characteristics of the goddess. Some texts associate her with the god Soma. Śrī-Lakṣmī, along with several other deities, attends Soma after he performs a great royal sacrifice.[17] The association of Lakṣmī with Soma is noteworthy for two reasons. First, in attending him after he has assumed the position of royal authority, she demonstrates one of her main characteristics, that of bestowing royal authority or being present where royal authority exists. Second, Soma is well known as the lord of plants and is often identified with the fertile sap that underlies vegetative growth. It is fitting that Śrī-Lakṣmī, who is similarly identified, should be associated with Soma in these texts. They complement and reinforce each other as symbols of the sap of existence.

A few texts say that Lakṣmī is the wife of Dharma. She and several other goddesses, all of whom are personifications of certain auspicious qualities, were given to Dharma in marriage by her father, Dakṣa. This association seems primarily to represent a thinly disguised "wedding" of Dharma (virtuous conduct) with Śrī-Lakṣmī (prosperity and well-being). The point of the association seems to be to teach that by performing dharma one obtains prosperity.[18]

A more interesting and fully developed association is between Śrī and the god Indra.[19] Several myths relate the theme of Indra's losing, acquiring, or being restored to the boon of Śrī-Lakṣmī's presence. In these myths it is clear that what is lost, acquired, or restored in the person of Śrī is royal authority and power. Indra is traditionally known as the king of the gods, the foremost of the gods, and he is typically described as a heavenly king. It is therefore appropriate for Śrī to be associated with him as his wife or consort. In these myths Śrī-Lakṣmī appears as the embodiment of royal authority, as a being whose presence is essential for the effective wielding of royal power and the creation of royal prosperity.

Several myths of this genre describe Śrī-Lakṣmī as being persuaded to leave one ruler for another. She is said, for example, to dwell with the demons Bali and Prahlāda. While she dwells with these demons they are demons in name only. Under her gracious presence they rule their kingdoms righteously, society operates smoothly, the lands are fertile, and the demon kings themselves shimmer with sublime inner and outer qualities. When she leaves Prahlāda, at Indra's request, the demon loses his luster and fears for his well-being.[20] Along with Śrī, the following

Śrī-Lakṣmī. Pratapaditya Pal, *Indo-Asian Art from the John Gilmore Ford Collection* (Baltimore: Walters Art Gallery, 1971), fig. 19. Reprinted by permission of the Walters Art Gallery.

qualities depart from Prahlāda: good conduct, virtuous behavior, truth, activity, and strength. With Śrī's departure, Prahlāda is left emptied of his royal might and his predilections toward virtuous conduct.

The myths concerning the demon Bali make clear the same association between Lakṣmī and victorious kings. In these myths Bali defeats Indra. Lakṣmī is attracted to Bali's winning ways and bravery and joins him, along with her attendant auspicious virtues. In association with the auspicious goddess, Bali rules the three worlds with virtue, and under his rule the three worlds prosper.[21] Only when Viṣṇu, at the request of the dethroned gods, tricks Bali into surrendering the three worlds does Śrī-Lakṣmī depart from Bali, leaving him lusterless and powerless.

Śrī-Lakṣmī's presence ensures a king more than ruling power. One of the myths associating her with Indra tells us that when she sat down next to Indra he began to pour down rain and the crops grew abundantly. Cows gave plenty of milk, all beings enjoyed prosperity, and the earth flourished.[22] Indra is associated with fertility in Vedic texts, and well into the medieval period festivals celebrated in his honor associated him with the fertility of the crops. From the earliest Vedic texts he is described as wielding the *vajra* (the thunderbolt) as his favorite weapon, and to the present day he is associated with bringing rain. As a couple, Śrī-Lakṣmī and Indra are a clear example of a common type of divine pair in the world's religions: a female earth goddess and a male sky/rain god. Together they combine to generate the fertility that is necessary to all life. In the *Vedas* the deities Dyaus and Pṛthivī are a good example of this type of divine pair and the reciprocal roles they play in generating and sustaining life. Śrī-Lakṣmī in association with Indra seems to represent a later version of the Dyaus-Pṛthivī couple. In this symbiotic relationship the male deity, associated with the sky, is said to fertilize the female deity with his rain. Indra also seems to have had phallic associations in his identification with the plow, and it seems appropriate that he would become associated with a goddess representing the fertile earth.[23]

Some traditions also associate Śrī-Lakṣmī with the god Kubera. Kubera is lord of the Yakṣas, a race of supernatural beings who in general frequent forests and uncivilized areas, and he is in particular the possessor and distributor of wealth. He is the possessor and guardian of the earth's treasures in the form of gems. Śrī's relationship to Kubera is appropriate insofar as each of them is preeminently associated with prosperity and wealth.[24] Where wealth and abundance are, one or the other deity, and probably both, is certain to be found. So the two deities become associated as a couple.[25] Śrī's identification through Kubera with the Yakṣas, in addition, emphasizes her identity with the mysterious powers of growth and fertility.[26] Yakṣas often play the part of fertility symbols in Indian art and generally are associated iconographically with trees, vines, and vegetative growth. They are often shown embracing trees, leaning against trees,[27] or pouring forth vegetation from their mouths or navels.[28] The identification of Śrī-Lakṣmī, the goddess who embodies the potent power of growth, with the Yakṣas is natural. She, like them, involves herself and reveals herself in the irrepressible fecundity of plant life.

Śrī-Lakṣmī's association with so many different male deities and with the notorious fleetingness of good fortune earned her a reputation for fickleness and inconstancy.[29] In one text she is said to be so unsteady that even in a picture she moves and that if she associates with Viṣṇu it is only because she is attracted to his many different forms (*avatāras*).[30] By the late epic period (ca. A.D. 400), however, Śrī-Lakṣmī becomes consistently and almost exclusively associated with Viṣṇu; as his wife she becomes characterized by steadfastness.[31] It is as if in Viṣṇu she has finally found the god she was looking for and, having found him, has remained loyal to him ever since.

Mythologically Śrī-Lakṣmī's association with Viṣṇu comes about in the context of the churning of the milk ocean by the gods and demons, who seek the elixir of immortality (*amṛta*). Lakṣmī does not figure at all in some versions of this story,[32] but in others she is the central focus of the myth.[33] What seems clear is that a myth concerning the churning of the ocean to obtain various valuable things existed from ancient times in India and that at some point Lakṣmī's origin was felt to be related to this mythological event. The interesting question is why Lakṣmī's origin makes sense in the context of this myth and how her association with Viṣṇu comes about in later versions of the myth.

An ancient Indian tradition asserts that creation proceeds from an infinite body of primordial water, that the world or the multitude of universes of later Hinduism ultimately arises from and rests upon this limitless expanse of waters. In its unrefined state this watery world is chaotic, or at least formless and overwhelming. Creation, or ordered existence, only takes place when this watery mass is somehow agitated, processed, or refined in such a way that form and growth take place. Within the watery formlessness resides the potency or essence of life, *rasa*, *amṛta*, or *soma*. When this potency is released by the primordial waters, creation can proceed.[34] The churning of the ocean by the gods and demons is intended to obtain the nectar of immortality, the essence of creative power that will make the churners immortal and grant them their status as ordainers and overseers of creation. The act of churning dramatically illustrates the process of distilling the essence of the primordial waters. By churning milk one thickens and refines it until it yields a richer substance—butter. Similarly, the milk ocean when churned yields valuable essences, among them, in most later versions of the myth, the goddess Śrī-Lakṣmī.

The role or place of Śrī-Lakṣmī in this myth of creation seems fairly clear. Although the nectar of immortality is described as a separate entity that arises from the churning of the ocean, Śrī-Lakṣmī has many and obvious associations with the sap of existence that underlies or pervades all plant and animal life. She herself represents the miraculous transformation of the formless waters into organic life.[35] The extent to which Śrī-Lakṣmī is necessary to the ongoing created order, and hence may be identified or associated with the essence of the creation, is indicated in some later variants of the myth. These versions tell us that Śrī-Lakṣmī disappears from the three worlds when Indra insults her. As a result, all sacrifices cease to be performed, all austerities are discontinued by the sages, all generosity ends, the sun and moon lose their brilliance, the gods lose their strength, and fire loses its heat.[36] In the absence of the goddess the worlds become dull and lusterless and begin to wither away. When she returns, the worlds again regain their vitality, and the society of humans and the order of the gods regain their sense of purpose and duty.

Most variants of the myth say that Śrī-Lakṣmī's association with Viṣṇu took place at the churning of the ocean. The relationship of Śrī and Viṣṇu seems appropriate in the context of the myth and at a general symbolic level in several ways. During her early history Śrī's attraction to powerful rulers among the gods (and demons) was firmly established. In the churning-of-the-ocean myth Viṣṇu is clearly the dominant god. He oversees the entire operation and actually makes the churning possible by providing two indispensable participants: Vāsuki, the cosmic serpent who is used as the churning rope, and the cosmic tortoise, upon which the churning stick rests. Furthermore, both Vāsuki and the tortoise are actually forms of Viṣṇu himself. When Śrī comes forth from the ocean, she is naturally attracted to Viṣṇu, the god who is obviously superior to the others. Conversely, Viṣṇu, as the divine overseer of the event, is the natural recipient of the treasures that result from the churning. As the master of ceremonies, Viṣṇu is entitled to the lovely goddess who emerges as a result of the efforts of the gods and demons.

Viṣṇu's royal nature is also significant in Śrī's association with him. By the medieval period (fifth through thirteenth century A.D.) Viṣṇu is considered the divine king par excellence. He is described as dwelling in a heavenly court, Vaikuṇṭha, and he is depicted iconographically as a mighty king. His primary role as king is to institute and maintain dharmic order. This he does by means of his various *avatāras*, who intervene in the world from time to time to combat the forces of disorder. Viṣṇu, however, is also present wherever righteous kings rule and maintain order. He maintains order on the earth, that is, through certain human agents, namely, righteous kings.[37] We noted earlier that kings cannot rule without the authority that is bestowed by Śrī. Where she is present, royal authority waxes strong. Where she is absent, would-be rulers become weak and ineffectual. The association of Śrī with Viṣṇu, the supreme divine king, as her husband is therefore fitting. She follows him when he becomes part of his human agents—the righteous kings—and she bestows on these kings her royal power, prosperity, and fertility. In effect Viṣṇu designates his human agents, and Śrī then empowers them, enabling them to be effective maintainers of Viṣṇu's cosmic scheme.

As Viṣṇu's wife, Lakṣmī loses her fickle nature. As the great cosmic king's queen she is depicted as a model Hindu wife, loyal and submissive to her husband. One of her most popular iconographic depictions shows her kneeling before Viṣṇu to massage his feet.[38] In her early history Śrī-Lakṣmī was strongly associated with growth and fecundity as manifested in vegetation. A teeming vitality animated her presence, a power that gave birth inexhaustibly to life. In her association with Viṣṇu her character seems more restrained. Although she does not lose her association with fertility and growth, she seems more clearly involved in or revealed in the order of dharma that her husband creates and oversees. When Viṣṇu assumes his various *avatāras* in order to uphold dharma, she incarnates herself as his helpmate, assuming an appropriate form as his spouse or consort. She thus assists and accompanies him in his world-maintaining role. The *Viṣṇu-purāṇa* says:

> . . . as Hari descends in the world in various shapes—so does his consort Śrī. Thus when Hari was born as a dwarf, as a son of Aditi, Lakṣmī appeared from a lotus; . . . when he was Rāghava, she was Sītā, and when he was Kṛṣṇa, she became Rukminī. In the other descents of Viṣṇu, she is his associate. If he takes a celestial form, she appears as divine; if a mortal, she becomes a mortal too, transforming her own person agreeably to whatever character it pleases Viṣṇu to put on. (1.9.142–146)[39]

Her role as a model wife typifies her more subdued nature. She is occupied in this role with household order. Indeed, she is said to cook food at the Jagannātha temple for those who come for *prasād*.[40] In her role as an ideal wife she exemplifies the orderliness of human society and human relations. Iconographic representations of Viṣṇu and Śrī together typically show her as subservient to Viṣṇu, which is in harmony with sexual roles as described in the *Dharma-śāstras*. She is usually shown as considerably smaller than Viṣṇu and as having only two arms instead of the four arms that she usually has when shown alone. Her submissive position is nicely conveyed in an image of the divine pair from Bādāmī in which Viṣṇu sits on a high stool while Lakṣmī sits on the ground and leans on him, her right hand placed on his knee.[41]

Reflecting her increasing association with social order, several texts locate Lakṣmī's presence in righteous behavior, orderly conduct, and correct social observance. She is said, for example, to live with those who tell the truth and are generous.[42] She dwells with those who have clean bodies and are well dressed,[43] who eat with moderation, who have intercourse with their wives on a regular basis (something prescribed in the Hindu law books), and who cover themselves when asleep.[44] In the *Mahābhārata* she says: "I dwell in truth, gift, vow, austerity, strength and virtue" (12.218.12). Orderly social relations and traditional social virtues attract Śrī-Lakṣmī, herself a model of social decorum as Viṣṇu's wife.

In association with Viṣṇu, Lakṣmī provides a picture of marital contentment, domestic order, and satisfying cooperation and beneficial interdependence between male and female. Most iconographic representations picture the pair as a smiling, happy couple; they are often shown touching each other intimately. In images of the Lakśmī-Nārāyaṇa type, Lakśmī is usually depicted seated on Viṣṇu's left thigh. Her right hand is around his neck while his left arm encircles her waist.[45] Sometimes the two are shown holding hands,[46] and it is not unusual for them to be shown gazing into each other's eyes.

The intimacy of the two, indeed, their underlying unity, is dramatically shown in images in which they are merged into one bisexual figure, Viṣṇu constituting the right half of the figure and Lakṣmī the left.[47] The interdependence of the two is the subject of a long passage in the *Viṣṇu-purāṇa*. There Viṣṇu is said to be speech and Lakṣmī meaning; he is understanding, she is intellect; he is the creator, she is the creation; she is the earth, he the support of the earth; she is a creeping vine, he is the tree to which she clings; he is one with all males, and she is one with all females; he is love, and she is pleasure (1.8.15 ff.).[48]

ŚRĪ-LAKṢMĪ IN THE PĀÑCARĀTRA AND ŚRĪ VAIṢṆAVA SCHOOLS

Śrī-Lakṣmī's association with Viṣṇu eventually leads to her playing important roles in the mythological and philosophic visions of the Pāñcarātra and Śrī Vaiṣṇava schools of thought and devotion. In the

Pāñcarātra school Lakṣmī comes to play the central role in the creation and evolution of the universe as the *śakti* of Viṣṇu. In the Pāñcarātra creation scenario Viṣṇu remains almost entirely inactive, relegating the creative process to Lakṣmī. After awakening Lakṣmī at the end of the night of dissolution, Viṣṇu's role in the creation of the universe is restricted to that of an inactive architect whose plan is put into effect by a builder. Lakṣmī alone acts, and the impression throughout the cosmogony is that she acts independently of Viṣṇu, although it is stated that she acts according to his wishes.[49]

The practical effect of Viṣṇu's inactive role in creation is that he becomes so aloof that Lakṣmī dominates the entire Pāñcarātra vision of the divine. In effect she acquires the position of the supreme divine principle, the underlying reality upon which all rests, that which pervades all creation with vitality, will, and consciousness. The *Lakṣmī-tantra*, a popular Pāñcarātra text, says that Lakṣmī undertakes the entire stupendous creation of the universe with only a one-billionth fraction of herself (14.3). So transcendent is she, so beyond the ability of the mind to circumscribe her, that only a miniscule fraction of her is manifest in the creation of the universe. Elsewhere in the same text she describes herself as follows:

> Inherent in the (principle of) existence, whether manifested or unmanifested, I am at all times the inciter (potential element of all things). I manifest myself (as the creation), I ultimately dissolve myself (at the time of destruction) and I occupy myself with activity (when creation starts functioning).
>
> I alone send (the creation) forth and (again) destroy it. I absolve the sins of the good. As the (mother) earth towards all beings, I pardon them (all their sins). I mete everything out. I am the thinking process and I am contained in everything. (50.65.67)[50]

Functionally Lakṣmī has taken over the cosmic functions of the three great male gods of the Hindu pantheon: Brahmā, Viṣṇu, and Śiva. In the Pāñcarātra vision, by creating, sustaining, and periodically destroying the universe, she completely dominates the divine, mythological landscape. She also occupies the central position as the object of devotion, the dispenser of grace, and the final bestower of liberation (50.131–132). Throughout the *Lakṣmī-tantra* it is she, not Viṣṇu, who is described as the object of devotion, the one who grants all desires and whose special mantra embodies salvific power. It is she, not Viṣṇu, whose form is described in detail and presented as the supreme object of meditation.[51]

Although Lakṣmī has been elevated functionally to a position of supreme divinity in the Pāñcarātra school and has been identified with various philosophic absolutes, she retains her nature as the goddess who both imbues creatures with illustriousness and well-being and pervades the creation as the sap of existence. At one point in the *Lakṣmī-tantra,* for example, she says of herself: "Like the fat that keeps a lamp burning I lubricate the senses of living beings with my own sap of consciousness" (50.110). Elsewhere she is said to be *prakṛti* (50.64, 96), the principle of nature in Hinduism which spontaneously creates all material reality. *Prakṛti* is the creation's dynamic aspect, which tends toward multiplication, diversification, and specificity.[52] It is an active, fertile principle that is similar to the sap of existence with which Lakṣmī is identified during her early history. Lakṣmī's identification throughout the Pāñcarātra system with Viṣṇu's *śakti* is also a way of declaring her association with fertile power. Although the idea of *śakti* is somewhat more refined and inorganic than *rasa, soma, amṛta,* or the powers of fertility, *śakti* does suggest unambiguously the idea of vigorous, dynamic power associated with life and growth. Despite her promotion, therefore, it is clear that Lakṣmī retains her essential character as a dynamic, positive force that underlies growth, fertility, and prosperity.

A central presupposition in Śrī Vaiṣṇavism is that Viṣṇu, the supreme deity for this school, is always accompanied by, attended by, or otherwise associated with his consort Śrī. But Śrī does not play the central cosmological role as she does in the Pāñcarātra school. In Śrī Vaiṣṇavism Viṣṇu is clearly the central actor on the mythological stage and is equated with the highest philosophic principles. Śrī-Lakṣmī has nevertheless acquired an important role among certain Śrī Vaiṣṇava theologicians as the mediator between Viṣṇu and his devotees.[53]

The central aim of the Śrī Vaiṣṇava devotee is to cultivate and perfect his inherent duty, which is to love his Lord, and in so loving his Lord to identify himself with God as closely as possible. The writings of some philosophers of the school say that in approaching the Lord and requesting purity and grace Lakṣmī acts as a mediating presence between the devotee and Viṣṇu. For Vedānta Deśika (A.D. 1268–1368) Lakṣmī seems indispensable in approaching Viṣṇu. She is described in his writings as a gracious mother who willingly intervenes with her often-stern husband on the devotee's behalf. "O Mother who resides on the lotus, hearken to my plea! I babble like a child; with your grace (*prasāda*) make the Lord who is your beloved listen to my [petition]."[54] Elsewhere he writes: "The mother . . . , whose nature is such that her grace is unmixed with any anger and is showered on all, does not spare any effort to make the punishing Lord be pleased with those who have committed several faults. She cools the heat of His anger, which arises because He is the father."[55]

Other Śrī Vaiṣṇava theologians share this view of Śrī as an intermediary between the sinful devotee and Viṣṇu. Periyavāccān Pillai (b. 1228) describes a conversation between Śrī and Viṣṇu in which Śrī acts as a devotee's advocate. Viṣṇu speaks first: "'Since beginningless time this human has been disobeying my laws and has been the object of my anger. If I condone his faults and accept them patiently, instead of punishing him, I will be disregarding the injunctions of *Śastra*.' Śrī replies: 'But if you punish the human, instead of saving him, your quality of grace will not survive.'"[56] In this passage Śrī takes the side of the devotee by arguing that if Viṣṇu does not save the sinner his reputation as merciful will be threatened. Her argument plays on Viṣṇu's own conception of himself. Elsewhere Śrī is said to resort to distracting Viṣṇu from his intention to punish a devotee by enticing him with her beauty. Maṇavāḷa Māmunikaḷ (1370–1443) says of Śrī: "She uses her beauty to entice and enslave [the Lord]. She makes eyes at Him, she lets her dress slip down a little."[57]

In Śrī Vaiṣṇavism Śrī embodies divine compassion. While Viṣṇu, as the mighty king of heavenly Vaikuṇṭha, may seem so awesome and transcendent as to be all but unapproachable to the lowly devotee, Śrī provides an aspect of the divine that is eminently approachable. In this role as mediator she considerably softens the Śrī Vaiṣṇava vision of the divine and allows feelings of intimacy and warmth to pervade the devotee's devotional moods toward the divine.

It should be noted that in Śrī Vaiṣṇavism the goddess is still renowned for bestowing all good things. Indeed, she is sovereignty.[58] It is fitting that as the mediator between Viṣṇu and the devotee she bestows on the devotee the most cherished of all boons, her husband's grace.

THE WORSHIP OF ŚRĪ-LAKṢMĪ

Śrī-Lakṣmī is today one of the most popular and widely venerated deities of the Hindu pantheon. Her auspicious nature and her reputation for granting fertility, luck, wealth, and well-being seem to attract devotees in every Indian village. "All of India's back country is the dominion of Lakṣmī, the goddess of the lotus. . . . She accompanies every mile traveled through central India, every visit to a temple. . . . Her likenesses are omnipresent on the walls and pillars, lintels and niches of sanctuaries, regardless of the deity of their specific dedication."[59]

Lakṣmī is worshiped throughout the year in a variety of festivals,[60] and she is the constant object of *vratas*, "religious vows," by means of which devotees ask her for a blessing in return for undertaking some act of devotion or piety on her behalf. The blessings requested vary according to the devotee and according to whether the *vrata* is undertaken during a festival in which certain kinds of blessings are traditional. The most common boons, however, have to do with marital fidelity or the longevity of one's spouse, the fertility of the crops, and the bestowal of material well-being.

The most important festival in which Lakṣmī is worshiped today (except in Bengal) is Dīpavalī (Dīvalī), which is held in the late autumn. Three important and interrelated themes are seen in this festival: Lakṣmī's association with wealth and prosperity, her association with fertility and abundant crops, and her association with good fortune in the coming year. Perhaps the most obvious indication that Lakṣmī is identified with prosperity is her popularity among merchants. During this festival it is customary for people, especially businessmen, to worship their account books.[61] It seems to be clearly understood by merchants that wealth will not arise without Lakṣmī's blessing or presence.

Agricultural motifs are also fairly clear in this festival as it is celebrated in some places. Cultivators are enjoined to worship their crops (which at this time of year have been harvested) and offer sacrifices of goats and sheep. "Moreover they visit the dunghill which is collected for manuring the field for future crops and fall prostrate and beg to fertilize their lands and to procure abundant crops. In the Decan and in Orissa the heap of cowdung is also worshiped by every householder on this day."[62]

Lakṣmī is also associated with crops and food in Orissa on the occasion of the Kaumudī-pūrṇimā festival. On these days women invoke Lakṣmī on a mound of new grain and recall a story in which Lakṣmī's disappearance results in the disappearance of crops and food and her return prompts the return of abundance.[63] The worship of Lakṣmī during Durgā Pūjā is also significant in terms of her association with agriculture. Although Durgā Pūjā as it is celebrated today in India is not primarily a harvest festival, there are many indications that the renewed vigor of the crops is still an aspect of the festival.[64]

The association of Lakṣmī with good fortune in the coming year is also a significant aspect of the Dīpavalī festival. During this festival end-of-the-year motifs are clear. At this time ghosts of the dead are said to return,[65] Bali, a demon, is said to emerge from the underworld to rule for three days, goblins and malicious spirits are about,[66] and gambling, profligate spending, and boisterous activity are commanded. Throughout the festival Lakṣmī is invoked to ward off the dangerous effects of the returned dead and the emergent demon king and his hosts and to bless the gambler with success that will betoken his good luck during the entire coming year. The banishment of Alakṣmī, the female spirit associated with bad luck and misfortune, is also associated with this festival. It is believed in many places that Alakṣmī is driven away for the coming year by lighting lamps, which is one of the most beautiful and characteristic features of this festival, and by making noise with pots and pans or instruments.[67] On another occasion in Bengal an image of Alakṣmī is made and ceremoniously disfigured by cutting off its nose and ears, after which an image of Lakṣmī is installed to signify the presence of good luck in the future.[68]

During Dīpāvalī people also replace the small clay images of Lakṣmī and Gaṇeśa which are revered in many homes and shops in North India. Lakṣmī's association with Gaṇeśa, the elephant-headed son of Śiva and Pārvatī, is prominent in North India. Indeed, it is more common to see Lakṣmī beside Gaṇeśa than beside Viṣṇu in most parts of North India today. This association represents the continuity of some important themes in Lakṣmī's character. Lakṣmī is often associated with elephants, the Gaja-Lakṣmī motif being ancient and consistent throughout her history. Her current association with Gaṇeśa probably suggests meanings similar to those inherent in the Gaja-Lakṣmī scenes. In addition, Gaṇeśa is a Yakṣa-type figure, associated with riches and good luck. It is appropriate that, like Kubera, he should be revered along with Lakṣmī, herself the embodiment of wealth and luck.

Another aspect of Lakṣmī is the focus of a summer festival in honor of her and Viṣṇu. This festival signals the point at which Viṣṇu is believed to fall asleep for several months. It is common to pray to Viṣṇu at this time to prevent the loss of one's wife or husband. In this festival Lakṣmī and Viṣṇu are the embodiment of marital harmony and bliss. Lakṣmī is understood to be the faithful, loving, and obedient wife.[69] At another festival in honor of her and Viṣṇu, Lakṣmī plays the role of a jealous wife and protector of the home. Viṣṇu is said to go off with another consort during this festival, and Lakṣmī, in anger over his unfaithfulness, breaks his vehicle and temporarily locks him out of their home (the temple).[70]

3

PĀRVATĪ

Rivaling Śrī-Lakṣmī in popularity in the Hindu tradition is the goddess Pārvatī. Unlike Śrī-Lakṣmī, Pārvatī has hardly any independent history of her own. Her identity and nature and nearly all her mythological deeds are defined or acted out vis-à-vis her consort/husband, the great ascetic god Śiva. Since epic times, when Pārvatī first appeared as a significant deity, she has been identified as a reincarnation of the goddess Satī, Śiva's first wife, who committed suicide because of an insult to her husband. So closely associated is Pārvatī with Satī that the two goddesses are usually treated as one, and their mythologies eventually come to sound very much alike. Both are defined in terms of their courtship and marriage with Śiva, and Pārvatī's mythology is almost always treated as the ongoing story of Satī.

In classical Hindu mythology the raison d'être of Pārvatī's (and Satī's) birth is to lure Śiva into marriage and thus into the wider circle of worldly life from which he is aloof as a lone ascetic living in the wilds of the mountains. This goddess (in both persons, as Satī and Pārvatī) represents the complementary pole to the ascetic, world-denying pole in the Hindu tradition. In her role as maiden, wife, and later mother (as Pārvatī) she extends Śiva's circle of activity into the realm of the householder, where his stored-up energy is released in positive ways.

As is the case with Lakṣmī, Pārvatī comes to represent certain philosophic absolutes in her association with Śiva. As his *śakti*, or embodied power, she becomes identified with the creative force of the cosmos and the underlying potency of things. Also like Lakṣmī she takes on a paradigmatic role as the ideal wife and mother. In fact, the act of suttee (Sanskrit *satī*), in which a Hindu widow immolates herself on her husband's funeral pyre as a final and consummate act of loyalty and devotion, is patterned on the goddess Satī, from whom the name of the act is derived. In some schools of Śaivism Pārvatī also assumes the role of ideal devotee. Finally, in Śaiva Siddhānta, a southern school of Śaivism, Pārvatī sometimes takes on the role of Śiva's embodied grace and thus comes to play a role somewhat similar to Śrī-Lakṣmī's role in Śrī Vaiṣṇavism.

EARLY REFERENCES TO PĀRVATĪ

The goddess Satī-Pārvatī does not appear in Vedic literature. Several references to Śiva's sister or wife do occur in Vedic texts, but the names for these deities only connect them tenuously, if at all, to the later Satī-Pārvatī. A being named Ambikā (a common epithet for several goddesses in the later tradition, especially Durgā) is called Śiva's sister in one passage,[1] while in another text she is said to be his consort.[2] Elsewhere in Vedic literature Śiva's wife is called Rudrāṇi. These references are never detailed enough to enable us to know if the deity named has any resemblance to the later, fully developed goddess Satī-Pārvatī.

The *Kena-upaniṣad* contains a goddess named Umā Haimavatī (3.12). This is one of the most common names of the later Satī-Pārvatī, but this reference does not associate the goddess with Śiva, nor does it associate her with mountains, except by name (Haimavatī meaning "she who belongs to Himavat," who is the Himalaya Mountains personified as a god). Her primary role in this text is that of a mediator who reveals the knowledge of *brahman* to the gods. She appears in the text suddenly, and as suddenly disappears. It is little more than conjecture to identify her with the later goddess Satī-Pārvatī, although quite naturally later writers do make the identification when describing the exploits of Satī or Pārvatī. To devotees of the goddess this early Upaniṣadic reference provides proof of her venerable history in the Hindu tradition; later texts that extol Śiva and Pārvatī retell the episode in such a way as to leave no doubt that it is Śiva's spouse who appears before the assembled gods in order to reveal to them the truth that Śiva is absolute reality and underlies them all.[3]

Both textual and archaeological evidence for the existence of Satī-Pārvatī appear by the epic period (400 B.C.–A.D. 400). Both the *Rāmāyaṇa* and *Mahābhārata* present Satī-Pārvatī as the wife of Śiva. Several important mythological events, though not told in detail, are referred to in the epics, and it is clear that the central themes of the later, developed mythology featuring Satī-Pārvatī are known to the epic writers. The *Mahābhārata* describes the destruction of Dakṣa's sacrifice (10.18; 12.274), mentions the birth of Kārttikeya and the defeat of the demon Tāraka (3.213–216; 13.83–84), and describes Śiva and Pārvatī as dwelling in the Himalayas, where they sport and play dice (13.140.43–44). Although not numerous, some images of Pārvatī, or at least a goddess associated with Śiva or a Śaiva symbol, appear on coins in this period.[4]

THE MYTHOLOGY OF SATĪ

Not until the plays of Kālidāsa (fifth to sixth century A.D.) and the *Purāṇas* (A.D. 350 through the thirteenth century) do we find the central myths of Satī and Pārvatī told in detail. Two distinct goddesses emerge in this fully developed mythology: Satī, the daughter of Dakṣa, who becomes Śiva's first wife, and Pārvatī, daughter of Himavat and his wife Menā, who is a reincarnation of Satī and becomes Śiva's second wife. Although the mythologies of the two goddesses (or the two lives of the same goddess) are similar in many details (and have probably influenced each other), each goddess (or each life of the goddess) is distinctive enough to be treated separately.

The goddess Satī sets out to win the great god Śiva for her husband.[5] In some versions of the myth Satī's quest is instigated by the god Brahmā, Dakṣa's father, who wants to humiliate Śiva because Śiva had insulted him earlier.[6] Śiva had laughed at Brahmā when Brahmā had lusted after his own daughter, and Brahmā vowed to seduce Śiva into the pangs of sexual passion. Elsewhere the motive is more vague. In the Rudra-saṁhitā of the *Śiva-purāṇa* Brahmā says that if Śiva is not involved in the created world the creation will lack auspiciousness (in fact Śiva means "auspicious") (2.11.27) or that the creation simply will not be able to continue (2.11.43). In fact, these latter reasons for involving Śiva in sex and marriage are more helpful in understanding the underlying meanings of the Satī myths than the more common reason of Brahmā's getting even with Śiva.

Satī is usually described as beautiful, but in most versions of her mythology it is her devotion and asceticism that attract Śiva's attention (2.16.39, 44, 50). At times she is tested by Śiva, or an agent of Śiva, but she always persists, and in the end Śiva grants her a boon for her austerities. She asks to marry him, and he agrees, having discovered at some point the presence of desire (*kāma*), which has made her extremely desirable. She insists upon a proper marriage involving rituals and guests, despite Śiva's impatience. Brahmā acts as the divine priest, and the two are duly married. At some point in the narrative, tension begins to develop between Dakṣa (Satī's father) and Śiva. The tension arises from Dakṣa's distaste for Śiva's odd appearance and strange habits. As a world renouncer Śiva does not behave according to the ways of the world, and his appearance is most unconventional (2.26.14–16).

Śiva and Satī retire to Śiva's mountain abode and dally there for many years. Dakṣa in the meantime plans a great sacrifice and invites all divine beings of any importance, except Śiva and Satī. Śiva is quite undisturbed by this deliberate snub. Satī, however, is furious at the insult to her husband (2.28). She storms off to her father's abode, where he snubs her. Outraged by the way in which her father has treated Śiva, she kills herself (2.29–30). Hearing the news of Satī's death, Śiva becomes angry and creates Vīrabhadra and, in some versions of the mythology, other fierce beings. The demons proceed to Dakṣa's sacrificial arena, where they defeat the assembled divine hosts and destroy the sacrifice. Dakṣa himself is usually said to be killed in the battle (2.32–37). Most versions of the story then tell of the reinstitution of the sacrifice and the resuscitation of Dakṣa (2.42.21–31). Śiva is included in the sacrifice along with the other gods, and the sacrifice proceeds smoothly (2.43).

In some versions of the myth, either before or after the reinstitution of the sacrifice, Śiva discovers Satī's body. He picks her up and, sobbing in grief, carries her about the universe. This causes cosmic disruptions, and Viṣṇu is summoned to end Śiva's grief. Viṣṇu follows the grieving Śiva about and gradually slices bits and pieces from Satī's body until nothing remains. The pieces of her corpse fall to the earth; wherever a bit of her body lands a sacred place, called a *pīṭha,* is established, where goddesses of various names and types become the objects of worship.[7] Realizing that Satī's corpse has disappeared, Śiva ends his grief and returns to his mountain retreat, where he retires into ascetic aloofness. In some versions Śiva comes to earth in search of Satī. Finding her yoni established at Kāmarūpa in Assam,[8] Śiva assumes the form of the *liṅga* and plunges himself into her, where the two remain conjoined permanently.[9]

In general terms the underlying theme or meaning of this myth seems fairly clear. The theme of Śiva's alternation between the poles of asceticism and eroticism[10] and the creative (sometimes destructive) tension that results from this alternation pervades the entire corpus of Śiva mythology. Underlying the mythology seems to be the assumption that Śiva's stored-up potency, which accumulates during asceticism, should be released into the world to invigorate or enliven creation. In the logic of this mythology Satī plays the role of luring Śiva from ascetic isolation into creative participation in the world. This theme is further developed and embellished in the Pārvatī cycle of myths in which Śiva actually becomes involved in an ongoing family situation and becomes a divine householder.

In the Satī myths Śiva's involvement in the world is most clearly suggested in the destruction and reinstitution of the sacrifice and his descent to earth to dwell with Satī's yoni in the form of the liṅga. In the Vedic tradition Śiva is an ambiguous deity at best. He has many fearsome and inauspicious qualities, and when offerings are made to him they are made outside inhabited areas.[11] The theme in the Satī myths of Śiva's exclusion from the sacrifice thus has considerable historical justification. Śiva was undoubtedly a non-Āryan indigenous deity who was looked upon with considerable suspicion by the Brahman custodians of the sacrificial cult. His association with world renunciation, asceticism, and the powers of fertility as symbolized by the liṅga probably marked him as a deity who belonged to the fringes of society from the point of view of the Brahman establishment. The antagonism between Śiva and Dakṣa probably reflects this underlying conflict. Eventually, of course, Śiva became one of the most important and dynamic deities in the Hindu pantheon. The reinstitution of the sacrifice with Śiva included among those who partake of it probably represents his incorporation into established Brahman religion.

Satī's devotion to Śiva and her outrage at the way he is treated eventually bring him within the sacrificial arena. He is indifferent to the doings of Dakṣa until Satī kills herself because of the insult to her husband. Satī comes from the realm of established religion, the order of dharma, and marries into the realm of asceticism, thus combining in herself the two opposing worlds. When she kills herself she precipitates a clash between these two worlds, between Dakṣa and Śiva, which is initially destructive but ultimately beneficial and creative. Satī's role is as a mediating influence between the two religious poles, both affirmed to be central, in the Hindu tradition. Her ability to involve Śiva in the sacrifice makes Śiva, previously aloof from the world, accessible in the sacrificial cult, the primary point of which is to maintain and nourish the creation.

Satī performs a similar feat when her body is cut to pieces and falls to earth. By following her to earth and embedding himself in her yoni, Śiva is literally brought down to earth. Where previously he dwelled in the mountains and engaged in austerities, indifferent to the ongoing creation, he now is fully engaged in the creation as symbolized by the conjunction of the yoni and liṅga. Satī, in her role as mediator, has succeeded in involving the great ascetic god in the creation by transforming him into the great god of sexual power and vigor. Again, her role has been primarily that of making Śiva accessible to the world by attracting him to her in the form of the yoni. While Śiva may continue to perform heroic asceticism in his mountain retreat in one of his several forms, he continues to be accessible to the world in the form of the liṅga. In the myths of Satī, this is her triumph.

The establishment of centers of worship on earth where pieces of Satī's body fell repeats the theme of making the divine accessible vis-à-vis Satī herself. In this myth the earth is sacralized (the earth being understood primarily as the Indian subcontinent). The earth itself is seen as the body of the goddess Satī. She becomes the earth and as such is made accessible to her devotees or to those who seek her powers.[12]

Satī's death is thus transformative. Through her death she provokes Śiva into a direct conflict with the sacrificial cult and then an accommodation with it. In this way Śiva is brought within the circle of dharma, within the order of established religion. Similarly, Satī's corpse, or pieces of her corpse, sacralize the earth. In dying she gives herself up to be accessible on earth to those who need her power or blessing. In transplanting or transforming herself into the earth, she also brings into the sphere of human society the invigorating power of Śiva in the form of the liṅga.

The Satī myth again reminds us of the archaic type of divine pair in which a male deity is associated with the sky and a female deity with the earth. Their union or marriage is necessary for life to be generated and sustained. Satī's identification with the earth and Śiva's identification with the distant Himalayas and their subsequent union as yoni and liṅga seem to be a variant on this theme. The main point of the Satī mythology is to bring about a marriage between these two deities so that creation may continue and prosper. The concluding chapter of Satī's mythology makes it clear that this has been accomplished. In the form of the yoni (all individual women) she attracts Śiva (all individual men) eternally.

The goddess Satī is also associated with the practice of widow suicide in Hinduism.[13] During the medieval period the custom of widows' burning themselves to death on their husbands' funeral pyres became accepted as the act of a faithful wife. The word *satī* (suttee) came to be applied to this practice. The term means "faithful wife," and its relation to the goddess Satī is clear in the sense that Satī is portrayed as a faithful wife of Śiva. It is not altogether clear, however, that Satī's suicide provides the mythological paradigm for suttee. Satī's suicide, although provoked by an insult to her husband, causes her husband considerable grief and outrage. The whole point of suttee is for the widow to follow her dead husband. She affirms in this act that she cannot live without him, that her entire identity is bound up with his. Satī's suicide, although perhaps the act of a faithful wife who cannot endure insults to her husband, results not in her maintaining a relationship with her husband but in her breaking that relationship.

THE MYTHOLOGY OF PĀRVATĪ

Pārvatī's name, which means "she who dwells in the mountains" or "she who is of the mountain," and her many epithets, such as Śailasutā (daughter of the mountain peaks), Giriputrī (daughter of the mountains), Girirājaputrī (daughter of the king of the mountains), Girīśā (mistress of the mountains), identify her with mountainous regions. It is quite possible that Pārvatī's early history and origin may lie with a goddess who dwelled in the mountains and was associated with non-Āryan tribal peoples. Such goddesses are sometimes referred to in Sanskrit texts.[14] Such a goddess would be an appropriate mate for Śiva, himself a deity who dwells in mountainous regions and on the fringes of society. Indeed, Pārvatī herself is described as a female forester in the company of Śiva, who is also described as a forester in the *Mahābhārata* (3.40.1–5). For the most part, however, Pārvatī's mythology does not describe her as a goddess associated with wild places or with people living on the fringes of culture. She is not usually included in lists of the group of goddesses called Mātṛkās (mothers), who are described as bloodthirsty, the bringers of disease, the speakers of foreign tongues, and fond of inaccessible places (9.45). If Pārvatī ever was associated with such a tradition, almost every trace of that identity is gone by the time we find her mentioned in the Hindu literary tradition.

Pārvatī's mythology is almost entirely dominated by her association with Śiva. Her nature, too, develops or is characterized by her relationship with Śiva. Although in certain Śākta texts she is said to transcend Śiva and to subsume within herself all male deities[15] or in other texts is identified with certain philosophic absolutes, for the most part these are late embellishments on her mythology and character and are the result of a theological effort on the part of devotees partial to various goddesses (the Śāktas) to assert the underlying unity of all goddesses.[16] Pārvatī is primarily the goddess who is Śiva's wife, she who won him as her husband after heroic efforts and who persuaded or provoked him into creating a child, who was necessary for the preservation of the world.

Most renditions of Pārvatī's mythology explain the goddess's birth as necessary for producing a child of Śiva.[17] The demon Tāraka has been granted the boon of being invincible to any creature except a child of Śiva. As Śiva is an ascetic, the gods have to find a woman or goddess capable of luring Śiva into a sexual encounter or marriage. Pārvatī is usually understood to be a reincarnation of Satī and sometimes is described as consenting to be reborn for the help of the gods when she is petitioned by them.[18] In some versions Pārvatī (and Satī) are understood to be manifestations of the supreme reality in the universe, the Mahādevī (great goddess), who condescends to incarnate herself for much the same reason that Viṣṇu does in his *avatāras*, to maintain the balance between dharma and *adharma*.[19] Sometimes the reason given by Pārvatī for her birth is her desire to reward Menā, the wife of Himavat, for her great devotion to Pārvatī in her former life as Satī.[20]

Pārvatī, then, is born to Himavat and Menā. She is usually described as dark and in some versions is given the name Kālī, "the dark one," because of her complexion.[21] She is also described as very beautiful. In some accounts she shows a keen interest in Śiva from the outset, repeating his name to herself and taking delight in hearing about his appearance and deeds. While she is a child a sage comes to her home and after examining the marks on her body predicts that she will marry a naked yogi.[22] When it becomes clear that she is destined to marry Śiva, her parents are usually described as feeling honored. Pārvatī is delighted, and she is sometimes said to remember Śiva from her past life as Satī.

At some point prior to or during Pārvatī's attempts to attract Śiva's attention for the purpose of marriage, the god Kāma is sent by the gods to awaken Śiva's lust. When he attracts Śiva's attention with sounds and scents of spring and tries to perturb Śiva with his intoxicating weapons, Śiva burns him to ashes with the fire from his middle eye. Although the gods and Pārvatī lament Kāma's destruction, it is clear later in the story that Kāma's powers were not destroyed when he was burned, for Śiva eventually falls in love with Pārvatī and recreates Kāma in bodily form at the request of Kāma's wife, Rati.[23]

Pārvatī persists in her quest to win Śiva as her husband by setting out to perform austerities. One of the most effective ways to achieve what a person wants in traditional Hinduism is to perform *tapas*, "ascetic austerities." If one is persistent and heroic enough, one will generate so much heat (also called *tapas*) that the gods will be forced to grant the ascetic a wish in order to save themselves and the world from being scorched. Pārvatī's method of winning Śiva is thus a common approach to fulfilling one's desires. It is also appropriate, however, in terms of demonstrating to Śiva that she can compete with him in his own realm, that she has the inner resources, control, and fortitude to cut herself off from the world and completely master her physical needs. By performing *tapas* Pārvatī abandons the world of the householder and enters the realm of the world renouncer, Śiva's world. Most versions of the myth describe her as outdoing all the great sages in her austerities. She performs all the traditional mortifications, such as sitting in the midst of four fires in the middle of summer, remaining exposed to the elements during the rainy season and during the winter, living on leaves or air only, standing on one leg for years, and so on.[24] Eventually she accumulates so much heat[25] that the gods are made uncomfortable and go to Śiva to persuade him to grant Pārvatī's wish so that she will cease her efforts.[26]

In some versions of the myth Pārvatī is tempted by an agent of Śiva, or by Śiva himself in disguise. She is told that Śiva's appearance is terrible and that his habits are uncivilized and inauspicious.[27] She is urged to desist from her desire to marry such a distasteful character. Pārvatī is never dissuaded from her purpose by these temptations, and as a result of her steadfastness Śiva agrees to marry her.

The marriage is duly arranged and elaborately undertaken. Śiva's marriage procession, which includes most of the Hindu pantheon, is often described at length. A common motif during the marriage preparations is Menā's outrage when she actually sees Śiva for the first time. She cannot believe that her beautiful daughter is about to marry such an outrageous-looking character; in some versions Menā threatens suicide and faints when told that the odd-looking figure in the marriage procession is indeed her future son-in-law.[28]

After the two are married they depart to Mount Kailasa, Śiva's favorite dwelling place, and immerse themselves completely in sexual dalliance, which continues uninterruptedly for long periods of time. Their lovemaking is so intense that it shakes the cosmos, and the gods become frightened.[29] In some versions the gods are also frightened at the prospect of what a child will be like from the union of two such potent deities. They fear the child's extraordinary powers. For whichever reason (sometimes the gods are simply impatient), the gods interrupt Śiva and Pārvatī's lovemaking. As a result Śiva spills his semen outside Pārvatī. The potent seed, which is extremely fiery and hot, passes from one container to another, the container varying in different versions of the myth, until it is finally contained in a suitable place, often the Ganges River, where it is incubated and born as the child Kārttikeya. Kārttikeya eventually finds his way back to his father and mother and by defeating the demon Tāraka rescues the world. Pārvatī accepts the child as her own, and sometimes we are told that her breasts ooze milk in affection for the child when she first sees him.[30]

A second child completes the divine family of Śiva and Pārvatī when Gaṇeśa is born. Pārvatī, desiring privacy, wishes to have a child of her own who will protect her from unwanted intrusions. She creates Gaṇeśa from the dirt and sweat of her body and commands him to guard the entrance to her house against any intruder. When Śiva himself tries to enter her apartments, Gaṇeśa refuses to admit him. Śiva becomes angry and decapitates the boy. Pārvatī is furious and demands that Gaṇeśa be restored to life. Śiva duly restores him to life by replacing his human head with an elephant head and puts him in charge of all his troops and heavenly attendants.[31]

For the most part Śiva and Pārvatī's married and family life is portrayed as harmonious, blissful, and calm. In iconography the two are typically shown sitting in happy, intimate embrace.[32] As a family the four deities are also typically shown in harmonious association.[33] A scene of the divine family in a painting from the Kangra school of art shows the foursome seated around a fire. Kārttikeya and Pārvatī are helping each other thread a garland of skulls, while Śiva and Gaṇeśa play idly with one of Śiva's serpent ornaments.[34] Many devotional hymns describe intimate family details, such as Kārttikeya's playing with Śiva's skull ornaments or mistaking Śiva's crescent moon for a lotus bud.

> He touches the garland made of skulls
> in hope that they are geese
> and shakes the crescent moon with eagerness to grasp
> a lotus filament.
> Thinking the forehead-eye a lotus flower,
> he tries to pry it open.
> May Skanda thus intent on play
> within his father's arms protect you.[35]

Śiva and Pārvatī do argue and insult each other from time to time. Bengali accounts of Śiva and Pārvatī often describe Śiva as an irresponsible, hemp-smoking husband who cannot look after himself. Pārvatī is portrayed as the long-suffering wife who complains from time to time to her mother but who always remains steadfast to her husband.[36] Sometimes the outcome of a game of dice results in a quarrel, particularly when Śiva loses his loincloth to Pārvatī and she laughs at him. In another incident Śiva becomes angry at her when she playfully covers his eyes with her hands from behind and the world is plunged into darkness.[37] On another occasion Pārvatī feels pique when Śiva calls her by the nickname Kālī (blackie), which Pārvatī takes as a slur on her appearance. She resolves to rid herself of her dark complexion and does so by performing austerities.[38] Having assumed a golden complexion she

Pārvatī with Gaṇeśa. Pratapaditya Pal, *Indo-Asian Art from the John Gilmore Ford Collection* (Baltimore: Walters Art Gallery, 1971), fig. 51. Reprinted by permission of the Walters Art Gallery.

then becomes known by the name Gaurī (the bright or golden one). In some versions of the myth her discarded, dark complexion or sheath gives birth to or becomes a warrior goddess who undertakes heroic feats of combat against demons.[39]

The presence of an alter ego or a dark, violent side to Pārvatī is suggested in several myths in which demons threaten the cosmos and Pārvatī is asked to help the gods by defeating the demon in question. Typically, when Pārvatī grows angry at the prospect of war, a violent goddess is born from her wrath and proceeds to fight on Pārvatī's behalf. This deity is often identified as the bloodthirsty goddess Kālī.[40] For the most part, however, the myths emphasize Pārvatī's milder side. So out of character is Pārvatī on the battlefield that another goddess, it seems, must be summoned to embody her wrath and dissociate this fury from Pārvatī herself.

TENSION AND RESOLUTION

The main theme of the Pārvatī cycle of myths is clear. The association between Pārvatī and Śiva represents the perennial tension in Hinduism between the ascetic ideal and the householder ideal. Pārvatī, for the most part, represents the householder. Her mission in almost all renditions of the myth is to lure Śiva into the world of marriage, sex, and children, to tempt him away from asceticism, yoga, and otherworldly preoccupations. In this role Pārvatī is cast as a figure who upholds the order of dharma, who enhances life in the world, who represents the beauty and attraction of worldly, sexual life, who cherishes the house and society rather than the forest, the mountains, or the ascetic life. In this role she repeats the feat of Satī in luring Śiva into an erotic relationship, which this time eventually brings him within the sacrificial, priestly order permanently. Pārvatī civilizes Śiva with her presence; indeed, she domesticates him. Of her role in relation to Śiva in the hymns of Māṇikkavācakar, a ninth-century poet-saint from South India, it has been said: "Śiva, the great unpredictable 'madman' (*pittaṉ, piccaṉ*), as Māṇikkavācakar occasionally addresses him . . . , is rendered momentarily sane (i.e., behaves in a socially acceptable manner) when in the company of the goddess. . . . Contact with his properly cultured spouse seems to connect him with ordinary social reality and temporarily domesticates him."[41]

The tension between Pārvatī and Śiva as representatives of the main types of religiosity in Hinduism is stated in various ways in the myths. Śiva is always said to have no family, no lineage, and no interest in progeny, which is one of the central concerns of the order of dharma and the householder's religion. Pārvatī, on the contrary, is born into an established family and longs for marriage, children, and a home. Śiva is associated with fire, which dries up or burns up the juices of life. His inner fire is so intense that in one myth he is shown to contain ashes in his veins instead of blood.[42] In one of the most famous of his myths he burns the god of lust to ashes with the fire from his middle eye. Pārvatī is associated with Soma, the deity or substance associated with the life essence of all plants. In many myths it is she who asks Śiva to revive Kāma, as she realizes that the god of sexual desire is at the root of the householder's life. In relation to Kāma, then, Śiva is a destructive fire, whereas Pārvatī is a refreshing, liquid glance: "While the fiery glance is Śiva, the Soma glance is Pārvatī, who revives Kāma when Śiva has burnt him."[43] Śiva is often said to wear on his body the ashes of the burnt Kāma. Kāma is resuscitated when Śiva embraces Pārvatī and the sweat from her body mingles with the ashes of the burned god.[44] Elsewhere it is said that when Kāma was burned by Śiva he entered the limbs of Pārvatī.[45] In the most general terms, Śiva as Agni is the fire that destroys the world at the end of each cosmic age. Pārvatī as Soma, in contrast, is the cosmic waters from which the world is inevitably reborn.

Throughout Hindu mythology it is well known that one of Śiva's principal functions is the destruction of the cosmos. In fact, Śiva has about him a wild, unpredictable, destructive aspect that is often mentioned. As the great cosmic dancer he periodically performs the *tāṇḍava*, an especially violent dance. Wielding a broken battle-ax, he dances so wildly that the cosmos is destroyed completely. In descriptions of this dance Śiva's whirling arms and flying locks are said to crash into the heavenly bodies, knocking them off course or destroying them utterly. The mountains shake and the oceans heave as the world is destroyed by his violent dancing.[46] Pārvatī, in contrast, is portrayed as a patient builder, one who follows Śiva about, trying to soften the violent effects of her husband.[47] She is a great force for preservation and reconstruction in the world and as such offsets the violence of Śiva. A seventeenth-century Tamil work pictures Pārvatī as a patient child who creates the worlds in the form of little houses. Śiva is pictured as constantly frustrating her purpose by destroying what she has so carefully built.

> The crazy old madman stands in front,
> dancing, destroying the beautiful little house that
> you have built in play.
> You don't become angry, but every time (he destroys
> it) you build it again.[48]

When Śiva does his violent *tāṇḍava* dance Pārvatī is described as calming him with soft glances, or she is said to complement his violence with a slow, creative step of her own.[49]

Pārvatī's goal in her relationship with Śiva is nothing less than the domestication of the lone, ascetic god whose behavior borders on madness.[50] Śiva is indifferent to social propriety, does not care about offspring, declares women to be a hindrance to the spiritual life, and is disdainful of the trappings of the householder's life.[51] Pārvatī tries to involve him in the worldly life of the householder by arguing that he should observe conventions if he loves her and wants her. She persuades him, for example, to marry her according to the proper rituals, to observe custom, instead of simply running off with her.[52] She is less successful, however, in getting him to change his attire and ascetic habits. She often complains of his nakedness and finds his ornaments disgraceful.[53] Usually prompted by her mother, Pārvatī sometimes complains that she does not have a proper house to live in. Śiva, as is well known, does not have a house but prefers to live in caves, on mountains, or in forests or to wander the world as a homeless beggar. Many myths delight in Śiva's response to Pārvatī's domestic pleas for a house. When she complains that the rains will soon come and that she has no house to protect her, Śiva simply takes her to the high mountain peaks above the clouds where it does not rain.[54] Elsewhere he describes his "house" as the universe and argues that an ascetic understands the whole world to be his dwelling place.[55] These philosophic arguments never satisfy Pārvatī, but she rarely, if ever, wins this argument and gains a house. In the final analysis, despite her success in involving Śiva in marital and family affairs, despite her initiating sexual desire in him, Śiva always remains in part antisocial and ascetic, a god who lives on the fringes of society.

The theme of Pārvatī's domesticating Śiva, or trying to domesticate him, is also seen in her tempering, or taming, his *tapas* and his sexual vigor, both of which are dangerous in excess. The theme of an ascetic's great austerities causing such heat that the world itself is scorched is common in Hindu mythology. The solution to this threat to the world is almost always either having a woman seduce the ascetic (women hardly ever play the role of the ascetic), granting a boon to the ascetic which distracts him from his asceticism, or granting the boon for which he undertook his asceticism in the first place. Śiva, too, does excessive *tapas* and thus threatens the world,[56] and it is Pārvatī's role to distract him from his asceticism or seduce him into erotic or domestic entanglements. In many myths Pārvatī is not so much Śiva's complement as his rival, tricking, seducing, or luring him away from ascetic practices.

Śiva's sexual vigor is also threatening to the world in quantity and intensity, and again it is Pārvatī who subdues, tames, or otherwise controls Śiva's immense sexual vitality.

> The sages cursed Śiva's *liṅga* to fall to the earth, and it burnt everything before it like a fire. Never still, it went to the underworld and to heaven and everywhere on earth. All creatures were troubled, and the sages went in desperation to Brahmā, who said to them, "As long as the *liṅga* is not still, there will be nothing auspicious in the universe. You must propitiate Devī so that she will take the form of the *yoni,* and then the *liṅga* will become still." They honoured Śiva, and he appeared and said, "If my *liṅga* is held in the *yoni,* then all will be well. Only Pārvatī can hold the *liṅga,* and then it will become calm." They propitiated him, and thus *liṅga*-worship was established.[57]

Śiva is a god of excesses, both ascetic and sexual, and Pārvatī plays the role of modifier. As a representative of the householder ideal she represents the ideal of controlled sex, namely, married sex, which is opposed to both asceticism and eroticism.

The theme of the conflict, tension, or opposition between the way of the ascetic and the way of the householder in the mythology of Pārvatī and Śiva yields to a vision of reconciliation, interdependence, and symbiotic harmony in a series of images that combine the two deities. Three such images or themes are central to the mythology, iconography, and philosophy of Pārvatī: (1) the theme of Śiva-*śakti,* (2) the image of Śiva as Ardhanārīśvara (the Lord who is half woman), and (3) the image of the liṅga and yoni.

The idea that the great male gods all possess an inherent power by which or through which they undertake creative activity is assumed in medieval Hindu mythology. When this power, or *śakti,* is personified it is always in the form of a goddess. Pārvatī, quite naturally, assumes the identity of Śiva's *śakti* in many myths and in some philosophic systems. In the role of Śiva's *śakti,* Pārvatī performs functions, or assumes meanings, which imply an underlying harmony or interdependent relationship between herself and Śiva. She is often identified with the force underlying and impelling creation. While Śiva remains more or less aloof in the creation of the world, Pārvatī as *śakti* is active, pervading the creation as its underlying strength and power.[58] In this active, creative role she is sometimes identified with *prakṛti* (nature), whereas Śiva is identified with *puruṣa* (pure spirit).[59] As *prakṛti,* Pārvatī represents the inherent tendency of nature to express itself in concrete forms and individual beings. In this task, however, whether as *śakti* or *prakṛti,* it is understood that Pārvatī either must be set in motion by Śiva or must act according to his will, wish, or design. She is not seen as antagonistic to him. Her role as his *śakti* is almost always interpreted as positive. Through Pārvatī, Śiva (the Absolute) is able to express himself in the creation. Without her he would remain inert, aloof, inactive. Just as in the mythology Pārvatī is necessary for involving Śiva in creation, so as his *śakti* she is necessary for his self-expression in creation. It is only in association with her that Śiva is able to realize or manifest his full potential. Without Pārvatī Śiva's great power does not, or cannot, manifest itself in creation. Pārvatī as *śakti* not only complements Śiva, she completes him.

A variety of images and metaphors are used to express the harmonious interdependence and close identity of Pārvatī as *śakti* and Śiva as the *śaktīmān*, the possessor of *śakti*. Śiva is said to be the male principle throughout creation, Pārvatī the female principle;[60] Śiva is the sky, Pārvatī the earth;[61] Śiva is subject, Pārvatī object;[62] Śiva is the ocean, Pārvatī the seashore;[63] Śiva is the sun, Pārvatī its light;[64] Pārvatī is all tastes and smells, Śiva the enjoyer of all tastes and smells;[65] Pārvatī is the embodiment of all individual souls, Śiva the soul itself;[66] Pārvatī assumes every form that is worthy to be thought of, Śiva thinks of all such forms;[67] Śiva is day, Pārvatī night;[68] Pārvatī is creation, Śiva the creator;[69] Pārvatī is speech, Śiva meaning;[70] and so on. In short, the two are actually one—different aspects of ultimate reality—and as such are complementary, not antagonistic.

The meaning of the Ardhanārīśvara form of Śiva is similar. The image shows a half-male, half-female figure. The right side is Śiva and is adorned with his ornaments; the left side is Pārvatī and adorned with her ornaments.[71] In the *Śiva-purāṇa* the god Brahmā is unable to continue his task of creation because the creatures that he has produced do not multiply. He propitiates Śiva and requests him to come to his aid. Śiva then appears in his half-male, half-female form. The hermaphrodite form splits into Śiva and Pārvatī, and Pārvatī, at Brahmā's request, pervades the creation with her female nature, which duly awakens the male aspect of creation into fertile activity.[72] Without its female half, or female nature,[73] the godhead as Śiva is incomplete and is unable to proceed with creation. To an even greater extent than the Śiva-*śakti* idea, the androgynous image of Śiva and Pārvatī emphasizes that the two deities are absolutely necessary to each other, and only in union can they satisfy each other and fulfill themselves. In this form the godhead transcends sexual particularity or, perhaps more accurately, includes both dimensions of sexual particularity. God is both male and female, both father and mother, both aloof and active, both fearsome and gentle, both destructive and constructive, and so on.

Ardhanārīśvara, the Lord as half woman. South Indian bronze, Choḷa, eleventh century A.D. Government Museum, Madras. Mario Bussagli and Calembus Sivaramamurti, *5000 Years of the Art of India* (New York: Harry Abrams, 1981), fig. 314, p. 255. Reprinted by permission of the publisher.

The image of the liṅga in the yoni, which is the most common image of the deity in Śiva temples,[74] similarly teaches the lesson that the tension between Śiva and Pārvatī is ultimately resolved in interdependence. Satī and Pārvatī as sexual objects succeed in tempering both Śiva's excessive detachment from the world and his excessive sexual vigor. In the form of the yoni in particular Satī-Pārvatī fulfills and completes, while at the same time tempering, Śiva's creative tendencies. As the great yogi who accumulates immense sexual potency he is symbolized by the liṅga. This great potency is creatively released in sexual or marital contact with Satī-Pārvatī. The ubiquitous image of the liṅga in the yoni symbolizes the creative release in the ultimate erotic act of power stored through asceticism. The erotic act is thus enhanced, made more potent, fecund, and creative, by the stored-up power of Śiva's asceticism. The liṅga and the yoni symbolize a creative interaction between the world of the ascetic, in which sexual abstinence is mandatory, and the life of the householder, in which sex is necessary.[75]

While many of the myths of Śiva and Pārvatī seem to accentuate the tension between the two, certain iconographic and philosophic themes concerning the divine pair show a preference for depicting or understanding them as in basic harmony. As a couple they are usually shown as affectionate. The half-male, half-female image also emphasizes the uniting of opposites. The lesson seems to be that the two poles that they represent, dharma and *mokṣa,* should not be isolated from each other. In relationship with Pārvatī, Śiva does not give up asceticism entirely, nor does Pārvatī give up asceticism entirely after having used it as a means of marrying Śiva. Nonetheless, the mutual bliss of Siva and Pārvatī also seems to teach that asceticism enhances the intensity of sexuality and makes the orderliness of the householder's world even more attractive. Held together, or in creative tension, yoga and *bhoga* (worldly or bodily pleasure), dharma and *mokṣa,* may be seen to complement and complete each other in the divine pair.

DEVOTION AND GRACE

Another important facet of Pārvatī is her role as a model of devotion to Śiva, as the devotee of the Lord par excellence. At several points in her mythology Pārvatī is described as devoted to Śiva, as unswerving in her attachment to him, and as incapable of being dissuaded from doting on him despite the most outrageous reports concerning his uncivilized, bizarre habits.[76] Her remarkably steadfast, indeed, stubborn, devotion to him is most obvious during her long period of asceticism when she undertakes heroic bodily mortifications in order either to be granted the boon of having Śiva for her husband or to attract the attention of Śiva himself.[77] In these scenes Pārvatī is portrayed as a devotee who seeks Śiva's attention and blessing; it is easy to see how she might become the paradigm for devotees of Śiva, which she does, for example, in the devotional hymns of Māṇikkavācakar, a Śaivite saint from Tamilnad.

Pārvatī appears in Māṇikkavācakar's hymns in the role of the ideal devotee, or in a position that the devotee longs to achieve, in at least two ways. First, Māṇikkavācakar uses the imagery of a love relationship, casting himself in the role of a woman who longs for her lover or husband, Śiva. In placing himself (and by extention other devotees) in this role, he identifies himself with Śiva's beloved, Pārvatī, who thus becomes the model, or vehicle, for devotion.[78] In this role Māṇikkavācakar imagines himself, along with women and goddesses, to be doing domestic chores for "her" husband.[79] Māṇikkavācakar approaches Śiva by assuming the role and duties of Pārvatī. In this way he is able to relate to Śiva in a most intimate way. Second, Māṇikkavācakar refers several times to the half-male, half-female image of Śiva and Pārvatī and sees in it the ultimate goal of the devotee, to be inextricably united with Śiva. In his longing to be with Śiva, to be consumed by and overcome by his Lord, Māṇikkavācakar sees in this image his desire graphically realized by Pārvatī.[80]

Another facet of Pārvatī is evident in Tamil Śaivism. Pārvatī tends to have a calming, civilizing effect on Śiva. Under her influence or in her presence, Śiva is often tamed, distracted from his wild, rude, mad behavior. In Māṇikkavācakar's hymns, for example, Śiva never appears before Pārvatī in his outrageous forms, such as the dancer in the cremation ground or the destroyer of Dakṣa's sacrifice.[81] In her presence, it seems, such behavior is inappropriate, and Śiva almost always behaves in properly domestic ways when she is present. Becalmed, Śiva is more attentive to the needs of his devotees (and to the needs and desires of his spouse) and more prone to grant them blessings. As the domesticator of Śiva, as the one who is able to distract him from his antisocial behavior and make him turn his attention to the world and to his devotees within the world, Pārvatī may be understood as playing the role of a mediator between the devotee and Śiva. She is a mediator in the sense that she is the one who awakens his grace or the one who is the key to activating his grace. Immersed in yoga, preoccupied with asceticism, dancing wildly with his ghastly companions in the cremation ground, Śiva is indifferent to his spouse, to the world, and to his devotees. In the presence of Pārvatī, in his role as her husband or Lord, Śiva is attentive to the world and to his devotees.

Although Pārvatī's role as intermediary is never developed in Śaivism to the extent that Śrī-Lakṣmī's role is developed in Śrī Vaiṣṇavism, Pārvatī does comes to be identified with Śiva's grace in Śaiva Siddhānta, a Tamil Śaivite school of thought and devotion.[82] In this school Śiva's grace (*aruḷ*) is said to play an active role, indeed, almost to have an identity of its own or an independent function. In its active role it is referred to as *aruḷ-catti* (*aruḷ-śakti*), "the power of grace." This power is sometimes personified, and when it is, it is identified with Pārvatī.[83] Furthermore, the *aruḷ-catti* is often said to reside inherently in every human being. Devotion is the means by which this power is awakened and provoked. The implication is that Pārvatī, in subtle form, resides within every human being.[84] She is awakened by means of devotion to Śiva, which expresses her most essential nature. Having been awakened, she infuses the devotee with her great devotion to Śiva, and thus the two, Pārvatī and the devotee, merge into one. So it is that Pārvatī's roles as ideal devotee and as Śiva's personified grace also merge into a unity.

Finally, Pārvatī often plays the role of the student in relation to Śiva. In many texts,[85] especially *Tantras*,[86] Pārvatī inquires of Śiva concerning a great many subjects: ritual, meditation, mythology, dharma, and philosophy. At her prompting or in response to her queries, Śiva reveals everything from the particulars of esoteric Tantric rituals to the nondual wisdom of Vedānta. Again, it is Pārvatī who succeeds in capturing Śiva's attention, in awakening his concern for the world, so that his great wisdom and knowledge, gained by his heroic eons of yogic meditation and brooding, can be revealed. In the role of curious student Pārvatī represents human beings who are anxious for and will benefit from all that Śiva reveals. In her role as student she again might be seen as a kind of mediator, one who coaxes from Śiva what is ultimately beneficial for human beings. Although Pārvatī is not the only one to whom Śiva gives instruction, she is by far the most common figure to be cast in this role.

4

SARASVATĪ

Sarasvatī is one of the few important goddesses in the *Vedas* who remain significant in later Hinduism.[1] In the *Vedas* her character and attributes are clearly associated with the mighty Sarasvatī River. She is the earliest example of a goddess who is associated with a river in the Indian tradition. As a river goddess she is praised for her ability both to cleanse and to fertilize. Later Vedic literature (the *Brāhmaṇas*) consistently associates her, even equates her, with the goddess of speech, Vāc. Increasingly in her later history her association with a river is deemphasized and her association with speech, poetry, music, and culture in general is affirmed. In classical and medieval Hinduism Sarasvatī is primarily a goddess of poetic inspiration and learning. She becomes associated with the creator god Brahmā as either his daughter or wife. In this role she is creative sound, which lends to reality a peculiar and distinctive human dimension. She becomes identified with the dimension of reality that is best described as coherent intelligibility. Sarasvatī to this day is worshiped throughout India and on her special day is worshiped by school children as the patron goddess of learning.

SARASVATĪ AS A RIVER

Sarasvatī as the embodiment of the Sarasvatī River is significant in both a historical and a theological sense. The religion of the Vedic Āryans was primarily a portable religion. It centered around a fire cult that did not require permanent temples or places of worship. The domestic hearth itself was a center of worship. By and large Vedic religion was appropriate for a nomadic people or for a people who only recently had ceased to be nomadic. In fact, the Āryans of the *Vedas* migrated into Northwest India sometime during the second millennium B.C.E. and gradually spread throughout the subcontinent in the course of many generations. The reverence given to Sarasvatī as the embodiment of a river in Northwest India is important because it indicates that the Āryans had begun to identify their culture with a specific geographical location and were beginning to settle down to a non-nomadic way of life.

The transition from a nomadic to an agricultural, village culture is central in the transition from the religion of the Vedic Āryans to classical Hinduism. In classical Hinduism India herself is affirmed to be the center of the world, the navel of the earth, the special and sacred location of the divine. This is dramatically specified in the sacrality of many individual features of the Indian subcontinent, especially the sacredness of the major rivers of the land.[2] The goddess Sarasvatī, then, represents a very early example of this tendency in the Hindu tradition toward affirming the land itself as holy. The river goddess Sarasvatī of the *Vedas* is a prototype of such important later river goddesses as Gaṅgā and Jumnā.

The river goddess Sarasvatī is also important in a theological or religious sense in that she suggests the sacrality inherent in rivers or water in general. While the symbolism of water is rich and complex in the religions of the world,[3] two typical associations are important in Vedic descriptions of Sarasvatī. First, she is said to bestow bounty, fertility, and riches. Her waters enrich the land so that it can produce. The waters of the river represent life itself in a dry environment, which Northwest India may have already been at the time of the Āryan migrations. Second, Sarasvatī represents purity, as does water, particularly running water. Although this characteristic is rarely mentioned directly vis-à-vis Sarasvatī, it is stated frequently in the *Vedas* that rituals were often performed on the banks of the Sarasvatī, which were held to be especially sacred for ritual purposes. This probably suggests the purifying powers of the river.

Saravatī's purifying power in the Vedic texts is also suggested in her association with medicine and healing. In the *Śatapatha-brāhmaṇa* in particular she is called upon to heal sickness and is referred to as a healing medicine.[4] In the *Ṛg-veda* she and the Aśvinas, twin gods often associated with healing, are said to heal the god Indra (10.131). As a divine physician, then, Sarasvatī is petitioned to cleanse the petitioner of disease.

A particularly Indian association with rivers is the imagery of crossing from the world of ignorance or bondage to the far shore, which represents the world of enlightenment or freedom. The religious quest in all three native Indian religions—Hinduism, Jainism, and Buddhism—is expressed by the metaphor of fording or crossing a wide stream. The river in this metaphor represents the state of transition, the period of rebirth, in which the spiritual sojourner undergoes a crucial metamorphosis. The river represents a great purifying power in which the pilgrim drowns his old self and is born anew, free and enlightened. This imagery is not expressly used in connection with Sarasvatī in the *Vedas*, but it may have been understood implicitly and may help to explain the association of Sarasvatī with inspiration, speech, and wisdom in her later history.

Although Sarasvatī's nature and characteristics are overwhelmingly associated with a mighty river, this is no ordinary river. Early Vedic references make it clear that the Sarasvatī River originates in heaven and flows down to the earth.[5] This idea, also affirmed in the case of such important later river goddesses as Gaṅgā, is a way of asserting the sacred nature of the rivers in question. The Sarasvatī (and later the Gaṅgā) represents an ever-flowing stream of celestial grace which purifies and fertilizes the earth. The earthly manifestation of Sarasvatī as a river thus represents only a partial disclosure of her being. Physical contact with her earthly manifestation, however, connects one with the awesome, heavenly, transcendent dimension of the goddess and of reality in general.

SARASVATĪ IN LATER HINDUISM

Saravatī's connection with a river steadily decreases in later Hinduism. Although she continues to be associated with a river in some late sources,[6] her characteristics and appearance increasingly bear little or no relation to a goddess who embodies the sacrality of a river.

As early as the *Brāhmaṇas* Sarasvatī is consistently identified with Vāgdevī, the goddess of speech. It is not at all clear what intrinsic connection between Sarasvatī and Vāgdevī led to this association. Perhaps the centrality of sacred speech in Vedic cult and the importance of Vedic rituals being performed on the banks of the Sarasvatī River led to the identification of the two goddesses. In any case, Sarasvatī increasingly becomes a goddess associated with speech, learning, culture, and wisdom; most post-Vedic references to her do not even hint that at one time she was identified with a river.

In later Hinduism Sarasvatī is sometimes said to have been born from the god Brahmā. Brahmā, desiring to create the world, goes into meditation, whereupon his body divides in two, half male and half female. Enraptured by his female half, who is Sarasvatī, Brahmā desires her, mates with her, and creates the demigod Manu, who subsequently creates the world.[7] A similar version of her origin is found in the

Brahma-vaivarta-purāṇa and the *Devī-bhāgavata-purāṇa*. According to these texts, Kṛṣṇa, who is identified with absolute reality (*brahman*), divides himself into male and female, *puruṣa* and *prakṛti*, spirit and matter, in order to proceed with creation. His female half takes on five forms or five *śaktis*, dynamic powers, one of which is Sarasvatī.[8] Her specific creative function in relation to the other *śaktis* is to pervade reality with insight, knowledge, and learning.[9] In relation to *prakṛti* she is said to be purely *sattvic*, spiritual.[10] These same texts also describe Sarasvatī's origin from the tip of Kṛṣṇa's *śakti*'s tongue. Suddenly, they say, a lovely girl appears dressed in yellow clothes, adorned with jewels, and carrying a book and a *vina* (lute).[11] Sarasvatī is also often said to have her origin in and to reside in the mouths or on the tongues of the god Brahmā (Brahmā has four or five heads).[12] That is, when Brahmā undertakes the creation of the world through creative speech, the goddess Sarasvatī is born in his mouths.

Sarasvatī is also said to have had her origin from the god Viṣṇu. In several places she is said to be his tongue or to be held in his mouth.[13] Her association with Viṣṇu makes her the co-wife of Lakṣmī in many myths. In this relationship Sarasvatī for the most part represents spiritual, ascetic, or religious goals and values, whereas Lakṣmī represents worldly well-being as manifest in wealth, material power, and fertility. In some texts the two goddesses do not get along very well, suggesting, perhaps, a tension between *bhukti* (sensual enjoyment) or dharma and *mukti* (spiritual liberation or perfection) in Hinduism.[14]

Although Sarasvatī's nature and appearance change dramatically from the Vedic period to later Hinduism as her association with a river decreases, she does maintain some characteristics of her earlier history, in a few cases even maintaining her association with a river.[15] She is associated, for example, with clouds, thunder, and rain and is said to be the presiding deity of rain.[16] In the *Vāmana-purāṇa* she is described as moving through the clouds and producing rain (40.14).[17] The *Vāmana-purāṇa* also identifies Sarasvatī with all waters (40.14). Her association with Soma in some texts[18] and with water in general suggests that Sarasvatī is identified with the underlying sap of vitality necessary for all living things, that she nourishes life and promotes fertility. These continued associations with water, and sometimes with rivers, indicate a certain continuity between the river goddess of the *Vedas* and the later goddess. Even in reference to her association with waters, though, Sarasvatī's character is much changed. In the later tradition she is not so much a river goddess as a goddess who manifests herself through the life-giving and purifying nature of all water: rain, rivers, ponds, and so on. Like Soma she pervades creation; she has transcended her association with a specific river.

Far more characteristic of the later Sarasvatī is her association with speech. Even in the *Ṛg-veda* she is called impeller of true and sweet speech and awakener of happy and noble thoughts (6.61.9). Such epithets as Vāgdevī (goddess of speech), Jihvāgrāvāsinī (dwelling in the front of the tongue), Kavijihvāgrāvāsinī (she who dwells on the tongues of poets), Śabdavāsinī (she who dwells in sound), Vāgīśā (mistress of speech), and Mahāvānī (possessing great speech)[19] are often used for Sarasvatī. Her mythological identification with the tongues of Brahmā, Kṛṣṇa, and Viṣṇu also underlines her identification with speech or creative sound.

The importance of speech in Hinduism is both ancient and central. The entire creative process is held to be distilled in the syllable *oṁ*, and the idea of creation proceeding from *śabda-brahman* (ultimate reality in the form of sound) is often mentioned in Hindu texts. The potency of speech and sound is also seen in the centrality of mantras in Hinduism. A mantra, which may consist of words or of sounds alone, is held to possess great power. Indeed, the mantra of a given deity is declared to be equivalent to the deity itself. To pronounce a mantra is to make the deity present. The name of the deity and the deity itself are equivalent. There resides in sound a potent quality, and this quality is embodied in the goddess Sarasvatī.

Speech is also important and revered because it permits communication between people. Speech, to a great extent, sets human beings apart from all animals. Speech is also associated with rationality and refinement. Speech represents coherent sound that permits the transmission of ideas, wisdom, and culture. As the embodiment of speech, then, Sarasvatī is present wherever speech exists. And so it is that she is preeminently associated with the best in human culture: poetry, literature, sacred rituals, and rational communication between individuals.

Sarasvatī is also identified with thought and intellect. Not only is she speech in the form of coherent sound, she is that which underlies or makes speech possible, namely, intelligence and thought. This association is indicated in such epithets for her as Smṛtiśakti (the power of memory), Jñañaśakti (the power of knowledge), Buddhiśaktisvarupīṇī (whose form is the power of intellect), Kalpanāśakti (who is the power of forming ideas), and Pratibhā (intelligence, or she who is intelligence).[20] As thought and intellect, Sarasvatī is thus identified with the distinctive ability that distinguishes human beings as special, reasoning. She represents the peculiar human ability to think, which is precisely the ability that has permitted human beings to create and imagine their innumerable cultural products, from cooking pots to philosophic systems.

Sarasvatī's association with science, learning, and knowledge further reinforces her nature as the goddess of speech and thought. She is called, for example, Vedagarbhā (the womb or source of the *Vedas* or knowledge), Sarvavidyāsvarūpiṇī (whose form is all the sciences), Sarvaśāstravasīnī (who dwells in all books), Granthakāriṇī (who causes books to be made), and many other such names.[21] As mind, intellect, and thought, she inspires the arts and sciences. She is also the accumulated products of human thought. She is the sum of the human intellectual tradition as preserved in the sciences. As the great goddess who bears culture, or who embodies culture, she is sometimes associated with the Brahmans, whose special duty is to preserve culture. She is manifest and especially revered in schools and wherever education takes place.

Sarasvatī is also said to underlie, inspire, or embody the arts. She is said to provide inspiration to poets and to be present wherever artistic excellence is evident. Poets often praise her assistance or ask for her help. She is said to be associated with the Gandharvas, a supernatural race that excels at dancing,[22] and she is often associated with music, both instrumental and vocal. In short, Sarasvatī is manifest wherever human culture exists. Inspiring and embodying both the arts and sciences in human culture, she represents the greatness of human civilization in all its richness and diversity.

Beyond Sarasvatī's associations with culture, which dominate her character, are certain cosmic associations or certain tendencies and epithets that suggest her primordial, absolute nature. Such names as the following identify Sarasvatī as a great, universal goddess whose functions extend to the creation of the worlds: Jaganmātā (mother of the world), Śaktirūpiṇī (whose form is power or *śakti*), and Visvarūpā (containing all forms within her).[23] It is fairly easy to imagine how Sarasvatī's character as the inspiration and embodiment of culture might lead to her assuming such cosmic characteristics. As the reality that permits human beings to achieve dominion over all other creatures, that permits or inspires the beauty and grace manifest in the arts, that has enabled human beings to achieve an almost godlike nature in the physical world as its masters and molders, this goddess of culture comes to be extolled or equated with the highest powers of the cosmos.

Sarasvatī's iconography illustrates her associations with culture, particularly the arts and sciences, and shows her to be a goddess who is for the most part set apart from the natural realm of growth, fertility, blood, and other phenomena often associated with or central in the iconography and mythology of other goddesses. She is usually depicted as having four hands, and the most common items held by her are a book, a lute (*vina*), a rosary, and a water pot.[24] The book associates her with the sciences and with learning in general. The lute associates her with the arts, particularly the musical arts, and the rosary and the water pot associate her with the spiritual sciences and with religious rites.[25]

Sarasvatī. Sixteenth century A.D. Rumtek Monastery, Sikkim. Madanjeet Singh, *Himalayan Art* (London: MacMillan, 1968), p. 20.

The predominant themes in Sarasvatī's appearance are purity and transcendence. She is almost always said to be pure white like snow, the moon, or the *kunda* flower[26] or to shine brilliantly and whitely like innumerable moons.[27] Her garments are said to be fiery in their purity, or they are described as white,[28] and she is sometimes said to be smeared with sandalwood paste.[29] Sarasvatī's gleaming white body and garments express well her purity and transcendence, and these themes are in keeping with her typical association with the *sattva guṇa*, the pure, spiritual thread of *prakṛti*.[30] Sarasvatī is rarely described as having fearsome aspects[31] and is usually portrayed as calm and peaceful. These qualities are conveyed in the serene, white images of her in Hindu art.[32]

Sarasvatī's transcendent nature, which removes her from the impurities of the natural world and its rhythms of growth and fertility, is also suggested in her vehicle, the swan. The swan is a symbol of spiritual transcendence and perfection in Hinduism. Spiritual masters and heroes are sometimes called supreme swans (*paramahaṁsa*) in that they have completely transcended the limitations and imperfections of the phenomenal world. Sarasvatī, astride her swan, suggests a dimension of human existence that rises above the physical, natural world. Her realm is one of beauty, perfection, and grace; it is a realm created by artistic inspiration, philosophic insight, and accumulated knowledge, which have enabled human beings to so refine their natural world that they have been able to transcend its limitations. Sarasvatī astride her swan beckons human beings to continued cultural creation and civilized perfection.

Sarasvatī is also typically shown seated on a lotus. Like the swan, the lotus seat of the goddess suggests her transcendence of the physical world. She floats above the muddy imperfections of the physical world, unsullied, pure, beautiful. Although rooted in the mud (like man rooted in the physical world), the lotus perfects itself in a blossom that has transcended the mud. Sarasvatī inspires people to live in such a way that they may transcend their physical limitations through the ongoing creation of culture.

The benefits to be derived from the worship of Sarasvatī, of the blessings that she is expected to bestow on her devotees, usually relate to the themes that we have noted as central to her character. She gives eloquence, wisdom, poetic inspiration, and artistic skill.[33] She removes speech defects and dumbness and grants charming speech and a musical voice.[34] Although she is sometimes said to grant wealth, long life, worldly enjoyments, and final salvation, she is primarily the goddess of wisdom and learning and specializes in promoting success among philosophers, scholars, and artists, who are her special devotees.

A persistent theme in the Hindu tradition is that human destiny involves the refinement of nature. Although the ultimate goal of the religious quest may be *mokṣa*, the complete release from the phenomenal world, Hindus affirm that being fully human necessitates molding, enhancing, and refining the natural world in order to make it habitable for human beings. Such important Hindu ideas as dharma, the *saṁskāras* (life-cycle rituals), and the *varna-jati* (caste) system all suggest this emphasis. The arts and sciences, however, seem to be the most obvious and concrete manifestations of this theme in the Hindu tradition. Artistic creation and the accumulated knowledge of the sciences, including philosophy, epitomize human culture and demonstrate the extraordinary ability of human beings to mold and refine the natural world into something beautiful and specially human. Sarasvatī presides over and inspires this dimension of being human in the Hindu tradition.

Many goddesses both within and outside the Hindu tradition gain their immense vitality and popularity through their associations with certain aspects of the natural world. Fertility, sexuality, growth, blood, and the sap of life in general seem to be embodied in many goddesses. Hinduism also attributes great power to goddesses. They are typically referred to as *śaktis* (powers), and several Hindu goddesses are particularly adept at warfare and are most at home on the battlefield. Several other Hindu goddesses seem to be particularly popular among women and to specialize in family and domestic blessings. Many goddesses provide models for the most significant female roles in Hindu culture, or at least they participate in these roles, albeit in ways that do not always conform to dharmic models. Sarasvatī has very few of these associations. Her pure, milky-white appearance and completely *sattvic* nature dissociate her from the mud of existence, from the vigorous, fecund sap of fertility. Her sexual encounters are not emphasized, and when her father/husband Brahmā does desire her, she seeks to flee from him. Her motherhood is usually only metaphorical: she is said to give birth to artistic creations by providing inspiration or to have given birth to the *Vedas* in the sense that she personifies wisdom. In the *Devī-bhāgavata-purāṇa* she is said to be ascetic in nature and to grant boons to those who perform asceticism (9.1.35). Her presence is therefore not usually sought in the home. She is not a domestic goddess. Nor is her presence sought in the fields, where fertility is crucial, or in the forests and mountains, where isolation from culture is desired in the quest for *mokṣa*. Her presence is sought in libraries and schools, by those who create and bear culture in the ongoing task of transforming the natural world into a refined and civilized habitation for human beings.

Throughout North India today Sarasvatī's special *pūjā* is celebrated in early spring. On this day images of the goddess are established in schools and universities, and special cultural programs take place. At Banares Hindu University there is a procession of faculty and students on this day (which corresponds to the anniversary of the university's founding). This is also the day when books, pens, musical instruments, and gurus are formally worshiped.

5

SĪTĀ

One of the most popular heroines in Hindu mythology is Sītā. She is known primarily as the wife of Rāma, the hero of the epic *Rāmāyaṇa*. As one of the protagonists of the *Rāmāyaṇa*, Sītā is revered as the model Hindu wife, who, although the victim of injustices, always remains loyal and steadfast to her husband. The divinity of Rāma and Sītā is not stressed in the early *Rāmāyaṇa* of Vālmīki (written sometime between 200 B.C. and A.D. 200), but they increasingly become identified as manifestations of the god Viṣṇu and his consort Śrī-Lakṣmī in later vernacular renditions of the tale. As early as the fourteenth century Rāma is praised as the supreme manifestation of the divine,[1] and in North India today millions of Hindus consider him and Sītā the supreme divine couple. Throughout this period of divinization, Sītā has achieved her status primarily in relation to Rāma. It is her wifely role, which has come to serve as a paradigm in Hindu mythology, legend, and folktale, which has defined Sītā and made her dear to so many Hindus. Sīta is the perfect model of wifely devotion.

Although Sītā is associated with the wife of Rāma in the minds of all Hindus today, a female divinity named Sītā was known prior to Vālmīki's *Rāmāyaṇa*, and this deity was associated with agricultural fertility. Just why Vālmīki associated the name of this deity with his heroine is not entirely clear, but that he did so consciously seems beyond doubt.

THE EARLY HISTORY OF SĪTĀ

The word *sītā* means "furrow," "the line made by the plow," and is the name of a goddess associated with plowed fields in Vedic literature.

In a hymn addressed to the lord of the fields, Kṣetrapati, Sītā is invoked as follows:

> Auspicious Sītā, come thou near:
> we venerate and worship thee
> That thou mayst bless and prosper us
> and bring us fruits abundantly.
>
> May Indra press the furrow down,
> may Pūshan guide its course aright.
> May she, as rich in milk, be drained for us
> through each succeeding year.[2]

In the *Kauśika-sūtra* Sītā is the wife of Parjanya, a god associated with rain. She is the "mother of gods, mortals and creatures" (7c)[3] and is petitioned for growth and prosperity (6).[4] In the *Parāskara-sūtra* Sītā is the wife of Indra, a god often associated with rain and fertility, and is offered cooked rice and barley in the sacrificial fire (2.17.1–19).[5] In the *Vājasaneyi-saṁhitā* Sītā is invoked when four furrows are drawn during a sacrificial ritual (12.69–72). This is reminiscent of plowing the ground upon which the fire altar is built during the Agnicayana ritual, an act apparently intended to ensure the abundance and fertility of the crops.[6] Sītā is also invoked as one of the names of the goddess Āryā in the *Harivaṁśa* (2.3.14).

> O goddess, you are the altar's center in the sacrifice,
> The priest's fee,
> Sītā to those who hold the plough,
> And Earth to all living beings.[7]

Sītā is not a very significant deity prior to the *Rāmāyaṇa* of Vālmīki. She is not mentioned very often and is overshadowed by much more popular goddesses associated with fertility, such as Śrī-Lakṣmī. Nevertheless, Sītā does seem to be part of a fundamental intuition concerning the fertility of the plowed earth and the necessity of a male power to awaken, arouse, and inseminate her. Underlying Sītā's connection with Indra, Parjanya, and other male deities associated with the inseminating effects of rain seems to be the basic perception that the ongoing fertility of the cosmos is the result of the interaction between the sky and the earth, between male and female, between the latent powers of the field and the inseminating effects of the plow, which opens the earth for the insertion of seeds into her fertile interior.

KINGS AND THE FERTILITY OF THE EARTH

Identification of Rāma's wife with a goddess of the plowed fields, with a goddess of fertility, seems to be related to the central role that kings in ancient India were assumed to play in promoting the fertility of the land.[8] The interrelation between fertility and the manly vigor and power of the ruler or king finds its prototype in the *Ṛg-veda*, where the mighty god Indra combats the demon Vṛtra, who withholds the creative, nourishing waters of creation. Indra having defeated the demon, the waters rush forth to fructify the earth and create a fertile, habitable cosmos fit for human civilization.[9]

The theme of the king's bringing forth the abundance and fertility of the earth is central in the myths concerning Pṛthu, the first human king. In these myths the necessity of a king is related in part to the chaotic and barren nature of the earth in the mythic past. Prior to Pṛthu's reign the earth was inhospitable, her terrain was impossible to cultivate, and her fertility remained untapped. The *Mahābhārata* describes Pṛthu as leveling the earth's mountains and hills to make her fit for agriculture and as milking the earth like a cow (7.69). As the legendary model for kings, one of Pṛthu's chief functions is to bring forth the fertility of the earth. According to the Pṛthu myths, the earth, although fertile and potent, does not or cannot yield the abundance of her interior without being stimulated, activated, or, in the image of the *Mahābhārata*, "milked" by a heroic, royal figure. Conversely, it is understood that the king's reign will not be fruitful, that he will not be successful, unless he can draw forth the richness of the earth. Just as the king is needed to activate or provoke the earth into life and fertility, so the earth's fruitfulness is necessary to the king's success as a ruler.

Certain myths and certain Vedic rituals indicate the theme of the king's winning the fruits of the earth. In various ways the king relates to, interacts with, or captures things that are related to the earth, such as cows. These acts symbolize the king's ability to draw forth from the earth her treasures and abundance. They symbolize the king's ability to "milk" the earth of her richness for the benefit of all living creatures.[10]

The myth of the churning of the ocean may also be understood in this vein.[11] Viṣṇu, as the cosmic ruler in this myth, usually plays the central role and dominates the action in his various forms: as the tortoise that provides the foundation for the churning stick; as the cosmic serpent, Vāsuki, who provides the churning rope; as the seductress Mohinī, who prevents the demons from partaking of the nectar of immortality; and as the leader of the gods. The central action of the myth is the churning of the ocean of milk to make it yield the nectar of immortality. Viṣṇu represents the active ruler who brings his power and ingenuity to bear on the passive fertility of the cosmos. The result of Viṣṇu's action is the drawing forth of representations of the abundance of the earth. Central among these are the nectar of immortality and the goddess Śrī-Lakṣmī. Śrī represents good luck, well-being, abundance, and fertility and is well known as dwelling wherever a righteous king reigns. She is sovereignty personified, and where she dwells there always exist wealth and abundance of all good things.

The *Rāmāyaṇa* takes care to portray Rāma as the ideal king and his rule as a model of social perfection. It is therefore not surprising that we would encounter the theme of Rāma relating to, interacting with, or winning the riches of the earth. In fact, his winning Sītā at her *svayamvara* (a suitor's contest for a bride), their subsequent marriage, and Rāma's regaining Sītā from the clutches of the demon Rāvaṇa should probably be understood as an expression of this basic and ancient pattern in Indian religion. It is clear in the *Rāmāyaṇa* that Sītā is no mere human being. Her birth is supernatural, and her abilities and appearance are exalted throughout the text. She is, for example, called *ayonijā*, "not born of a womb" (1.66; 2.30), and in appearance she is often likened to Śrī-Lakṣmī (5.12).[12] The nature of her birth (as well as her name) also makes it clear that Sītā fits the theme of the mutual and necessary interaction between a king and the earth, which alone leads to fertility and abundance. According to the *Rāmāyaṇa*, Sītā is literally unearthed when her father, King Janaka, is plowing (1.66). Given Janaka's position as a great king, ruler of Videha, it seems extremely unlikely that he was simply in the fields farming when Sītā was discovered. What is more likely is that Janaka was involved in some royal ritual, part of which involved the king's plowing the earth to bring about fertility.[13] It is also probable that the act of the king's plowing the field was likened to sexual intercourse, a symbolic coupling of the king (and the powers he represented or contained) with the latent powers of the earth.[14] The effectiveness of the ritual plowing, then, is manifest in the birth of Sītā, the earth's personified fertility, abundance, and well-being, which has been brought forth by Janaka.

The marriage of Rāma and Sītā represents a further interplay between a vigorous, virtuous, powerful king and a woman who symbolizes the fecund forces of the earth, a woman who is literally the child of the earth. Their marriage institutes a relationship in which Sītā is, as it were, plowed by Rāma the king. The ultimate result of this auspicious relationship between kingly virility and earthly fertility is the inauguration of Rāmrājya, "the rule of Rāma," an idealized reign in which harmony, longevity, order, fruitful crops, and all social, political, and economic virtues dominate society to the exclusion of all ills.

Sītā. South Indian bronze, early Choḷa, ca. 1000 A.D. Government Museum, Madras. C. Sivaramamurti, *South Indian Bronzes* (New Delhi: Lalit Kala Akademi, 1963), fig. 41. Reprinted by permission of the publisher.

Interposed between the marriage of Rāma and Sītā and the inauguration of Rāmrājya is the central part of the epic narrative in which Rāma is banished from the capital city, Sītā is abducted by the villain Rāvaṇa, and Rāma and his allies defeat Rāvaṇa and recapture Sītā. During Rāma's exile, Ayodhya, the capital of Rāma's kingdom, is desolate. The citizens bemoan Rāma's absence, and in all respects the situation is contrasted with the times when Rāma was present there.[15] Doubly traumatic is the situation later in the forest when Sītā is kidnapped and separated from Rāma. At one point Rāma is reduced to a blubbering, half-maddened wreck and must be returned to sobriety by the appeals of his brother Lakṣmaṇa, who tells him it is unmanly and improper to lament so.[16]

In summary, traditional Indian religion viewed the king as a figure who could stimulate, activate, or somehow draw forth from the earth her creative potential. Indeed, it was held that without the king's beneficial influence, without the manly vigor of the king, the earth's fecundity would remain untapped; the earth would remain unproductive. The king entered into a relationship with the earth in which he could stimulate her, a relationship that was understood as not unlike a marriage. "This marital relation of the ruler to the earth is directly expressed in the word *Bhupati* 'lord of the earth,' i.e. king."[17] In the *Rāmāyaṇa* Rāma's wife is associated with the powers of the earth, or the earth itself, through her name and through her unusual birth. Underlying Sītā's epic character and personality is the ancient fertility goddess associated with the plowed field, who was worshiped for abundant crops and who was ritually activated by rulers in certain contexts. Sītā, the epic heroine, has ancient roots, and one important dimension of her character associates her with the primordial powers of the earth.

THE IDEAL WIFE

Sītā is defined in the *Rāmāyaṇa* and in the subsequent cult of Rāma almost entirely in relation to her husband. She is portrayed as the ideal Hindu wife, whose every thought revolves around her husband. For Sītā Rāma is the center of her life. She is always steadfast in her loyalty to him. His welfare, reputation, and wishes are uppermost in her mind. The *Manu-dharma-śāstra* describes the ideal wife as a woman who always remains faithful to her husband, no matter what his character might be: "Though destitute of virtue, or seeking pleasure elsewhere, or devoid of good qualities, a husband must be constantly worshiped as a god by a faithful wife" (5.154).[18] The same text, commenting on the necessity for protecting women throughout their lives, says: "Her father protects her in childhood, her husband protects her in old age; a woman is never fit for independence" (9.3).[19] Sītā is the ideal *pativratā*, the wife devoted entirely to her husband. In her selfless devotion and sexual fidelity the *pativratā* nourishes an inner heat that both purifies her and provides her with a destructive weapon that can be used against those who might threaten her purity.[20] This inner heat generated as a result of marital fidelity seems to be similar to *tapas* in the context of asceticism. *Tapas* is both the act of doing asceticism, or something virtuous, and the result of doing that action, namely, an inner heat or fire.

Sītā's mythological role as the ideal wife and *pativratā* is illustrated in several incidents in the *Rāmāyaṇa*. When Rāma is told by his father that he will not inherit the kingdom and that he must go into exile in the forest for fourteen years, he prepares to leave Sītā behind in the city of Ayodhya because he thinks that she could not bear the ordeals and discomforts of the forest. She is grief stricken at this plan and delivers a long discourse to him on her desire to go into exile with him. The point to which she returns often is that a husband is a god to his wife and that apart from him a wife might as well commit suicide, so meaningless would be her existence. She threatens to kill herself unless he relents and allows her to go with him to the forest. She begins her plea with these words:

> O Son of an illustrious monarch, a father, a mother, a brother, a son or a daughter-in-law enjoy the fruit of their merits and receive what is their due, a wife alone follows the destiny of her consort, O Bull among Men; therefore, from now on, my duty is clear, I shall dwell in the forest! For a woman, it is not her father, her son, nor her mother, friends nor her own self, but the husband, who in this world and the next is ever her sole means of salvation. If thou dost enter the impenetrable forest to-day, O Descendant of Raghu, I shall precede thee on foot, treading down the spiky Kusha Grass. . . . I shall willingly dwell in the forest as formerly I inhabited the palace of my father, having no anxiety in the Three Worlds and reflecting only on my duties towards my lord. Ever subject to thy will, docile, living like an ascetic, in those honey-scented woodlands I shall be happy in thy proximity, O Rama, O Illustrious Lord. (2.27)[21]

Rāma replies to her by describing all the dangers and discomforts of the forest and tells her that he cannot bear to inflict these things on her, that she must stay behind in the comfort of the city under the protection of her in-laws. She replies by saying:

> The hardships described by thee, that are endured by those who dwell in the forest, will be transmuted into joys through my devotion to thee. . . . separated from thee I should immediately yield up my life. . . . Deprived of her consort a woman cannot live, thou canst not doubt this truth where I am concerned. . . . O Thou of pure soul, I shall remain sinless by following piously in the steps of my consort, for a husband is a God. (2.29)[22]

In her utter loyalty to Rāma she compares herself to Sāvitrī, who followed her husband to the realm of the dead, and says that she has never seen the face of another man, even in her thoughts (2.30). She says that the forest discomforts will be enjoyed by her as pleasures as long as she can be with him. She sums up her plea to Rāma by saying: "To be with thee is heaven, to be without thee is hell, this is the truth!" (2.30).[23]

When Rāvaṇa abducts Sītā and takes her to Laṅka, he keeps her prisoner in a garden surrounded by demonesses. Several long descriptions portray Sītā's pitiful condition in the absence of Rāma. Through a series of metaphors Vālmīki tries to capture both Sītā's great beauty and her great grief. The latter has clearly eclipsed the former but cannot altogether hide it. In the words of the *Rāmāyaṇa* she was

> resplendent with a radiance which now shone but dimly so that she seemed like a flame wreathed in smoke.
>
> . . . she resembled a lotus pool stripped of its flowers. Oppressed, racked with grief, and tormented, she was like unto Rohini pursued by Ketu. . . .
>
> Entangled in a mighty web of sorrow, her beauty was veiled like a flame enveloped in smoke or a traditional text obscured by dubious interpretation or wealth that is melting away or faith that is languishing or hope that is almost extinguished or perfection unattained on account of obstacles or an intellect which is darkened or fame tarnished by calumny. (5.15)[24]

Musing on her appearance, Hanuman, the loyal monkey ally of Rāma, says: "For a woman the greatest decoration is her lord and Sita, though incomparably beautiful, no longer shines in Rama's absence" (5.16).[25]

Although her beauty is dimmed, although she lacks the presence of Rāma, who alone gives her life meaning, she is described throughout this section of the narrative as constantly remembering Rāma. Keeping him always in her mind, she is sometimes described as shining beautifully as a result of this steadfastness. "Though that blessed one was shorn of her beauty, yet her soul did not lose its transcendency, upheld as it was by the thought of Rāma's glory and safeguarded by her own virtue" (5.17).[26]

Rāvaṇa comes to the garden and proposes that Sītā abandon Rāma and take him as her husband. She is shocked at this suggestion and refuses. Rāvaṇa then threatens that he will give her two months to agree to his wishes. If, after that time, she refuses, he will cut her up and have her for breakfast (5.22). Sītā shows great pride and courage in the face of Rāvaṇa's threats. At one point she tells him that if she wished she could burn him to ashes with the fire that she has accumulated from her chastity (5.22). She refuses to do so, she says, simply because she has not been given Rāma's permission.

When Hanuman finds Sītā in her garden prison he proposes to return her to India by carrying her on his back. Given Sītā's predicament and her longing to see Rāma again, it would be natural for her to accept this offer of rescue joyfully. She does not agree to return with Hanuman, however, because to do so would mean touching another male besides her husband, which would violate her devotion to Rāma. She also refuses to accept Hanuman's offer because it would mean that Rāma would not obtain the glory involved in rescuing her. Sītā displays in this scene her habit of always thinking of Rāma first. His welfare and reputation are uppermost in her mind. To her it would be wrong to think of her own safety first if it would mean adversely influencing Rāma's reputation or opportunity for fame and glory (5.37).

Rāvaṇa attempts to persuade Sītā to accept him as her new husband by having his court magician create a head that resembles Rāma's and a bow like Rāma's. Taking these to Sītā, Rāvaṇa claims that Rāma has been defeated in battle and slain. In her shock and lamentation Sītā's chief thought is that it must have been some fault of hers which resulted in Rāma's untimely and undignified death. A virtuous woman sustains her husband and prevents his untimely death. Only some shortcoming or unvirtuous act, she thinks, can explain the tragedy. She begs Rāvaṇa to take her to the body of her husband and slay her there so that she can be united with him in death (6.31–32).

After Rāma defeats Rāvaṇa, Sītā's loyalty to her husband is severely tested. Sītā is brought before Rāma, and she beams with joy at seeing him. He, however, scowls at her and announces that he has only undertaken the defeat of Rāvaṇa in order to uphold his family's honor and not out of love for her. He says that it would be lustful and ignoble for him to take her back after she had spent time under the control of another man. He disclaims her and even invites her to associate with one of his brothers or one of the surviving demon heroes. He concludes this frosty interview with her by saying: "Assuredly Rāvaṇa, beholding thy ravishing and celestial beauty, will not have respected thy person during the time thou didst dwell in his abode" (6.17).[27]

Sītā is shocked at this accusation and protests her innocence, saying that although it is true that Rāvaṇa handled her, she could have done nothing to prevent it, that he abducted her by means of superior strength, and that throughout her ordeal and stay in Laṅka she remained completely faithful to her husband and thought of him constantly. Grieved by Rāma's false accusations, she asks Lakṣmaṇa to make a funeral pyre for her. Having displeased Rāma and having been renounced by him publicly, she wishes to die (6.118). When the fire has been kindled Sītā prepares to enter it by circumambulating Rāma and then addressing Agni, the god of fire, with the words: "As my heart has never ceased to be true to Raghava, do thou, O Witness of all Beings, grant me thy protection! As I am pure in conduct, though Rāma looks on me as sullied, do thou, O Witness of the Worlds, grant me full protection!" (6.118).[28] Because of her innocence and purity, Agni refuses to harm her and returns her to Rāma so unscathed that even her flower garland remains unwithered by the heat of the flames. Rāma, convinced of her purity, accepts her back and says that he will protect her forever (6.120).

Back in Ayodhya, however, when everyone is living happily ever after and the glorious era of Rāmrājya is under way, Rāma hears that his citizens are gossiping about Sītā and are unhappy that he accepted her back after she was under Rāvaṇa's control. To stop this gossip and to set a stainless example for his subjects, Rāma decides to banish Sītā from his kingdom, even though he has just learned of her pregnancy. He commands his brother Lakṣmaṇa to take Sītā to a deserted place and abandon her (7.45). When Lakṣmaṇa tells Sītā of Rāma's decision, her predilection is again to blame some fault of her own, either in this life or a past life, for bringing about her ill luck. She does not blame Rāma, nor does it seem to occur to her that he might be in the wrong (7.48). She asks Lakṣmaṇa to send Rāma this message:

> O Raghava, thou knowest I am truly pure and that I have been bound to thee in supreme love, yet thou hast renounced me in fear of dishonour, because thy subjects have reproached and censured thee, O Hero. . . . As for me, I am not distressed on mine own account, O Prince of Raghu, it is for thee to keep thy fair name untarnished! The husband is as a God to the woman, he is her family, and her spiritual preceptor, therefore, even at the price of her life, she must seek to please her lord. (7.48)[29]

The test of Sītā. Kulu, about 1720 A.D. Jagdish and Kamla Mittal Museum of Indian Art, Hyderabad. *In the Image of Man: The Indian Perception of the Universe through 2000 Years of Painting and Sculpture*, Hayward Gallery, London, March 25–June 13, 1982 (London: Weidenfeld and Nicolson, 1982), fig. 386, p. 73. Reprinted by permission of the publisher.

After Sītā has given birth to twin sons and has spent several years in exile in a forest hermitage, Rāma summons her back to Ayodhya to undergo an ordeal that will absolve him of all shame and demonstrate her innocence once and for all. Although he himself is convinced of her innocence, he demands a public ordeal in order to convince his subjects. Sītā agrees, but it seems that she no longer relishes life; she asks, on the basis of her purity and loyalty to Rāma, to be taken back into the bosom of her mother, the goddess Earth. She says: "If, in thought, I have never dwelt on any but Rāma, may the Goddess Madhavi receive me!" (7.97).[30] As she finishes this act of truth, a throne rises from the ground supported by serpents. Earth embraces Sītā, seats her on the throne, and then the throne and Sītā sink back into the ground (7.97). Although Rāma angrily demands Sītā's return, the earth remains silent and closed, and Rāma lives out his life in sorrow. He does not marry again and has a golden image of Sītā made, which he uses in her place at religious rituals requiring the presence of a wife.

Sītā's self-effacing nature, her steadfast loyalty to her husband, and her chastity make her both the ideal Hindu wife and the ideal *pativratā*. In a sense Sītā has no independent existence, no independent destiny. In all things she sees herself as inextricably bound up with Rāma. Apart from him her life is meaningless. Throughout the *Rāmāyaṇa* she constantly thinks of Rāma and his welfare and always remains faithful to him despite provocations on his part. Although Rāma is considered the ideal king, he is not a very good husband to Sītā. He would be perfectly willing to leave her behind for fourteen years during his exile, he entertains doubts about her chastity while she was under Rāvaṇa's control, he allows her to undergo an ordeal by fire, he exiles her from his kingdom to stop the gossip of the citizens and to protect his own reputation, and finally he demands that she undergo a public ordeal. Throughout all this Sītā remains steadfast and usually tries to blame herself instead of Rāma for events that cause her suffering and separation from Rāma. In her loyalty and chastity, furthermore, it is understood that she supports and nourishes Rāma's strength and reputation. A common Hindu belief is that a man is strengthened, indeed, is made nearly invulnerable, by his wife's chastity, whereas he is weakened and endangered by her faithlessness. Thus when Rāvaṇa shows Sītā Rāma's head and bow, she immediately blames herself. Although she cannot remember being faithless in act or thought, she assumes that she must have been at some time (perhaps in a past life) in order for Rāma to meet such an untimely end. It does not occur to her that some fault of Rāma's own might have led to his misfortune.

Although in Hinduism there are differing marital-role expectations and traditions concerning where brides are expected to live after marriage, it is generally true that the good woman and ideal wife should express submission and docility to her in-laws. Speaking of the training of girls in Mysore, M. N. Srinivas says:

> It is the mother's duty to train her daughter up to be an absolute docile daughter-in-law. The *summum bonum* of a girl's life is to please her parents-in-law and her husband. If she does not "get on" with her mother-in-law, she will be a disgrace to her family, and cast a blot on the fair name of her mother. The Kannada mother dins into her daughter's ears certain ideals which make for harmony (at the expense of her sacrificing her will) in her life.[31]

In the Hindu tradition a woman is taught to understand herself primarily in relation to others. She is taught to emphasize in the development of her character what others expect of her. It is society that puts demands on her, primarily through the agents of relatives and in-laws, and not she who places demands on society that she be allowed to develop a unique, independent destiny. A central demand placed on women, particularly vis-à-vis males, is that they subordinate their welfare to the welfare of others. Hindu women are taught to cultivate an attitude that identifies their own welfare with the welfare of others, especially that of their husbands and children.

> In the *bratas*, the periodical days of fasting and prayer which unmarried girls keep all over India, the girl's wishes for herself are almost always in relation to others; she asks the boons of being a good daughter, good wife, good daughter-in-law, good mother, and so forth. Thus, in addition to the "virtue" of self-effacement and self-sacrifice, the feminine role in India crystallizes a woman's connections to others, her embeddedness in a multitude of familial relationships.[32]

In inculcating the nature of the ideal woman in India, Sītā plays an important role, perhaps the dominant role of all Hindu mythological figures. The *Rāmāyaṇa*, either in its original Sanskrit version or in one of several vernacular renditions, is well known by almost every Hindu. Many of the leading characters have come to represent Hindu ideals. In the context of the Daśa Puttal Vrata, for example, Bengali girls wish that "I shall have a husband like Rāma, I shall be *sati* like Sītā, I shall have a Devara [younger brother-in-law] like Lakshman. I shall have a father-in-law like Dasaratha; I shall have a mother-in-law like Kousalya."[33]

Sītā represents all the qualities of a good woman and ideal wife. Although other goddesses, such as Pārvatī and Lakṣmī, and other heroines from Hindu mythology, such as Sāvitrī and Damayantī, express many of these qualities, Sītā is by far the most popular and beloved paradigm for wifely devotion, forbearance, and chastity.

> From earliest childhood, a Hindu has heard Sita's legend recounted on any number of sacral and secular occasions; seen the central episodes enacted in folk plays like the *Ram Lila;* heard her qualities extolled in devotional songs; and absorbed the ideal feminine identity she incorporates through the many everyday metaphors and similes that are associated with her name. Thus, "She is as pure as Sita" denotes chastity in a woman, and "She is a second Sita," the appreciation of a woman's uncomplaining self-sacrifice. If, as Jerome Bruner remarks, "In the mythologically instructed community there is a corpus of images and models that provide the pattern to which the individual may aspire, a range of metaphoric identity," then this range, in the case of a Hindu woman, is condensed in one model. And she is Sita.[34]

IDEAL DEVOTEE AND INTERMEDIARY

After Vālmikī's *Rāmāyaṇa,* Rāma increasingly ascended to a position of supreme deity for many Hindus. Today in India he is one of the most popular deities and is the recipient of fervent devotion from millions of devotees. The shift in Rāma's status from that of a human hero or incarnation of Viṣṇu in Vālmikī's *Rāmāyaṇa* to that of the lord of the worlds is evident in the sixteenth-century Hindi work of Tulsī Dās, the *Rāmcarit-mānas,* an extremely popular devotional work in North India. Although the central narrative remains the same, even in most particulars, Tulsī Dās frequently alters the story in such a way that opportunities are afforded to express devotion to Rāma as the Lord. Throughout the text it is clear that the central point of the narrative is Rāma's descent to the earth in order to provide his devotees a chance to worship him.[35]

In the process of Rāma's elevation to divine supremacy, Sītā also underwent certain changes. Her status becomes similarly elevated when Rāma becomes identified with the highest god. In his poem *Kavitāvalī* Tulsī Dās refers to Sītā as the world's mother and to Rāma as the world's father (1.15).[36] Elsewhere in the poem Rāma and Sītā are praised in fervent, devotional language by village women who see them walking along the road. The two are compared to various divine couples, and the very sight of them has redemptive effects (2.14–25; 7.36). In another of Tulsī Dās's works Rāma and Sītā are worshiped and addressed in devotional tones: "My mind now tells me that save for Rāma's and Sītā's feet I shall go nowhere else."[37] In his invocation to his *Rāmcaritmānas* Tulsī Dās invokes several deities and includes this verse to Sītā: "Hail to Rama's own beloved Sita, victor o'er all suff'ring, / Mistress of birth, life, death, and of all happiness the giver."[38] In the popular folk dramas of North India, the Rām Līlās, in which whole villages act out the story of Rāma over the course of several weeks, the actors playing the roles of Rāma and Sītā are worshiped by the spectators as deities.[39]

Consistent with her role in Vālmīki's *Rāmāyaṇa* as the ideal wife who subordinates herself to her husband, Sītā never achieves the position of a great, powerful, independent deity. Even compared to such goddesses as Lakṣmī and Pārvatī, who in most respects are portrayed as ideal wives in Hindu mythology, Sītā lacks an identity, power, and will of her own. She remains in Rāma's shadow to such an extent that she is often hardly visible at all. Sītā is rarely mentioned in such devotional works as Tulsī Dās's *Kavitāvalī* and *Vinaya-patrikā*. Hanuman and Lakṣmaṇa, in fact, are mentioned more often than she is. And when Rāma's consort is specified, Tulsī Dās often prefers to identify her as Lakṣmī, not as Sītā.[40] In fact, Tulsī Dās expresses devotion more often to Pārvatī and Gaṅgā as goddesses than he does to Sītā.[41]

In popular Hinduism today Sīta is revered as a deity, and in the numerous Rām Līlā performances throughout the Hindi-speaking area of North India the actor who plays Sītā (all actors are males) is worshiped as a deity. But Sītā is rarely worshiped in her own right. It would be very unusual to find a temple dedicated to Sītā alone. In Rāma and Hanuman temples an image of Sītā is installed alongside or between Rāma and Lakṣmaṇa, where she receives worship along with her husband and brother-in-law. Though she is honored along with Rāma, it is understood that she is not his equal.

If Sītā does not assume the role of a popular, powerful goddess more or less equal to her husband Rāma, she does play two important roles in the context of devotion to Rāma: the role of intermediary and the role of ideal devotee. Addressing her as world mother, Tulsī Dās petitions Sītā to act as his advocate before Rāma.[42] She is not approached directly for divine blessing but as one who has access to Rāma, who alone dispenses divine grace. Again, consistent with her subordinate position vis-à-vis Rāma in the *Rāmāyaṇa*, consistent with her role as one who always subordinates her will to his, Sītā here acts primarily as a messenger between Rāma and his devotees. In her loyalty and devotion she has gained the Lord's ear, and because of this she is sometimes approached by his devotees for help in seeking Rāma's favor.

Sītā also assumes the role of devotee in the later Rāma cult and thus assumes a place as model to Rāma's devotees. Although Hanuman is the most popular model of Rāma devotion in the later Rāma cults, Sītā is often pictured as an ardent devotee. In the *Rāmcarit-mānas*, for example, she is typically pictured as intoxicated by the appearance of Rāma and steadfastly devoted to him. Indeed, in the *Rāmcarit-mānas* Tulsī Dās has sometimes altered the narrative in such a way as to emphasize Sītā's devotion and love for Rāma. For example, in the Vālmikī *Rāmāyaṇa* Sītā pleads to accompany Rāma to the forest by appealing to law and custom. She argues that a wife's duty is to be with her husband. In the *Rāmcarit-mānas*, however, Rāma and others argue that religious custom and law dictate that she should stay behind and take care of her in-laws. Backing up these arguments are other reasons why she should stay behind, including the argument that someone as delicate as Sītā could not endure the difficulties of the forest life. Sītā's reply does not dwell on the social norm that a wife always be with her husband, as in the Vālmīki *Rāmāyaṇa*, but on the unbearable agony that separation from her husband will inflict. It is not her sense of duty but her love for and devotion to Rāma which give Sītā's plea its force and passion in the *Rāmcarit-mānas*.[43]

Sītā's role as devotee, like her role as intermediary, casts her in a subsidiary positon vis-à-vis Rāma. He is the supreme deity, the object of devotion; she is the ideal devotee, the model for the human devotee. Wifely devotion has here become a metaphor for ideal devotion to God.

6

RĀDHĀ

Rādhā, like Sītā, is understood primarily in relation to a male consort. Throughout her history Rādhā has been inextricably associated with the god Kṛṣṇa. Unlike Sītā, however, Rādhā's relationship to Kṛṣṇa is adulterous. Although she is married to another, she is passionately attracted to Kṛṣṇa. Rādhā's illicit relationship with Kṛṣṇa breaks all social norms and casts her in the role of one who willfully steps outside the realm of dharma to pursue her love. In contrast to Sītā, who is the model of wifely devotion and loyalty, whose foremost concern is the reputation and well-being of her husband, Rādhā invests her whole being in an adulterous affair with the irresistibly beautiful Kṛṣṇa.

This relationship takes place during Kṛṣṇa's youth or adolescence, before his adult years, when he marries Rukminī, Satyabhāmā, and others, and before his part in the *Mahābhārata* war. Rādhā and Kṛṣṇa's love affair takes place in the cowherd village of Vraja and in the woods and bowers of Vṛndāvana. In many ways the setting is idyllic, removed from the pragmatic world of social duty, a setting often described as filled with natural beauty, where spring is eternal, and where the vigor and excitement of youth are expressed through Kṛṣṇa's sports. In most ways Vraja is heaven on earth.[1]

But all is not blissful fulfillment for Rādhā. Her liaison with Kṛṣṇa is brief, and even at its passionate height Kṛṣṇa arouses Rādhā's jealousy by consorting with other lovers. The theme of love in separation is a dominant one in their relationship (particularly from Rādha's point of view) and counterbalances the frenzy and ecstasy of their union.

Rādhā's popularity develops primarily in the context of devotion to Kṛṣṇa. In religious movements in which devotion to the cowherd god is central, such as the Bengal Vaiṣṇavas and the Vallabhācārins, Rādhā becomes the model of love for the Lord. It is primarily Kṛṣṇa devotees who write poems celebrating the many nuances of Rādhā and Kṛṣṇa's love; for these devotees Rādhā's frenzied love for Kṛṣṇa is an emotion and an attitude to be emulated. The love affair of Rādhā and Kṛṣṇa in this devotional context becomes a metaphor for the divine-human relationship. Rādhā represents the human devotee who gives up everything in order to cling to the Lord, and Kṛṣṇa represents God, irresistibly beautiful and attractive. The aim of Kṛṣṇa devotees is to develop or uncover the Rādhā dimension within themselves, that tendency within all human beings to devote themselves entirely and passionately to Kṛṣṇa.

THE EARLY HISTORY OF RĀDHĀ

Rādhā does not appear as a fully developed figure until quite late in the Hindu tradition. Prior to Jayadeva's *Gītagovinda* (twelfth century) she is mentioned in only a few brief references.[2] The *Padma-, Brahmavaivarta-,* and *Devī-bhāgavata-purāṇas,* which describe her affair with Kṛṣṇa in detail, are all considered late. Although the early references are few and although they never supply lengthy descriptions of Rādhā, her character is nevertheless clearly suggested.

In these passages Rādhā is a lovesick girl or woman who is overcome by her emotions. The *Veṇīsaṁhāra* of Bhaṭṭa Nārāyaṇa (antedates A.D. 800) describes Rādhā as being angered while making love to Kṛṣṇa and as leaving him while choking on her tears.[3] In the *Dhvanyalokālocana* of Abhinavagupta (early tenth century) Rādhā weeps pitifully when Kṛṣṇa leaves the village of Vraja for Mathurā, where he begins his adult life.[4] She is described in Kṣemendra's *Daśāvatāracarita* (1066) as barely able to speak when Kṛṣṇa leaves for Mathurā.

> With tears, flowing away like life in Mādhava's desertion,
> Falling on her breasts' firm tips, Rādhā was like a laden
> kadamba tree
> As tears were strewn by her endless sighing and trembling
> gait—
> Darkened by the delusion that was bound to all her hopes,
> She became like the new rainy season engulfed in darkness.[5]

Although the adulterous aspect of her love is not mentioned explicitly in any of these early references, the centrality of love in separation (*viraha*) is clear in almost every one. In later texts it is the illicit nature of Rādhā's love for Kṛṣṇa that usually necessitates long periods of separation and dictates that she cannot leave with him when he goes away to

Mathurā or later to Dvāraka; it is probable that the authors of these earlier passages also understood Rādhā to be married to another man, to be *parakīyā* (belonging to another) in her relationship with Kṛṣṇa.

Another characteristic of Rādhā is clear in these early references: she is always associated with Kṛṣṇa. None of the references shows interest in Rādhā per se. It is only her love for Kṛṣṇa, or his love for her, which is mentioned. In several of these texts Kṛṣṇa is as hopelessly impassioned and maddened by love as Rādhā. When he mounts his chariot to leave Vraja he is described in Kṣemendra's *Daśāvatāracarita* as looking longingly for a sight of Rādhā, as being disconsolate, and as sighing unhappily.[6] In the *Siddhahemaśabdānuśāna* of Hemacandra (1088–1172) we read:

> Though Hari sees every person with full regard,
> Still his glance goes wherever Rādhā is—
> Who can arrest eyes ensnared by love?[7]

Prior to her appearance as a fully developed heroine in Jayadeva's *Gītagovinda*, then, Rādhā is known to the Indian literary tradition as a young girl who is passionately in love with Kṛṣṇa; that love is often expressed in terms of separation from him, which suggests an illicit quality to their affair.

THE *GOPĪ* TRADITION

Another historical thread is important in understanding Rādhā's central role in Jayadeva's writing and in the later devotional movements of North India. This is the mythological tradition surrounding Kṛṣṇa's sojourn in Vraja and his dalliance there with the *gopīs*, the cowherd women of the village. This tradition dates back to the *Harivaṁśa* (ca. A.D. 500) and is a central part of most later Vaiṣṇava *Purānas*. The most popular and detailed rendering of the tradition prior to Jayadeva is found in the *Bhāgavata-purāṇa*, written in South India sometime during the tenth century.[8] According to this mythological tradition, Kṛṣṇa's father spirits him away from Mathurā, where he was born, to escape the threat of his murderous uncle, Kaṁsa. Kṛṣṇa's father leaves the infant in the home of Nanda and Yaśodā, a cowherd couple, who raise the child as their own in the village of Vraja. On reaching maturity Kṛṣṇa leaves Vraja, returns to Mathurā, and slays Kaṁsa. According to early renditions of this tradition, Kṛṣṇa is an incarnation of Viṣṇu, and the purpose of his incarnation as Kṛṣṇa is to slay Kaṁsa, who is oppressing the earth with his wickedness. The primary focus of the narrative in the *Bhāgavata-purāṇa,* however, and the central interest of the later devotional traditions in North India, is Kṛṣṇa's sojourn in Vraja, where he sports with his young companions and, on reaching adolescence, dallies with the women of the village.

The village women dote on Kṛṣṇa as a child. They tolerate and are often amused by his pranks. But their interest in him changes to passionate longing when he grows older. They are all married women, but none is able to resist Kṛṣṇa's beauty and charm. He is described as retiring to the woods, where he plays his flute on autumn nights when the moon is full. Hearing the music, the women are driven mad with passion and give up their domestic roles and chores to dash away to be with Kṛṣṇa in the bowers of Vṛndāvana. They jump up in the middle of putting on their makeup, abandon their families while eating a meal with them, leave food to burn on the stove, and run out of their homes to be with Kṛṣṇa. They are so distraught and frenzied as they rush to his side that their clothes and jewelry come loose and fall off (10.29.3–7).

In the woods the *gopīs* sport and play with Kṛṣṇa. They make love in the forest and in the waters of the Jumna River. In some accounts of the tradition Kṛṣṇa is said to multiply himself so that each woman has a Kṛṣṇa to herself. The mood is joyous, festive, and erotic. The text makes no attempt to deny the impropriety of the *gopīs'* leaving their husbands and abandoning their social responsibilities in order to make love to Kṛṣṇa. Kṛṣṇa even teases some of the women for behaving illicitly (10.29.26–27).

No mention is made of Rādhā in any of these early accounts of the *gopī* tradition. The *gopīs,* in fact, are not mentioned by name but are usually treated as a group. In general, Kṛṣṇa is portrayed as sporting with many women at once. The *Bhāgavata-purāṇa* mentions a favorite *gopī.* Kṛṣṇa goes off with her alone, but when she begins to feel proud of herself for being singled out by Kṛṣṇa and asks him to carry her, he disappears, reducing her to tears and remorse (10.30.35–38). The lesson seems clear: Kṛṣṇa's love is not exclusive. He loves all the cowherd women and encourages them all to love him in return.

The role of the cowherd women in the context of devotion is made fairly clear in the *Bhāgavata-purāṇa* itself. The nature of true devotion, the text says, is highly emotional and causes horripilation, tears, loss of control, and frenzy (11.14.23–24). Those who love the Lord truly behave like the *gopīs.* They let nothing come between themselves and the Lord. When they hear his call they abandon everything to be with him. Even though they are married and have household duties to attend to, even though they incur the censure of society, they rush off to be with Kṛṣṇa when they hear his call. So too should the ardent devotee behave in loving Kṛṣṇa. In their disregard for normal social roles, in their extreme emotion and frenzy, the *gopīs* serve as an appropriate metaphor for the divine-human love affair. Rādhā, as we shall see, inherits this role in the later devotional movements, particularly in Bengal.

RĀDHĀ AS BELONGING TO ANOTHER (*PARAKĪYĀ*)

Not until Jayadeva's *Gītagovinda* in the twelfth century do we find a sustained rendition of Rādhā as the central figure in the love drama between Kṛṣṇa and the cowherd women of Vraja. In this poem the tradition of Rādhā as Kṛṣṇa's favorite and the tradition of the *gopīs* came together to form the central heroine of the text. The poem is dominated by the lovesick Rādhā, who ventures out at night to search the woods for her lover, Kṛṣṇa. Several familiar allusions to Vraja and to Kṛṣṇa's foster parents make it clear that the context of the drama is set in the cowherd village described in the earlier *gopī* tradition. The whole flavor of the poem, however, lacks the festive, joyful, carnival-like atmosphere of earlier descriptions of Kṛṣṇa's love play with the cowherd women. The *Gītagovinda* is written almost entirely from Rādhā's point of view, and the dominant emotion is love in separation (*viraha*).

The texts in the *gopī* tradition prior to Jayadeva focused primarily on the external characteristics of the women's attachment to Kṛṣṇa. Frenzy, horripilation, frantic haste, and shuddering characterize the *gopīs* when they hear Kṛṣṇa's flute and dally with him in the woods. With Rādhā the focus changes to the internal, shifting moods of a specific woman. Whereas the early *gopī* tradition concentrated on exterior landscapes, painting lush pictures of Kṛṣṇa's dalliance with hundreds of smitten women in the woods of Vṛndāvana, the *Gītagovinda* through the heroine Rādhā explores interior landscapes and paints moody pictures of obsessive love. Almost the entire *Gītagovinda* deals with Rādhā separated from and searching for Kṛṣṇa. She experiences longing, jealousy, and sorrow. The overall mood is not that of joyful union, although the two do unite blissfully at the end of the poem, but of love in separation, which causes Rādhā pain. In the flowering bowers of Vṛndāvana, amid the joyful celebration of spring throughout the natural world, Rādhā is tormented by her love.

> When spring came, tender-limbed Rādhā wandered
> Like a flowering creeper in the forest wilderness,

Seeking Krishna in his many haunts.
The god of love increased her ordeal,
Tormenting her with fevered thoughts,
And her friend sang to heighten the mood.[9]

Although Rādhā's marital status is not specified in the *Gītagovinda*, there are hints that she belongs to another man.[10] The whole drama takes place at night in the woods and is surrounded by secrecy. It is not a relationship that takes place under the approving eye of society. Whether or not Rādhā is married to another man, Kṛṣṇa certainly is not married to her and consorts with other women, which makes Rādhā jealous. The whole mood suggests that Rādhā's love for Kṛṣṇa is illicit, that she has no formal claim on him, and that in order to be with him she must risk the dangers of the night, the woods, and public censure.

Rādhā's illicit love for Kṛṣṇa is the central theme in the poetry of Vidyāpati (1352–1448) and Caṇḍīdās (ca. fourteenth to fifteenth century). Both authors make it clear that she is married to another man and that she risks social ostracism by pursuing her affair with Kṛṣṇa. Vidyāpati describes Rādhā as a woman of noble family, but he portrays Kṛṣṇa as a common villager. In loving Kṛṣṇa Rādhā sacrifices her status and reputation.

I who body and soul
am at your beck and call,
was a girl of noble family.
I took no thought for what would be said of me,
I abandoned everything.[11]

Many poems portray Rādhā as torn between seeking out Kṛṣṇa and protecting her reputation. Her love for him totally possesses her but is extremely dangerous to reveal. The matter is put succinctly by Rādhā at one point: "If I go [to Kṛṣṇa] I lose my home / If I stay I lose my love."[12] As always happens when Rādhā is so torn, she decides in favor of going to Kṛṣṇa, in this case despite a full moon that lights up the village and forest so that she fears she will be discovered.

The theme of Rādhā's abandoning her social duty to love Kṛṣṇa is central in the poems of Caṇḍīdās. Caṇḍīdās describes Rādhā as a forthright, strong-willed woman who, although married to a man named Āyāna, does not hesitate to incur the wrath of her family and village to be with Kṛṣṇa. In Caṇḍīdās's poems Rādhā is not secretive about her illicit love, although the dire social consequences of her adultery are mentioned repeatedly. Realizing that it will entail social censure, she

Rādhā and Kṛṣṇa. Kangra, 1785 A.D. Victoria and Albert Museum. Philip Rawson, *Oriental Erotic Art* (New York: A and W Publishers, 1981), fig. 44, p. 50.

knowingly and willfully makes a choice to love Kṛṣṇa; having made that choice she is not inclined to keep her adultery a secret.

> Casting away
> All ethics of caste
> My heart dotes on Krishna
> Day and night.
> The custom of the clan
> Is a far-away cry
> And now I know
> That love adheres wholly
> To its own laws.[13]

Rādhā is rebellious in her attitude, cursing her fate and the society that would keep her married to her husband, whom she describes as a dolt, and away from Kṛṣṇa. Impatient and angry with her painful situation, she threatens to burn down her house, which represents a social identity and destiny that would keep her away from her beloved.

> I throw ashes at all laws
> Made by man or god.
> I am born alone,
> With no companion.
> What is the worth
> Of your vile laws
> That failed me
> In love,
> And left me with a fool,
> A dumbskull [Āyāna]?
>
> My wretched fate
> Is so designed
> That he is absent
> For whom I long.
> I will set fire to this house
> And go away.[14]

In the sixteenth century a devotional movement centered on the worship of Kṛṣṇa arose in Bengal. At the center of this movement was Caitanya (1486–1533), who in his own devotion to Kṛṣṇa imitated the emotional traumas of the lovesick Rādhā. In the subsequent history of the movement Rādhā continued to play a central role as the devotee par excellence of Kṛṣṇa. According to the theologians of the movement, a devotee may approach the Lord in a variety of moods or modes: the contemplative mood, in which the Lord is approached as transcendent; the mood of the servant, in which the Lord is approached as a master; the mood of a friend; the mood of a parent; and the mood of the lover. Furthermore, the theologians have ranked these moods. The least worthy modes of approach to Kṛṣṇa emphasize his transcendent qualities of lordship; the most worthy modes maximize the intimacy between the devotee and Kṛṣṇa. The mood of the lover is affirmed to be the best approach, the mood most cherished by the Lord himself, and of all lovers of the Lord Rādhā is affirmed to be Kṛṣṇa's favorite. Throughout the poetry, literature, and devotion of the movement, Rādhā plays a central role. Her *parakīyā* (belonging to another man) status vis-à-vis Kṛṣṇa is also maintained in the mythology, worship, and theology of the Bengal Vaiṣṇavas.

What seems clear is that the Bengal Vaiṣṇavas and other devotional movements that center on Kṛṣṇa devotion, such as the Vallabhācārins,[15] understand quite well that the adulterous nature of Rādhā's love for Kṛṣṇa is appropriate as a devotional metaphor. In fact, the superiority of illicit love is argued by the Bengal Vaiṣṇava theologians in some detail. Their main point is that illicit love is given freely, makes no legal claims, and as such is selfless. Married love, they argue, functions according to rights and obligations in which both partners have specific expectations of each other, including sexual gratification. Married love, it is argued, is characterized by *kāma* (sexual lust), while Rādhā's love, illicit and adulterous though it may be, is characterized by *prema* (selfless love for the beloved).[16] And selfless love is what Kṛṣṇa desires.

The illicit nature of Rādhā's love is deemed appropriate for other reasons as well. Because of the adulterous nature of her love, Rādhā must overcome many obstacles in order to satisfy her love. The impediments put in her way serve to increase that love. The long periods of separation, far from cooling her emotions, serve to enhance her feelings. Married love, in contrast, operates without any obstacles or impediments. There is very little separation, and it can become routine and boring. Rādhā's love for Kṛṣṇa is full of risk, insecurity, painful separation, and hence periodic thrills of union. As a metaphor of the divine-human relationship, the illicit nature of Rādhā's love is held to be superior to any example of married love. The devotional attitude held in highest esteem by the Bengal Vaiṣṇavas is characterized by uncontrolled frenzy, weeping, and ecstatic feelings. The Lord's presence is held to be surpassingly beautiful and irresistible and its effect on the devotee devastating. The devotee, however, in responding to the Lord's presence, can never count on binding the Lord through love. Kṛṣṇa is always free to come and go, and the devotee often spends long periods in painful separation from Kṛṣṇa. These feelings and experiences, seen as rare in married love, are epitomized in Rādhā's adulterous love.

It is probably not surprising that some Bengal Vaiṣṇavas were tempted to argue that Rādhā was *svakīyā* (married to Kṛṣṇa) in her affair with Kṛṣṇa. An adulterous sexual affair at the center of their devotional mythology was understandably embarrassing to some devotees. The illicit nature of Rādhā's love, however, her *parakīyā* status, eventually came to be declared the orthodox position. The issue was even the subject of a formal debate in 1717. The proponents of the *parakīyā* position were declared the winners.[17]

Given Rādhā's central position in Bengal Vaiṣṇavism it is understandable that she herself tended to become an object of devotion and the subject of metaphysical speculation in the writings of the movement. The sixteenth-century dramas of Rūpa Gosvāmin, the leading theologian of the movement, cast Rādhā in the familiar role as the foremost lover of the Lord, the paradigm of complete devotion. Her mind is totally obsessed with Kṛṣṇa to the point that, in pique, she tries in vain to forget him. Her utter preoccupation with him is contrasted to those mere fleeting glimpses that sages and ascetics attain of the Lord after arduous meditation and spiritual exercises.

> Seeking to meditate for a moment upon Krishna,
> The sage wrests his mind from the objects of sense;
> This child [Rādhā] draws her mind away from Him
> To fix it on mere worldly things.
> The *yogī* yearns for a tiny flash of Krishna in his heart;
> Look—this foolish girl strives to banish Him from hers![18]

Rādhā has also achieved the position of receiving devotion herself in these plays. The most sustained example in Rūpa's plays is the devotion of Kṛṣṇa himself to Rādhā. He is often pictured doting on Rādhā, concentrating his mind on her with the single-minded attention of a yogi and losing sleep because of her.[19] Just as Rādhā in her total preoccupation with Kṛṣṇa sees him everywhere, so Kṛṣṇa is similarly entranced and sees Rādhā everywhere. "Radha appears before me on every side; how is it that for me the three worlds have become Rādhā?"[20] And just as Rādhā makes gestures of adoration toward Kṛṣṇa in the dramas, so too Kṛṣṇa makes worshipful gestures to Rādhā, which indicate to the audience Rādhā's status as a being worthy of reverence.

Other characters in the plays also revere Rādhā. The elderly go-between, Paurṇamasī, Rādhā's two female friends, Lalitā and Viśākhā, and Kṛṣṇa's foster mother, Yaśodā, all admire and dote on Rādhā in various moods that are held appropriate for devotion to Kṛṣṇa.[21] In many cases Rādhā's own emotions toward Kṛṣṇa are echoed in the emotions of Rādhā's friends toward her. Lalitā, for example, cries in grief at the thought of Rādhā's leaving, just as Rādhā grieves at the thought of Kṛṣṇa's leaving.[22] Rūpa's aim in the drama seems clear: he is portraying Rādhā as worthy of devotion by Kṛṣṇa devotees. In doing this, however, he is not detracting from the centrality of Kṛṣṇa himself, who throughout the dramas is the object of Rādhā's passion.

Rādhā's status as a being worthy of worship by Kṛṣṇa devotees is explained in the philosophic teachings of the Bengal Vaiṣṇavas. Kṛṣṇa, the ultimate godhead, includes within himself various *śaktis*, powers through which he reveals and displays himself. For example, by means of certain *śaktis* he creates the world. His essential nature, however, is displayed through his *svarūpa śakti* (own form). Within this *svarūpa śakti* are contained other *śaktis*, the most essential of which is the *hlādinī śakti*, the *śakti* of bliss. This *śakti* is understood to be the most refined essence of the godhead, Kṛṣṇa in his most sublime and complete form. And this *hlādinī śakti* is identified with none other than Rādhā herself.[23]

If Rādhā is Kṛṣṇa, if Kṛṣṇa is Rādhā—which is the import of this theological doctrine—then Rādhā is essentially divine and as such worthy of the devotee's adoration. From the point of view of the devotee, Rādhā's centrality to devotion is not limited to her role as a model to be imitated or an ideal to be pursued. She herself may now be doted on with efficacious results, as she herself is part of, indeed, is the essence of, the godhead. In this theological vision Rādhā has assumed the position of Kṛṣṇa's eternal *śakti*. Her role as the ideal human devotee is necessarily played down as her divine status as Kṛṣṇa's *śakti* is emphasized. On the model of other divine couples—Śiva-Pārvatī, Rāma-Sītā, Viṣṇu-Lakṣmī—Rādhā assumes the position of a heavenly deity whom the devotee supplicates.

Another significant implication of this theological vision is that Rādhā is no longer necessarily seen as *parakīyā* to Kṛṣṇa. Although their dalliances may be described as illicit, although Rādhā is said to be married to another man, ultimately she is an aspect of Kṛṣṇa's own being and thus really belongs to him. His sport with her is an eternal self-dalliance by which or in which he is enabled to appreciate his own paramount beauty.[24]

Although the theology of the Bengal Vaiṣṇavas provides an avenue for reinterpreting Rādhā as belonging to Kṛṣṇa and not to another man, the movement steadfastly resisted playing down the illicit, adulterous dimension of Rādhā's love for Kṛṣṇa and even declared the *parakīyā* position the orthodox doctrine. From the devotional point of view, Rādhā's love for Kṛṣṇa would lose some of its intensity, fervor, and passion if she were understood to be married to him. To this day, among Kṛṣṇa devotees for whom the mode of the lover is the most sublime approach to Kṛṣṇa, it is understood that Rādhā's love for Kṛṣṇa, which is always described as selfless love (*prema*), expresses itself without any formal obligation or legal duty on her part. Her love is spontaneous and complete. In her relationship with Kṛṣṇa she gains nothing (from the worldly point of view), losing her reputation, pride of family, and so on. She clearly goes against the ways of the world to express her emotions. It is as an adulteress that these dimensions of her love are best expressed. Rādhā loves Kṛṣṇa *in spite* of everything, not because she has an obligation to him.

RĀDHĀ AS BELONGING TO KṚṢṆA (*SVAKĪYĀ*)

Although Rādhā's position as Kṛṣṇa's legal, divine consort never became very popular in Kṛṣṇa devotional movements, there is a sustained rendition of Kṛṣṇa mythology in which Rādhā is cast in this role. The *Brahma-vaivarta-purāṇa* assumes Rādhā's status as a goddess.[25] She is inextricably associated with Kṛṣṇa philosophically as his *śakti*, as his underlying power or that dimension of himself that empowers him, indeed, enables him, to create the world and display himself in his various forms. Several passages compare Rādhā to Kṛṣṇa in such a way that her status is affirmed to be comparable, equal, or even superior to his own. For example, a familiar analogy likens Rādhā to the clay with which Kṛṣṇa, the potter, creates the world.[26] She is identified with *prakṛti*, the primordial matter or substance of creation; Kṛṣṇa is identified with *puruṣa*, the spiritual essence of reality that stirs *prakṛti* to evolve into various forms. Elsewhere the two are identified on the analogy of attribute and substance. Kṛṣṇa says to Rādhā:

> As you are, so am I; there is certainly no difference
> between us.
> As whiteness inheres in milk, as burning in fire,
> my fair Lady,
> As smell in earth, so do I inhere in you always.[27]

Another passage describes the two as initially forming an androgynous figure, of which Kṛṣṇa is one half and Rādhā the other. Rādhā says to Kṛṣṇa:

I have been constructed by someone out of half your body;
Therefore there is no difference between us, and my
heart is in you.
Just as my Self (Ātman), heart, and life has been placed
in you,
So has your Self, heart, and life been placed in me.[28]

The text elevates Rādhā to such an extent that in several places it states that she is superior in status to Kṛṣṇa himself. In one passage, for example, Kṛṣṇa is speaking to Rādhā and says that all things in the universe have some kind of support, that without some kind of support they could not exist. His support, he concludes, is Rādhā, upon whom he rests eternally.[29] She alone, by implication, has no support and as such is the supreme reality. In another place Kṛṣṇa likens Rādhā to his *ātman*: "You are my life; I am dead without you."[30] In another passage Rādhā is called mother of the world and Kṛṣṇa father of the world. The mother, however, is declared to be the guru of the father and as such is said to be worshiped as supreme.[31]

Rādhā's elevated status, her role as cosmic queen equal to or superior to Kṛṣṇa, gives her a central role in the cosmogony in the *Brahma-vaivarta-purāṇa*. In one version of creation Kṛṣṇa desires to create and so divides himself into two, male and female. The two undertake sexual intercourse for a long time, during which his sighs and the sweat from her body create the winds and primordial oceans. Eventually he ejaculates into her; after bearing his seed for many years, she gives birth to a golden egg, the universe itself. The egg floats in the cosmic waters for a long time, then splits, and the god Viṣṇu is born; he in turn creates innumerable worlds.[32] As creator of the universe we find Rādhā playing a role that is extremely atypical of her earlier history, namely, the role of mother. Nowhere in earlier literature is Rādhā a mother. In the *Brahma-vaivarta-purāṇa*, however, she is often called by names that suggest her motherly role vis-à-vis the created world. She is called mother of Viṣṇu (Mahāviṣṇormātṛ, Mahāviṣṇudhātrī), mother of the world (Jaganmātṛ, Jagadambikā), and mother of all (Sarvamātṛ).[33]

Rādhā's personal relationship to Kṛṣṇa has also undergone significant changes in this text. In earlier literature her relationship to him was consistently described as nonpossessive and was characterized by love in separation. These qualities stemmed in good measure from the illicit nature of their love, in which neither could exert legal or formal controls over the other. As a woman married to another man, Rādhā owed Kṛṣṇa nothing. In the *Brahma-vaivarta-purāṇa*, however, in which the two are understood to be eternally related to each other as husband and wife (or as god and goddess), Rādhā's love takes on a possessive quality. As the queen of the cosmos, as consort of the great god Kṛṣṇa, she is described as surrounded and worshiped by millions of cowherd devotees and as acting the part of the chaste and jealous wife of Kṛṣṇa. At several points in the text Rādhā discovers Kṛṣṇa dallying with other women. Her reaction is always the same: she is outraged, jealous, and vengeful. She terrifies Kṛṣṇa in her rage and curses her rivals to miserable fates. In one case a woman named Virājā is so scared of Rādhā's wrath that she commits suicide.[34] Rādhā's love is described in many episodes as cruel, selfish, and demanding. In several cases she nags Kṛṣṇa about which consort he loves best and is only contented when he flatters her.[35] In contrast to earlier descriptions of her love for Kṛṣṇa, in the *Brahma-vaivarta-purāṇa* she is a selfish, vindictive, and insecure wife who makes life miserable for Kṛṣṇa, herself, and the other women of heavenly Vraja. If Rādhā has gained metaphysical promotion in the *Brahma-vaivarta-purāṇa*, it seems to have been at the expense of losing her intrinsic appeal as the lovesick girl of Vraja, who is unable to make any claims on her lover. The Rādhā of the *Brahma-vaivarta-purāṇa* has lost her innocence, her intensity, and a considerable part of her charm.

Nevertheless, although most Kṛṣṇa devotional movements rejected this portrait of Rādhā as *svakīyā* (the text is undoubtedly quite late, dating from the fifteenth or sixteenth century), a few small groups revere Rādhā in her role as cosmic queen. Both the Rādhāvallabhins and the Sakhībhavas, movements that arose sometime during the sixteenth century in and around Brindaban in North India, place Rādhā in a position similar to her position in the *Brahma-vaivarta-purāṇa*. The Rādhāvallabhins in their actual devotion concentrate on Rādhā more than on Kṛṣṇa. The Sakhībhavas express their piety by concentrating on becoming servants or friends of Rādhā. In their rituals they dress like women and express their devotion by doting on Rādhā and serving her in every way. The attitude of these movements is nicely expressed in the words of one of their members: "Krishna is the servant of Rādhā. He may do the coolie-work of building the world, but Rādhā sits as Queen. He is at best but her Secretary of State. We win the favor of Krishna by worshipping Rādhā."[36]

7

DURGĀ

One of the most impressive and formidable goddesses of the Hindu pantheon—and one of the most popular—is the goddess Durgā. Her primary mythological function is to combat demons who threaten the stability of the cosmos. In this role she is depicted as a great battle queen with many arms, each of which wields a weapon. She rides a fierce lion and is described as irresistible in battle. The demon she is most famous for defeating is Mahiṣa, the buffalo demon. Her most popular epithet is Mahiṣa-mardinī, the slayer of Mahiṣa, and her most common iconographic representation shows her defeating Mahiṣa.

At a certain point in her history Durgā becomes associated with the god Śiva as his wife. In this role Durgā assumes domestic characteristics and is often identified with the goddess Pārvatī. She also takes on the role of mother in her later history. At her most important festival, Durgā Pūjā, she is shown flanked by four deities identified as her children: Kārttikeya, Gaṇeśa, Sarasvatī, and Lakṣmī.

It also seems clear that Durgā has, or at least at some point in her history had, a close connection with the crops or with the fertility of vegetation. Her festival, which is held at harvest time, associates her with plants, and she also receives blood offerings, which may suggest the renourishment of her powers of fertility.

THE WARRIOR GODDESS

Although several Vedic deities play central roles as demon slayers and warriors, no goddesses are cast in this function in Vedic literature. The name Durgā is mentioned in Vedic literature,[1] but no goddess resembling the warrior goddess of later Hinduism is to be found in these early texts.

Around the fourth century A.D. images of Durgā slaying a buffalo begin to become common throughout India.[2] By the medieval period (after the sixth century) Durgā has become a well-known and popularly worshiped deity. Her mythological deeds come to be told in many texts, and descriptions of and injunctions to undertake her autumnal worship are common in several late *Upa-purāṇas*.[3]

Durgā's historical origin seems to be among the indigenous non-Āryan cultures of India. In addition to there being no similar goddesses among the deities of the Vedic tradition, many early references to Durgā associate her with peripheral areas such as the Vindhya Mountains, tribal peoples such as the Śabaras, and non-Āryan habits such as drinking liquor and blood and eating meat.[4] Although Durgā becomes an establishment goddess in medieval Hinduism, protecting the cosmos from the threat of demons and guarding dharma like a female version of Viṣṇu, her roots seem to be among the tribal and peasant cultures of India, which eventually leavened the male-dominated Vedic pantheon with several goddesses associated with power, blood, and battle.

Hindu mythology includes several accounts of Durgā's origin. She is sometimes said to arise from Viṣṇu as the power that makes him sleep or as his magical, creative power. In the *Viṣṇu-purāna* Viṣṇu enlists her aid to help delude a demon king who is threatening the infant Kṛṣṇa (5.1.93). In the *Devī-māhātmya* she comes to the aid of the god Brahmā and ultimately of Viṣṇu himself when Brahmā invokes her to leave the slumbering Viṣṇu so that Viṣṇu will awaken and fight the demons Madhu and Kaitabha (1). The *Skanda-purāṇa* relates that once upon a time a demon named Durga threatened the world. Śiva requested Pārvatī to slay the demon. Pārvatī then assumed the form of a warrior goddess and defeated the demon, who took the form of a buffalo. Thereafter, Pārvatī was known by the name Durgā (2.83).[5] A similar account of her origin occurs in myths relating her defeat of the demons Śumbha and Niśumbha. Durgā emerges from Pārvatī in these accounts when Pārvatī sheds her outer sheath, which takes on an identity of its own as a warrior goddess.[6]

The best-known account of Durgā's origin, however, is told in connection with her defeat of the demon Mahiṣa. After performing heroic austerities, Mahiṣa was granted the boon that he would be invincible to all opponents except a woman. He subsequently defeated the gods in battle and usurped their positions. The gods then assembled and, angry at the thought of Mahiṣa's triumph and their apparent inability to do anything about it, emitted their fiery energies. This great mass of light and strength congealed into the body of a beautiful woman, whose splendor spread through the universe. The parts of her body were formed from the male gods. Her face was formed from Śiva, her hair from Yama, her arms from Viṣṇu, and so on. Similarly, each of the male deities from whom she had been created gave her a weapon. Śiva gave her his trident, Viṣṇu gave her his *cakra* (a discus-like weapon), Vayu his bow and arrows, and so on. Equipped by the gods and supplied by the god Himalaya with a lion as her vehicle, Durgā, the embodied strength of the gods, then roared mightily, causing the earth to shake.[7]

The creation of the goddess Durgā thus takes place in the context of a cosmic crisis precipitated by a demon whom the male gods are unable to subdue. She is created because the situation calls for a woman, a superior warrior, a peculiar power possessed by the goddess with which the demon may be deluded, or a combination of all three. Invariably Durgā defeats the demon handily, demonstrating both superior martial ability and superior power. On the battlefield she often creates female helpers from herself. The most famous of these are the goddess Kālī and a group of ferocious deities known as the Mātṛkās (mothers), who usually number seven.[8] These goddesses seem to embody Durgā's fury and are wild, bloodthirsty, and particularly fierce.[9] Durgā does not create male helpers, and to my knowledge she does not fight with male allies. Although she is created by the male gods and does their bidding and although she is observed and applauded by them, she (along with her female helpers and attendants) fights without direct male support against male demons—and she always wins.

Durgā's distinctive nature, and to a great extent probably her appeal, comes from the combination of world-supportive qualities and liminal characteristics that associate her with the periphery of civilized order.[10] In many respects Durgā violates the model of the Hindu woman. She is not submissive, she is not subordinated to a male deity, she does not fulfill household duties, and she excels at what is traditionally a male function, fighting in battle. As an independent warrior who can hold her own against any male on the battlefield, she reverses the normal role for females and therefore stands outside normal society. Unlike the normal female, Durgā does not lend her power or *śakti* to a male consort but rather *takes* power from the male gods in order to perform her own heroic exploits.[11] They give up their inner strength, fire, and heat to create her and in so doing surrender their potency to her.

Many renditions of Durgā's mythological exploits highlight her role reversal by portraying her male antagonists as enamored of her and wanting to marry her. They have no wish to fight her at all, assume that she will be no match for them in battle, and proceed to make offers of marriage to her.[12] In some variants of the myth Durgā explains to her antagonist and would-be suitor that her family has imposed a condition on

Durgā slaying Mahiṣa. Miniature painting from School of Nupur, about 1765 A.D. Victoria and Albert Museum. Marguerite-Marie Deneck, *Indian Art* (London: Paul Hamlyn, 1967), fig. 46.

her marriage, namely, that her husband must first defeat her in battle. The suitor is unable to do this, of course, and is annihilated in his attempt. In some forms of the myth the goddess rejects the offer of marriage with fierce, combative language, foretelling how she will tear her would-be suitor to pieces in battle. The antagonist, however, insists on interpreting this language as a metaphor for love play and blindly insists on trying to overcome the goddess in battle.[13] In the Mahiṣa myth as told in the *Devī-bhāgavata-purāṇa*, for example, a long dialogue takes place between Durgā and the demon in which Mahiṣa insists that as a woman the goddess is too delicate to fight, too beautiful for anything but love play, and must come under the protection and guidance of a man in order to fulfill her proper proclivities (5.16.46–65).

Because Durgā is unprotected by a male deity, Mahiṣa assumes that she is helpless (5.12.14–30), which is the way that women are portrayed in the *Dharma-śāstras*.[14] There women are said to be incapable of handling their own affairs and to be socially inconsequential without relationships with men. They are significant primarily as sisters, daughters, and mothers of males and as wives. Nearly all forms of Durgā's mythical exploits portray her as independent from male support and relationships yet irresistibly powerful. She is beautiful and seductive in appearance, but her beauty does not serve its normal function, which is to attract a husband. It serves to entice her victims into fatal battle.

In short, this beautiful young woman who slays demons seeking to be her lovers and who exists independent from male protection or guidance represents a vision of the feminine that challenges the stereotyped view of women found in traditional Hindu law books. Such a characterization perhaps suggests the extraordinary power that is repressed in women who are forced into submissive and socially demeaning roles. In her role reversal Durgā exists outside normal structures and provides a version of reality that potentially, at least, may be refreshing and socially invigorating.[15]

Durgā's liminal nature is also evident in her favorite habitats and in some of her favorite habits. Nearly all of Durgā's myths associate her with mountains, usually the Himalayas or the Vindhyas. One of her common epithets is Vindhyavāsinī, "she who dwells in the Vindhya Mountains." These mountainous regions are areas considered geographically peripheral to civilized society and inaccessible except through heroic efforts. The Vindhyas, in particular, are also regarded as dangerous because of the violent and hostile tribal peoples who dwell there. Indeed, Durgā is said to be worshiped by tribal groups such as the Śabaras. In this worship, furthermore, she is said to receive (and to enjoy) meat and blood, both of which are regarded by civilized Āryan society as highly polluting. In the *Devī-māhātmya* Durgā is also described as quaffing wine during battle in her fight with Mahiṣa (3.33) and as laughing and glaring with reddened eyes under its influence. In the concluding scene of the *Devī-māhātmya* her devotees are instructed to propitiate her with offerings of their own flesh and blood (13.8). Durgā's preference for inaccessible dwelling places, her worship by tribal peoples, her taste for intoxicating drink, meat, and blood, her ferocious behavior on the battlefield, and her preference for the flesh and blood of her devotees convey a portrait of a goddess who stands outside the civilized order of dharma; her presence is to be found only after stepping out of the orderly world into the liminal space of the mountainous regions where she dwells.

Reinforcing Durgā's tendencies to the antistructural or liminal are certain associations with negative, or at least inauspicious, qualities or powers such as sleep, hunger, and *māyā* (in the sense of delusion). In the Mahiṣa episode of the *Devī-māhātmya* she is called she whose form is sleep (5.15), she whose form is hunger (5.16), she whose form is shadow (5.17), and she whose form is thirst (5.19).

These associations are particularly emphasized in versions of the myth that tell of Durgā's aid to Brahmā and Viṣṇu against the demons Madhu and Kaitabha. In this myth as told in the *Devī-māhātmya* Madhu and Kaitabha are born from Viṣṇu's ear wax. They threaten to kill the god Brahmā, who in turn has been born from a lotus sprung from Viṣṇu's navel. Brahmā appeals to the goddess in the form of sleep to come forth from Viṣṇu so that he will awaken and slay the demons. Throughout the episode the goddess is called Mahāmāya, the power that throws people into the bondage of delusion and attachment (1.40). Indeed, Viṣṇu is successful in slaying Madhu and Kaitabha only because the goddess deludes them into offering Viṣṇu a boon; he accepts and asks that they permit him to slay them (1.73–74). She is also called great delusion (Mahāmohā) (1.58); the great demoness (Mahāsurī) (1.58); the black night, the great night, the night of delusion (1.59); darkness (Tāmasī) (1.68); the force that seizes those of knowledge and leads them to delusion (1.42); and the cause of bondage in the world (1.44). The entire Madhu-Kaitabha episode as told in the *Devī-māhātmya* hinges on Viṣṇu's helplessness as long as he is pervaded by the goddess, whose primary effect on him is to keep him unconscious. In this episode, then, the goddess has numbing, deluding, dark qualities, even though she is called by many positive terms. Again, Durgā's role vis-à-vis Viṣṇu seems exactly the opposite of the normal role of a goddess as a male deity's *śakti*, the power that enables the god to act in the world. In this myth Viṣṇu is only enabled to act when the goddess *leaves* him. She does not empower, enliven, or strengthen Viṣṇu; she puts him to sleep, reducing him to powerlessness.

Counterbalancing Durgā's liminal, peripheral nature, which at times seems to threaten dharmic stability and to inhibit the spiritual quest for *mokṣa,* is her role as protectress of the cosmos. Dominating her mythology is her role as the destroyer of demons who have usurped the position of the gods. As a great warrior she is created by the gods and acts on their behalf. While she is often said to transcend the male gods who create her and to excel them on the battlefield, she acts for their welfare. In doing this she acts to maintain or restore cosmic harmony and balance.

The theology underlying Durgā's appearances and exploits is clear in the *Devī-māhātmya,* the most famous text extolling her deeds. Durgā is said to underlie or pervade the cosmos; to create, maintain, and periodically destroy it according to the rhythmic sequences of Hindu cosmology (12.33–35); and to assume different forms from time to time when cosmic balance is threatened by enemies of the lesser gods (11.38–51). The *Devī-māhātmya* puts the matter succinctly: "Though she is eternal, the goddess becomes manifest over and over again to protect the world" (12.32).

The *Devī-māhātmya* itself relates three of Durgā's cosmic interventions on behalf of the gods: the battle with Madhu and Kaitabha; the battle with Mahiṣa and his army; and the battle with Śumbha and Niśumbha and their generals, Caṇḍa, Muṇḍa, and Raktabīja. The text also refers specifically to five other appearances of the goddess (11.38–51) and implies that she is incarnate in many more forms (12.32). The myths that are told in detail in the *Devī-māhātmya* conform to a structure that underlines Durgā's role as the upholder and protector of the dharmic order. Because the myths are cast in traditional structure, they also make the point that Durgā transcends the great male gods of the Hindu pantheon, who in other texts usually have the central role in these myths.

The structure to which the demon-slaying myths of Durgā conform is found throughout Hindu mythological texts and is consistent despite the specific deity who is featured in the myth. In basic outline the structure is as follows: (1) a demon gains great power through doing austerities, is granted a boon as a reward, and becomes nearly invincible; (2) the demon defeats the gods and takes over their positions; (3) the gods prepare their revenge by creating a special being who can defeat the demon despite the boon, or else the lesser gods petition one of the great deities (Śiva, Viṣṇu, or a great goddess) to intervene on their behalf; (4) the battle takes place and often includes the creation of helpers by the hero or heroine; (5) the demon is defeated, either slain or made subservient to the gods; (6) the gods praise the demon slayer.[16] In the Madhu and Kaitabha myth and the myth of Śumbha and Niśumbha, Durgā is petitioned to help the gods, whereas in the Mahiṣa myth she is specially created by the gods. In the Mahiṣa and Śumbha and Niśumbha myths the goddess takes a direct, active part in the battle itself, demonstrating her superior martial skills against her opponents. In the Śumbha and Niśumbha myth she also creates helpers in the form of ferocious goddesses. In all three episodes the gods collectively praise Durgā during the battle or after she has defeated the demons.

The theology underlying Durgā's cosmic interventions and the structure of the demon-slaying myths thus conform to well-known Hindu ideas and forms. The idea of a deity's descending to the world from time to time in various forms to maintain the balance of cosmic order is a central Vaiṣṇavite idea. Ever since the time of the *Bhāgavad-gītā* the idea of Viṣṇu's descending to the world in different forms in order to combat disorder has been well known in the Hindu tradition. Durgā, in the *Devī-māhātmya,* is heir to this *avatāra* theology. In fact, in many ways Durgā is a female version of Viṣṇu. She, like him, creates, maintains, and destroys the world; intervenes on a cosmic scale whenever disorder threatens to disrupt the world in the form of certain demons; and is approached by the other gods as their savior in times of distress. This conformity to a well-known type of theology does not detract from Durgā's appeal, power, or prestige. On the contrary, by creating her in this familiar role and by telling her myths according to a familiar structure, the author of the *Devī-māhātmya* underlines Durgā's supremacy and might.[17]

Durgā's role as cosmic queen is complemented by her role as a personal comforter who intervenes on behalf of her devotees. Near the end of the *Devī-māhātmya,* after the world has been restored to order, Durgā herself says that she is quick to hearken to the pleas of her devotees and that she may be petitioned in times of distress to help those who worship her. She mentions specifically forest fires, wild animals, robbers, imprisonment, execution, and battle as some threats from which she will save her devotees (12.24–28). At the end of the *Devī-māhātmya,* after being petitioned by two of her devotees (part of whose petition has included offering their own blood to the goddess), she appears before them and grants their desires. To one she returns his wealth and kingdom and to the other she grants ultimate liberation (13.11–15). Durgā, then, is not just a powerful, transcendent force whose sole concern is maintaining the cosmic rhythms, who is moved to action only when the

Durgā. South Indian bronze, early Choḷa, ca. 1000 A.D. Government Museum, Madras. C. Sivaramamurti, *South Indian Bronzes* (New Delhi: Lalit Kala Akademi, 1963), plate 50. Reprinted by permission of the publisher.

world itself is threatened. She is attentive to the needs of her devotees and intervenes on their behalf if asked to do so. She is a personal savior as well as a great battle queen who fights to defeat the enemies of the gods.

Durgā's distinctive nature also has to do with her identification with certain important Hindu philosophic ideas. The *Devī-māhātmya* and other texts extolling Durgā state that she is identical with or associated with *śakti, māyā,* and *prakṛti.* This is to say that in some way Durgā represents a dramatic illustration of these ideas or that these ideas can be discerned in her nature. *Śakti* is almost always understood to be the underlying power of the divine, the aspect of the divine that permits and provokes creative activity. *Śakti,* furthermore, is almost always understood to be a positive force. When viewed in concrete form, *śakti* is usually personified as a goddess. A common belief is that without his *śakti,* without his female counterpart, a male deity is ineffective, weak, and immobilized. Durgā's creation by the assembled male deities in the Mahiṣa episode dramatically depicts the goddess as *śakti.* Although the energy and heat that the deities contribute to her formation is called *tejas,* not *śakti,* it is clear that the male gods are contributing their strength and vigor to the goddess, who epitomizes power, action, and strength in the battle with the demon.[18] Durgā, particularly in her role as battle queen, is action and power personified and as such is a fitting representation of the idea of *śakti.*

Durgā as a personification of *māyā* is most clearly seen in the Madhu and Kaitabha episode, in which she deludes the demons so that Viṣṇu can slay them and in which she is repeatedly referred to as Mahāmāyā and as Viṣṇu's *māyā. Māyā* has negative connotations in Hindu philosophy and mythology, as does Durgā, particularly in this episode. *Māyā* is that which deludes individuals into thinking themselves to be the center of the world, the power that prevents individuals from seeing things as they really are. *Māyā* is that which impels individuals into self-centered, egotistical actions. *Māyā* is the sense of ego, personal identity, and individuality which clouds the underlying unity of reality and masks one's essential identity with *brahman* or some exalted being such as Viṣṇu, Śiva, or Durgā. *Māyā,* however, may also be understood as a positive, creative force not unlike *śakti. Māyā* may be understood as the power that enables a deity to display or embody himself or herself and therefore as the power that enables a deity to act.

When Durgā is called Māyā, or equated or associated with it, both connotations—delusion and creation—are suggested. Like Viṣṇu, Durgā creates the world through her extraordinary power, but then she bewitches the creatures she has created. Underlying this apparently incomprehensible "game" is the idea of divine *līlā* (sport, play, or dalliance), according to which the gods never act out of necessity but only out of a sense of play.[19] Unlike mere mortals, the gods (in this case Durgā) act not from pragmatic motives but only to amuse themselves or to display themselves. The way in which Durgā's defeat of Mahiṣa is often depicted in Indian art suggests this theme. Typically she is shown bringing a blizzard of weapons to bear on the hapless demon, who is half-emerging in his human form from the carcass of his former buffalo form. Durgā's many arms are all in motion, and she is a perfect vision of power in action. Her face, however, is calm and shows no sign of strain. For her this is mere sport and requires no undue exertion. It is a game for her, it is *līlā*.[20] She enters into the cosmic struggle between the lesser gods and the demons because it pleases her, not out of any sense of compulsion.

Durgā's identification with *prakṛti* and with the earth itself makes another theological point. *Prakṛti* is the physical world as well as the inherent rhythms within this world that impel nature to gratify and produce itself in its manifold species. *Prakṛti* is both the primordial matter from which all material things come and the living instincts and patterns that imbue the material world with its proclivities to sustain and recreate itself in individual beings. As *prakṛti*, then, Durgā is inextricably associated with the physical world, the world she creates, sustains, and protects in her various forms. Durgā's identification with the world is unambiguous. The *Devī-māhātmya* makes a point at several places to say that she *is* the world, she *is* all this (11.2–3, 5–6). As the earth itself she conveys cosmic stability. She is the foundation of all creatures and that which nourishes all creatures. As the embodiment of the earth she supports, protects, and mothers all beings. As Śākambharī she provides the world with food from her own body (11.45). In her role as cosmic queen, warrior goddess, and demon slayer, Durgā in effect protects herself in her aspect as the earth itself. As immanent in the world Durgā is equated with the earth. As transcendent, she is the heavenly queen who descends from time to time to maintain harmony on earth.

Durgā's association or identification with *śakti*, *māyā*, and *prakṛti* lends to the great demon-slaying goddess an immediate, tangible dimension. As an expression of these ideas she is identified with the creation itself. Her presence is affirmed to pervade and underlie the actual world in which people live, and her power and strength are affirmed to imbue all creatures with the will to prosper and multiply.

THE WORSHIP OF DURGĀ

One of the most important festivals in North India is Durgā Pūjā, which is celebrated in the autumn during the month of Āśvin. The festival takes place over a period of nine days and is often called the Navarātra festival. The central image of the festival shows Durgā slaying Mahiṣa. The iconographical details of the images are usually faithful to the scene as described in the *Devī-māhātmya* and other scriptures. Durgā has many arms, each of which bears a weapon; she stands on her lion vehicle; and she is thrusting her trident into the chest of Mahiṣa, who is in human form, half-emerged from the carcass of a slain buffalo. During the festival it is customary to recite the *Devī-māhātmya* in its entirety several times.[21] The Durgā Pūjā festival clearly asserts Durgā's central role as a battle queen and the regulator of the cosmos. In part, at least, the festivities celebrate Durgā's defeat of Mahiṣa and the restoration of cosmic order.

This festival, in which Durgā is worshiped in the form of a mighty warrior goddess, seems to be, or to have been until recently, part of a pattern of worship undertaken by rulers for success in battle. The festival of Dasarā, which falls on the tenth *tithi* (lunar day) of the bright half of Āśvin and thus immediately follows Durgā Pūjā (which occupies the first through ninth *tithis* of the bright half of Āśvin), was in many parts of India primarily an occasion in which to celebrate military might and royal power and to petition for military success in the coming year. Worship of weapons was also a part of the festival in many cases.

Writing in the early nineteenth century, when the festival of Dasarā was still widely undertaken, the Abbé Dubois wrote of the celebrations in Mysore:

> The *Dasarā* is likewise the soldier's feast. Princes and soldiers offer the most solemn sacrifices to the arms which are made use of in battle. Collecting all their weapons together, they call a Brahmin *purohita*, who sprinkles them with *tirtham* (holy water) and converts them into so many divinities by virtue of his *mantrams*. He then makes *puja* to them and retires. Thereupon, amidst the beat of drums, the blare of trumpets and other instruments, a ram is brought in with much pomp and sacrificed in honour of the various weapons of destruction. This ceremony is observed with the greatest solemnity throughout the whole Peninsula. . . . It is known by the special name of *ayuda-puja* (sacrifice to arms), and is entirely military.[22]

Alexander Forbes, who wrote in the second half of the nineteenth century, described Dasarā among the Rajputs: "The Rajpoot chiefs, on the evening of Dussera, worship also the *Fort-Protectress,* the goddess Gudeychee. On their return from the Shumee worship into the city, they join together in bands, brandishing their spears, galloping their horses, and enacting in other ways the part of an army taking the field."[23]

Although the worship of a goddess is not always part of Dasarā celebrations, there are many indications in ritual and mythological texts that the annual (usually autumnal) worship of a warrior goddess, often specified to be Durgā, was part of festivals associated with military success. Mantras to be uttered by kings on the occasion of Dasarā, for example, sometimes invoke a goddess. In the *Dharmasindhu* the king is to speak this prayer: "May Aparājitā [the unconquerable one] wearing a striking necklace and resplendant golden girdle and fond of doing good bestow victory on me."[24] In the *Nirnayasindhu* this prayer is to be said at the time of blessing weapons: "O goddess, ruling over gods! may my army divided into four sections (elephants, chariots, horsemen, and foot-soldiers) attain to the position of having no enemy left in this world and may victory come to me everywhere through your favour."[25]

An eleventh- or twelfth-century Jain text, the *Yaśatilaka* of Somadeva, mentions the worship of Aparājitā, who is also called Ambikā. She is said to give victory in war and to be present in the king's weapons.[26] The text also says that she is worshiped on Mahānavamī, which is the last day of Durgā Pūjā. Some *Purāṇas,* furthermore, say that *nīrājana,* the worship of weapons, is held on Mahānavamī.[27] In the Prakrit drama *Gauḍavaho,* King Yaśovarman undertakes a military campaign in the autumn. Shortly after beginning his march he reaches the Vindhya Mountains and there undertakes the worship of the goddess Vindhyavāsinī (she who dwells in the Vindhyas), an epithet of Durgā in some texts.[28]

The worship of Durgā also came to be associated with the military success of both the Pāṇḍava brothers in the *Mahābhārata* and Rāma in the *Rāmāyaṇa.* Although her worship by the heroes was not part of either epic tradition initially (the incidents are not found in the critical editions of either epic), a tradition has developed that insists that the worship of Durgā was necessary to the success of the heroes in both epics. Durgā is worshiped twice in the *Mahābhārata*: in Viratā-parva 6 by Yudhiṣṭhira and in Bhīṣma-parva 23 by Arjuna. In the latter case the occasion of Durgā's praise is clear. The setting is just before the great battle that is the highpoint of the entire epic. Kṛṣṇa instructs Arjuna as follows: "O one having great arms, standing in the face of battle, say a hymn to Durgā for the purpose of defeating your enemies" (4.6.2). The hymn that Arjuna then offers is full of references to Durgā's military might and prowess. The goddess appears to Arjuna and promises him victory, after which the text says that anyone who hears or recites the hymn will be victorious in battle.

The placement of the second hymn to Durgā in Virāṭa-parva is more difficult to understand. The Pāṇḍava brothers have just emerged from twelve years of exile in the forest and are about to begin a year of life in the world during which they must remain in disguise lest their enemies discover them. Before entering the city of Virāṭa and taking up their disguises they hid their weapons in a *śami* tree near a cremation ground. Yudhiṣṭhira asks Durgā for protection from being discovered during the coming year and for later success against their enemies. She appears at the end of the hymn and grants his wishes. It seems that the hymn was placed at this point in the text because worship of a *śami* tree on the outskirts of a town is often a part of Dasarā festivals.[29] The author or editor of the hymn probably thought this an appropriate place to insert a hymn to Durgā for military success.

The association of Durgā with Rāma's success in battle over Rāvaṇa in the *Rāmāyaṇa* tradition, although not part of Vālmīki's *Rāmāyaṇa*, has become a well-known part of the Rāma story throughout India. In the *Kālikā-purāṇa* we are told:

> In former times, the great Goddess was waked up by Brahmā when it was still night, in order to favour Rāma and to obtain the death of Rāvaṇa.
>
> On the first day of the bright half of the month of Āśvina, she gave up her sleep and went to the city of Laṅkā, where Raghu's son formerly lived.
>
> When she came there, the great Goddess caused Rāma and Rāvaṇa to be engaged in battle, but Ambikā herself remained hidden. . . .
>
> Afterwards, when the seventh night had gone by, Mahāmāyā, in whom the worlds are contained, caused Rāvaṇa to be killed by Rāma on the ninth day. . . .
>
> After the hero Rāvaṇa had been killed on the ninth day, the Grandfather of the worlds (Brahmā) together with all the gods held a special worship for Durgā.
>
> Afterwards the Goddess was dismissed with Śabara-festivals, on the tenth day; Indra on his part held a lustration of the army of the gods for the appeasement of the armies of the gods and for the sake of prosperity of the kingdom of the gods. . . .
>
> All the gods will worship her and will, on their part, lustrate the army; and in the same way all men should perform worship according to the rules.
>
> A king should hold a lustration of the army in order to strengthen his army; a performance must be made with charming women adorned with celestial ornaments; . . .

> After one has made a puppet of flour for Skanda and Viśākha, one should worship it in order to annihilate one's foes and for the sake of enjoying Durgā.[30]

In the *Devī-bhāgavata-purāṇa* Rāma is despondent at the problems of reaching Laṅka, defeating Rāvaṇa, and getting back his beloved Sītā. The sage Nārada, however, advises him to call on Durgā for help. Rāma asks how she should be worshiped, and Nārada instructs him concerning the performance of Durgā Pūjā or Navarātra. The festival, which Nārada assures Rāma will result in military success, is said to have been performed in previous ages by Indra for killing Vṛtra, by Śiva for killing the demons of the three cities, and by Viṣṇu for killing Madhu and Kaitabha (3.30.25-26). Rāma duly performs Durgā's worship, and she appears to him mounted on her lion. She asks what he wishes, and when he requests victory over Rāvaṇa she promises him success (3.30). The traditions of Rāma's inaugurating Durgā Pūjā for the purpose of defeating Rāvaṇa is also found in the *Bṛhaddharma-purāṇa* (1.21-22) and the Bengali version of the *Rāmāyaṇa* by Kṛttivāsa (fifteenth century).[31] Bengali villagers tell of a tradition in which it was customary to worship Durgā during the spring. Rāma, however, needed the goddess's help in the autumn when he was about to invade Laṅka. So it was that he worshiped her in the month of Āśvin and inaugurated autumnal worship, which has become her most popular festival. "When Rāma . . . came into conflict with Rāvan . . . Rāma performed the pūjā when he was in trouble, without waiting for the proper time of the annual pūjā. He did the pūjā in the autumn, and later this pūjā became the most popular ritual of the goddess."[32]

Durgā's association with military prowess and her worship for military success undoubtedly led to her being associated with the military success of both sets of epic heroes sometime in the medieval period. Her association with these great heroes in turn probably tended to further promote her worship by kings for success and prosperity.

Durgā's association with military might is probably also part of a tradition, most evident in recent centuries, in which goddesses give swords to certain rulers and in which swords are named for goddesses. In the *Devī-purāṇa* it is said that the goddess may be worshiped in the form of a sword (98). Śivaji, the seventeenth-century Marathi military leader, is said to have received his sword from his family deity, the goddess Bhavānī. One account of how Śivaji obtained his sword is phrased as if Śivaji himself were speaking:

> I received that famous sword very early in my career as a token of a compact with the Chief Gowalker Sawant. It had been

> suggested to me on my way to the place where it was being kept that I should take it by force, but remembering that tremendous storms are sometimes raised by unnecessary trifles, I thought it better to leave it to its owner. . . . In the end the wise chief brought the sword to me as a sign of amity even when he knew that its purchase-price was not to be measured in blood. From that day onward the sword, which I reverently named after my tutelary deity *Bhavāni,* always accompanied me, its resting place when not in use generally being the altar of the goddess, to be received back from her as a visible favour from heaven, always on the *Dasara* day when starting out on my campaigns.[33]

In other legends concerning Śivaji's sword the goddess Bhavānī speaks directly to Śivaji, identifies herself with his sword, and is described as entering his sword before battle or before urging Śivaji to undertake the task of murdering his enemy, Afzalkhan.[34]

The Paṇḍyan prince Kumāra Kampaṇa (fourteenth century), before going to battle against the Muslims in the Madura area, is said to have been addressed by a goddess who gave him a sword: "A goddess appeared before him and after describing to him the disastrous consequences of the Musselmen invasions of the South and sad plight of the Southern country and its temples exhorted him to extirpate the invaders and restore the country to its ancient glory, presenting him at the same time with a divine sword."[35]

A sacred sword also belonged to the Rajput kingdom of Mewar. The sword was handed down from generation to generation and was placed on the altar of the goddess during Navarātra.[36] According to legend, the founder of the dynasty, Bappa, undertook austerities in the woods. Near the end of his ascetic efforts a goddess riding a lion appeared to him: "From her hand he received the panoply of celestial fabrication, the work of Viswacarma. . . . The lance, bow, quiver, and arrows; a shield and sword . . . which the goddess girded on him with her own hand."[37]

The autumnal worship of Durgā, in which she is shown in full military array slaying the demon Mahiṣa in order to restore order to the cosmos, thus seems to have been part of a widespread cult that centered around obtaining military success. The central festival of this cult took place on Dasarā day, immediately following the Navarātra festival, and included the worship of weapons by rulers and soldiers. The worship of a goddess for military success, though not always a part of the Dasarā festival, was associated with the festival. Indeed, the two festivals, Navarātra and Dasarā, probably were often understood to be one continuous festival in which the worship of Durgā and the hope of military success were inseparably linked.

Although the military overtones of Durgā Pūjā are apparent, other themes are also important during this great festival, and other facets of Durgā's character are brought out by the festival. Durgā Pūjā is celebrated from the first through the ninth days of the bright half of the lunar month of Āśvin, which coincides with the autumn harvest in North India, and in certain respects it is clear that Durgā Pūjā is a harvest festival in which Durgā is propitiated as the power of plant fertility. Although Durgā Pūjā lacks clear agricultural themes as celebrated today in large cities such as Calcutta or as celebrated by those with only tenuous ties to agriculture, there are still enough indications in the festival, even in its citified versions, to discern its importance to the business of agriculture. A central object of worship during the festival, for example, is a bundle of nine different plants, the *navapattrikā*, which is identified with Durgā herself.[38] Although the nine plants in question are not all agricultural plants, paddy and plantain are included and suggest that Durgā is associated with the crops.[39] Her association with the other plants probably is meant to generalize her identification with the power underlying all plant life: Durgā is not merely the power inherent in the growth of crops but the power inherent in all vegetation. During her worship in this form, the priest anoints Durgā with water from auspicious sources, such as the major holy rivers of India. He also anoints her with agricultural products, such as sugarcane juice[40] and sesame oil,[41] and offers to her certain soils that are associated with fertility, such as earth dug up by the horns of a wild boar, earth dug up by the horns of a bull, and earth from the doors of prostitutes.[42] It seems clear that one theme of this aspect of the worship of Durgā is to promote the fertility of the plants incorporated into the sacred bundle and to promote the fertility of crops in general.

At another point in the ceremonies a pot is identified with Durgā and worshiped by the priest. Edible fruit and different plants from those making up the *navapattrika* are placed in the pot.[43] The pot, which has a rounded bottom, is then firmly set up on moist dough. On this dough are scattered five grains: rice, wheat, barley, "mas (*Phaseolus Roxburghii, Wight*)," and sesame.[44] As each grain is scattered on the dough, a priest recites the following invocation: "Om you are rice [wheat, barley, etc.], om you are life, you are the life of the gods, you are our life, you are our internal life, you are long life, you give life, om the Sun with his rays gives you the milk of life and Varuna nourishes you with water."[45] The pot contains Ganges water in addition to the plants; in a prayer the priest identifies the pot with the source of the nectar of immortality (*amṛta*), which the gods churned from the ocean of milk.

Durgā, then, in the form of the pot, is invoked both as the power promoting the growth of the agricultural grains and as the source of the power of life with which the gods achieved immortality. In the forms of the *navapattrikā* and the *ghaṭa* (pot) Durgā reveals a dimension of herself that primarily has to do with the fertility of the crops and vegetation and with the power that underlies life in general. In addition to granting freedom from troubles and bestowing wealth on those who perform her *pūjā*, Durgā is also affirmed to grant agricultural produce,[46] and at one point in the festival she is addressed as she who appeases the hunger of the world.[47]

Durgā's beneficial influence on crops is also suggested at the very beginning of the festival when her image is being set up. The image is placed on a low platform or table about eighteen inches high. The platform is set on damp clay, and the five grains mentioned above are sprinkled in the clay. Although not specifically stated, it appears that the presence of the goddess is believed to promote the growth of these seeds.[48] Furthermore, on the eighth day of the festival the priest worships several groups of deities while circumambulating the image of Durgā. Among these are the *kṣetrapālas*, deities who preside over cultivated fields.[49]

Two other distinctive features of Durgā Pūjā suggest its importance as a festival affecting the fertility of the crops: the animal sacrifices and the ribald behavior that is specifically mentioned in certain religious texts as pleasing to the goddess. Certainly the sacrifice of an animal, particularly when that animal is a buffalo, suggests the reiteration of the slaying of Mahiṣa by Durgā. But the custom of offering other animals such as goats and sheep and the injunctions to offer several victims during the festival suggest that other meanings are also intended. These blood sacrifices occupy a central role in Durgā Pūjā. Durgā's thirst for blood is established in various texts,[50] and this thirst is not limited to the battlefield. Her devotees are said to please her with their own blood,[51] and she is said to receive blood from tribal groups who worship her.[52] Furthermore, other goddesses to whom Durgā is closely affiliated, such as Kālī, receive blood offerings in their temples daily with no reference at all to heroic deeds in battle. Blood offerings to Durgā therefore seem to contain a logic quite apart from the battlefield, or at least quite apart from the myth of the goddess's slaying of Mahiṣa on behalf of cosmic stability.

My suggestion is that underlying blood sacrifices to Durgā is the perception, perhaps only unconscious, that this great goddess who nourishes the crops and is identified with the power underlying all life needs to be reinvigorated from time to time. Despite her great powers she is capable of being exhausted through continuous birth and the giving of nourishment. To replenish her powers, to reinvigorate her, she is given back life in the form of animal sacrifices. The blood in effect resupplies her so that she may continue to give life in return. Having harvested the crops, having literally reaped the life-giving benefits of Durgā's potency, it is appropriate (perhaps necessary) to return strength and power to her in the form of the blood of sacrificial victims. This logic, and the association of blood sacrifices with harvest, is not at all uncommon in the world's religions. It is a typical ceremonial scenario in many cultures, and it seems likely that at one time it was important in the celebration of Durgā Pūjā.[53]

Promotion of the fertility of the crops by stimulating Durgā's powers of fecundity also seems to underlie the practice of publicly making obscene gestures and comments during Durgā Pūjā. Various scriptures say that Durgā is pleased by such behavior at her autumnal festival,[54] and such behavior is suggested in the wild, boisterous activities that accompany the disposal of the image of Durgā in a river or pool.[55] The close association, even the interdependence, between human sexuality and the growth of crops is clear in many cultures;[56] it is held to be auspicious and even vital to the growth of crops to have couples copulate in the fields, particularly at planting and harvest time. Again, the logic seems to be that this is a means of giving back vital powers to the spirit underlying the crops. The sexual fluids, like blood, are held to have great fertilizing powers, so to copulate in the fields is to renourish the divine beings that promote the growth of the crops. While such outright sexual activity is not part of Durgā Pūjā, the sexual license enjoined in some scriptures is certainly suggestive of this well-known theme.

Another facet of Durgā's character emerges in Durgā Pūjā but is not stressed in the texts casting her in the role of battle queen; that is her domestic role as the wife of Śiva and mother of several divine children. In North India, which is primarily patrilocal and patriarchal in matters of marriage, it is customary for girls to be married at an early age and to leave their parents' home when quite young. This is traumatic for both the girl and her family. In Bengal, at least, daughters customarily return to their home villages during Durgā Pūjā. The arrival home of the daughters is cause for great happiness and rejoicing, and their departure after the festival is over is the occasion for painful scenes of departure. Durgā herself is cast in the role of a returning daughter during her great festival, and many devotional songs are written to welcome her home or to bid her farewell. These songs contain no mention whatsoever of her roles as battle queen or cosmic savior. She is identified with Pārvatī, who is the wife of Śiva and the daughter of Himalaya and his wife Mena. In this role Durgā is said to be the mother of Gaṇeśa, Kārttikeya, Sarasvatī, and Lakṣmī.

The dominant theme in these songs of welcome and farewell seems to be the difficult life the goddess/daughter has in her husband's home in contrast to the warm, tender treatment she receives from her parents when she visits them. This theme undoubtedly reflects the actual situation of many Bengali girls, for whom life in their husband's village can be difficult in the extreme, particularly in the early years of their marriage when they have no seniority or children to give them respect and status in the eyes of their in-laws. Śiva is described as inattentive to his wife and as unable to take care of himself because of his habit of smoking hemp and his habitual disregard for social convention.[57] The songs contrast the poverty that Durgā must endure in her husband's care with the way that she is spoiled by her parents. From the devotee's point of view, then, Durgā is seen as a returning daughter who lives a difficult life far away from home. She is welcomed warmly and provided every comfort. The days of the festival are ones of intimacy between the devotee and the goddess, who is understood to have made a long journey to dwell at home with those who worship her. The clay image worshiped during Durgā Pūjā may show a mighty, many-armed goddess triumphing over a powerful demon, but many devotees cherish her as a tender daughter who has returned home on her annual visit for family succor, sympathy, and the most elaborate hospitality. This theme places the devotee in the position of a family member who spoils Durgā with every sort of personal attendance in order to distract her from her normal life with her mad husband, Śiva. At the end of Durgā Pūjā, when the image of the goddess is removed from its place of honor and placed upon a truck or some other conveyance to be carried away for immersion, many women gather about the image to bid it farewell, and it is a common sight to see them actually weeping as the goddess, their daughter, leaves to return to her husband's home far away.

The sacrifice of a buffalo to Durgā is practiced in South India too. While agricultural fertility and her cosmic victory on behalf of divine order are themes in this ceremony, Tamil myths and rituals emphasize a quite different aspect of her character. In the *Purāṇas*, and in North Indian traditions, there is an implied sexual tension between Durgā and Mahiṣa, her victim. In the South this sexual tension is heightened and becomes one of the central themes of Durgā's defeat of Mahiṣa. In fact, most Southern myths about Durgā identify Mahiṣa as her suitor, her would-be husband. Independent in her unmarried state, Durgā is portrayed as possessing untamed sexual energy that is dangerous, indeed, deadly, to any male who dares to approach her.[58] Her violent, combative nature needs to be tamed for the welfare of the world. Mahiṣa is unsuccessful in subduing her and is lured to his doom by her great beauty. A central point of the South Indian myths about Durgā and Mahiṣa is that any sexual association with the goddess is dangerous and that before her sexuality can be rendered safe she must be dominated by, made subservient to, defeated by, or humiliated by a male.[59] In most myths she eventually is tamed by Śiva.[60]

The South Indian tradition of Durgā as a dangerous, indeed, murderous, bride who poses a fatal threat to those who approach her sexually contrasts sharply with the North Indian tradition of Durgā Pūjā, which stresses Durgā's character as a gentle young wife and daughter in need of family tenderness. The South Indian role suggests again the liminal aspect of the goddess. Unlike the weak, submissive, blushing maiden of the *Dharma-śāstras*, Durgā presents a picture of determined, fierce independence, which is challenged only at great risk by her suitors.

8

KĀLĪ

The goddess Kālī is almost always described as having a terrible, frightening appearance. She is always black or dark, is usually naked, and has long, disheveled hair. She is adorned with severed arms as a girdle, freshly cut heads as a necklace, children's corpses as earrings, and serpents as bracelets. She has long, sharp fangs, is often depicted as having clawlike hands with long nails, and is often said to have blood smeared on her lips. Her favorite haunts heighten her fearsome nature. She is usually shown on the battlefield, where she is a furious combatant who gets drunk on the hot blood of her victims, or in a cremation ground, where she sits on a corpse surrounded by jackals and goblins.

Many texts and contexts treat Kālī as an independent deity, unassociated with any male deity. When she is associated with a god, however, it is almost always Śiva. As his consort, wife, or associate, Kālī often plays the role of inciting him to wild behavior. Kālī's association with Śiva, unlike Pārvatī's, seems aimed at exciting him to take part in dangerous, destructive behavior that threatens the stability of the cosmos. Kālī is particularly popular in Bengal, although she is known and worshiped throughout India. In Bengal she is worshiped on Dīpāvalī. In this festival, and throughout the year at many of her permanent temples, she receives blood offerings. She is also the recipient of ardent devotion from countless devotees, who approach her as their mother.

EARLY HISTORY

The earliest references to Kālī in the Hindu tradition date to the early medieval period (around A.D. 600) and usually locate Kālī either on the battlefield or in situations on the periphery of Hindu society. In the

Agni- and *Garuḍa-purāṇas* she is mentioned in invocations that aim at success in war and against one's enemies. She is described as having an awful appearance: she is gaunt, has fangs, laughs loudly, dances madly, wears a garland of corpses, sits on the back of a ghost, and lives in the cremation ground. She is asked to crush, trample, break, and burn the enemy.[1] In the *Bhāgavata-purāṇa* Kālī is the patron deity of a band of thieves whose leader seeks to achieve Kālī's blessing in order to have a son. The thief kidnaps a saintly Brahman youth with the intention of offering him as a blood sacrifice to Kālī. The effulgence of the virtuous youth, however, burns Kālī herself when he is brought near her image. Emerging from her image, infuriated, she kills the leader and his entire band. She is described as having a dreadful face and large teeth and as laughing loudly. She and her host of demons then decapitate the corpses of the thieves, drink their blood until drunk, and throw their heads about in sport (5.9.12–20).

Bāṇabhaṭṭa's seventh-century drama *Kādambarī* features a goddess named Caṇḍī, an epithet used for both Durgā and Kālī, who is worshiped by the Śabaras, a tribe of primitive hunters. The worship takes place deep in the forest, and blood offerings are made to the goddess.[2] Vākpati's *Gauḍavaho* (late seventh or early eighth century) portrays Kālī as an aspect of Vindhyavāsinī (an epithet of Durgā). She is worshiped by Śabaras, is clothed in leaves, and receives human sacrifices (verses 285–347).[3] In Bhavabhūti's *Mālatīmādhava*, a drama of the early eighth century, a female devotee of Cāmuṇḍā, a goddess who is very often identified with Kālī, captures the heroine, Mālatī, with the intention of sacrificing her to the goddess. Cāmuṇḍā's temple is near a cremation ground. A hymn to the goddess describes her as dancing wildly and making the world shake. She has a gaping mouth, wears a garland of skulls, is covered with snakes, showers flames from her eyes that destroy the world, and is surrounded by goblins.[4]

Somadeva's *Yaśatilaka* (eleventh to twelfth century) contains a long description of a godess called Caṇḍamārī. In all respects she is like Kālī, and we may understand the scenario Somadeva describes as suggestive of Kālī's appearance and worship at that time. The goddess adorns herself with pieces of human corpses, uses oozings from corpses for cosmetics, bathes in rivers of wine or blood, sports in cremation grounds, and uses human skulls as drinking vessels.[5] Bizarre and fanatical devotees gather at her temple and undertake forms of ascetic self-torture. They burn incense on their heads, drink their own blood, and offer their own flesh into the sacrificial fire.[6]

Kālī's association with the periphery of Hindu society (she is worshiped by tribal or low-caste people in uncivilized or wild places) is also seen in an architectural work of the sixth to eighth centuries, the *Māna-sāra-śilpa-śāstra*. There it is said that Kālī's temples should be built far from villages and towns, near the cremation grounds and the dwellings of Caṇḍālas (very low-caste people) (9.289).

Kālī's most famous appearances in battle contexts are found in the *Devī-māhātmya*. In the third episode, which features Durgā's defeat of Śumbha and Niśumbha and their allies, Kālī appears twice. Early in the battle the demons Caṇḍa and Muṇḍa approach Durgā with readied weapons. Seeing them prepared to attack her, Durgā becomes angry, her face becoming dark as ink. Suddenly the goddess Kālī springs from her forehead. She is black, wears a garland of human heads and a tiger skin, and wields a skull-topped staff. She is gaunt, with sunken eyes, gaping mouth, and lolling tongue. She roars loudly and leaps into the battle, where she tears demons apart with her hands and crushes them in her jaws. She grasps the two demon generals and in one furious blow decapitates them both with her sword (7.3–22). Later in the battle Kālī is summoned by Durgā to help defeat the demon Raktabīja. This demon has the ability to reproduce himself instantly whenever a drop of his blood falls to the ground. Having wounded Raktabīja with a variety of weapons, Durgā and her assistants, a fierce band of goddesses called the Mātṛkās,[7] find they have worsened their situation. As Raktabīja bleeds more and more profusely from his wounds, the battlefield increasingly becomes filled with Raktabīja duplicates. Kālī defeats the demon by sucking the blood from his body and throwing the countless duplicate Raktabījas into her gaping mouth (8.49–61)

In these two episodes Kālī appears to represent Durgā's personified wrath, her embodied fury. Kālī plays a similar role in her association with Pārvatī. In general, Pārvatī is a benign goddess, but from time to time she exhibits fierce aspects. When this occurs, Kālī is sometimes described as being brought into being. In the *Liṅga-purāṇa* Śiva asks Pārvatī to destroy the demon Dāruka, who has been given the boon that he can only be killed by a female. Pārvatī then enters Śiva's body and transforms herself from the poison that is stored in Śiva's throat. She reappears as Kālī, ferocious in appearance, and with the help of flesh-eating *piśācas* (spirits) attacks and defeats Dāruka and his hosts. Kālī, however, becomes so intoxicated by the blood lust of battle that she threatens to destroy the entire world in her fury. The world is saved when Śiva intervenes and calms her (1.106). Kālī appears in a similar context elsewhere in the same text. When Śiva sets out to defeat the demons of the three cities, Kālī is part of his entourage. She whirls a trident, is adorned with skulls, has her eyes half-closed by intoxication from drinking the blood of demons, and wears an elephant hide. She is also praised, however, as the daughter of Himalaya, a clear identification with Pārvatī. It seems that in the process of Pārvatī's preparations for war, Kālī appears as Pārvatī's personified wrath, her alter ego, as it were (1.72.66–68).

The *Vāmana-purāṇa* calls Pārvatī Kālī (the black one) because of her dark complexion. Hearing Śiva use this name, Pārvatī takes offense and undertakes austerities in order to rid herself of her dark complexion. After succeeding, she is renamed Gaurī (the golden one). Her dark sheath, however, is transformed into the furious battle queen Kauśikī, who subsequently creates Kālī in her fury. So again, although there is an intermediary goddess (Kauśikī), Kālī plays the role of Pārvatī's dark, negative, violent nature in embodied form (25–29).

Kālī makes similar appearances in myths concerning both Satī and Sītā. In the case of Satī, Kālī appears when Satī's father, Dakṣa, infuriates his daughter by not inviting her and Śiva to a great sacrificial rite. Satī rubs her nose in anger and Kālī appears.[8] Kālī also appears in other texts when Satī, in her wrath over the same incident, gives birth to or transforms herself into ten goddesses, the *Dasamahāvidyās*. The first goddess mentioned in this group is usually Kālī.[9] In the case of Sītā, Kālī appears as her fierce, terrible, bloodthirsty aspect when Rāma, on his return to India after defeating Rāvaṇa, is confronted with such a terrible monster that he freezes in fear. Sītā, transformed into Kālī, handily defeats the demon.[10]

In her association with Śiva Kālī's tendency to wildness and disorder persists. Although she is sometimes tamed or softened by him, at times she incites Śiva himself to dangerous, destructive behavior. A South Indian tradition tells of a dance contest between the two. After defeating Śumbha and Niśumbha, Kālī takes up residence in a forest with her retinue of fierce companions and terrorizes the surrounding area. A devotee of Śiva in that area becomes distracted from doing austerities and petitions Śiva to rid the forest of the violent goddess. When Śiva appears, Kālī threatens him, claiming the area as her own. Śiva challenges her to a dance contest and defeats her when she is unable (or unwilling) to match his energetic *tāṇḍava* dance.[11]

Although this tradition says that Śiva defeated and forced Kālī to control her disruptive habits, we find few images and myths depicting her becalmed and docile.[12] Instead, we find references or images that show Śiva and Kālī in situations where either or both behave in disruptive ways, inciting each other, or in which Kālī in her wild activity dominates an inactive or sometimes dead Śiva.[13]

In the first type of relationship the two appear dancing together in such a way that they threaten the world. Bhavabhūti's *Mālatīmādhava* describes the divine pair as they dance wildly near the goddess's temple. Their dance is so frenzied that it threatens to destroy the world. Pārvatī stands nearby, frightened.[14] Here the scenario is not a dance contest but a mutually destructive dance in which the two deities incite each other. This is a common image in Bengali devotional hymns to Kālī. Śiva and Kālī complement each other in their madness and destructive habits.

> Crazy is my Father, crazy my Mother,
> And I, their son, am crazy too!
> Shyama [the dark one, an epithet of Kālī] is my
>   Mother's name.
> My Father strikes His cheeks and makes a hollow sound:
> *Ba-ba-boom! Ba-ba-boom!*
> And my Mother, drunk and reeling,
> Falls across my Father's body!
> Shyama's streaming tresses hang in vast disorder;
> Bees are swarming numberless
> About her crimson Lotus Feet.
> Listen, as She dances, how Her anklets ring![15]

Iconographic representations of Kālī and Śiva nearly always show Kālī as dominant. She is usually standing or dancing on Śiva's prone body, and when the two are depicted in sexual intercourse, she is shown above him. Although Śiva is said to have tamed Kālī in the myth of the dance contest, it seems clear that she was never finally subdued by him and is most popularly represented as a being who is uncontrollable and more apt to provoke Śiva to dangerous activity than to be controlled by him.

In general, then, we may say that Kālī is a goddess who threatens stability and order. Although she may be said to serve order in her role as slayer of demons, more often than not she becomes so frenzied on the battlefield, usually becoming drunk on the blood of her victims, that she herself begins to destroy the world that she is supposed to protect. Thus even in the service of the gods, she is ultimately dangerous and tends to get out of control. In association with other goddesses, she appears to represent their embodied wrath and fury, a frightening, dangerous dimension of the divine feminine that is released when these goddesses become enraged or are summoned to take part in war and killing. In relation to Śiva, she appears to play the opposite role from that of Pārvatī. Pārvatī calms Śiva, counterbalancing his antisocial or destructive tendencies. It is she who brings Śiva within the sphere of domesticity and who, with her soft glances, urges him to moderate the destructive

Kālī and Śiva. Ann and Bury Peerless. Philip Rawson, *Oriental Erotic Art* (New York: A and W Publishers, 1981), fig. 16, p. 22.

aspects of his *tāṇḍava* dance.[16] Kālī is Śiva's "other" wife, as it were, provoking him and encouraging him in his mad, antisocial, often disruptive habits. It is never Kālī who tames Śiva but Śiva who must becalm Kālī. Her association with criminals reinforces her dangerous role vis-à-vis society. She is at home outside the moral order and seems to be unbounded by that order.

THE LATER HISTORY AND THE SIGNIFICANCE OF KĀLĪ

Given Kālī's intimidating appearance and ghastly habits, it might seem that she would never occupy a central position in Hindu piety, yet she does. She is of central importance in Tantrism, particularly left-handed Tantrism, and in Bengali Śākta devotionalism. An underlying assumption in Tantric ideology is that reality is the result and expression of the symbiotic interaction of male and female, Śiva and *śakti,* the quiescent and the dynamic, and other polar opposites that in interaction produce a creative tension. Consequently, goddesses in Tantrism play an important role and are affirmed to be as central to discerning the nature of reality as the male deities are. Although Śiva is usually said to be the source of the *Tantras,* the source of wisdom and truth, and Pārvatī, his spouse, to be the student to whom the scriptures are given, many of the *Tantras* emphasize the fact that it is *śakti* that pervades reality with her power, might, and vitality and that it is she (understood in personified form to be Pārvatī, Kālī, and other goddesses) who is immediately present to the adept and whose presence and being underlie his own being. For the Tantric adept it is her vitality that is sought through various techniques aimed at spiritual transformation; thus it is she who is affirmed as the dominant and primary reality.

Although Pārvatī is usually said to be the recipient of Śiva's wisdom in the form of the *Tantras,* it is Kālī who seems to dominate Tantric iconography, texts, and rituals, especially in left-handed Tantra. In many places Kālī is praised as the greatest of all deities or the highest reality. In the *Nirvāṇa-tantra* the gods Brahmā, Viṣṇu, and Śiva are said to arise from her like bubbles from the sea, endlessly arising and passing away, leaving their source unchanged. Compared to Kālī, proclaims this text, Brahmā, Viṣṇu, and Śiva are like the amount of water in a cow's hoofprint compared to the waters of the sea.[17] The *Nigama-kalpataru* and the *Picchilā-tantra* declare that of all mantras Kālī's is the greatest.[18] The *Yoginī-tantra,* the *Kāmākhyā-tantra,* and the *Niruttara-tantra* all proclaim Kālī the greatest of the *vidyās* (the manifestations of the Mahādevī, the "great goddess") or divinity itself; indeed, they declare her to be the essence or own form (*svarūpa*) of the Mahādevī.[19] The *Kāmadā-tantra* states unequivocally that she is attributeless, neither male nor female, sinless, the imperishable *saccidānanda* (being, consciousness, and bliss), *brahman* itself.[20] In the *Mahānirvāṇa-tantra*, too, Kālī is one of the most common epithets for the primordial *śakti*,[21] and in one passage Śiva praises her as follows:

> At the dissolution of things, it is Kāla [Time] Who will devour all, and by reason of this He is called Mahākāla [an epithet of Śiva], and since Thou devourest Mahākāla Himself, it is Thou who art the Supreme Primordial Kālikā.
>
> Because Thou devourest Kāla, Thou art Kālī, the original form of all things, and because Thou art the Origin of and devourest all things Thou art called the Adyā [primordial] Kālī. Resuming after Dissolution Thine own form, dark and formless, Thou alone remainest as One ineffable and inconceivable. Though having a form, yet art Thou formless; though Thyself without beginning, multiform by the power of Māyā, Thou art the Beginning of all, Creatrix, Protectress, and Destructress that Thou art. (4.30–34)[22]

Why Kālī, in preference to other goddesses, attained this preeminent position in Tantrism is not entirely clear. Given certain Tantric ideological and ritual presuppositions, however, the following logic seems possible. Tantrism generally is ritually oriented. By means of various rituals (exterior and interior, bodily and mental) the *sādhaka* (practitioner) seeks to gain *mokṣa* (release, salvation). A consistent theme in this endeavor is the uniting of opposites (male-female, microcosm-macrocosm, sacred-profane, Śiva-*śakti*). In Tantrism there is an elaborate, subtle geography of the body that must be learned, controlled, and ultimately resolved in unity. By means of the body, both the physical and subtle bodies, the *sādhaka* may manipulate levels of reality and harness the dynamics of those levels to the attainment of his goal. The *sādhaka*, with the help of a guru, undertakes to gain his goal by conquest—by using his own body and knowledge of that body to bring the fractured world of name and form, the polarized world of male and female, sacred and profane, to wholeness and unity.

Sādhana (spiritual endeavor) takes a particularly dramatic form in left-handed (*vāmācāra*) Tantrism. In his attempt to realize the nature of the world as completely and thoroughly pervaded by the one *śakti*, the *sādhaka* (here called the "hero," *vīra*) undertakes the ritual of the *pañca-tattva*, the "five (forbidden) things" (or truths). In a ritual context and under the supervision of his guru, the *sādhaka* partakes of wine, meat, fish, parched grain (perhaps a hallucinogenic drug of some kind), and illicit sexual intercourse. In this way he overcomes the distinction (or duality) of clean and unclean, sacred and profane, and breaks his bondage to a world that is artificially fragmented. He affirms in a radical way the underlying unity of the phenomenal world, the identity of *śakti* with the whole creation. Heroically, he triumphs over it, controls and masters it. By affirming the essential worth of the forbidden, he causes the forbidden to lose its power to pollute, to degrade, to bind.[23]

The figure of Kālī conveys death, destruction, fear, terror, the all-consuming aspect of reality. As such she is also a "forbidden thing," or the forbidden par excellence, for she is death itself. The Tantric hero does not propitiate, fear, ignore, or avoid the forbidden. During the *pañcatattva* ritual, the *sādhaka* boldly confronts Kālī and thereby assimilates, overcomes, and transforms her into a vehicle of salvation. This is particularly clear in the *Karpūrādi-stotra*, a short work in praise of Kālī, which describes the *pañcatattva* ritual as performed in the cremation ground (*śmaśāna-sādhana*). Throughout this text Kālī is described in familiar terms. She is black (verse 1), has disheveled hair and blood trickling from her mouth (3), holds a sword and a severed head (4), wears a girdle of severed arms, sits on a corpse in the cremation ground (7), and is surrounded by skulls, bones, and female jackals (8). It is she, when confronted boldly in meditation, who gives the *sādhaka* great power and ultimately salvation. In Kālī's favorite dwelling place, the cremation ground, the *sādhaka* meditates on every terrible aspect of the black goddess and thus achieves his goal.

> He, O Mahākālī, who in the cremation-ground, naked, and with dishevelled hair, intently meditates upon Thee and recites Thy *mantra*, and with each recitation makes offering to Thee of a thousand *Akaṇda* flowers with seed, becomes without any effort a Lord of the earth.
>
> O Kālī, whoever on Tuesday at midnight, having uttered Thy *mantra*, makes offering even but once with devotion to Thee of a hair of his *Śakti* [his female companion] in the cremation-ground, becomes a great poet, a Lord of the earth, and ever goes mounted upon an elephant. (15–16)[24]

The *Karpūrādi-stotra* clearly makes Kālī more than a terrible, ferocious slayer of demons who serves Durgā or Śiva on the battlefield. In fact, she is by and large dissociated from the battle context. She is the supreme mistress of the universe (12), she is identified with the five elements (14), and in union with Śiva (who is identified as her spouse)[25] she creates and destroys the worlds. Her appearance has also been modified, befitting her exalted position as ruler of the world and the object of meditation by which the *sādhaka* attains liberation. In addition to her terrible aspects (which are insisted upon), there are now hints of another, benign dimension. So, for example, she is no longer described as emaciated or ugly. In the *Karpūrādi-stotra* she is young and beautiful (1), has a gently smiling face (18), and makes gestures with her two right hands that dispel fear and offer boons (4). These positive features are entirely apt, as Kālī no longer is a mere shrew, the distillation of Durgā's or Pārvatī's wrath, but is she through whom the hero achieves success, she who grants the boon of salvation, and she who, when boldly approached, frees the *sādhaka* from fear itself. She is here not only the symbol of death but the symbol of triumph over death.

Kālī also attains a central position in late medieval Bengali devotional literature.[26] In this devotion Kālī's appearance and habits have not changed very much. She remains terrifying in appearance and fearsome in habit. She is eminently recognizable. Rāmprasād Sen (1718–75), one of her most ardent devotees, describes his beloved Kālī in almost shocked tones:

> O Kālī! why dost Thou roam about nude?
> Art Thou not ashamed, Mother!
> Garb and ornaments Thou hast none; yet Thou
> pridest in being King's daughter.
> O Mother! is it a virtue of Thy family that
> Thou placest thy feet on Thy Husband?
> Thou are nude; Thy Husband is nude; you both
> roam cremation grounds.
> O Mother! we are all ashamed of you; do put on
> Thy garb.
> Thou hast cast away Thy necklace of jewells,
> Mother, and worn a garland of human heads.
> Prasāda says, "Mother! Thy fierce beauty has
> frightened Thy nude Consort."[27]

The approach of the devotee to Kālī, however, is quite different in mood and temperament from the approach of the Tantric *sādhaka*. The Tantric adept, seeking to view Kālī in her most terrible aspect, is heroic in approach, cultivating an almost aggressive, fearless stance before her. The Tantric adept challenges Kālī to unveil her most forbidding secrets. The devotee, in contrast, adopts the position of the helpless child when approaching Kālī. Even though the child's mother may be fearsome, at times even hostile, the child has little choice but to return to her for protection, security, and warmth. This is just the attitude Rāmprasād expresses when he writes: "Though she beat it, the child clings to its mother, crying 'Mother.'"[28]

Why Kālī is approached as mother and in what sense she is perceived to be a mother by her devotees are questions that do not have clear or easy answers. In almost every sense Kālī is *not* portrayed as a mother in the Hindu tradition prior to her central role in Bengali devotion beginning in the eighteenth century. Except in some contexts when she is associated or identified with Pārvatī as Śiva's consort, Kālī is rarely pictured in motherly scenes in Hindu mythology or iconography. Even in Bengali devotion to her, her appearance and habits change very little. Indeed, Kālī's appearance and habits strike one as conveying truths opposed to those conveyed by such archetypal mother goddesses as Pṛthivī, Annapūrṇā, Jagaddhātrī, Śatāksī, and other Hindu goddesses associated with fertility, growth, abundance, and well-being.[29] These goddesses appear as inexhaustible sources of nourishment and creativity. When depicted iconographically they are heavy hipped and heavy breasted. Kālī, especially in her early history, is often depicted or described as emaciated, lean, and gaunt. It is not her breasts or hips that attract attention. It is her mouth, her lolling tongue, and her bloody cleaver. These other goddesses, "mother goddesses" in the obvious sense, give life. Kālī takes life, insatiably. She lives in the cremation ground, haunts the battlefield, sits upon a corpse, and adorns herself with pieces of corpses. If mother goddesses are described as ever fecund, Kālī is described as ever hungry. Her lolling tongue, grotesquely long and oversized, her sunken stomach, emaciated appearance, and sharp fangs convey a presence that is the direct opposite of a fertile, protective mother goddess. If mother goddesses give life, Kālī feeds on life. What they give, she takes away.

Although the attitude of the devotee to Kālī is different from that of the Tantric hero, although their paths appear very different, the attitude and approach of the devotee who insists upon approaching Kālī as his mother may reveal a logic similar to that of the Tantric hero's. The truths about reality that Kālī conveys—namely, that life feeds on death, that death is inevitable for all beings, that time wears all things down, and so on[30]—are just as apparent to the devotee as they are to the Tantric hero. The fearfulness of these truths, however, is mitigated, indeed is transformed into liberating wisdom, if these truths can be accepted. The Tantric hero seeks to appropriate these truths by confronting Kālī, by seeking her in the cremation ground in the dead of night, and by heroically demonstrating courage equal to her terrible presence. The devotee, in contrast, appropriates the truths Kālī reveals by adopting the attitude of a child, whose essential nature toward its mother is that of acceptance, no matter how awful, how indifferent, how fearsome she is. The devotee, then, by making the apparently unlikely assertion that Kālī is his mother, enables himself to approach and appropriate the forbidding truths that Kālī reveals; in appropriating these truths the devotee, like the Tantric adept, is liberated from the fear these truths impose on people who deny or ignore them.

Through devotion to Kālī the devotee becomes reconciled to death and achieves an acceptance of the way things are, an equilibrium that remains unperturbed in Kālī's presence. These themes are expressed well in this song of Rāmprasād's:

> O Mother! Thou has great dissolution in Thy hand;
> Śiva lies at Thy feet, absorbed in bliss.
> Thou laughest aloud (striking terror); streams of
> blood flow from Thy limbs.
> O Tārā, doer of good, the good of all, grantor of safety,
> O Mother, grant me safety.
> O Mother Kālī! take me in Thy arms; O Mother Kālī!
> take me in Thy arms.
> O Mother! come now as Tārā with a smiling face and
> clad in white;
> As dawn descends on dense darkness of the night.
> O Mother! terrific Kālī! I have worshiped Thee alone
> so long.
> My worship is finished; now, O Mother, bring down Thy
> sword.[31]

Rāmprasād complains in many of his songs that Kālī is indifferent to his well-being, that she makes him suffer and brings his worldly desires to naught and his worldly goods to ruin.

> Mother who art the joy of Hara's [Śiva's] heart, and who dost bring to naught the hopes of men, thou hast made void what hope was left to me.
>
> Though I place my soul an offering at thy feet, some calamity befalls. Though I think upon thy loveliness, unceasing death is mine.
>
> Thou dost frustrate my desires, thou art the spoiler of my fortunes. Well do I know thy mercy, Mother of mine.

> Great were my desires, and I spread them all out as a salesman does his wares. Thou didst see the display, I suppose, and didst bring confusion upon me. . . .
> My wealth, my honour, kith and kin, all have gone, and I have nothing now to call my own.
> What further use is there for me? Wretched indeed am I.
> I have sought my own ends, and now there is no limit to my grief.
> Thou who dost take away sorrow, to me most wretched hast thou given sorrow. And I must all this unhappy lot endure.[32]

He complains that she does not behave in the ways mothers are supposed to behave, that she does not hearken to his pleas.

> Can mercy be found in the heart of her who was born of the stone [a reference to her being the daughter of Himālaya]?
> Were she not merciless, would she kick the breast of her lord?
> Men call you merciful, but there is no trace of mercy in you, Mother.
> You have cut off the heads of the children of others, and these you wear as a garland around your neck.
> It matters not how much I call you "Mother, Mother." You hear me, but you will not listen.[33]

To be Kālī's child, Rāmprasād often asserts, is to suffer, to be disappointed in terms of worldly desires and pleasures. Kālī does not give what is normally expected. She does allow her devotee/child, however, to glimpse a vision of himself that is not circumscribed by physical and material limitations. As Rāmprasād says succinctly: "He who has made Kālī . . . his only goal easily forgets worldly pleasures."[34] Indeed, that person has little choice, for Kālī does not indulge her devotees in worldly pleasures. It is her very refusal to do so that enables her devotees to reflect on dimensions of themselves and of reality that go beyond bodily comfort and world security.

An analysis of the significance of Kālī to the Hindu tradition reveals certain constants in her mythology and imagery. She is almost always associated with blood and death, and it is difficult to imagine two more polluting realities in the context of the purity-minded culture of Hinduism. As such, Kālī is a very dangerous being. She vividly and dramatically thrusts upon the observer things that he or she would rather not think about. Within the civilized order of Hinduism, within the order of dharma, blood and death are acknowledged—it is impossible not to acknowledge their existence in human life—but they are acknowledged within the context of a highly ritualized, patterned, and complex social structure that takes great pains to handle them in "safe" ways, usually through rituals of purification. These rituals (called *saṁskāras*, "refinements") allow individuals to pass in an orderly way through times when contact with blood and death are unavoidable. The order of dharma is not entirely naive and has incorporated into its refined version of human existence the recognition of these human inevitabilities.

But the Hindu *saṁskāras* are patterned on wishful thinking. Blood and death have a way of cropping up unexpectedly, accidentally, tragically, and dangerously. The periodic flow of menstrual blood or the death of an aged and loved old woman (whose husband has cooperatively died before her) are manageable within the normal order of human events. But the death of an infant or a hemorrhage, for instance, are a threat to the neat vision of the order of dharma.[35] They can never be avoided with certainty, no matter how well protected one thinks one is.

Kālī may be one way in which the Hindu tradition has sought to come to terms, at least in part, with the built-in shortcomings of its own refined view of the world. It is perhaps best and even redemptive to recognize that the system does not work in every case. Reflecting on the ways in which people must negate certain realities in their attempts to create social order, anthropologist Mary Douglas writes:

> Whenever a strict pattern of purity is imposed on our lives it is either highly uncomfortable or it leads into contradiction if closely followed, or it leads to hypocrisy. That which is negated is not thereby removed. The rest of life, which does not tidily fit the accepted categories, is still there and demands attention. The body, as we have tried to show, provides a basic scheme for all symbolism. There is hardly any pollution which does not have some primary physiological reference. As life is in the body it cannot be rejected outright. And as life must be affirmed, the most complete philosophies . . . must find some ultimate way of affirming that which has been rejected.[36]

Kālī puts the order of dharma in perspective, perhaps puts it in its place, by reminding Hindus that certain aspects of reality are untamable, unpurifiable, unpredictable, and always a threat to society's feeble attempts to order what is essentially disorderly: life itself.

Kālī's shocking appearance and unconventional behavior confront one with an alternative to normal society. To meditate on the dark goddess, or to devote oneself to her, is to step out of the everyday world of predictable dharmic order and enter a world of reversals, opposites, and contrasts and in doing so to wake up to new possibilities and new frames of reference. In her differentness, strangeness, indeed, in her perverseness, Kālī is the kind of figure who is capable of shaking one's comforting and naive assumptions about the world. In doing this she allows a clearer perception of how things really are.[37]

Kālī allows (or perhaps forces) better perception by enabling one to see the complete picture. She allows one to see behind the bounteousness of the other goddesses who appear in benign forms. Kālī reveals the insatiable hunger that logically must lie behind their amazing fecundity and liberality. Similarly, Kālī permits individuals to see their overall roles in the cosmic drama. She invites a wider, more mature, more realistic reflection on where one has come from and where one is going. She allows the individual to see himself or herself as merely one being in an endless series of permutations arising from the ever-recurring cycles of life and death that constitute the inner rhythms of the divine mother. As cycling and recycled energy, as both the creation and the food of the goddess, the individual is permitted to glimpse social roles and identities in perspective, to see them as often confining and as obscuring a clear perception of how things really are and who he or she really is. Kālī reveals that ultimately all creatures are her children and also her food and that no social role or identity can remove the individual from this sacrificial give and take. While this truth may appear grim, its realization may be just what is needed to push one over the threshold into the liberating quest for release from bondage to *saṁsāra*.

The extent to which Kālī invites or provokes one over the threshold from order to antistructure is seen in the roles she requires of those who would establish any intimacy with her.[38] Iconographically, it is Śiva who participates in the most intimate relations with Kālī. In probably her most famous pose, as Dakṣiṇakālī, she stands or dances upon Śiva's prone body in the cremation ground. His eyes are closed in bliss, sleep, trance, or death—it is difficult to say which. His attitude is utterly passive and, whether he is dead or not, his appearance corpselike. The myth that explains the origin of this pose says that once upon a time Kālī began to dance out of control on the battlefield after having become drunk on the blood of her victims. To stop her rampage, Śiva lay down on the battlefield like a corpse so that when she danced on his body she would stop, recognizing him as her husband. It is thus as a corpse, as one of her victims, that Śiva calms Kālī and elicits her grace.[39]

In another myth it is the infant Śiva who calms Kālī and stops her rampage by eliciting motherly emotions from her. In this story Kālī again has defeated her enemies on the battlefield and begun to dance out of control, drunk on the blood of those she has slain. To calm her and protect the stability of the world, Śiva appears in the midst of the battlefield as an infant, crying out loudly. Seeing the child's distress, Kālī stops her dancing, picks him up, and kisses him on the head. Then she suckles him at her breasts.[40]

Both the dead and infants have a liminal nature. Neither has a complete social identity. Neither fits neatly or at all into the niches and structures of normal society. To approach Kālī it is well to assume the identity of a corpse or an infant. Having no stake in the orderly structures of society, the devotee as corpse or infant is free to step out of society into the liminal environment of the goddess. The corpse is mere food for her insatiable fires, the infant mere energy, as yet raw and unrefined. Reduced to either extreme, one who approaches Kālī in these roles is awakened to a perception of reality that is difficult to grasp within the confines of the order of dharma and a socialized ego.

9

THE MAHĀDEVĪ

There is a tendency in many texts, myths, and rituals concerning goddesses to subsume them all under one great female being. This goddess has many names, but her most common designation is simply Devī (goddess) or Mahādevī (great goddess). The early Hindu tradition tended to speak of discrete goddesses—Śrī, Pārvatī, Sītā, and so on.[1] Sometime in the medieval period, however, the tendency to think of all goddesses as related beings began to dominate certain texts. Perhaps the earliest example of this trend is the *Devī-mahātmyā*, which is usually dated around the sixth century.[2]

Affirmation of a unity underlying all goddesses is usually expressed in one of two ways. First, a particular goddess, such as Pārvatī or Lakṣmī, will be affirmed as the highest deity, or perhaps the consort or *śakti* of the highest deity, and all other goddesses will be understood as portions or manifestations of her. This approach is also seen in the case of male deities and often involves a sectarian desire to demonstrate the superiority of one deity over others. The second way in which the unity of all goddesses is asserted is by assuming the existence of one transcendent great goddess who possesses most classical characteristics of ultimate reality as understood in the Hindu tradition and then subsuming all particular goddesses under her as partial manifestations of her.

It is often difficult to separate these two approaches. In the former case, the particular goddess who is elevated to supremacy, be she Pārvatī, Durgā, or Lakṣmī, will be given all the attributes of ultimate reality but at the same time will keep most of her distinctive mythology and appearance. In the latter case, when the supreme goddess is described concretely, the description will often be similar to the appearance of a specific goddess well known in the tradition. That is, the author will usually betray a preference for a particular goddess tradition in actually describing the supreme goddess, and she will tend to appear more like one goddess than another. Both approaches, however, tend to assert a definite theological position, namely, that underlying all female deities there is a unified power or essence. This power, furthermore, tends to display itself in almost innumerable forms, for a variety of purposes.

CENTRAL THEOLOGICAL AND PHILOSOPHICAL CHARACTERISTICS

An underlying theological assumption in texts celebrating the Mahādevī is that the ultimate reality in the universe is a powerful, creative, active, transcendent female being. The *Lalitā-sahasranāma* gives many names of the Mahādevī, and several of her epithets express this assumption. She is called, for example, the root of the world (Jagatīkandā, name 325), she who transcends the universe (Viśvādhikā, 334), she who has no equal (Nirupamā, 389), supreme ruler (Parameśvarī, 396), she who pervades all (Vyāpinī, 400), she who is immeasurable (Aprameyā, 413), she who creates innumerable universes (Anekakoṭibrahmāṇḍajananī, 620), she whose womb contains the universe (Viśvagarbhā, 637), she who is the support of all (Sarvādhārā, 659), she who is omnipresent (Sarvagā, 702), she who is the ruler of all worlds (Sarvalokeśī, 758), and she who supports the universe (Viśvadhāriṇī, 759). In the *Devī-bhāgavata-purāṇa,* which also assumes the ultimate priority of the Mahādevī, she is said to be the mother of all, to pervade the three worlds, to be the support of all (1.5.47–50), to be the life force in all beings, to be the ruler of all beings (1.5.51–54), to be the only cause of the universe (1.7.27), to create Brahmā, Viṣṇu, and Śiva and to command them to perform their cosmic tasks (3.5.4), to be the root of the tree of the universe (3.10.15), and to be she who is supreme knowledge (4.15.12). The text describes her by many other names and phrases as it exalts her to a position of cosmic supremacy.

One of the central philosophic ideas underlying the Mahādevī, an idea that in many ways captures her essential nature, is *śakti. Śakti* means "power"; in Hindu philosophy and theology *śakti* is understood to be the active dimension of the godhead, the divine power that underlies the godhead's ability to create the world and to display itself.[3] Within the totality of the godhead, *śakti* is the complementary pole of the divine tendency toward quiescence and stillness. It is quite common, furthermore, to identify *śakti* with a female being, a goddess, and to identify the other pole with her male consort. The two poles are usually understood to be interdependent and to have relatively equal status in terms of the divine economy.[4]

Silver mask of Devī. Sixteen or seventeenth century A.D. Madanjeet Singh, *Himalayan Art* (London: MacMillan, 1968), p. 143.

Texts or contexts exalting the Mahādevī, however, usually affirm *śakti* to be a power, or *the* power, underlying ultimate reality, or to be ultimate reality itself. Instead of being understood as one of two poles or as one dimension of a bipolar conception of the divine, *śakti* as it applies to the Mahādevī is often identified with the essence of reality. If the Mahādevī as *śakti* is related to another dimension of the divine in the form of a male deity, he will tend to play a subservient role in relation to her.[5] In focusing on the centrality of *śakti* as constituting the essence of the divine, texts usually describe the Mahādevī as a powerful, active, dynamic being who creates, pervades, governs, and protects the universe. As *śakti*, she is not aloof from the world but attentive to the cosmic rhythms and the needs of her devotees.

In a similar vein the Mahādevī is often identified with *prakṛti* and *māyā*. Indeed, two of her most common epithets are Mūlaprakṛti (she who is primordial matter) and Mahāmāyā (she who is great *māyā*). These ideas have negative connotations in certain schools of Hindu philosophy. Sāṁkhya philosphy and yogic spiritual techniques describe *prakṛti* as the web of matter in which one's spiritual essence, *puruṣa* (literally, the male), is enmeshed. Yogic exercise aims at reversing the spontaneous tendencies of *prakṛti* to reproduce and specify itself. In the quest for liberation *prakṛti* represents that from which one seeks freedom. Similarly, most schools of Hindu philosophy identify *māyā* with that which prevents one from seeing things as they really are. *Māyā* is the process of superimposition by which one projects one's own ignorance on the world and thus obscures ultimate truth. To wake up to the truth of things necessarily involves counteracting or overcoming *māyā*, which is grounded in ignorance and self-infatuation. Liberation in Hindu philosophy means to a great extent the transcendence of embodied, finite, phenomenal existence. And *māyā* is often equated precisely with finite, phenomenal existence.[6] To be in the phenomenal world, to be an individual creature, is to live enveloped in *māyā*.

When the Mahādevī is associated with *prakṛti* or *māyā*, certain negative overtones sometimes persist. As *prakṛti* or *māyā* she is sometimes referred to as the great power that preoccupies individuals with phenomenal existence or as the cosmic force that impels even the gods to unconsciousness and sleep.[7] But the overall result of the Mahādevī's identification with *prakṛti* and *māyā* is to infuse both ideas with positive dimensions. As *prakṛti* or *māyā*, the Devī is identified with existence itself, or with that which underlies all existent things. The emphasis is not on the binding aspects of matter or the created world but on the Devī as the ground of all things. Because it is she who pervades the material world as *prakṛti* or *māyā*, the phenomenal world tends to take on positive qualities. Or perhaps we could say that a positive attitude toward the world, which is evident in much of popular Hinduism, is affirmed when the Devī is identified with *prakṛti* and *māyā*. The central theological point here is that the Mahadevī is the world, she is all this creation, she is one with her creatures and her creation. Although a person's spiritual destiny ultimately may involve transcendence of the creation, the Devī's identification with existence per se is clearly intended to be a positive philosophic assertion. She is life, and to the extent that life is cherished and revered, she is cherished and revered.

As *śakti, prakṛti,* and *māyā,* the Devī is portrayed as an overwhelming presence that overflows itself, spilling forth into the creation, suffusing the world with vitality, energy, and power. When the Devī is identified with these well-known philosophic ideas, then, a positive point is being made: the Devī creates the world, she is the world,[8] and she enlivens the world with creative power. As *śakti, prakṛti,* and *māyā,* she is not understood so much as binding creatures to finite existence as being the very source and vitality of creatures. She is the source of creatures—their mother—and as such her awesome, vital power is revered.

The idea of *brahman* is another central idea with which the Devī is associated. Ever since the time of the *Upaniṣads, brahman* has been the most commonly accepted term or designation for ultimate reality in Hinduism. In the *Upaniṣads,* and throughout the Hindu tradition, *brahman* is described in two ways: as *nirguṇa* (having no qualities or beyond all qualities) and *saguṇa* (having qualities). As *nirguṇa,* which is usually affirmed to be the superior way of thinking about *brahman,* ultimate reality transcends all qualities, categories, and limitations. As *nirguṇa, brahman* transcends all attempts to circumscribe it. It is beyond all name and form (*nāma-rūpa*). As the ground of all things, as the fundamental principal of existence, however, *brahman* is also spoken of as having qualities, indeed, as manifesting itself in a multiplicity of deities, universes, and beings. As *saguṇa, brahman* reveals itself especially as the various deities of the Hindu pantheon. The main philosophical point asserted in the idea of *saguṇa brahman* is that underlying all the different gods is a unifying essence, namely, *brahman*. Each individual deity is understood to be a partial manifestation of *brahman,* which ultimately is beyond all specifying attributes, functions, and qualities.

The idea of *brahman* serves well the attempts in many texts devoted to the Devī to affirm her supreme position in the Hindu pantheon. The idea of *brahman* makes two central philosophic points congenial to the theology of the Mahādevī: (1) she is ultimate reality itself, and (2) she is the source of all divine manifestations, male and female (but especially female). As *saguṇa brahman,* the Devī is portrayed as a great cosmic queen enthroned in the highest heaven, with a multitude of deities as the agents through which she governs the infinite universes. In her ultimate essence, however, some texts, despite their clear preference for the Devī's feminine characteristics, assert in traditional fashion that she is beyond all qualities, beyond male and female.[9]

MYTHOLOGICAL CHARACTERISTICS AND FUNCTIONS

The central role the Devī plays in mythology is that of creator and queen of the cosmos. When she is portrayed in her own form (*sva-bhāva*), she is usually described as a beautiful young woman in regal attire surrounded by thousands of attendants and seated on a throne in the highest heaven.[10] As cosmic queen she oversees or performs directly the three primary cosmic functions of creation, preservation, and destruction. The world is said to be destroyed when she blinks her eyes and to be recreated when she opens her eyes.[11]

Many Hindu mythological texts attribute the three cosmic functions to Brahmā (creation), Viṣṇu (preservation), and Śiva (destruction). While texts extolling the Devī often picture these three male deities in their familiar roles, it is made clear that the male gods only act according to the Devī's will and at her command.[12] Some myths make the point that the great male gods are entirely dependent on the Devī for their strength and power and that if she withdraws her power they are impotent and helpless.[13] The *Devī-bhāgavata-purāṇa* also makes it clear that the traditional heavenly abodes of these deities are far below and inferior to the Devī's heaven. Indeed, the text asserts that there are innumerable Brahmās, Viṣṇus, and Śivas, whose tasks are to govern the innumerable universes that ceaselessly bubble forth from the inexhaustibly creative Devī (3.4.14–67). In the *Lalitā-sahasranāma* the Devī is called she from whose ten fingernails spring the ten forms of Viṣṇu (Karānguli-nakhotpanna-nārāyana-dasākṛtiḥ, 80). In the *Saundaryalaharī* the entire universe is formed from a tiny speck of dust from the Devī's foot. Brahmā takes that speck and from it fashions worlds that Viṣṇu, in his form as the many-headed cosmic serpent, can barely support with his thousand heads (verse 2). In a particularly humbling scene for the male deities, the Devī is described in her heaven as seated upon a couch, its four legs consisting of the great male deities of the Hindu pantheon.[14] The point is clear: the great male gods still have important roles to play, but ultimately they are the servants of the Devī and do her bidding. She has created them, indeed, she has created innumerable copies of each of them, and they act as her cosmic agents, overseeing the universes she has created.

Although the male deities are frequently portrayed as carrying out their traditional cosmological functions at the Devī's command, she herself is also often pictured as taking an active role in the cosmic processes. She is ever attentive to the world, particularly to her devotees, and in various forms she acts to uphold cosmic order and protect her creatures. Although her concern is that of a mother for her children, hence a passionate and ever-watchful concern, her favorite role as protector and preserver of the cosmos is that of the warrior, a traditionally male role. Many of her epithets emphasize this aspect of her character. The *Lalitā-sahasranāma* calls her she who slays demons (Rākṣasaghnī, 318), she who grants boons to great warriors (Mahāvīrendravaradā, 493), ruler of armies (Caturaṅgabaleśvarī, 691), she who is worshiped by warriors (Vīrārādhya, 777), and mother of warriors (Vīramātā, 836).

The Devī's most famous mythological exploits usually involve the defeat of demons who have taken over the world and displaced the gods from their positons as rulers of the cosmos. The three episodes featuring the goddess Durgā are particularly popular in texts celebrating the Mahādevī, and she is identified with Durgā in various renditions of the tales. To a great extent Durgā is the Devī's most common or favorite form, and Durgā's exploits are the most commonly celebrated events in Devī mythology. From the point of view of Mahādevī theology the two are essentially the same deity. The account of Durgā's defeat of Mahiṣa in the *Devī-bhāgavata-purāṇa*, for example, explicitly states that the Devī, though *nirguṇa* in her ultimate essence, assumes for her pleasure a great variety of forms in order to maintain cosmic order and that her form as Durgā is simply one of those forms, though undoubtedly a very important one.[15] As Durgā, the Mahādevī is typically described as a ferocious, invincible warrior who descends into the world from time to time to combat evil of various kinds, especially demons who have stolen the positions of the gods.

As Durgā, the Mahādevī is in many ways like the great god Viṣṇu. Viṣṇu is usually pictured as a cosmic king who oversees the stability of the world. When the world is threatened by demons, he descends in different forms to combat the danger. The Mahādevī is also said to assume forms appropriate to cosmic threats. Viṣṇu is traditionally said to have ten *avatāras*. In each universal cycle he takes ten different forms to combat ten different demons. The Mahādevī, too, is said to have ten forms, the Dasamahāvidyās (the ten great scenes or insights). These ten forms include several well-known Hindu goddesses, and like the Vaiṣṇavite idea of *avatāras* the ten forms of the Devī effectively bring together distinct strands under a unifying great deity.[16] From the point of view of Devī theology and cosmology the Hindu goddesses are varying manifestations of the Devī's activity on behalf of the world. Durgā, Lakṣmī,

Pārvatī, and other goddesses are all understood to be parts of a transcendent divine economy that is governed by the the Devī in her own form (*svabhāva*) or in her aspect as *brahman*. This economy, with a few important exceptions, is oriented toward upholding and protecting the world.

The Devī, like Viṣṇu, also plays the role of protector and preserver in less grand, cosmic ways by making periodic and dramatic appearances on behalf of her individual devotees. In this role she plays the savior. Her devotees Samādhi and Suratha propitiate her in the closing scene of the *Devī-māhātmya*. She appears before them and graciously grants their desires (13.7–16). In the *Devī-bhāgavata-purāṇa* when her devotee Sudarśana is surrounded by his enemies and prays to her for help, she appears as a great warrior riding on her lion and quickly routs them (3.23.18–41). She appears to aid Rāma when he prays to her for help in defeating Rāvaṇa. She enpowers him to build a bridge from India to Laṅka and announces that she will cause him to defeat Rāvaṇa (3.30.43–61). In the *Devī-bhāgavata-purāṇa*'s account of the well-known story of Hariścandra, who is reduced to poverty and the pitiable status of an outcaste, the Devī answers Hariścandra's prayer by appearing and restoring him to his former state and reviving his child from the dead (7.27.1–7). The Mahādevī, then, though typically pictured as a distant, awesome figure who sits in majesty on a heavenly throne surrounded by divine attendants, is responsive to the pleas of her individual devotees and is quick to come to their aid in times of distress. She is understood to be an approachable, motherly figure who is never deaf to the cries of her children.

AUSPICIOUS AND TERRIBLE FORMS

Another important feature of Mahādevī mythology and theology is the insistence that she assumes both benign and terrible forms. Most texts extolling the Devī are preoccupied with her benign and auspicious forms, but many texts affirm that she has several manifestations that are dreadful, dangerous, or bloodthirsty.[17] In the *Devī-bhāgavata-purāṇa* (7.33.21–56), in a passage reminiscent of the scene in the *Bhāgavad-gītā* when Arjuna asks to see Kṛṣṇa's cosmic form, the gods ask the Devī for a glimpse of her universal form. She obliges, and the gods are stunned and terrified by what they behold. She assumes a form having thousands of heads, eyes, and feet. Her entire body blazes with fierce, destructive flames, and her teeth make horrible grinding noises. Her eyes blaze with flames brighter than millions of suns, and the gods tremble as they see her consume the universes. They plead with her to resume her gentle form, which she does, reappearing as a beautiful woman with a soft and gentle body and a smiling face. The *Kurma-purāṇa* describes the Devī, who is identified primarily with Pārvatī, as showing her cosmic form to Himavat. She blazes brightly, has dreadful teeth, wears a tiger skin, is armed with many weapons, and is of terrible form. When Himavat trembles with fear at her sight, she changes her appearance, presenting herself to him in her beautiful, tranquil, approachable form (11.67–73, 214–217). The *Mahānirvāna-tantra* describes her as drenched in blood from grinding up the world at the time of dissolution; the next verse says that she protects all beings, dispels fear, and grants blessings (13.9–10).

Many epithets in the *Lalitā-sahasranāma* emphasize the Devī's graciousness, and her physical appearance from head to toe is described as surpassingly beautiful (13–51). Other names, however, suggest a destructive side to her nature: she who is seated on a throne of five corpses (Pañcapretāsanāsīnā, 249), the terrible one (Bhairavī, 276), she who destroys (Saṁhārinī, 268), she who has flaming tusks (Daṁṣṭrojjvalā, 488), she who is a great devourer (Mahāgrāsā, 752), she who is a great eater (Mahāsanā, 753), and she who is wrathful (Pracaṇḍā, 827). The Devī is also often referred to by names that suggest her thirst for intoxicants: she who is drunk with the wine of dates (Vāruṇīmadavihvalā, 333), she whose eyes roll about from drinking wine (Madaghūrṇitaraktākṣī, 432), and she who is fond of wine (Madhuprītā, 510). Other names suggest that the Devī is mad: she who is mad, or drunk (Mattā, 576), or causes madness or bewilderment; she who bewilders all (Sarvamohinī, 703).

The *Āryāstava*, a hymn to the Devī in the *Harivaṁśa*, similarly juxtaposes the Devī's auspicious and terrible characteristics. She is said to be success itself (*siddhi*), life (*jīvanam*), victory (*vijayā*), mercy, nourishment, and many other auspicious things. She is also described as the night of death (Kālarātri), she who is fond of violence and quarreling (Kalahapriyā), she who is death (Niṣṭhā), and she who is fond of offerings of meat and wine (Surāmaṅgsabalipriyā).[18]

Before reflecting on the meaning of the juxtaposition of the Devī's auspicious and terrifying aspects, it may be helpful to clarify what the two facets of the Devī are. The Devī's auspicious aspect is manifest in several of the goddesses we have already discussed: Lakṣmī, Pārvatī, Satī, and Pṛthivī. In these and other forms she displays positive roles: fertility, the protection and establishment of dharmic order, cultural creativity, wifely duty, and material abundance. Three other roles are also important in connection with the Devī's auspicious forms: (1) her role as granter of wisdom, learning, and liberation, (2) her role as the embodiment of female beauty and the exciter of desire, and (3) her role as the source of food and nourishment.

In the *Āryāstava* she is called liberation (*mukti*), she who speaks of the knowledge of *brahman*, and she who is the knowledge of *brahman*.[19] A hymn addressed to the Devī in the *Mahābhārata* calls her liberation and knowledge of *brahman* as well as mother of the *Vedas*.[20] Another hymn of the *Mahābhārata* calls her intelligence and knowledge and says that she destroys ignorance and all of mankind's fetters.[21] In the *Lalitā-sahasranāma* she is called she who is great intelligence (Mahābuddhi, 223), she whose form is a mass of knowledge (Vijñānabhanarūpiṇi, 253), she who is wisdom itself (Prajñātmikā, 261), she who releases creatures from bondage (Paśupāśavimocinī, 354), she who removes darkness (Tamopahā, 361), intelligence (Mati, 445), she who removes bonds (Bandhamocanī, 546), knowledge (Vidyā, 549), she who is knowledge of the *ātman* (Ātmavidyā, 583), she who is great and auspicious knowledge (Mahāvidyā and Śrīvidyā, 584 and 585), she whose form is the guru (Gurumūrti, 603), she who bestows knowledge (Jñānadā, 643), she who gives salvation (Muktidā, 736), she who bestows heaven and liberation (Svargāpavargadā, 764), she whose form is truth, wisdom, and bliss (Satyajñānānandarūpā, 791), she who brings peace to people consumed by birth, death, and decrepitude (Janmamṛtyujarātaptajanavisrāntidāyinī, 851), she who removes all misfortune (Sarvāpadivinivārinī, 913), and she who is the lamp that dispels the darkness of ignorance (Ajñānadhvāntadīpikā, 993).

In many ways the Devī assumes the role and displays the characteristics of Sarasvatī as the granter of wisdom and learning. She is associated with practical knowledge and civilization in general. The Devī in this aspect is not a goddess revealed in nature but a goddess associated with culture. Her association with spiritual knowledge, wisdom, and liberation also makes the point that the Devī transcends the world she creates, that she not only underlies the world and is its creator but is the means to transcend the world, which is the ultimate spiritual goal in Hinduism.

Many texts extolling the Devī emphasize her extraordinary beauty. It is common for hymns that praise her to describe her physical appearance from head to toe. The *Saundaryalaharī*, perhaps the most famous hymn praising the Devī, dotes on each physical detail of her body, devoting verses 42–88 to her physical praise. The *Lalitā-sahasranāma* similarly describes her every feature in names 13–51. These texts emphasize the desirability of actually seeing or visualizing the Devī, which is a redemptive event in itself and is longed for by her devotees. Even though the Devī's devotees never approach her as lovers, almost invariably preferring to come to her in the mood of children, her physical appearance is held to epitomize feminine beauty and to arouse those deities who are associated with her, especially Śiva. She is also often given epithets that identify her with sexual desire, and the hymns that praise her make the point that she reveals herself or is manifest in the sexual attraction of creatures, that she is identified with the power of sexuality. The *Saundaryalaharī* says that Kāma's great power, by which he arouses all creatures to sexual desire, was given by a glance of the Devī (verse 6). Her sexually stimulating effect is vividly described in the same text:

> A worn-out old man, distasteful to the sight,
> sluggish in love's art,
> if he but fall within a side glance from you, there
> run after him by the hundreds,
> with hair ribbons flying loose and clothes slipped from
> their jarlike breasts,
> young women, their girdles violently bursting and their
> garments dropped down.[22]

Several names in the *Lalitā-sahasranāma* stress the Devī's physical beauty or her association with sexual vitality: the beautiful one (Ramyā, 307), loveliness (Kāntā, 329), she who has beautiful eyes (Vāmanayanā, 332), she who has beautiful hair (Vāmakesī, 351), she whose form is Rati (Ratirūpā, 315; Rati is the wife of the god Kāma; her name literally means "sexual intercourse"), the one who is desired (Kāmyā, 321), she who is filled with the erotic sentiment (Sṛṅgārarasasaṁpūrṇā, 376), she whose form is the desire of women (Lolākṣīkāmarūpiṇī, 454), she who causes emotion (Kṣobhiṇī, 466), enchantress (Mohinī, 562), she whose form is sexual desire (Kāmarūpiṇī, 796), and she who overflows with desire and pleasure (Kāmakelitaraṅgitā, 863).

The Devī's association or identification with life and the rhythms of the physical world is clear in her aspect as instigator of desire. As *prakṛti* and *śakti*, the Devī impels creation forward. In the *Lalitā-sahasranāma* she is called vitality (Ojovatī, 767), she who gives life (Prāṇadā, 783), and she whose form is life (Prāṇarūpiṇī, 784). The immediate, dramatic, forceful expression of this impulse is sexual attraction, which characterizes most created beings and often powerfully dominates human beings. Although the male deity Kāma is traditionally given the role of instigator of sexual desire in Hindu mythology, the Devī nonetheless is often celebrated as manifesting herself wherever sexual desire appears. In the texts that praise her, Kāma acts as her agent and is empowered by her sexual vitality.[23]

The Devī's association with nourishment and food is another of her distinctive characteristics. As she is often identified with the earth itself (she is called Mahī and Dharā, "earth," in the *Lalitā-sahasranāma*, 718 and 955) it is not surprising that the Devī is also identified with food, which comes from the earth. The *Lalitā-sahasranāma* calls her she who gives food (Annadā, 669) and nourishment (Puṣṭi, 444). Texts celebrating the Mahādevī relate a myth concerning a great drought that resulted in a dreadful famine.[24] In desperation the Brahmans approached the Devī and begged her for relief. The Devī obligingly appeared in a form having many eyes. Seeing the pitiful condition of her creatures, she began to weep. She cried for nine nights, causing heavy rains to fall on the earth from her eyes. The rivers again flowed, the lakes and ponds were filled, and life once more returned to the earth in abundance.[25] In this manifestation she is called Satākṣī (she who has one hundred eyes), Śākambharī (she who bestows vegetables), and Annapūrṇā (she who is full of food). Images of Satākṣī show her carrying various kinds of food.[26] Images of Annapūrṇā typically show her holding a cooking pot and spoon.[27] Her most popular festival in Banaras takes place in the fall and celebrates her role as the sustainer of life. During the Annakutā (food mountain) festival, a mountain of food is indeed constructed and fills her temple.[28] In the spring during a festival that associates her with the sprouting rice, her image and temple are decorated with green rice sprouts.[29] Another well-known epithet of the Devī which emphasizes her nourishing aspect is Jagaddhātrī, which may mean either "she who supports the world" or "world nurse."[30]

A basic human perception seems to underlie the Devī's association with food. The mysterious power by which apparently lifeless seeds produce vegetation when inserted into the earth impresses itself on people as revealing an awesome, potent presence associated with the solid earth itself. It is natural, furthermore, that this presence be apprehended as a female in whom the same mysterious fertile powers are evident. The earth and the Devī possess an immense reservoir of power that can renourish declining vigor and make it fresh and new. Crops, food—all living things that teem upon the surface of earth—are the natural bubblings of the great fertile power that resides in the earth and is identified with the Devī. As *śakti* (power) and *prakṛti* (the tendency of nature to specify and multiply), the Devī manifests herself in infinite concrete organisms that in turn feed more complex organisms, and so the continued impulse of life is sustained and maintained by the Devī as food. As food, or as the giver or source of food, the empahsis is on the Devī's benign, fructifying aspects. The other side of her nature, however, is that in her bloodthirsty forms she demands to be renourished by blood and ultimately by the lives of all creatures.[31]

Although the Devī's auspicious, benign forms tend to dominate her character, sometimes to the extent that no fierce or destructive aspects appear,[32] most texts that celebrate her insist that she possesses fierce or terrible forms that are associated with war, blood, destruction, death, and hunger. The terrible forms of the Devī often arise in the context of one of her most fundamental protective roles, guardian of the cosmos in the form of a formidable warrior. Sometimes the Devī, in one of her auspicious, gentle forms, will be petitioned to defeat a demon on behalf of the gods. Hearing of the demon's activity, or perhaps simply contemplating the idea of war, the Devī takes on a fierce, terrible form and proceeds to enter into battle.[33] Sometimes her fierce forms only arise once she has actually entered the battle. Having worked herself up, having gotten the taste of blood and death, or provoked by the insults of her enemies, the Devī transforms herself,[34] splits herself,[35] or multiplies herself[36] into a ferocious goddess or goddesses and tears into her enemies with awful glee.[37] Although ostensibly performing a positive function in these scenes, the Devī's terrible forms betray qualities that often threaten the world and suggest dangerous, uncontrollable facets of her character. More often than not the ferocious goddess (or goddesses) loses control. She is described as rending her enemies limb from limb, tearing their flesh with her teeth, and drinking their blood, which then intoxicates her. Thirsting for more blood or dancing drunkenly out of control, she herself becomes a threat to the cosmos and must be tamed or subdued.[38] In these instances the terrible forms of the Devī appear to represent her personified wrath, her destructive power intensified, or her loss of temper and control.

The context of combat arouses an aspect of the Devī that delights in the blood lust of battle and is reminiscent of the berserk qualities of warriors by which they undertake bloodcurdling deeds. In this aspect the Devī is dangerous, even to her own allies. She is all-consuming. She lacks finesse. Typically she does not use weapons, such as a bow and arrow, spear, or chariot. She uses her own formidable teeth and sharp nails to tear her enemies to pieces. It is not the art of war that delights her in this aspect but the blood lust of battle. It is the clamor, tumult, terror, and frenzy of the battlefield which please and excite her and summon her into existence in the first place. She is the distillation of the furious, raw, savage power and lust of the frenzied warrior, and as such she is truly a terrible being, feared by her enemies, to be sure, but a threat to the overall stability of the world itself.

Many fierce, terrible goddesses also exist outside the battle context. They are not related in any clear way to the Mahādevī's central role as cosmic guardian, but they are definitely affirmed to be aspects of her being. Besides their terrible appearances and fierce natures, their most distinctive characteristic is often their taste for blood. There are many examples from all over India of goddesses who are worshiped with blood sacrifices.[39] The tradition of goddesses who are pleased with blood—and particularly human blood, often the blood of their most ardent devotees—dates back at least to medieval times in Hinduism.[40] Although human sacrifice is not usually sanctioned in texts extolling the Devī, there are several indications that human sacrifice was performed in her honor. The *Kālikā-purāṇa* devotes a whole chapter to sacrifices acceptable to the Devī and includes human beings as particularly pleasing to her (71.73). A goddess named Kesai Khati (eater of raw flesh) was worshiped in Assam, and sometimes human sacrifices were made to her.[41] The *Maṇimēkalai*, a Tamil epic, describes the temple of a goddess which has an altar surrounded by posts from which human heads are hung.[42] In Bhavabhūti's *Mālatīmādhava* a devotee of the goddess Cāmuṇḍā kidnaps the heroine with the intention of sacrificing her to the goddess.[43] The hero of the *Varāṅgacarita* is also kidnapped, in this case by tribal people, to be sacrificed to a forest goddess (13.58).[44] In the not-too-distant past the goddess Kāmākhyā was offered 140 human heads when her new temple was dedicated.[45]

Iconography and literature contain many examples of people who sacrifice their own blood and pieces of their flesh to goddesses; ritual suicide, usually self-decapitation, is also well documented as an act of devotion to goddesses.[46] The *Kālikā-purāṇa* says that the Devī is satisfied when her devotees offer flesh from near their hearts (71.74 ff.); the *Kumārī-tantra* says that one who offers his own blood to the Devī will achieve royalty.[47] In the *Devī-māhātmya* two devotees of the Devī petition her to grant them boons, and as part of their spiritual exercises they offer their own blood and pieces of their flesh (13.8).

Although to my knowledge there exists no textual sanction for ritual suicide to the Devī, many cases of self-immolation as an act of devotion to goddesses have been noted.[48] In Kṣemendra's *Bṛhatkathā-mañjarī* a washerman and his brother-in-law cut off their heads in a fit of devotional fervor to the goddess Gaurī. In an inscription dated A.D. 991 from the Kannada area we hear of a loyal subject named Katega who offered his head to the goddess Guṇḍadabbe to fulfill a vow when the king succeeded in fathering a son.[49] Four similar scenes from Pallava and early Chola sculpture depict kneeling male devotees offering their heads to a four-armed goddess.[50] In the Tamil epic *Śilappadihāram* the goddess Aiyai, who is worshipped by hunters, is adorned with snakes, tiger's teeth, and a leopard skin and is armed with a bow. She receives blood sacrifices and accepts the blood that flows from the severed heads of her devotees.[51]

Human sacrifices and self-immolation to goddesses represent only the extreme aspect of the blood offerings to these deities and were probably never widely practiced. Animal sacrifices, however, are a very common part of the worship of local goddesses throughout India. Goats are sacrificed daily to Kālī at the Kālīghāt temple in Calcutta to the present day, and this is nothing unusual in terms of her worship elsewhere in Bengal and India. On her festival day in the autumn in Bengal goats are sacrificed to her at temporary shrines set up all over the state. Similarly, during Durgā Pūjā goats and sometimes buffaloes are offered in great numbers to the goddess wherever she is worshiped. An inscription from South India mentions daily offerings of sheep to Cāmuṇḍā.[52] Māriyamman, the popular village goddess of South India, recieves blood offerings at her festivals.[53] Indeed, so common is blood sacrifice to goddesses in South India that the practice has been singled out as one of the characteristic aspects of local worship of goddesses in the South: "The village deities are almost universally *worshiped with animal sacrifices.* Buffaloes, sheep, goats, pigs, and fowls are freely offered to them, sometimes in thousands."[54]

The centrality of blood offerings to goddesses is all the more remarkable in light of the emphasis in much of the Hindu tradition, both Brahmanic and popular, on *ahiṁsa,* "noninjury." Despite the insistence on noninjury as an ethic to be followed by all Hindus (except where their traditional occupations make this impossible), and despite outspoken criticism of animal sacrifice by influential Hindu figures in recent times,[55] goddesses throughout India continue to receive blood offerings. It seems clear that the practice of offering goddesses animal (and sometimes human) sacrifices is extremely ancient[56] and also central to the meaning and logic of their worship. In the eyes of their devotees these goddesses, usually fierce in nature, need or demand blood and will not bless their devotees unless they receive blood from them. As in the case of Kālī discussed in chapter 8, the underlying intuition or perception in these cults seems to be that these goddesses, who are associated with fertility, must be periodically renourished. In order to give life, they must receive life back in the form of blood sacrifices.

In addition to being associated with battle and blood sacrifice, the terrible forms of the Mahādevī (or those terrible goddesses who are incorporated into Mahādevī mythology) are often associated with destruction, death, and hunger. Their untamed, wild behavior threatens cosmic stability. In Somadeva's *Yaśastilaka* the goddess Caṇḍamārī is described as follows:

> The impetuous movements of the goddess are such that the waters of the ocean are splashed by the heavy impact of her feet; the moon (on her forehead) is terrified by the horrid mass of her matted hair, entwined with madly excited serpents; while the bells of her club ring out as the human skulls, swaying at her side, move to and fro; and the mountains are laid low by her massive hands as she vehemently waves them in an outburst of joy at the destruction of demons.[57]

A hymn of praise to the goddess Camuṇḍā in Bhavabhūti's *Mālatīmādhava* describes her as dancing so wildly that she threatens to destroy the world. She has a gaping mouth, wears a garland of skulls that laugh and terrify the worlds, is covered with snakes, showers flames from her eyes that destroy the worlds, and is surrounded by fiends and goblins.[58] In Ratnakara's *Haravijaya* the goddess Camuṇḍā does a dance that destroys the world. As she dances she plays a musical instrument whose shaft is Mount Meru, whose string is the cosmic serpent Śeṣa, and whose gourd is the crescent moon. She tunes this great instrument during the deluge that destroys the world and then plays it during the night of the end of the world.[59]

Appropriate to the wild, destructive natures of these goddesses is the association with death and places of death. The *Mānasāra-śilpa-śāstra*, a text on architecture, specifies that temples to Kālī should be built far from villages and towns, near cremation grounds (9.289). In Tantric worship of Kālī it is not uncommon for texts to recommend confronting her in cremation grounds, which are well known as one of her favorite haunts.[60] Cāmuṇḍā is also typically described as haunting cremation grounds. In the *Mālatīmādhava* of Bhavabhūti a devotee of Cāmuṇḍā propitiates her in a temple adjacent to a cremation ground.[61] A South Indian image of Camuṇḍā is described as follows: "She holds a skull-mace (*khaṭṭvāṅga*), a snake, a wine cup (*modaka bhāṇḍa*) in her different hands. She has a third eye and below her is a jackal gnawing at the left hip of a corpse lying on the floor."[62] The goddess Tripura Bhairavī is described in the *Kālikā-purāṇa* as wearing red clothes and as having four arms, a red complexion, and a dazzling appearance. She stands on a corpse and wears garlands of skulls on her head and around her neck and waist. Her eyes show she has been drinking liquor (74.90–94). The goddess Śivadūtī is similarly described in the *Kālikā-purāṇa*. Her teeth are red, her hair is matted, and she wears skulls as a garland, snakes as ornaments, and a panther skin as clothing. She places a foot on a corpse and the other on a jackal and is surrounded by thousands of jackals (63.104–108).[63] The goddess Carmamuṇḍā is also said to have a fearful form. She is black, fond of meat and wine, and surrounded by ghosts. She is seated on a corpse and holds in her hands a noose and a pot full of blood.[64] A particularly gruesome description of Caṇḍamārī from Somadeva's *Yaśastilaka* vividly shows the association of these terrible goddesses with death and cremation grounds.

> Garlands of human skulls are her head-ornaments. Corpses of children are her ear-ornaments. The elbows of dead men are her earrings. Balls made from the bones of dead bodies form her necklaces. The oozings from the leg-bones of corpses serve as her cosmetics. Skeletons play the part of toy-lotuses in her hands. Rivers of wine are the streams wherein she performs her evening ablutions. Charnel-fields are her pleasure grounds. The ashes of funeral pyres are her face-ornament. Raw hides constitute her robe. The intestines of dead bodies form her girdle. The bosoms of dead men are her dancing floor. She plays with heads of goats as with balls. Her water-sports take place in lakes of blood. The blazing fires of cremation-grounds serve as her votive lamps at night. Human skulls are the vessels she eats from. Her greatest pleasure is when living creatures of all kinds are sacrificed at her altar.[65]

These goddesses are also often described as lean, skinny, or emaciated. They are also said to have prominent teeth or fangs. There is a clear emphasis on these goddesses' ever-hungry and all-consuming nature. They rip and tear their way through the world, seeking to satisfy a primordial hunger that is the opposite of the ever-fruitful forms of the Mahādevī, which perpetually give birth to all creatures. Some of the terrible goddesses have epithets that emphasize their hungry natures. In the *Devī-māhātmya* the Devī mentions one of her incarnations named Raktadantikā (the red-toothed one) (11.42). The goddess Danturā (she having fangs) is described as having "bare canine teeth, rounded eyes, ghastly smile, emaciated body, lean and pendulous breasts, sunken belly and peculiar sitting posture."[66] An image of Cāmuṇḍā adorning a temple in Bubhaneśvar is so emaciated in appearance that her bones are all clearly visible. Her eyes pop from her head, her breasts are withered, and her expression is fierce.[67] Another awesome image of Cāmuṇḍā is found at Jajpur in Orissa. She is described in this sculpture as follows:

> She has four arms, emaciated body and shrunken belly showing the protruding ribs and veins, skull-garland (*muṇḍamālā*), her corpse seat (*pretāsana . . .*), bare teeth and sunken eyes with round projecting eye-balls, bald head with flames issuing from it. She holds in her back hands a *kartṛ* (chopper) and a *śūla*, while her front right and left ones hold a *kapāla* and a *muṇḍa* (human head) respectively; the skull on the armlet on

her right hand has a grinning smile on its face, while the severed head in her left hand has a life-like expression.[68]

The juxtaposition of auspicious and terrible qualities in most portraits of the Mahādevī underlines one of her central features. She *is* the world in the form of a great being. The world, as perceived through the person of the Devī, is a living organism. In her auspicious forms the Devī represents the world as unceasingly fruitful, full of awesome energy that pervades and nourishes all creatures. In her aspect as mother she is understood to dote on her children, to spoil them with all the bounties at her disposal. As food she gives herself to be eaten by her creatures, and as the essence of sexual desire she prompts all creatures to take part in the great dance of continued creation and life.

The mother herself, however, must also be nourished. She must eat, for her energy is not inexhaustible. If she were only to give birth to and nourish her creatures she would soon grow weak, and creation would cease. This seems to be the perception underlying the insistence in Mahādevī theology that she possesses a variety of terrible manifestations. The Mahādevī needs to be renourished as continually as she gives birth. Her awesome creative power must be matched by her awesome hunger. The intuition here seems to be that there is only so much energy in the world, there is only so much energy possessed by the Mahādevī. If she gives her fertile power at one point, she must be renourished at another point. The world in Mahādevī theology is perceived as a steady-state system.

> In this view . . . any gain somewhere is a loss somewhere else, every loss a gain. The world is a body, and just as its blood must continually flow both out and back, so at every cell in that body the life-blood must continually both arrive and depart. Any local blockage and eventually something has to give. The world is an economy, an integrated system of ongoing exchanges, and excessive hoarding anywhere in the system, by either producers or consumers, creates trouble—and again, eventually something has to give. In such a system there is, over the long run, no getting without giving.[69]

The Mahādevī gives unstintingly. She is indeed life itself. But she must receive back unstintingly too. She is also death itself, which is always necessary to sustain life. The Devī's auspicious and ferocious aspects, her associations with life on the one hand and with death on the other, do not teach primarily that she is a two-faced, ambivalent being who is unpredictable in her activity and nature. Her two facets are clearly interrelated; indeed, each facet demands the existence of the other.

Insofar as the Devī is this world, she reveals a basic truth that is at the very heart of things: namely, that life, metabolism, nourishment necessitate continual massive killing and death. Food that sustains life is only procured through death and killing. Life and death constitute a process of giving and getting, a process through which the energy of the Mahādevī is continuously recycled.

10

THE MĀTṚKĀS

THE EARLY HISTORY OF THE MĀTṚKĀS

Certain groups of goddesses occupy an important place in the Hindu perception of the divine feminine. A band of divinities known simply as the Mātṛkās, "mothers," is among the most significant groups of goddesses. Early references to the Mātṛkās date to around the first century A.D., but they rarely specify their number; the implication in some passages is that they are innumerable. The goddesses are only mentioned as a group, and it is as a group that they function and are characterized in almost all references throughout the tradition. In most early references the Mātṛkās have inauspicious qualities and are often described as dangerous. In the medieval period their number and names become more standardized. They are usually said to number seven, although some texts mention eight or sixteen. In this period the Mātṛkās also take on names and characteristics that associate them with important male gods in the Hindu pantheon. They also come to play a protective role vis-à-vis the world in later mythology, although some of their early inauspicious, wild characteristics tend to persist in these accounts.

Although some scholars have sought to demonstrate that the Mātṛkās were known in Vedic literature,[1] the earliest clear descriptions of a group of goddesses known as Mātṛkās appear in the *Mahābhārata*. The sections in which these references occur do not belong to the earliest layers of the epic and probably date to around the first century A.D. Several groups of female beings are called Mātṛkās in the *Mahābhārata*. The Vana-parva mentions a group of goddesses called the mothers of the world (215.16). They are sent by Indra to kill the youth Kārttikeya shortly after his birth. When they approach the child, however, their breasts ooze milk, and they ask him to adopt them as his mothers (215.18). Two of these goddesses are described. One is said to have been born of anger and to carry a spike in her hand. The other is said to be bad tempered, of red complexion, the daughter of the sea, and to live on blood. Although only these two goddesses are described, it seems likely that the others (the text does not specify how many there are) are also characterized by inauspicious qualities and habits (215.21–22).

In a subsequent episode in the story of Kārttikeya's birth, a host of ferocious and terrifying goddesses are born from the child when Indra strikes him with his thunderbolt. Among this host of fierce goddesses are Kākī, Halimā, Mālinī, Bṛhalī, Āryā, Palālā, and Vaimitrā. Although Kārttikeya adopts them as his mothers and divides them into *śiva* and *aśiva* spirits, good and evil spirits, they are collectively characterized as stealing children.[2]

The dangerous nature of the Mātṛkās is elaborated and underlined later in the narrative of Kārttikeya. The wives of six sages, who have been unjustly accused of having been Kārttikeya's real mothers and consequently have been divorced by their husbands for being adulterous, come to Kārttikeya and appeal to him to adopt them as his mothers. As a group they are called the Mahāmātṛkās (great mothers). He agrees to become their adopted son and then asks them if there is anything else they wish. They make two requests. The first is to be recognized and worshiped as great goddesses throughout the world. The second request is to live off the children of men because they themselves have been divorced and therefore cheated of the possibility of having their own children. Kārttikeya is reluctant to allow these women to destroy children and says he finds it painful to grant their request. He asks them to protect children instead of harming them, and they agree. In the closing lines of his speech to them, however, as he gives them their functional mandate, he says to them: "In your various forms may you torment children until they reach sixteen years old. I grant you an imperishable, violent nature. You shall live happily with that (nature) worshiped by all."[3]

Another list of female spirits is mentioned in the following episode of the story. Ten spirits are named, and all of them serve inauspicious functions or are described in fierce terms. They are Vinatā, Pūtanā, Raksasī, Aditi (or Revati), Diti, Surabhi, Saramā, Kadrū, Lohitayani, and Āryā. All but two of these goddesses (Vinatā and Lohitayani) devour or afflict children or pregnant women. They like flesh, drink strong liquor, and lurk in the confinement chamber (where birth takes place) for the first ten days of a child's life. The text repeats the idea that these beings afflict children until the age of sixteen, whereafter they act as positive influences.[4]

Chapter 45 of the Śalya-parva of the *Mahābhārata* tells of the elevation of Kārttikeya to supreme command of the divine army. In keeping with the description of the Mātṛkās from the Vana-parva is a description of a host of female beings (ninety-two names are given, but the text says there are many more besides those actually named) who are said to be among Kārttikeya's hosts when he confronts the demon armies in battle. As a group this host of Mātṛkās is characterized in different ways, and although some are said to be lovely of form, cheerful, fair of skin, and youthful, they are generally characterized by inauspicious qualities. They have long nails, large teeth, and protruding lips; they inspire their foes with terror; they are like Indra in battle; they live in trees, at crossroads, in caves, on mountains, at springs, in burning grounds; and they speak a variety of languages. Some of them are dark.

Most references in the *Mahābhārata* to groups of divinities called Mātṛkās make it clear that these goddesses were understood to be dangerous. Their physical descriptions emphasize their fearsome natures, and their behavior is consistently said to be violent. Although they eventually end up serving Kārttikeya in one way or another, as his mothers or as his allies in battle, their initial task in the Vana-parva is to kill him. In fact, one of the main points emphasized in the association of Kārttikeya with the Mātṛkās is the danger that they represent to newborn children. The infant Kārttikeya is particularly vulnerable to these beings. The Mātṛkās are most attracted to children and express their wrathful, dangerous natures primarily against children. Although Kārttikeya is portrayed as transforming these goddesses into benign presences, indeed, into mothers who protect infants, the transformation is sometimes unconvincing, for example, when he refuses the request of the sages' wives to destroy children but then commands them a few verses later to torment children until the age of sixteen (219.22–23).

Goddesses who are inimical to children are found elsewhere in the Indian religious traditions. The goddess Hārītī, who is mentioned in several Buddhist sources, was well known in the Magadha area of North India, where the Buddha lived and preached. She is described as stealing children from the people of Rājagṛha and feeding herself and her many sons on them. Her name literally means "she who steals." The Buddha transformed her into a benign being and promised her that pious people in the future would worship her and make images of her and her children in their homes.[5]

A demon goddess named Jarā is described in the Sabhā-parva of the *Mahābhārata* (16.40–17.5). When two sisters each give birth to half a child, they abandon the deformed creatures at a crossroads. Jarā, who feeds on flesh and blood, takes the children away. Inadvertently, however, she combines the two infants into a whole being. She gives the whole child to the king of the area, and in gratitude he orders that she be worshiped throughout the region at a great festival in her honor.

The demoness Pūtanā, who is actually named in one of the lists of the Mātṛkās in the *Mahābhārata,* where she is described as a stalker of the night and evil in her ghastly shape,[6] seeks to kill the infant Kṛṣṇa by poisoning her breasts and then asking Kṛṣṇa's mother if she might suckle the child. She disguises herself as an attractive woman, but when Kṛṣṇa sucks the life from her and she dies, she is revealed in her true form as an ugly hag.[7]

The goddess Jyeṣṭhā, although not specifically said to harass children, may well have been another goddess of this type. She is described as having "large pendulous breasts descending as far as her navel, with a flabby belly, thick thighs, raised nose, hanging lower lip, and is in colour as ink."[8] According to the *Liṅga-purāṇa* she is born when the gods and demons churn the ocean of nectar to obtain immortality. She is given as a wife to the sage Dussaha, who soon discovers that his unattractive wife cannot bear the sound or sight of any kind of pious activity. When he complains to Viṣṇu, Viṣṇu tells Dussaha to go with his wife only to places where inauspicious things occur, hence Jyeṣṭhā's popular epithet Alakṣmī, "she who is inauspicious." Among places specifically mentioned where she should reside are homes where family members quarrel and where the elders eat food while disregarding the hunger of their children (2.6). Eventually Jyeṣṭhā is abandoned by her husband. She complains to Viṣṇu that she cannot sustain herself without a husband. He dictates that she will be sustained by offerings from women (2.6.83–87). Although the text does not say so, it is probably to be understood that Jyeṣṭhā will not enter the homes of those who propitiate her.

Behind child-afflicting goddesses such as the Mātṛkās is probably the belief that women who die childless or in childbirth linger on as inimical spirits who are jealous of other women and their children and whose jealousy is appeased by stealing or harming their children.[9] Worship of the Mātṛkās is aimed primarily at keeping them away. Not referring to one's children as beautiful or attractive and marking children with collyrium to hide their beauty are practices probably related to keeping these goddesses from noticing one's children lest their jealousy be aroused and they harm the children. To make much of one's children might attract the Mātṛkās' attention and risk incurring their dread afflictions.

Despite the name Mātṛkās, then, and despite the fact that Hindu iconography usually shows them holding small children, early in their history they represent inimical spirits who are particularly attracted to small children. Although they, and goddesses like them, are described as being thwarted and even transformed in nature by such powerful heroes as Kārttikeya and the Buddha, in fact the Mātṛkās continue to threaten children and must be worshiped to forestall their afflictions.

The references to the Mātṛkās in the *Mahābhārata* also make it clear that they were initially associated with non-Āryan, or at least non-Brahmanic, traditions. They are said to speak a variety of languages, to be dark, and to live in peripheral areas such as mountains and caves.[10] Their association with Kārttikeya in the epic, and later with Śiva, reinforces this point. Kārttikeya is a deity who only enters the Brahmanic tradition at the time of the epic, and Śiva is well known as possessing many non-Brahmanic attributes and tendencies.[11]

It is hard to resist the conclusion that the groups of goddesses called Mātṛkās in the *Mahābhārata* represent the many village goddesses throughout India who are widely worshiped by the common people and who are often associated with disease or the prevention of diseases, especially those that afflict children. Such deities are not found in the Vedic pantheon but are probably indigenous to a non-Brahmanic, if not pre-Āryan, religious universe. The Brahman editors of the *Mahābhārata* probably apprehended such goddesses with considerable suspicion. The epic does not yet admit a theology or mythology in which goddesses play a central part, and the Mātṛkās are depicted as dangerous, often malevolent, and are associated with a divine newcomer (Kārttikeya) and peripheral geographical places. Although the Mātṛkās probably are grounded in village-goddess cults that are central to the majority of common folk in India, the epic is suspicious of their powers and tends to emphasize their inauspicious aspects and peripheral associations.[12]

THE MĀTṚKĀS IN THE LATER TRADITION

The popularity of the Mātṛkās in the postepic period (after A.D. 400) is attested by the many casual references to them in literary works. The *Naṭya-śāstra* recommends that the Mātṛkās be worshiped prior to setting up the theater and stage for dance performances (13.66).[13] Both the *Cārudatta* of Bhāsa and the *Mṛcchakaṭika* of Śūdraka refer to offerings made to the Mātṛkās at crossroads.[14] The *Harṣacarita* of Bāṇabhaṭṭa mentions an ascetic who dwells at an old *matṛ-gṛha*, a "house (or temple) of the Mothers," where young nobles perform rites on behalf of the king's health. "There young nobles were burning themselves with lamps to propitiate the Mothers."[15] In the *Kādambarī* the queen Vilāsavatī wishes to have a son. She performs a variety of rites and resorts to a nearby shrine to the Mātṛkās, "in whom faith was displayed by the people."[16] The many literary references to the Mātṛkās in the postepic period are echoed by their numerous images and by the many inscriptions that mention them and their temples.[17]

The number and names of the Mātṛkās become increasingly standardized in the postepic period until a more-or-less standard list of seven goddesses begins to become synonymous with the Matṛkās. The appearance of these seven goddesses is quite modified from the Mātṛkās of the epic. In the medieval period they are patterned (at least in appearance) on male deities of the Hindu pantheon. Furthermore, they are usually portrayed in mythology as combating demons who threaten the gods or the stability of the cosmos. Thus, in some ways, the Mātṛkās seem to have been Brahmanized and domesticated.

Perhaps the best-known mythological account of the Mātṛkās in the medieval period is found in the third episode of the *Devī-māhātmya*. There the demons Śumbha and Niśumbha, who have usurped the gods from their positions, are confronted in battle by the Devī. When the demon armies approach her, the male gods, who are watching from the sidelines, create *śaktis*, female counterparts of themselves, to help the Devī on the battlefield. Seven such *śaktis* are created, and in appearance they closely resemble the male gods from whom they are said to arise: Brahmāṇī, created from the god Brahmā, holds a rosary and water pot; Māheśvarī, created from Śiva, is seated on a bull, holds a trident, wears serpent bracelets, and is adorned with the crescent moon; Kaumarī, created from Kārttikeya, rides a peacock and holds a spear; Vaiṣṇavī, created from Viṣṇu, is seated on Garuda and holds a conch, *cakra* (discus), mace, bow, and sword; Vārāhī, created from the boar *avatāra* of Viṣṇu, has the form of a boar; Narasiṁhī, created from the man-lion *avatāra* of Viṣṇu, has the form of a woman-lion and throws the stars into disarray with the shaking of her lion's mane; and Aindrī, created from the god Indra, holds a thunderbolt and is seated on an elephant (8.11–20). Charging into the fray, this group of *śaktis*, collectively called the Mātṛkās (8.38, 44, 49, 62), tears into the demon army and begins to slaughter them. Along with Kālī (who is also called Cāmuṇḍā), Śivadūtī (a goddess formed from the *śakti* of the Devī), and the Devī herself, the Mātṛkās devastate the demons. After the battle the Mātṛkās dance, drunk with the blood of their victims (8.62). This description of the Mātṛkās is repeated with very little variation in the *Devī-bhāgavata-purāṇa* (5.28–29) and the *Vāmana-purāṇa* (30).

Despite the names, appearances, and origins of the Mātṛkās in the *Devī-māhātmya* and *Devī-bhāgavata-purāṇa* accounts, it seems clear that they are to be understood not primarily as the divine consorts or the

Vārāhī, one of the Mātṛkās. Thirteenth or fourteenth century A.D. Pratapaditya Pal, *Nepal, Where the Gods are Young* (New York: Asia Society, 1975), fig. 70, p. 102. Reprinted by permission of Eric D. Morse.

śaktis of the male deities but rather as extensions or forms of the Devī herself. Indeed, in the later episode of the *Devī-māhātmya,* after Niśumbha has been killed by the Devī and her female cohorts, the demon Śumbha challenges the Devī to single combat, in effect complaining about her many female allies. In response to his challenge, she absorbs into herself all the Mātṛkās. She refers to them as just so many of her different forms (10.2.–5). In the *Vāmana-purāṇa* account of the Mātṛkā episode the situation is even clearer. There the Mātṛkās arise from the different parts of the Devī's body and not from the male gods at all, although they are described and named after the male deities (30.3–9).

The different versions of this episode do not stress the individuality of the seven goddesses. By and large the seven act as a group and share the same characteristics: they fight ferociously and get drunk on blood. In the *Matsya-purāṇa* the Mātṛkās appear in a slightly different context. They are created by Śiva to combat the demon Andhaka, who has the ability to duplicate himself from each drop of blood that spills from him when he is wounded.[18] The Mātṛkās are instructed to drink up his blood and thus defeat him. This they gladly agree to do. Although the traditional seven Mātṛkās are mentioned in the text at the head of the list of goddesses, roughly 190 names are given, along with the comment that there are many others.[19] It is difficult to escape the conclusion that the *Puraṇa* writers are primarily describing a group of goddesses whose individual members are not significant in themselves.[20] This is also quite in keeping with references to the Mātṛkās in the *Mahābhārata.* By restricting their number and relating them to male gods, the *Purāṇa* writers have to some extent brought the Mātṛkās into the mainstream literary and mythological tradition.

The *Purāṇa* writers have also sought to modify the inimical character of the Mātṛkās by describing their primary role as the Devī's (or Śiva's) assistants in combating demons. In the Purāṇic accounts they are seen as primarily fierce, effective warriors who protect the stability of the world by combating demons. They are understood as extensions of the Devī in her role as guardian of the cosmic order. The wild, inimical, bloodthirsty character of the Mātṛkās is not entirely hidden in these accounts, however, and probably testifies to the fact that they have not changed much over the centuries and are in some ways the same dangerous beings mentioned in the *Mahābhārata.* Their taste for blood, for instance, remains in some of the Purāṇic accounts. The *Devī-māhātmya* also describes the Mātṛkās as getting drunk on the blood of their victims (8.62).

Similarly, in the *Matsya-purāṇa* account the Mātṛkās, at Śiva's command, defeat Andhaka. They are described as terrible in appearance and as drinking the blood of the demons they slay. After the battle the

Mātṛkās announce that they will now proceed to devour all the gods, demons, and people of the world. Śiva commands them not to do this, but they ignore him and begin a rampage of destruction. Śiva summons Narasiṁha, Viṣṇu's man-lion *avatāra*, who creates a host of benign goddesses; they in turn calm down the terrible Mātṛkās and stop their destruction. At the end of the episode it is said that Śiva's own terrible form as Bhairava is enshrined with the images of the Mātṛkās at the place where this battle took place (179.8–90).

In the *Varāha-purāṇa* the Devī, who is called Vaiṣṇavī in this account of the creation of the Mātṛkās, is doing asceticism on Mount Mandara. At one point she loses her concentration; from her distracted mind are created several beautiful female attendants, who later become the Devī's helpmates on the battlefield when she fights demons. Although the Mātṛkās are described as lovely in this account, it is important to note that they are born when the Devī loses control of her concentration. This suggests the Mātṛkās' essentially uncontrolled natures. Born from lack of mental control, they lack control themselves.[21]

The malevolent nature of the Mātṛkās also seems clear in several passages from the *Bhāgavata-purāṇa*. When the races and species of beings created by Viṣṇu are listed, the Mātṛkās are mentioned with the *uragas, rākṣasas, piśācas, bhūtas,* and other dangerous kinds of beings (2.10.37–39).[22] It is difficult not to suppose that the Mātṛkās, like these other beings, are terrible in character. Elsewhere in the *Bhāgavata-purāṇa* they are mentioned with the *bhūtas, ḍakinīs, vetālas, pretas, piśācas,* and other malign beings as part of Śiva's army (10.63.6 ff.).[23] Again, from the context, it appears certain that the Mātṛkās are understood as a dangerous group of goddesses. When Kṛṣṇa kills the demoness Pūtanā, who has tried to kill the baby god by suckling him with her poisoned nipples, the cowherd women carry out protective rites to keep Kṛṣṇa safe from future harm. At the end of their rituals, they say: "May the Ḍākinīs, the Jatādhārīs, . . . the goblins, the Mātṛs, the Piśācas, . . . etc. [and] other evil omens and calamities dreamt of, the slayers of the old and the young, and these and other evil spirits be destroyed, being terrified at the recital of the name of Viṣṇu" (10.6.27–29).[24]

In the *Viṣṇudharmottara-purāṇa*, after the Mātṛkās defeat the demon Andhaka, the text dwells at length on how the evil influences of the Mātṛkās can be avoided (1.227).[25] The *Varāha-purāṇa* relates them to vices or inauspicious emotions: "Yogisvarī is the symbol of lust, Māhesvarī of anger, Vaiṣṇavī of greed, Kaumarī of attachment, Brahmāṇī of pride, Aindrī of jealousy, Cāmuṇḍā of depravity and Vārāhī of envy" (17.33–37).[26]

Although the Mātṛkās are reduced to seven, eight, or sixteen goddesses, each related to a male deity of the Hindu pantheon, and although they are made to serve a role supportive of the dharmic order in many Purāṇic accounts, throughout their history they remain primarily a group of goddesses, unspecified in number, who are inimical in nature and particularly dangerous to children. None of the Mātṛkās is significant by herself, either as an independent goddess or as the spouse or *śakti* of her male counterpart.[27] The restriction of the number of Mātṛkās and their association with male deities, then, is artificial and to some extent arbitrary. The Mātṛkās are primarily an independent group of goddesses who have violent natures, are associated with diseases, and are particularly prone to afflict small children. Many local or village goddesses are also associated with diseases that afflict children, are routinely served with blood, and are held to have violent natures. It is quite likely that the Mātṛkās of the Hindu literary tradition beginning with the *Mahābhārata* can be identified with those goddesses, who are so central to the religious life of most Hindu villagers.[28]

11

TĀRĀ, CHINNAMASTĀ, AND THE MAHĀVIDYĀS

THE MAHĀVIDYĀS

The Mahāvidyās (great revelations or manifestations) are a group of ten goddesses who are mentioned rather late in the Hindu literary tradition. Although some of the goddesses in this group are individually important and date back to a much earlier time (Kalī, for example), the group as a whole seems to be a medieval iconographic and mythological expression of an aspect of Mahādevī theology. An important point in Mahādevī theology is the Devī's tendency to display or manifest herself in a great variety of forms.[1] Many myths about the Devī describe her as producing goddesses from different parts of her body,[2] and she often announces to her petitioners that she assumes different forms at different times in order to maintain cosmic stability.[3] All ten of the Mahāvidyās are often depicted in goddess temples throughout India today. They seem to be fairly well known to many Hindus. They do not seem to be individually revered when shown as a group but rather seem to represent a common way of expressing the idea that the particular goddess who dwells in the temple takes many forms.

The ten Mahāvidyās, at least in part, are probably a Śākta version of the central Vaiṣṇava idea of Viṣṇu's ten *avatāras*, who appear from time to time to maintain the order of dharma. Indeed, the *Guhyātiguhya-tantra* gives a list of the Mahāvidyās and identifies each one with an *avatāra* of Viṣṇu, stating that the *avatāras* of Viṣṇu arose initially from the different Mahāvidyās. Kālī is said to have become Kṛṣṇa, Chinnamastā to have become Narasiṁha, and so on.[4] The Devī, like Viṣṇu, is understood in Mahādevī theology to be the creator and maintainer of cosmic order. Indeed, one might argue that the authors of some Śākta texts extolling the Devī have patterned her quite self-consciously on Viṣṇu himself.[5] The ten Mahāvidyās, however, are more than a Śākta version of the Vaiṣṇava ten *avatāras*, or at least the Mahāvidyās differ significantly from the *avatāras* in appearance and function.

The origin of the ten Mahāvidyās in Hindu mythology takes place in the context of the story of Satī and Śiva. Satī's father, Dakṣa, decides to perform a great sacrifice and invites all the inhabitants of the heavenly spheres to attend. The only couple he does not invite are Śiva and Satī. Dakṣa does not like his son-in-law because of Śiva's uncivilized habits and disheveled appearance and so purposely neglects to invite him to the sacrifice. Śiva is not offended by this social slight, but his wife Satī is greatly insulted and announces to Śiva that she will go to the sacrifice to disrupt it. Śiva is not pleased to hear this and forbids her to attend the sacrifice. Satī is unable to change Śiva's mind and eventually loses her temper. First she assumes a dreadful form,[6] and then she multiplies herself into ten forms, the Mahāvidyās: Kālī, Tārā, Chinnamastā, Bhuvaneśvarī, Bagalā, Dhūmāvatī, Kamalā, Mātaṅgī, Ṣoḍaśī, and Bhairavī.[7]

The ten forms that Satī takes are not consistently described, and some of the forms, such as Kālī and Tārā, have several manifestations. The following descriptions, however, are typical of the way in which each of the forms is described.

Kālī has a fierce countenance, is naked, dwells in the cremation ground, holds a severed head and a bloodied cleaver, has disheveled hair, and sports a garland of decapitated heads and a girdle of severed arms.[8]

When Tārā is included in the list of Mahāvidyās, she is described as nearly identical with Kālī. Tārā is dark, rests her left foot on a corpse, wears a tiger skin and a necklace of severed heads, laughs terribly, has her hair in a single matted braid, stands on a funeral pyre, and is pregnant.[9]

Chinnamastā stands in a cremation ground on the copulating bodies of Kāma and Rati (sometimes Rādhā and Kṛṣṇa), the god of sexual lust and his wife. She has decapitated herself with a sword, which she holds in one hand. In her other hand she holds a platter bearing her severed head. Three jets of blood spurt from her neck and stream into the mouths of two female attendants and into the mouth of her own severed head.[10]

Bhuvaneśvarī is said to nourish the three worlds and is described as holding a piece of fruit in one of her four hands. Her breasts are large and ooze milk. She has a bright, light complexion, smiles pleasantly, and holds a goad and a noose.[11]

Bagalā has the head of a crane, is seated on a throne of jewels, is yellow, and in one hand holds a club with which she beats an enemy while another of her hands is pulling her enemy's tongue.[12]

Dhūmāvatī has a pale complexion, is tall, and has a stern, unsmiling expression. Dressed as a widow, she wears dirty clothes, her hair is disheveled, she has no teeth, her breasts are long and pendulous, she is afflicted with hunger and thirst, her nose is large and crooked, she has a quarrelsome nature, she holds a winnowing fan, and she rides a crow.[13]

Kamalā is described as a beautiful woman of golden complexion who is surrounded by elephants pouring pitchers of water over her. She is seated on a lotus and holds two lotuses in her hands. She is in most respects portrayed like the goddess Lakṣmī, one of whose epithets, in fact, is Kamalā.[14]

Mātaṅgī is black. Her eyes roll in intoxication, and she reels about like an impassioned elephant.[15]

Ṣoḍaśī is a girl of sixteen with a red complexion. She is shown astride the prone body of Śiva, with whom she is having intercourse. They are on a pedestal made of the gods Brahmā, Viṣṇu, Rudra, and Indra. Ṣoḍaśī is identified with Tripurasundarī in some lists of the Mahāvidyās.[16]

Bhairavī (also known as Tripura Bhairavī) has a reddish complexion and wears a garland of severed heads, holds a rosary and a book in two of her four hands, and makes the signs of fearlessness and conferring boons with her other two hands. Her breasts are smeared with blood.[17] In the *Kālikā-purāṇa* Tripura Bhairavī is said to have eyes that roll from intoxication and to stand on a corpse (74.90–94).

Śiva is frightened by Satī's fearful appearance and the terrible forms that she has assumed, which completely surround him. He gives her permission to go to her father's sacrifice if she will withdraw them. In the *Mahābhāgavata-purāṇa* account Satī takes the form of Kālī, goes to her father's sacrifice, and then kills herself. In this account Dakṣa is said to weep at the sight of his daughter in the form of Kālī, who is dark, naked, and disheveled (8–9). In the Madhya-khanda of the *Bṛhaddharma-purāṇa* Satī assumes her own benign form before going to the sacrifice (6–7).

The mythological context of the appearance of the Mahāvidyās makes it clear that they are meant to be fearsome deities. Even though a few of the goddesses who belong to this group are described as beautiful and unthreatening, for the most part they are formidable and fearsome. Furthermore, the fearsomeness of the goddesses does not seem to be related to upholding the cosmic order.[18] They are not described as warriors, and the goddesses mentioned (with the exception of Kālī) are not known for playing the roles of warriors. In this respect the Mahāvidyās are not mere feminine versions of the Vaiṣṇava *avatarās*, most of whom appear precisely to defeat demons who threaten the world. In no clear way are the Mahāvidyās said to play the role of guardians of cosmic order. Their primary function in the myth is to frighten Śiva so that Satī may have her own way. The emphasis is on their terrible appearance, which causes Śiva to tremble and attempt to flee.

The Mahāvidyās also play the role of asserting Satī's power as greater than that of Śiva. In the context of the myth he is simply no match for her. By means of the Mahāvidyās she overpowers him. It is difficult to escape the conclusion that the authors of these myths were trying, at least in part, to assert the superiority of the Devī over Śiva (and by implication other male gods as well). Although the Devī plays the part of the gracious, submissive wife in her form as Satī, willingly submitting herself to her husband Śiva, she contains fearsome, independent aspects that easily overwhelm Śiva when they do appear. Satī's transformation into a dreadful form, and then into several dreadful forms, dramatically alters the traditional myth of Satī, in which she remains loyal and subordinate to Śiva throughout her life. These late versions of the myth show Satī exerting her will over Śiva, scaring him into submission when he resists her.

The fearsomeness of these goddesses also seems to be related to the context in which they are propitiated. Most of these deities are known primarily in Tantric literature; even the goddess Kālī, who is well known outside Tantrism, plays an important part in Tantric texts and practices. In the *Bṛhaddharma-purāṇa* Satī in her dreadful form commands Śiva to give mantras and instructions for worshiping the Mahāvidyās.[19] In both that account and the *Mahābhāgavata-purāṇa* Satī announces that she has appeared in these dreadful forms so that her devotees not only may achieve ultimate release (*mokṣa*) but may achieve desires and invoke magical powers over others. Both texts specifically mention *mārana*, rituals causing the destruction of enemies; *uccāṭaṇa*, rituals causing a person to stop what he is doing; *kṣobhaṇa*, rituals causing shaking and emotional disturbance; *mohana*, rituals causing infatuation, loss of consciousness, or delusion; *drāvaṇa*, rituals causing people to flee; *jṛmbhaṇa*, rituals causing people to yawn or become slack; and *stambhana*, rituals causing people to become paralyzed.[20] The specific powers are not related to specific goddesses in the texts; it seems that these powers are associated with the goddesses' fearsome aspects and terrifying powers in general. Just as the appearance of the Mahāvidyās causes Śiva to be overcome by these various emotions, so these goddesses will subdue, defeat, or terrify the enemies of the adept or devotee who invokes them.

Although the Mahāvidyās act primarily as a group in the Purāṇic myths, terrifying Śiva together, three of the Mahāvidyās are important individually: Kālī, Tārā, and Chinnamastā. Kālī, who is almost always mentioned first in lists of the Mahāvidyās, has an ancient history in the Hindu tradition and is an important goddess in many parts of India. Her association with the Mahāvidyās, particularly as the first in the list of ten, sets the tone for the rest of the goddesses, who for the most part are fearsome beings. Kālī's appearance in this myth is typical of her appearance elsewhere. She appears as Satī's personified wrath, just as in other myths she appears as the personified wrath of goddesses such as Durgā and Pārvatī.[21]

TĀRĀ

The goddess Tārā does not figure prominently in the Hindu tradition. Her place in Tibetan Buddhism, however, is central and quite ancient. Her appearance in the list of the Mahāvidyās can probably be explained, at least in part, by the religious communication that existed for centuries between Tibet and Bengal (where the texts that mention the Mahāvidyās were written). Many important Buddhist missionaries to Tibet came from Bengal, and Buddhists continued to be mentioned in Bengali texts until the sixteenth century.[22] In the late medieval period, when such texts as the *Mahābhāgavata-purāṇa* and the *Bṛhaddharma-purāṇa* were written, Tārā was probably fairly well known in Bengal. Rāmprasād Sen, the eighteenth-century Bengali devotee of Kālī, often used the name Tārā as an epithet of Kālī, and it seems clear that for him the two goddesses were more or less the same and that he understood Tārā to be as much a Hindu goddess as a Buddhist goddess.

The earliest reference to Tārā is found in Subandhu's *Vasavadattā*, which was probably written around the middle of the seventh century. The reference occurs as part of a pun and situates Tārā in the context of Buddhist devotion. The passage reads: "The Lady Twilight was seen, devoted to the stars and clad in red sky, as a Buddhist nun (is devoted to Tārā and is clad in red garments)."[23] In Buddhist Tantric mythology Tārā belongs to the family of the Dhyāni Buddha Amoghasiddhi, but she is also related to the bodhisattva Avalokiteśvara, who is in the family of the Dhyāni Buddha Amitābha. In one account all the creatures lament the thought of Avalokiteśvara's abandoning them as he is about to achieve *nirvāṇa*. Hearing them, Avalokiteśvara sheds a tear of compassion for all beings. That tear becomes Tārā, who is thus understood to be the essence of the essence of compassion.[24] As we shall see, Tārā's essential nature in Tibetan Buddhism is that of a compassionate savior who rescues her devotees from peril. Her inclusion in the Amitābha family therefore seems fitting, since both Amitābha and Avalokiteśvara are renowned for their great compassion.

Tibetan Buddhists know other legendary or mythological accounts of Tārā's origin. One legend identified Tārā with the wives of the first great Tibetan king, Songsten gampo (A.D. 617–650). The king himself is said to have been an incarnation of Avalokiteśvara, while his Chinese wife is said to have been an incarnation of Green Tārā and his Nepalese wife an incarnation of White Tārā (there are several different forms of Tārā, as we shall see).[25] Another Tibetan legend says that the Tibetan people arose from the union of a monkey and a rock ogress. This legend is ancient and pre-Buddhist in origin. By the fourteenth century, when Buddhism had come to dominate Tibet, however, the monkey had come to be identified with Avalokiteśvara and the rock ogress, despite her lustful nature, with an incarnation of the goddess Tārā.[26] What is interesting about these Tibetan legends is that they associate Tārā with the origins of the Tibetan people and the Tibetan royal line. They affirm that Tārā is dear to the Tibetan people in a special way. She is in a historical or legendary sense their queen and mother.[27]

Historically, the cult of Tārā in Tibetan Buddhism dates to the eighth century, that is, to around the time when Buddhism was introduced to Tibet from India. Until the time of Atīśa (eleventh century), however, the worship of Tārā does not seem to have been very widespread in Tibet. Atīśa is traditionally associated with bringing the cult of Tārā to Tibet, and biographical accounts emphasize his many visions of Tārā and his special devotion to her. Atīśa is credited with having translated a series of Sanskrit texts concerning Tārā into Tibetan. The texts were soon circulated as a coherent cycle and came to be known by the name *Cheating Death*.[28] Another text that was to become very popular in Tibet was also brought there in the eleventh century. The master Darmadra brought to Tibet and translated the text *Homages to the Twenty-one Tārās*, which to this day is well known to most Tibetans.[29]

Despite Tārā's many forms and functions it seems clear wherein lies her extraordinary power and appeal. She is approached primarily as a savior, as a being who specializes in spectacular, dramatic appearances when her devotees call on her in dire circumstances. Like Durgā,[30] Tārā is often said to rescue her devotees from such desperate predicaments as being lost in an impenetrable forest, foundering in a storm at sea, being under threat of imminent execution, or being trapped and bound in prison.[31] The many folk stories about Tārā show her typically appearing at the request of her devotees to dramatically rescue them from the jaws of certain death.[32] Tārā's compassion for suffering beings, then, is revealed primarily in her role as the cheater of death. In this sense her chief blessing to her devotees is a long life, and other stories emphasize that regular worship of Tārā brings about longevity.[33] In Tibetan monastic traditions, when novices are initiated into the ceremonies in honor of Tārā, the rituals are referred to as an "initiation into life."[34] Unlike goddesses who are associated with life as embodiments of fertility, Tārā is approached primarily as the one who protects, preserves, and saves life. She is not a fertility goddess (although she does give her blessing in this form from time to time)[35] but a greatly compassionate being who cannot tolerate the suffering of her devotees.

Tārā's devotees approach her with great love and devotion. Tibetan Tantric Buddhism is in many respects a heroic, fierce religion involving arduous spiritual exercises. Her worship introduces into it a theme of great tenderness. An example of this devotional tenderness is the poem the *Cry of Suffering to Tārā* by the lama Lozang tenpe jets'en:

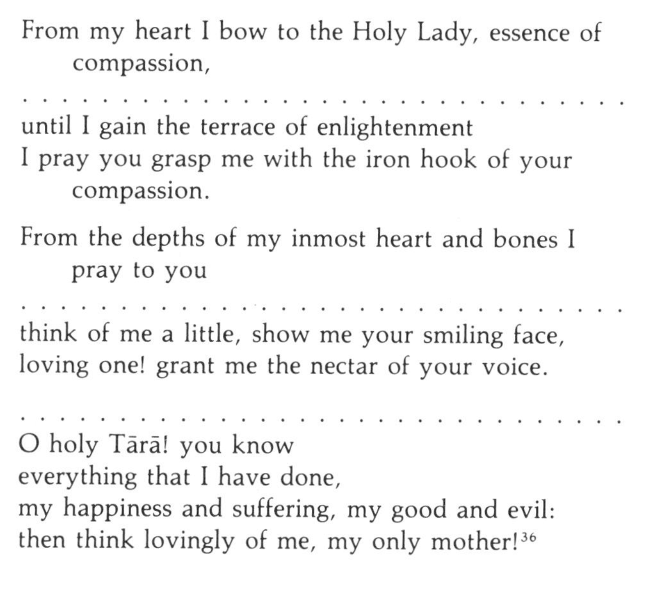

From my heart I bow to the Holy Lady, essence of
    compassion,

. . . .

until I gain the terrace of enlightenment
I pray you grasp me with the iron hook of your
    compassion.

From the depths of my inmost heart and bones I
    pray to you

. . . .

think of me a little, show me your smiling face,
loving one! grant me the nectar of your voice.

. . . .

O holy Tārā! you know
everything that I have done,
my happiness and suffering, my good and evil:
then think lovingly of me, my only mother![36]

Tārā's charm and approachability are evident in her appearance and personality. Although she is often depicted in regal attire, she is usually said to be a girl of sixteen or younger. She is playful, energetic, and possesses a sense of humor. A modern story about her appearance to a young Tibetan couple whom she rescued from starvation describes her as follows:

> Presently a bright light fell upon his eyes and, starting up in alarm, he beheld Tara seated negligently on the table, swinging her legs like a child with more energy than she knew what to do with. However, even as he lept up to prostrate himself, her body began to glow with light. The window behind her was dissolved in these rays and, in its place, he saw the peak of a lofty hill covered with lush green grass wherein glittered innumerable points of light as though it were bestrewn with gems. Beyond and stretching to the horizon was an expanse of deep blue water capped by magnificent white waves which, breaking on the shore below, emitted rainbow-colored clouds of spray. These clouds, rising to the hilltop, filled the air with millions upon millions of glittering particles like multi-coloured jewels. Meanwhile, the table had become a moon disc resting on a huge and many-petalled lotus, whereon Tara sat, still negligently and with the air of a young girl having fun, but now clad in shining silks and golden ornaments like the daughter of the Emperor of the Sky. She was smiling at him with a mixture of archness and contempt.[37]

Although Tārā's primary appeal seems to be as the cheater of death, the prolonger of life, and although she is primarily popular as a charming, playful young girl, she does have a variety of forms, some of which are fierce, even terrifying. The *Homages to the Twenty-one Tārās,* probably her most popular hymn of praise, contains several verses that invoke Tārā in fierce forms.

> Homage, Lady who annihilates the heroes of Māra,
> TURE, the terrible lady,
> slaying all enemies
> by frowning the brows of her lotus face.
>
> . . . .
>
> Homage, Lady who strikes the earth with her hand,
> who pounds upon it with her feet,
> shattering the seven underworlds
> with the sound of HŪṂ made by her frowning brows.
>
> . . . .
>
> Homage, Lady who strikes with the feet of TURE,
> whose seed is the form of the syllable HŪṂ,
> shaking Mount Meru, Mandāra, Kailāśa,
> and all the triple world.[38]

Tārā. Eleventh century A.D. Pratapaditya Pal, *Nepal, Where the Gods are Young* (New York: Asia Society, 1975), fig. 37, p. 55. Reprinted by permission of William H. Wolff.

A particularly fierce form of Tārā is Tārā Kurukullā.[39] She is described as follows:

> Homage and praise to her
> who stands in the dancing pose
> haughty with furious rage,
> who has a diadem of five skulls,
> who bears a tiger's skin.
> I pay homage to the red one,
> bearing her fangs, whose body is frightful,
> who is adorned with the five signs of ferocity,
> whose necklace is half a hundred human heads,
> who is the conqueress of Māra.[40]

Tārā Kurukullā's special power lies in her ability to subjugate and destroy evil spirits or one's personal enemies.[41] The rituals in which Kurukullā is invoked involve the goddess's coming to reside in the practitioner himself. The rituals thus require a strong and accomplished adept, for Kurukullā is a potent force. The adept dresses in red garments and visualizes himself taking on the form of the goddess. Then he recites her mantra ten thousand times. Then he makes certain offerings to her and asks her to subjugate the person or demon who is the object of the rituals.

> When these preliminaries are complete, when he has firmly grasped the vivid appearance and ego of the goddess, the visualization is ready to be performed. Light radiates forth from a HRĪḤ in the practitioner's heart and places the person to be subjugated, naked and with unbound hair, upon a wind maṇḍala arisen from YAṂ: that is, the seed of wind transforms into the round shape symbolic of the air element, and this wind propels forward the person to be subjugated; he is bound around the neck by a noose radiated from the practitioner's—Kurukullā's—lotus flower, drawn forward by an iron hook stuck into his heart, summoned by the strength of the mantra, and laid down helpless upon his back before the practitioner's feet. If the person to be subjugated is male, the text adds, Kurukullā's iron hook is stuck into his heart; if female it is stuck into her vagina.[42]

Other fierce forms of Tārā include Mahāmāyā-vijayavāhinī Tārā,[43] Bhīmadevī, who is also called the blue she-wolf,[44] and Mahācinatārā. Mahācinatārā (also known as Ugratārā) is described in both Buddhist and Hindu sources. She is described in the Buddhist work *Sādhanamālā*.

> The worshiper should conceive himself as (Māhacina-Tārā) who stands in the Pratyālīḍha attitude, and is awe-inspiring with a garland of heads hanging from the neck. She is short and has a protruding belly, and her looks are terrible. Her complexion is like that of the blue lotus, and she is three-eyed, one-faced, celestial and laughs horribly. She is in an intensely pleasant mood, stands on a corpse, is decked in ornaments of snakes, has red and round eyes, wears the garments of tiger-skin round her loins, is in youthful bloom, is endowed with the five auspicious symbols, and has a protruding tongue. She is most terrible, appears fierce, with bare canine fangs, carries the sword and the Kartri in the two right hands and the Utpala and Kapāla in the two left. Her Jaṭāmukuṭa of one coil is brown and fiery and bears the image of Akṣobhya within it.[45]

An almost identical description of Mahācinatārā is given in the *Tantrasāra* of Kṛṣṇānanda Āgamavāgīśa, a seventeenth-century compilation of *dhyāna-mantras* written in Bengal. Even though it is a Hindu work, the *Tantrasāra* description includes the reference to an image of Akṣobhya adorning her crown.[46]

Several other Hindu Tantric texts describe Tārā as fierce, and the goddess's appearance in these texts differs only in a few particulars from Kālī's. Such works as the *Tārārahasyavṛttikā*, the *Rudra-yāmala*, and the *Tārā-tantra* describe Tārā as "short of stature, bedecked with ornaments of serpents of various colour, bearing garlands composed of fifty human heads, severed afresh from bodies, and bleeding freely. The *devi* stands with one foot on a dead body . . . in the funeral ground."[47] Completing Tārā's fierce description in the *Tārā-tantra*, in which barely any resemblance to the benign Tārā of Tibet remains, is her delight in receiving both the blood of sacrificial animals and the blood of her devotees. The devotees' blood, which is to be taken from specified parts of the body such as the forehead, hands, breast, head, or area between the eyebrows, is said to be far more pleasing to the goddess than the blood of an animal victim (5.15). Throughout the text Tārā is to be worshiped in the context of left-handed Tantric rites, in which wine, meat, and illicit sex play an important role.

Tārā's association with Kālī in the devotional works of Ramprasād Sen also makes it clear that the Tārā known in Hindu Bengal was a fierce goddess quite different from the gentle, youthful, playful forms of Tārā so popular in Tibet. I have a contemporary lithograph of the Mahāvidyās that shows Kālī and Tārā adjacent to each other and almost identical in appearance. Both are dark, nearly naked, have protruding tongues, hold bloodied cleavers in the upper left hand, have a garland of severed heads (the heads of Kālī's garland are freshly cut, while the heads of Tārā's garland are skulls), have disheveled hair, and stand or dance on an identical prone male body (or corpse). Tārā's inclusion in the list of Mahāvidyās thus does not seem to derive from her essential popularity in Tibetan Buddhism as a gentle, compassionate deity who cheats death. The Hindu Mahāvidyā Tārā is modeled on Tārā's fierce forms such as Kurukullā and Mahācinatārā.

The Hindu Mahāvidyā Tārā's association with ceremonies that terrify, disable, stultify, and enchant people[48] immediately brings to mind Tārā Kurukullā's employment in rituals of subjugation in Tibetan Buddhism. Although the ritual context of worship of the Hindu Mahāvidyās is not clear, it may well be that these fierce goddesses are utilized in rituals similar to the ones featuring the fierce Tārā Kurukullā in Tibet. One of the underlying assumptions of the Tārā Kurukullā rituals of subjugation seems to be that if one wishes to exert power over another person, or if one wishes to protect oneself from supernatural beings, the most effective kind of deity one can employ is fierce and terrifying. Such beings as Tārā Kurukullā, it seems, dramatically express the aggressive emotions that must accompany rituals of subjugation and also reassure the person seeking protection from equally fierce, hostile demons.

In any case, the effect of the appearance of the Mahāvidyās on the great god Śiva is impressive. He is terrified and immediately agrees to what Satī wishes. He is subjugated by these goddesses in the same way that Tārā Kurukullā subjugates enemies when properly invoked.

CHINNAMASTĀ

Chinnamastā, like Tārā, is also popular in Tantric and Tibetan Buddhism. In Buddhism she is known as Vajrayoginī. The Buddhist Tantric text, the *Sadhanamālā*, describes her as follows:

> Vajrayoginī . . . carries in her left hand her own head severed by herself with her own Kartri held in her right hand. Her left hand is raised upwards while the right is placed below. She is nude, and her right leg is stretched while the left is bent down. He (the worshipper) should also meditate on the streams of

> blood issuing from the severed body as falling into the mouth of the severed head and into the mouths of the two Yoginīs on either side of her.
>
> He (the worshipper) should also conceive the two Yoginīs to the left and right . . . , both of whom carry the Kartri in their left and right hands respectively. . . . Their left and right legs respectively are stretched forward, while the other legs are bent, and they have disheveled hair. On all sides, between the two Yoginīs and in the firmament there is the awful cremation ground.[49]

The Hindu deity Chinnamastā is similarly depicted. In most Hindu renditions three jets of blood spurt from the cut stump of her neck. One jet streams into the goddess's own mouth, while the other two flow into the mouths of the two flanking *yoginīs*. The goddess usually holds her own head on a platter, as if about to make an offering of it. Beneath the goddess the god Kāma, personifying sexual desire, and his wife, Rati, are engaged in sexual intercourse, she usually on top. They are stretched out on a lotus, and the backdrop is often a cremation ground.[50]

Chinnamastā is probably the most dramatic, stunning representation in the Hindu pantheon of the truth that life, sex, and death are part of an interdependent, unified system. The stark contrasts and reversals of what one would normally expect to see in this iconographic scenario—the gruesome decapitation, the copulating couple, the cremation ground, all arranged in a quite delicate, harmonious pattern—jolt the viewer into an awareness of the truth that life feeds on death, is nourished by death, necessitates death, and that the ultimate destiny of sex is to perpetuate more life, which in turn will decay and die in order to feed more life. As arranged in most renditions, the lotus and the copulating couple appear to provide a powerful life force for the goddess, who is standing on the back of the copulating woman. The couple, vigorously participating in the ultimate act of affirming life, convey a strong, insistent, vital urge to the goddess. They pump her with energy, as it were. And at the top, like an overflowing fountain, her blood spurts from her severed neck, the life force leaving her, but streaming into the mouths of her devotees (and into her own mouth) to nourish and sustain them.[51] The cycle is starkly portrayed: life (the lovemaking couple), death (the decapitated goddess), and nourishment (the flanking *yoginīs* drinking her blood).

The images of most fierce goddesses, such as Kālī, show the goddess severing the heads of others and demanding their blood as nourishment. The practice of sacrificing one's head to a goddess, usually

Chinnamastā. Contemporary. First published in *L'Art du Mithila* (Paris: Les Presses de la Connaissance/Editions sous le Vent, 1985). Reprinted by permission of Editions sous le Vent.

Durgā or Kālī,[52] is also often attested in Indian literature and art. The message (or at least one of the messages) is that the goddess, representing the vital forces of the cosmos, needs regular nourishment; sacrificing oneself to her is a way of acknowledging that one is obliged to give life back to her because one has received life from her. These images convey the truth that the goddess is ever hungry and demands blood in order to remain satisfied.

The Chinnamastā image reverses these images but ultimately teaches the same truth. Chinnamastā is shown not taking or receiving the heads or blood of others but taking her own head and drinking her own blood. She is shown being nourished or sustained not by death (or sacrifice) but by the copulating couple beneath her. She is shown not being fed by her devotees but feeding them with her blood. Chinnamastā, however, does not teach different truths from those conveyed by Kālī and Durgā. She simply represents the alternate phase of an ever-recurring sequence. The cosmic process, the rhythms of creation and destruction, the universal economy, is a harmonious alternation of giving and taking, of life and death. Kālī's need for blood, or conversely the ever-fecund, ever-bountiful giving of goddesses such as Annapūrṇā or Śatākṣī, represents only one aspect of the process of giving and taking. Chinnamastā, in her shocking way, presents both aspects together and in such a way that the viewer can grasp the interconnectedness of the different stages in the process. Chinnamastā takes life and vigor from the copulating couple, then gives it away lavishly by cutting off her own head to feed her devotees. Such is the way of things in a world where life must be sustained by organic matter, where metabolism is maintained only by ingesting the corpses of other beings.

The image of Chinnamastā, like the formula of the ten Mahāvidyās itself, does not seem to be very old. The *Sādhanamālā*, containing a description of the headless Vajrayoginī, probably dates to not much later than the twelfth century, and mention of the Hindu ten Mahāvidyās is even more recent than that.[53] It has been suggested, however, that Chinnamastā may have earlier prototypes in India.[54] Several examples have been discovered in India of nude goddesses squatting or with their thighs spread to display their sexual organs. These figures, some very ancient, often have their arms raised above their bodies and are headless or faceless. Their headless condition is not the result of subsequent damage but an intentional part of the image. The combination of nudity and headlessness, it has been suggested, suffices to indicate that the Chinnamastā figure may have some roots in this more ancient figure.[55]

These early nude figures, however, are particularly one-sided in what they convey. The arresting iconographic feature of these images is their sexual organs, which are openly displayed. If the headlessness of the figures suggests death, it lacks the force of the Chinnamastā icon. More likely, the headlessness of the nude figures simply focuses attention on their physiology. Although the Chinnamastā image includes an emphasis on sexual vigor, life, and nourishment, the central theme is the shocking self-decapitation.

Other nude goddess figures have been suggested as possible prototypes of Chinnamastā. One of these is the fierce, disheveled goddess Koṭavī. Koṭavī is usually associated with battlefields and is sometimes included among lists of the Mātṛkās.[56] She sometimes is an opponent of Viṣṇu, and in the *Viṣṇu-purāṇa* (5.32–33) and *Bhāgavata-purāṇa* (10.63.20) she is described as naked, disheveled, and of such an awful appearance that Viṣṇu has to turn his head away from her lest he become incensed by her. In this myth she tries to protect the demon Bāṇāsura, who is her son in the *Bhāgavata-purāṇa* account. Although descriptions of Koṭavī emphasize her nudity and her wild appearance, she seems very different in character from Chinnamastā. Her typical haunt is the battlefield, not the cremation ground (although both are places of death), and she seems to be a fierce demoness whose primary role is to terrify or distract enemies during battle. Her character is usually malevolent, while Chinnamastā's character, although fierce perhaps, is not said to be malevolent.

A South Indian hunting goddess called Koṟṟavai is similar in name and character to Koṭavī. She is fierce, bloodthirsty, and wild. Again, it has been suggested that she may be another expression of the type of goddess that inspired Chinnamastā.[57] J. N. Tiwari sums up her nature.

> . . . Koṟṟavai was perhaps the earliest and the most widely worshipped goddess of the ancient Dravidian people. She was essentially a goddess of the semi-nomadic hunting tribes of South India who invoked her for success in cattle-raids and appeased her with bloody sacrifices. As presented in the Tamil heroic poems, there is no marked element of fertility in the character of Koṟṟavai, who remains primarily a goddess of war and victory.[58]

The Chinnamastā image is striking primarily because her self-decapitation rivets the viewer's attention. She is not a warrior goddess, and unlike Koṟṟavai she does not receive blood sacrifices; rather, she gives her own blood to her devotees. Although Tiwari is to be commended for drawing our attention to the nude, squatting goddesses and to the naked, fierce goddesses Koṭavī and Koṟṟavai, for each of whom he gives a thorough description from many and differing sources, none of the figures seems to be overwhelmingly similar to Chinnamastā. There are many goddesses and demonesses in the Hindu tradition who haunt battlefields, are nude, are fierce and bloodthirsty in nature, or have a clear association with fertility. Chinnamastā, however, seems to be the only goddess who decapitates herself in order to nourish her devotees.

Although Chinnamastā is easily recognized by most Hindus and although her image, along with the other Mahāvidyās, is fairly common in goddess temples, she is not popularly worshiped by most Hindus. She is almost always associated with heroic, Tantric religious practice. The only temple dedicated to Chinnamastā that I have been able to locate is in the courtyard of a large Durgā temple in Rāmnagar across the Ganges River from Banaras. The priests at the Durgā temple told me that the temple had been established by a Tantric *sādhu* and that the people who worshiped the image were primarily Tantrics in pursuit of *siddhis* or supernatural powers.

12

GODDESSES AND SACRED GEOGRAPHY

EARTH AS A GODDESS/INDIA AS A GODDESS

An important aspect of the reverence for the divine feminine in the Hindu tradition is an awe for the sacrality of the land itself and for the Indian subcontinent as a whole. The most ancient expression of this in the Hindu tradition is found in the *Ṛg-veda* and its several hymns that praise the goddess Pṛthivī. It is clear that the hymns to Pṛthivī are grounded in reverence for the awesome stability of the earth itself and the apparently inexhaustible fecundity possessed by the earth.[1] When Pṛthivī is described, characterized, or otherwise praised, the earth itself is usually the object of the hymn. Pṛthivī is the earth in a literal sense as much as she is a goddess with anthropomorphic characteristics.

An underlying implication of perceiving the earth as a great and powerful goddess is that the world as a whole, the cosmos itself, is to be understood as a great, living being, a cosmic organism. This idea is expressed in the central creation myth of the *Brāhmaṇas*, which feature the deity Prajāpati. The world was created, according to this scenario, when Prajāpati undertook great austerities and subsequently released his immense stored-up energy.[2] This great vigor became the underlying substance of the world, pervading it with life and energy. The aim of Vedic sacrificial ritual in the context of this myth is to reconstitute, replenish, rebuild, or reinvigorate Prajāpati by gathering his dispersed energy. By gathering, nurturing, and feeding Agni (who is identified with Prajāpati's released power), the participants in these rites understand that they are renewing Prajāpati. Vedic rituals therefore become part of an ongoing cycle in which Prajāpati creatively releases his ascetic power[3] into the world and is then continually renourished in the sacrificial cult.[4]

The idea of the earth as a personified goddess and the idea that the cosmos as a whole is a living being persist and are central in later Hindu mythology. Pṛthivī continues to be mentioned in medieval mythological texts, and reverence for Bhūdevī (whose name literally means "the goddess who is the earth") becomes an important aspect of Vaiṣṇavite mythology and iconography. When Bhūdevī complains that she is being oppressed by a certain demon, Viṣṇu, attentive to the welfare of the earth, assumes the appropriate form and rescues the earth from her predicament.[5] Iconographically it is common to see Viṣṇu flanked by Śrī-Lakṣmī on one side and Bhūdevī on the other.[6] Bhūdevī's primary role in medieval mythology, however, does not seem to be as the underlying, stable, broad ground that supports all creatures or as the source of inexhaustible fertility. These aspects of the earth, expressed in early hymns to Pṛthivī, are found in other goddesses, such as Śākambharī, Lakṣmī, and the Mahādevī.[7] Bhūdevī's primary role is that of an injured supplicant who is being oppressed by wicked rulers.[8]

Texts extolling the Mahādevī contain many examples of her identification with the world or the cosmos. The Mahādevī is often identified with *prakṛti*, primordial matter or nature (see chapter 9 above).[9] The stuff of creation, the basic matter of the world, is affirmed to be a divine being. In the *Devī-māhātmya* the world is said to be filled by her (11.5); she is said to constitute every created thing (11.6): In the *Devī-bhāgavata-purāṇa* she is said to be present everywhere in the universe, from Brahmā to each blade of grass (1.9.31–32). The Devī herself proclaims to Viṣṇu that everything that is seen is she (1.15.52). At the time of the dissolution the Devī is said to withdraw the world into her womb and then to exist as the seed of the universe until the next creation, when she grows and blossoms forth (3.3.54–55). She is said to appear in the form of the universe. As a spider weaves its web, the Devī creates the universe out of her own body (3.4.41; 4.19.10). In the *Lalitā-sahasranāma* she is called she whose form is all (Sarvamayī, 203), she whose body is matter (Kṣetrasvarūpā, 341), she who is the world (Jadātmikā, 419), she whose womb contains the universe (Viśvagarbhā, 637), and she whose form is all existing things (Bhūmarūpā, 666). She is also called Mahī (718) and Dharā (955), two common names for the earth.

The identification of the Devī with matter, the earth, or the cosmos is often expressed by identifying parts of the world with parts of her body. The *Devī-bhāgavata-purāṇa* calls the earth the Devī's loins (5.8.72). The same text speaks of the oceans as her bowels, the mountains as her bones, the rivers as her veins, and the trees as her body hair. The sun and moon are her eyes, and the nether worlds are said to be her hips, legs, and feet (7.33.21–41).[10] Somadeva's *Yaśastilaka* describes the goddess Aparājītā as having the stars for pearls in her hair, the sun and moon for eyes, the heavenly rivers as her girdle, and Mount Meru as her

The goddess Earth. Nineteenth century A.D. National Museum, Bankok. Mario Bussagli and Calembus Sivaramamurti, *5000 Years of the Art of India* (New York: Harry Abrams, 1981), fig. 211, p. 185. Reprinted by permission of the publisher.

body.[11] In a Gupta inscription Kumarāgupta is said to rule over the whole earth, whose "marriage-string is the verge of the four oceans; whose large breasts are (the mountains) Sumeru and Kailāsa; [and] whose laughter is the full-blown flowers showered forth from the borders of the woods."[12]

The image of the earth, or at least of India, as a great goddess in the Gupta inscription is part of a Gupta ideology that was inspired to a great extent by Vaiṣṇava mythology and theology. The Gupta rulers saw themselves as divine instruments of Viṣṇu, the cosmic king. Like Viṣṇu they understood themselves as protecting the earth and cosmic stability in general. The boar *avatāra* of Viṣṇu, who rescues the earth by diving into the primordial waters where she has been taken by a demon and raising her up on his tusk,[13] was particularly popular among the Guptas and probably represented a mythological model that expressed their understanding of their political role.[14]

The fundamental conviction that the earth itself, or the Indian subcontinent itself, is a goddess, indeed, that she is one's mother, pervades the modern cult of Bhārat Mātā (Mother India), in which all Indians are called sons or children of India and are expected to protect their mother without regard for personal hardship and sacrifice. One of the earliest and probably still the most popular literary expressions of this theme is Bankim Chandra Chatterjee's novel *Ānandamath,* written in the late nineteenth century when the Indian independence movement was beginning to become powerful. The novel is set in Bengal in the late eighteenth century during a great famine. The action centers around a conflict between a band of militant Hindu ascetics and the Muslim rulers of Bengal (and eventually their British allies). The ascetics have renounced wealth, prestige, and even their families to devote themselves to the service and freedom of their motherland, Bengal. They are worshipers of Viṣṇu's man-lion *avatāra,* a particularly ferocious aspect of the divine, while at the same time being devoted to the mother, who is worshiped in concrete form in images of Durgā and Kālī.[15] In the context of the novel it is clear that it is not Durgā herself, or Kālī herself, who is the object of reverence on the part of the ascetics (and the author). Kālī's image is interpreted as the present condition of the mother; that is, the mother, under the domination of foreigners, has become naked, poor, and disheveled. Mahendra, the hero of the work, is told as he gazes on her image that the severed arms that adorn her waist as a girdle are the arms of devotees who will have to be sacrificed before the mother can be freed from her foreign yoke.[16] For purposes of the novel, Kālī's appearance—naked, disheveled, and in disarray—becomes a symbol of the present condition of the motherland: a place of sickness, death, poverty, and exploitation.

The band of ascetics are known as the children, and their battle cry is "hail to the mother" (*bande mātāram*). All of the children have vowed to serve the mother and have sworn not to return to their families until she is saved.[17] When the hero, Mahendra, asks who this mother is, he receives this explicit answer from one of the leaders of the children: "'We own no other mother,' retorted Bhavānanda; 'they say, "the mother and the land of birth are higher than heaven." We think the land of birth to be no other than our mother herself. We have no mother, no father, no brother, no wife, no child, no hearth or home, we have only got the mother.'"[18]

Bhavānanda elaborates his answer to Mahendra's question by singing a hymn in praise of the mother, which is clearly a hymn of praise to the motherland. This hymn became known as the "Bande Mātāram" and was very popular during the independence movement in India.

Hail thee mother! To thee I bow!
Who with sweetest water o'erflows
With dainty fruits is rich and endowed
And cooling whom the south wind blows;
Who's green with crops as on her grow;
To such a mother down I bow!

With silver moon beams smile her nights
And trees that in her bloom abound
Adorn her; and her face doth beam
With sweetest smiles, sweet's her sound!
Joy and bliss she doth bestow;
To such a mother down I bow.

Resounding with triumphal shouts
from seventy million voices bold
With devotion served by twice
As many hands that ably hold
The sharp and shining rapier bold,
—Thou a weakling we are told!

Proud in strength and prowess thou art,
Redeemer of thy children thou;
Chastiser of aggressive foes;
Mother, to thee thy child I bow.

Thou are knowledge, thou my faith,
Thou my heart and thou my mind.
Nay more, thou art the vital air
That moves my body from behind.

Of my hands thou are the strength,
At my heart devotion thou,
In each temple and each shrine,
To thy image it is we bow.

Durga bold who wields her arms
With half a score of hands,
The science-goddess, Vani too,
And Lakshmi who on lotus stands,—
What are they but, mother, thou,
To thee in all these forms I bow!

To thee! Fortune-giver, that art
To fault unknown, beyond compare,
Who dost with sweetest waters flow
And on thy children in thy care
Dainty fruits dost rich bestow,
To thee, mother, to thee I bow!

To thee I bow, that art so green
And so rich bedecked; with smile
Thy face doth glow; thou dost sustain
And hold us—still unknown to guile!
Hail thee mother! To thee I bow![19]

Independent India still cultivates this theme of the motherland as a goddess. The Indian national anthem, composed by Rabindranath Tagore and first sung in 1911 at the Indian National Congress in Calcutta, is in the same vein as Chatterjee's "Bande Mātāram."

Thou art the ruler of the minds of all people,
Dispenser of India's destiny.
Thy name rouses the hearts of Punjab, Sind, Gujarat
 and Maratha,
Of Dravida and Orissa and Bengal.
It echoes in the hills of Vindhyas and Himalayas,
 mingles in the music of Jamuna and Ganges
 and is chanted by the waves of the Indian Sea.
They pray for thy blessings and sing thy praise.
The saving of all people waits in thy hand,
Thou dispenser of India's destiny.
Victory, victory, victory to thee.[20]

Concrete expressions of this reverence for India as a feminine deity are not difficult to find in modern India. In Banaras, the spiritual capital of Hinduism, there is a temple dedicated to Bhārat Mātā. Inside the temple, in the place where there would ordinarily be an anthropomorphic image of the goddess, there is a large, colored relief map of the Indian subcontinent. It is to this large map that pilgrims show reverence.[21] Insofar as the nation-state represents, is identified with, or is associated with the land itself, it is due reverence. For the land itself is a sacred, nourishing, redemptive presence to those who are born from it and are nourished by it.

THE ŚĀKTA *PĪṬHAS*

The myth and cult of the Śākta *pīṭhas* is another vivid expression of the Hindu intuition that the Indian subcontinent itself is a goddess. India is covered with sacred places associated with prominent geographical features of the country. Mountains, hills, rivers, caves, and other sites having some geographical or natural peculiarity are often affirmed to possess sacred power or to be places where one may make contact with the divine. These sites are usually called *tīrthas*, a term that means a place where one fords a river. The term is significant in regard to sacred places in two senses: (1) it indicates that rivers themselves are often the site of sacred power, and (2) such places are sites where one may cross over from the realm of the profane to the sacred, from the human to the divine, from this world to another world.[22] In many cases these sites are associated with deities who are well known in the Hindu tradition and who have an elaborate mythology and cult independent of the sacred site in question. In other cases it seems that the object of sacrality, that which lends the site power, is the place itself and not so much the deity who is associated with the place.[23]

While it is difficult to establish historically how a given site has become popular as a sacred place, it seems clear that in many cases an awe or reverence for the geographical place itself was crucial in distinguishing it.[24] Arduous pilgrimages to remote sites where the central religious rite is to bathe in the waters of a pool or river, enter a cave, or have a view of some geographical feature indicate that the great attraction of many sacred places is tied to the geography of the place. Although temples are often found in such places, the environment rather than the temple itself is usually the object of the pilgrim. The temple simply serves to mark, specify, or objectify the sacrality of the local geography. The temple does not enhance the sacrality of the place so much as the place enhances the sacrality of the temple.

Underlying the extraordinary number of sacred sites associated with geographical places in India seems to be the intuition that the land, the earth, or the Indian subcontinent itself is an immense source or repository of sacred power. Looking at a map of the Indian subcontinent on which only the most famous sacred places are marked, we see that India bubbles with sacrality in every region.[25] To a great extent these many *tīrthas*, which are associated with Hindu mythology and epic history, have given India its sense of cultural and historical unity. India has rarely been under central rule. For the most part she has been ruled by several competing kingdoms. The sacrality of the land itself, rather than a unified political tradition, has cultivated among most Hindus the strong sense of Mother India.

> The whole of India's sacred geography, with its many *tīrthas*—those inherent in its natural landscape and those sanctified by the deeds of gods and the footsteps of heroes—is a living geography. As such it has been central for the shaping of an Indian sense of regional and national unity. The recognition of India as sacred landscape, woven together north and south, east and west, by the paths of pilgrims, has created a powerful sense of India as Bhārat Mātā—Mother India.[26]

Many sacred sites are specifically associated with, identified with, or presided over by a goddess. The pervasiveness of sites sacred to goddesses is suggested by the number of towns and villages that have names associated with different goddesses.

> . . . in this vast country, holy resorts of the goddess are innumerable and the popularity of her cult is proved even in the place-names of India. Referring to the Panjab region Prof. Niharranjan Ray observed: "Very few people pause to consider this social phenomenon, or to consider the significance of such toponyms in these regions as, for instance, Ambala which is derived from Amba, one of the many names of Durgā, Chandigarh which is named after Caṇdī, . . . Kalka which is a vulgarisation of Kālikā, Simla which is Śyāmalā Devī in its anglicised version. A careful and close look at the postal directories of the Punjab, Hariyana and Himachal would yield a long list of such toponyms from which one may draw one's own conclusion. Besides, throughout these regions one still finds a countless number of small, lowly shrines with all but shapeless or crude forms placed on their altars, which worshippers, lowly village folks, describe as Manasā, Caṇḍī, Kālī, Naynā, Durgā, etc."[27]

Many of these sites associated with goddesses are called *pīṭhas*, "seats." Why the term *pīṭha* is used for those sites in preference to the more traditional and common term *tīrtha* is not entirely clear. *Pīṭha* is preferred, perhaps because it tends to emphasize the rootedness of the goddesses associated with these places. Many of the goddesses are preeminently tied to the locales in which they are worshiped. They are perceived to be not so much transcendent, heavenly beings as beings whose power is firmly grounded in the earth itself. It may be, too, that the term *pīṭha* is appropriate to those aspects of Devī theology which emphasize her association with the earth itself and her motherly nature, which casts her in the role of an ever-present, nurturing presence. Perhaps the point of the term is to emphasize that the Devī is to be understood as firmly located in this world, both in the sense of being identified with it and in the sense of being oriented toward such worldly concerns of her devotees as fertility, well-being, and long life.[28] While the term *tīrtha* has connotations of crossing from this world to another world, the term *pīṭha* connotes a fixed point, and by extension the fixedness of the goddesses worshiped at these sites.

Sometime in the medieval period an attempt was made to affirm the basic unity of all *pīṭhas* sacred to goddesses.[29] The assumption behind this attempt was that the Mahādevī underlies all the particular manifestations of goddesses residing at the many *pīṭhas*. Mythologically this idea was expressed by adding an episode to the myth of Satī's self-destruction at Dakṣa's sacrifice. In the expanded version of the myth Śiva arrives at Dakṣa's sacrifice having received the news that Satī has killed herself. He picks up her body and, racked with grief, begins to wander the cosmos. He is so distraught by Satī's death and so grieved by the presence of her corpse that he completely ignores his divine responsibilities. His sobbing and grief threaten the stability of the world. Viṣṇu is called upon to remedy the situation. He enters Satī's body by yoga or else slices pieces of her body off bit by bit, but in one way or another he disposes of her body a bit at a time.[30] When Śiva discovers that Satī's body is gone, he recovers his divine composure and stops grieving. Where the parts of Satī's body fell, sacred places called *pīṭhas* were then established. The number of *pīṭhas* varies from 4 to 110 in the different accounts of the tale.[31]

In most accounts of this myth and in most lists of the *pīṭhas*, Satī's yoni is said to have fallen and been enshrined at Kāmagiri in the region of Kāmarūpa in Assam, where the goddess is worshiped as Kāmākhyā. Although goddess worship is undoubtedly ancient in this part of India[32] and although Kāmarūpa is mentioned in the Allahabad pillar inscription of Samudragupta (middle of the fourth century), the present temple of

Kāmākhyā near Gauhati does not date beyond the sixteenth century. In the seventeenth century the Ahom kings of Assam encouraged the worship of Kāmākhyā on a grand scale, and her centrality in the *pīṭha* mythology probably originates around this time. In the Kāmākhyā temple at Kāmagiri, the central image of the goddess is a yoni carved in stone and smeared with red paste symbolizing blood.[33] Rituals are done at the temple each month to signify the Devī's menstruation. This famous center of goddess worship, in short, reveres and enshrines a sacred place that is affirmed to be the creative orifice of a goddess whose larger body is the earth itself or at least the local mountain and region.

According to this myth, then, the Indian subcontinent has been sacralized by the remains of Satī. India is in effect her burial ground.[34] The subcontinent is sown with the pieces of Satī's body, which make the land especially sacred.[35] The myth also stresses that the numerous and varied *pīṭhas* and goddesses worshiped at them are part of a larger, unified whole. Each *pīṭha* represents a part of Satī's body or one of her ornaments;[36] taken together, the *pīṭhas* found throughout India constitute or point toward a transcendent (or, perhaps better, a universally immanent) goddess whose being encompasses, underlies, and unifies the Indian subcontinent as a whole. In short, the Indian subcontinent *is* the goddess Satī.

Although the myth speaks of the dismemberment of Satī's corpse, the emphasis at the *pīṭhas* is not on the worship of Satī's relics but on the worship of living goddesses, who are all understood as manifestations of the living Mahādevī. The point is not so much that India is the reliquary of the Devī's corpse as it is that India is the Devī's living body. The myth provides a vantage point from which the many local and regional goddess cults throughout India may be understood as part of a larger, unified vision in which each act of devotion to a local goddess becomes an act of reverence to the divinity of India as a whole.

THE GANGES AND THE SACRALITY OF RIVERS

Geographical sacrality in the Hindu tradition is also dramatically expressed in the reverence shown to almost every river of the Indian subcontinent. This reverence extends all the way back to the *Ṛg-veda*, where the idea is expressed that earthly rivers have their origin in heaven. In the *Ṛg-veda* the Sarasvatī River is praised as a mighty goddess who blesses her devotees with health, long life, and poetic inspiration.[37] The earthly Sarasvatī River is said to be only a partial manifestation of the goddess Sarasvatī, for she is said to exist in heaven as well as on earth. The earthly river is an extension or continuation of divine waters that flow from heaven to earth. In Ṛg-vedic cosmology the creation of the world or the process of making the world habitable is associated with the freeing of the heavenly waters by Indra. Indra's enemy Vṛtra is said to have withheld these waters, thus inhibiting creation. When Indra defeats Vṛtra the waters rush onto the earth like mother cows eager to suckle their young (10.9). The rivers of the earth are therefore seen as being necessary to creation and as having a heavenly origin. They are brought to earth by the heroic act of a god who defeats a demon who has hoarded the waters and kept them from fertilizing and nourishing the earth in the form of rivers.[38]

Reverence for rivers in the Hindu tradition is nowhere more intense than in the case of the Ganges. Like the Sarasvatī River in the Vedic tradition, the Ganges is said to have its origin in heaven. Many myths concerning the descent of the Ganges to earth emphasize this point. The oldest and probably best known concerns the restoration of the sixty thousand sons of King Sagara. According to this myth, Sagara's sons were dull-witted and impetuous, and while searching the world for their father's sacrificial horse they insulted and disturbed the tranquillity of the great sage Kapila. In anger, Kapila burned them all to ashes with the fire that he had generated as the result of his great austerities. Sagara's descendants, despite their piety and ascetic efforts, were unable to restore their incinerated forefathers until the saintly and mighty Bhagīratha, the great-great-great-grandson of Sagara, undertook the task. Giving his kingdom over to a trusted minister, Bhagīratha went to the Himalayas to do heroic austerities. After he had physically mortified himself for centuries, the Ganges appeared in bodily form and granted his wish: she would descend to the earth, provided that someone could be found to break her mighty fall, which otherwise would destroy the earth itself. Śiva was persuaded to receive the Ganges on his head, and so the great heavenly river descended to earth, her mighty fall softened by Śiva's massive tangle of hair. In his hair she became divided into many streams, each of which flowed to a different region of earth and sanctified that area. Her principal artery emerged from Śiva's hair and came to India, and under Bhagīratha's guidance it cut a channel to where the ashes of Sagara's sons were piled. Moistened by her waters, the souls of the sixty thousand sons were purified and freed to undertake their journey to the land of their fathers, where they could be duly honored by their descendants.[39]

Other accounts of the Ganges' descent feature Viṣṇu and sometimes Kṛṣṇa. After assuming his dwarf *avatāra* to trick the demon Bali, Viṣṇu strides across the cosmos to appropriate it for the gods. On his third stride his foot strikes the vault of heaven and breaks it. The Ganges

River pours through the hole and eventually finds its way to earth. Falling on Mount Meru, the cosmic axis, the Ganges divides into four parts, and as it flows onto the four world continents it purifies the world in every direction.[40] In some versions of the myth the god Brahmā, who is said to hold the heavenly Ganges in his water pot, pours the Ganges on Viṣṇu's foot when it stretches into the heavenly sphere.[41] In still other versions of the myth Viṣṇu becomes liquified when he hears a particularly sublime song sung in his praise, and in this form he enters Brahmā's water pot, which contains the Ganges, and thus sacralizes her.[42]

In one way or another, these myths about the Ganges' coming to earth stress the river's heavenly origin, her essentially divine nature, and her association with the great male deities Brahmā, Viṣṇu, and Śiva. Spilling out of heaven from Viṣṇu's foot, containing Viṣṇu's liquified essence according to some myths, and falling onto Śiva's head, where she meanders through his tangled locks, the mighty Ganges appears in this world after having been made more sacred by direct contact with Viṣṇu and Śiva. The river then spreads the divine potency of these gods into the world when she flows onto the earthly plane. She gives their sacred presences to the earth in liquid form.[43] The myths make clear that the earthly Ganges is only a limited part of the cosmic river that flows in heaven and descends to other regions and worlds as well as this one. As mighty as the Ganges appears here, the earthly river is only a limited aspect of a reality that transcends this world. The Ganges, these myths insists, points beyond itself to a transcendent, cosmic dimension that locates the source of the river in a divine sphere.

Another important theme in the reverence for rivers in Hinduism is the purifying quality of rivers and of running water in general. The purity-conscious Hindu social system, in which pollution is inevitably accumulated in the course of a normal day, prescribes a ritual bath as the simplest way to rid oneself of impurities. This act consists of little more than pouring a handful of cold water over one's head and letting it run down one's body. Moving, flowing, or falling water is believed to have great cleansing power; a mere sprinkling of water over one's head or a dip in a stream is sufficient to remove most kinds of daily pollution accumulated through normal human intercourse with those in a state less pure that one's own.[44] Like fire, the other great natural purifying element in Hinduism,[45] water is affirmed to contain intrinsic powers of purification, particularly when in motion.

The most awesome manifestations of moving water in the Hindu context are the great rivers of the Indian subcontinent. Ever moving, ever the same, apparently inexhaustible, such rivers as the Jumna, Cauvery, Narmada, Brahmaputra, and Ganges are revered in particular for their great purifying powers. The myths concerning the heavenly origin

The goddess Gaṅgā. Sena, twelfth century A.D., Bengal. C. Sivaramamurti, *Gaṅgā* (New Delhi: Orient Longman, 1976), fig. 29, p. 62.

of such rivers as the Ganges make the point that the mighty rivers of India are in essence uncontaminated by the impurities of the world, that they arise and for the most part flow in celestial realms before falling to earth. Once descended to earth, however, these same rivers literally wash away the accumulated impurities of the realms they traverse. As a handful of water sprinkled over a person's head cleanses that person, so the river cleanses the entire world when she falls on Mount Meru. The Ganges, Jumna, Cauvery, and countless other rivers and streams are understood to perform a continuous, gracious process of purifying the earth and her inhabitants.

The physical evidence of this continuous process of purification is the clarity of a river's swiftly flowing source compared to its broad, sluggish, murky mouth before it enters the sea. A river may take on an increasingly impure appearance the farther it travels from its source. Rivers like the Ganges are nevertheless held to be equally purifying from source to mouth. While the source of the Ganges and the place where it breaks out of the mountains onto the plains are important pilgrimage sites, the lower Ganges also has many places of great sanctity. Banaras itself, perhaps the most sacred site in all of India, is far downstream on the Ganges. Though great removers of pollution, the rivers remain uncontaminated by what they remove, staying ever pure, ever potent, ever gracious to all those who come to them for purification.

Although all rivers are revered as removers of pollution, the Ganges is preeminent among India's rivers as a purifying power. Hymns extolling the Ganges repeatedly emphasize the miraculously purifying powers of her waters. The *Agni-purāṇa* says that the river makes those regions she flows through into sacred ground, that bathing in her waters is an experience similar to being in heaven, that those afflicted with blindness and other ailments become like gods after bathing in her waters, that the Ganges has made pure thousands of impure people who have seen, touched, or drunk her waters.[46] To die while being immersed in the Ganges results in *mokṣa*, final spiritual liberation. Being brushed by a breeze containing even a drop of Ganges water erases all sins accumulated over lifetimes.[47] In the *Bṛhaddharma-purāṇa* a sinful king is said to have been spared an untimely death because he lived for a while with a merchant who used to bathe in the Ganges.[48] The *Mahābhāgavata-purāṇa* tells the story of a robber who, though sent to hell after death, was subsequently sent to Śiva's heaven because his flesh was eaten by a jackal who had drunk Ganges water (74).

In the Gupta and early medieval periods it was common for the personified images of the Ganges and Jumna to flank the doorways of temples.[49] The Ganges' role as threshold figure in these periods probably had to do with both her (and the Jumna's) purificatory powers. The Ganges' heavenly origin and descent to the earth made her an intermediary between the earthly and heavenly realms. She is a continuous, liquid link between the two worlds. Her location at the thresholds of temples was appropriate in that she connected and formed a transition between the worlds of men and gods. Her position at the doorways of temples probably also indicated her role as remover of pollution. Before entering the sacred realm of the gods, which a temple represents, devotees should cleanse themselves of worldly impurities. Crossing the threshold of a temple flanked by images of the goddesses Gaṅgā and Yamunā, devotees probably were symbolically cleansed in the purificatory waters of these rivers.

The Ganges' location as a threshold figure in medieval temples also suggests the threshold function of the physical Ganges River (and other rivers). The most common name for a sacred place in Hinduism is *tīrtha,* which means a place for crossing over from one place to another, especially a place for crossing a river, a fording place. As applied to sacred places the term signifies a place at which one may cross from one plane of reality to another, in particular, a place where one can cross from the earthly plane to the divine plane, or from the limited human sphere to the unconditioned divine sphere. As a sacred place, as a *tīrtha,* the Ganges is prototypical. Her waters are affirmed to orginate in heaven and to flow in a continuous stream into the earthly sphere. The Ganges is often called she who flows in the three worlds (Triloka-pathagaminī).[50] She is a liquid *axis mundi,* a pathway connecting all spheres of reality, a presence at which or in which one may cross over to another sphere of the cosmos, ascend to heavenly worlds, or transcend human limitations. As Diana Eck has so nicely put it: "It is because the Gaṅgā descended in her *avataraṇa* that she is a place of ascent as a *tīrtha.*"[51] Flowing out into the world, the Ganges moves according to rhythms and currents that originate in heaven. Her waters have had physical contact with the great gods Viṣṇu and Śiva. She is a sacred bridge to those realms from which she has come.

The Ganges' role as a mediator between this world and the divine worlds, as a place at which or in which crossings may be made, is clear in the context of death rituals.[52] A strong and widespread Hindu belief is that to die in the Ganges, or to have a few drops of Ganges water poured on one's lips just prior to death, is to gain immediate liberation.[53] Although any part of the Ganges is believed to have this redemptive power, the cult of seeking to die in contact with the Ganges is most active in Banaras, where special hostels for the dying accommodate the thousands of pious Hindus who make a final pilgrimage from all over

India to die on the banks of the Ganges there.[54] The Ganges is understood to be a particularly accessible bridge from one mode of being to the other, a sure crossing point in the difficult transition from life to death or from bondage to liberation.

Another strong and widespread belief in India is that having their ashes or bones thrown into the Ganges guarantees the dead a safe journey to the realm of the ancestors. Against this background the story of the redemption of Sagara's sons makes sense. Cursed to eternal banishment from the realm of the ancestors, the souls of Sagara's sons can only reach the goal of the dead by means of contact with the Ganges, which provides them a special route to heaven. In this role the Ganges is known especially by the epithet Svārga-sopana-saranī (she who is a flowing staircase to heaven).[55] Pious Hindus make a pilgrimage to various points on the banks of the Ganges to cast the ashes of their ancestors and kin onto the waters of the Ganges so that they, like the sons of Sagara, will be ensured a successful transition to the realm of the dead. Just as the mighty waters of the Ganges are envisioned in Hindu cosmology as continuously descending from heaven to earth, so a continuous procession of souls is ascending the Ganges to transcendent realms.[56]

The Ganges as the surest access between the worlds of the living and the dead is also seen in *śrāddha* and *tarpaṇa* rituals, which are performed in honor of ancestors. These rites frequently stipulate Ganges water as desirable. The intention of these rites is to nourish the ancestors, the *pitṛs,* in the heavenly sphere. The use of Ganges water may be understood both as nourishing the ancestors directly and as representing the means by which the other offerings to the ancestors will reach the desired realm. The use of Ganges water guarantees the efficacy of the rites by making the Ganges present as a *tīrtha,* a crossing point from the world of the living to the world of the dead.

A particularly strong motif in reverence to the Ganges is her presence to her devotees as a mother. Gaṅgā Mā, "Mother Ganges," is probably the river's most popular epithet. Like a mother or as a mother the Ganges is here in the world to comfort her children. She is tangible, approachable, and all-accepting. All who approach her for comfort and blessing are enveloped by her yielding, redemptive waters. She is the distilled essence of compassion in liquid form. No one is denied her blessing. Jagganātha, the author of the *Gaṅgā Laharī,* probably the most famous hymn in praise of the Ganges, was outcast by his fellow Hindus for having a love affair with a Muslim woman. He says that he was even shunned by untouchables and madmen. He declares that he was so despicable, so polluted, that none of the *tīrthas* was able to cleanse him.[57] The Ganges alone was willing to accept him and cleanse him, and he in gratitude praises her as a loving mother:

> I come to you as a child to his mother.
> I come as an orphan to you, moist with love.
> I come without refuge to you, giver of sacred rest.
> I come a fallen man to you, uplifter of all.
> I come undone by disease to you, the perfect physician.
> I come, my heart dry with thirst, to you, ocean of
> sweet wine.
> Do with me whatever you will.[58]

The Ganges' maternal aspect is seen especially in her nourishing qualities. Her waters are sometimes likened to milk or *amṛta*, the drink of immortality.[59] "The concept of the river in India is that of a sustaining mother. The stream of the river carries *payas*. The word *payas* stands for both water and milk. Appropriately this has been used in relation to the river as the stream that sustains the people, her children, with water, as a mother sustains her babies with her milk."[60] Her waters are life-giving, nourishing to all those who bathe in or drink them.[61] Her waters have miraculous vivifying powers. The ashes of Sagara's sons, and the ashes of the dead in general, are enlivened, invigorated, or otherwise made strong enough by the touch of her waters to make the journey to heaven.

As a mother, the Ganges nourishes the land through which it flows, making it fertile. Historically, the land along the banks of the Ganges has been intensely cultivated. It is particularly fertile because of the sediment periodically deposited by the flood waters of the river and because of irrigation. Images of the Ganges often show her carrying a plate of food and a *pūrṇakumbha*, an overflowing pot.[62] Mother Ganges is depicted as a being overflowing with food and life-giving waters, as one who continually nourishes all she comes in contact with. As giver of food and as water that makes fields rich with crops, the Ganges bestows her blessings concretely in this world. She makes the earth abundant with crops and thereby sustains and enriches life. As the bestower of worldly blessings the Ganges is particularly approached to ensure healthy crops and to promote fertility in women. "Today in Bihar, at the start of the plowing season, before the seeds are sown, farmers put Ganga water in a pot and set it in a special place in the field to ensure good harvest. Among those who live along the river, a newly married woman unfolds her sari to Ganga and prays for children and the long life of her husband."[63]

The waters of the Ganges are also often used to restore the health of sick people.[64] The miraculous restorative powers of the Ganges is the subject of many stories. In one of the Buddhist *Jataka* tales we read of a parrot who lived in a fig tree. The tree's fruit sustained the bird and also provided him shelter. Over the years the parrot became exceedingly devoted to the tree, which had acted as his benefactor throughout his life. Hearing of the devotion of the parrot, the king of the area wished to test the bird's fidelity and magically dried up the tree. But the bird remained. Impressed with the bird's loyalty the king granted the parrot a wish. The bird asked that the tree be restored. Thereupon the king "took up the water from the Ganges in his hand and dashed it against the fig-tree stump. Straightaway the tree rose up rich in branch and stem, with honey-sweet fruit, and stood a charming sight, like the bare Jewel-Mountain."[65]

The Ganges' relationship with Śiva suggests a structure similar to the rhythmic interdependence of opposites in Śiva's relationship with Pārvatī.[66] The Ganges, like Pārvatī, her co-wife, represents the cool, nourishing, fertile dimension of reality that calms, contains, or offsets the fierce, hot, destructive powers of Śiva. The most dramatic expression of this relationship is found in the myth concerning the birth of Kārttikeya. When Śiva spills his semen it is so powerfully hot that it cannot be contained even by Agni himself. After passing through a series of containers, none of which is able to contain it for long, the semen falls into the Ganges and is cooled there. Within the cooling womb of Mother Ganges the semen takes on embryonic form, and the war god Kārttikeya is duly born.[67]

The practice in many Śiva temples of pouring Ganges water on Śiva's liṅga also suggests the cooling, calming effect of the Ganges. Śiva's fiery, hot, hard character is complemented and made accessible by the soft, cooling effect the Ganges has on him. The pouring of Ganges water on the liṅga, which goes on continuously from dawn till dusk in some temples,[68] is also reminiscent of the Ganges' descent from heaven onto Śiva's head. Śiva's consent to accept the mighty weight of the Ganges to break her fall to earth effectively involves him in worldly matters, drawing him away from isolated meditation. The Ganges' meandering course through Śiva's locks and through the regions of the earth physically connects the aloof god's presence with the earth. By tangibly connecting Śiva with the earth the Ganges extends his presence into the world. In a quite physical and literal way the Ganges acts as Śiva's *śakti*, permitting his redemptive presence to spread to the world and his devotees, who yearn for his grace. By means of the Ganges Śiva's otherwise dangerous, destructive, fierce presence is transmitted into an approachable reality accessible to all.[69]

Behind the many myths that exalt the Ganges as a great goddess and associate her with Śiva, Viṣṇu, Brahmā, and other deities lies an enduring reverence for the river itself. Behind the lofty hymns of praise that affirm the Ganges' miraculous powers to effect renewed health, fertility, a safe journey to the land of the ancestors, and spiritual liberation, there is a fundamental affection for the physical river that meanders across the North Indian plains. The extent to which it is the physical Ganges River itself that is adored by Hindus is evident in the persistent habit of pilgrims to see, touch, be sprinkled with, and bathe in the river's waters. It is not anthropomorphic images of the Ganges that attract reverence and worship, although such images are common enough. It is the river itself that is worshiped. Devotees honor other deities by draping a garland around the neck of the image. They worship the Ganges by stringing the garland of flowers across the river itself. Similarly, while it is auspicious to circumambulate the image of a deity, some adventurous devotees circumambulate the Ganges by traveling up one bank and down the other along her entire course.[70] In Diana Eck's phrase, the Ganges is an "organic symbol," not a narrative symbol. In the case of the Ganges, and in the case of the Hindu reverence for the sacrality of the land, the organic *is* the sacred.

> For the Gaṅgā's significance as a symbol is not exhaustively narrative. First, she is a river that flows with waters of life in a vibrant universe. Narrative myths come and go in history. They may shape the cosmos and convey meaning for many generations, and then they may gradually lose their hold upon the imagination and may finally be forgotten. But the river remains, even when the stories are no longer repeated. The river flows on, bringing life and conveying the living tradition, even to those of this age for whom everything else is demythologized.[71]

Reverence for and worship of the Ganges is yet another vivid affirmation that the geography of India itself is somehow redemptive, that simply being in contact with this place, dwelling upon it, imbues people with salvific strength.

13

VILLAGE GODDESSES

India today is primarily a village culture. The majority of Hindus live in villages of under a hundred thousand people, and there is little doubt that this has always been the case in the Indian subcontinent. In the context of village life one of the most (if not the most) significant and powerful divine presences is the *grāmadevatā*, a deity who is especially identified with the village and toward whom the villagers often have a special affection. It is not uncommon, in fact, for there to be several *grāmadevatās* in a village, each of whom may have a specialized function.[1] These village deities, more numerous than Indian villages themselves, are naturally diverse in character. Their names alone suggest diverse characteristics and functions.[2] Some of these deities have a regional reputation, or at least the name of a certain *grāmadevatā* will be well known or popular throughout an entire region. The goddesses Māriyamman in South India and Manasā in North India are examples of this regional popularity. Other village deities may be known only to one small village. The goddess Periyapālayattamman, whose name means simply "the mother (or mistress) of the village Periyapālayam," is relatively unknown outside that village near Madras in South India.[3] Often the village deity will share the names or epithets of deities from the Sanskrit pantheon and will be identified with these deities in the minds of villagers. But this does not necessarily mean that the village deity will bear many similarities to the "great" god in question. It may indicate little more than a conscious attempt to relate the village deity to a wider religious universe or to make the local deity recognizable to curious outsiders. In most cases where such an identification exists the *grāmadevatā* differs markedly from the "great" deity with whom it shares a name.[4]

Despite the number and variety of *grāmadevatās*, several typical characteristics of these local deities have been noted. First, they usually are female. Speaking of South India, Henry Whitehead says that "*village deities,* with very few exceptions, *are female.* . . . All over Southern India . . . the village deities are almost exclusively female. In the Tamil country, it is true, most of them have male attendants, who are supposed to guard the shrines and carry out the commands of the goddesses; but their place is distinctly subordinate and almost servile."[5]

Second, these deities are usually not represented by anthropomorphic images. They are usually represented by uncarved stones, trees, or small shrines that do not contain an anthropomorphic image. Sometimes no shrine is present at all except during special festivals, when temporary structures will be built to house or represent the deity.[6]

Third, these deities, goddesses for the most part, capture the primary interest of the villagers and tend to be worshiped with more intensity than the great gods of the Hindu pantheon. Although the great gods are acknowledged to be in charge of distant, cosmic rhythms, they are only of limited interest to most villagers, many of whom traditionally were not allowed within the precincts of the temples of these deities in the first place. The village goddess, in contrast, engages the villagers directly by being associated with their local, existential concerns.[7] She is perceived to be *their* deity and to be concerned especially with *their* well-being and that of their village.

Finally, these village deities are often directly associated with disease, sudden death, and catastrophe. When the village is threatened by disaster, particularly epidemics, the local goddess is usually said to be manifesting herself. She erupts onto the village scene along with diasters that threaten the stability, and even the survival, of the village. Furthermore, her role vis-à-vis such epidemics or disasters is ambivalent. She is perceived both as inflicting these diseases and as protecting the village from them.

THE LOCAL ROOTEDNESS OF THE VILLAGE GODDESSES

One of the most persistent themes found in the myth, cult, and worship of village goddesses is their being rooted in specific, local villages. The village is the special place of the deity. She is the mother or mistress of the village, as suggested by a name popular in the South, Amman, meaning "mother, mistress, or lady."[8] Although it is common to speak of the goddess of such-and-such a village, it is probably more accurate to think of the village as belonging to the goddess. Theologically the village goddess predates the village. She created it. As its center and source she is often associated with a "navel stone" located somewhere in the village.[9] Sometimes she is represented only by a head placed directly on the ground. This may suggest that her body is the village itself, that she is rooted in the soil of the village.[10] The village and the villagers might be understood as living within or upon the body of the village goddess.

The close identity of the goddess with her village is also seen in her role as guardian of the village's boundaries. Her shrines or symbols are often erected at the boundaries of the village, where she acts to protect it from invasions of evil spirits and outsiders in general. Another expression of the intimate identity of the goddess with her village is her symbolic marriage to representatives of the village during her ceremonies.[11] Although the goddess is sometimes said to have a husband or a male consort or guardian, her real associate in a marriagelike arrangement is the village itself rather than a male deity. The two, the goddess and the village, are tied to each other, dependent on each other; in short, they are married to each other and nourish each other.

Another indication of the identity of village and goddess is the participation of almost all members of a village in the goddess's festivals. In the case of the high or great gods, worship is often restricted to certain castes, usually the higher ones, or such deities may be particularly worshiped by *sampradāyas* or movements that have restricted membership. The village goddess, however, is approached by the natural grouping of the local village itself and all those who constitute it. She is the goddess of the whole village, the physical place as well as the social and economic organism. Nearly all castes are represented at her festivals and to some extent mix freely. Her worship is a community effort, although particular castes may play more important ritual roles than others.[12] The extent of the all-inclusive nature of local-goddess worship in villages is indicated by the participation of Brahmans and Muslims in these festivals.[13] The point is that the local goddess is not so much a Hindu deity or a deity specially related to a caste or occupation, or even to a specific phenomenon such as disease, although all of these things might be the case to some extent. The point is that from the villagers' point of view the goddess is specifically their deity, their lady, as it were, who has their particular needs at heart.

The local rootedness of village goddesses, their special and narrow association with particular villages, is also suggested in the tendency during festivals in their honor to exclude outsiders. The exclusion of outsiders seems to be associated with the idea that they might benefit from the power of the goddess, which is intended for the local village. Her power is believed to be for her village, not for outsiders. Sometimes, too, the symbol or image of a disease or epidemic will be escorted to the border of a village and symbolically passed on to another village.[14] The village and its immediate surroundings thus represent for the villager a more or less complete cosmos within which life in all its fullness and complexity can be lived out in an orderly and fruitful way. The central divine power impinging on or underlying this cosmos is the village goddess, and the extent to which order and fertility dominate the village cosmos is bound up with the relationship between the goddess and the villagers. Village life is her business and their business, and the role of outsiders is sometimes seen to be irrelevant or disruptive.

The basic relationship between the village goddess and her village seems quite straightforward. In return for the worship of the villagers the goddess ensures good crops, timely rain, fertility, and protection from demons, diseases, and untimely death. The arrangement is a local one with little or no room for outsiders. The power of the goddess does not extend beyond the village, so villagers leave her jurisdiction and protection when they venture beyond it. The relationship is localized and aims not so much at individual welfare as the welfare of the whole.

In fact, relations between village goddesses and their villages are more complicated. This is made clear by the association of these goddesses with disease and disruption, an identification that gives them an ambivalent character. For these goddesses are not usually peaceful, benign, and calm presences. Rather, they tend to be wild, rambunctious, independent, demanding, and destructive in their habits. This is evident in both their mythology and their ceremonies.

MYTHOLOGICAL THEMES

An important theme in myths concerning the origin of village goddesses is the injustice done to women by men. Two of the best-known myths concerning the origin of the popular goddess Māriyamman in South India include this motif. In one version a young Brahman girl is courted by and eventually married to an untouchable who has disguised himself as a Brahman. On discovering the trick, the woman becomes furious and kills herself. She is transformed into a goddess and in her divine form punishes the untouchable by burning him to ashes or otherwise humiliating or humbling him.[15] Another version of Māriyamman's origin identifies her with an extremely pious, pure wife who is married to a devout holy man. She is so pure that she can perform miraculous tasks such as making jars out of loose sand and boiling water simply by placing a pot of water on her head. One day, however, she sees two *gandharvas* making love and feels envy for them. Thereupon she loses her miraculous powers. Discovering this and suspecting sexual disloyalty, her husband commands their son to kill his mother. The son obeys his father and decapitates his mother. Eventually she is restored to life, but in the process her head and body get transposed with those of an untouchable woman. Māriyamman is thus understood to have a Brahman head and an untouchable body, which is significant in terms of both her ambivalent nature and her role as a village goddess exemplifying the social status quo in which Brahmans are at the head of the social system.[16]

Myths concerning the origins of other village goddesses also include this motif of injustice done to women by males. Kaṇṇagi, the heroine of the Tamil epic *Śilappadihāram,* is portrayed as faultlessly faithful to her husband despite his lecherous and unfaithful behavior. Ordinarily Kaṇṇagi's faithfulness would guarantee the well-being and long life of her husband, for according to folk tradition a wife's faithfulness ensures her husband's welfare, whereas her unfaithfulness causes him harm. If a man's wife is faithful, he is virtually immune from harm—such is the belief promulgated in both the folk and Sanskrit traditions. Kaṇṇagi's husband, however, is unjustly accused by the king of Madurai of having stolen an anklet and is executed. Kaṇṇagi proves her husband's innocence, tears off her breast, which becomes blistering hot, and burns the city of Madurai in her wrath. She subsequently becomes a goddess.[17] Again we see the theme of a woman who has been treated unjustly by males expressing her outrage in an act of violent destruction and being transformed into a goddess.

Another set of myths relating the origin of village goddesses takes place entirely in the divine sphere but contains a similar theme. In the beginning is the great goddess Ammavaru. In her desire to create she produces three eggs, from which are born the three great gods: Brahmā, Viṣṇu, and Śiva. When she wants to marry these deities to promote the continuation of creation, they refuse, saying that it would be improper for a mother to have sex with her sons. But one or the other of the gods finally agrees to marry her if she will give him her middle eye, which is symbolic of her primordial power. She agrees, but having given up her power to the god she is destroyed by him. From her body are created the many *śaktis* who become village goddesses.[18]

These myths, with their theme of village goddesses' having suffered injustices at the hands of men, help us to understand certain central characteristics of village goddesses: namely, the fiercely ambivalent nature of these goddesses, which manifests itself in sudden outbursts of rage, and the goddesses' relative independence from or superiority over male consorts. Such goddesses' terrible retributive wrath continues to be expressed in festivals in which a male animal, often identified as a "husband," is sacrificed. These goddesses are angry deities and need appeasing. Furthermore, they rarely provide a traditional model for women in their relationships with males. The village goddesses are often not married at all, and if they are, they dominate their male consorts—the reverse of what sexual roles should be according to Indian cultural models.[19] It could be said of these fiercely independent goddesses that they have "learned their lesson,"[20] that they have learned that they only receive injustice from males; consequently they are determined to remain independent from men in their transformed positions as goddesses. This theme of the goddesses' using and abusing males is suggested at certain points in local-goddess festivals. The goddesses still need males to invigorate them, but they ensure that the males will not dominate them or threaten their powers. At the end of the festival, in fact, it is not uncommon for the male to be symbolically destroyed, humiliated, or cast out of the village.

Another kind of mythical theme that emphasizes the village goddesses' independence appears in the stories concerning Kaṉṉiyākumari. Kaṉṉiyākumari is prohibited from marrying Śiva for various reasons. Although she is described as distressed at being prevented from enjoying Śiva as her husband, the myths underline Kaṉṉiyākumari's perpetual virginity and her formidable power. Her great power seems to be directly related to her unmarried state and her celibacy. In the context of Tamil culture a woman's virginity, through which she withholds her sexual energy, is more or less equivalent to the building up of *tapas* in males when they retain their semen, which is magically transformed into powerful heat.[21] Quite simply, Kaṉṉiyākumari is much more powerful as an unmarried maiden than she would be as a married woman. Although reluctantly unmarried, her independence from males gives her great power.

The great power possessed by goddesses and females who are independent of males is also a theme in many myths current in South India in which female deities are subjugated or tamed by gods. Probably the two best-known examples of this theme feature Mīnākṣī, the goddess enshrined in Madurai, and the fiercely wild goddess Kālī. In the mythology concerning Mīnākṣī the goddess is born with three breasts. Her disconcerted parents are instructed to raise the child like a male. She is brought up like a boy and ascends her father's throne when he dies. She then undertakes a campaign to subdue the entire world. She and her armies are invincible in battle until she comes to Mount Kailasa and challenges Śiva himself. Seeing Śiva, Mīnākṣī's entire character is transformed. She becomes shy, and "as soon as she caught sight of him, her third breast disappeared, and, overcome with modesty, innocence, and shyness, she began to scrape the ground shyly with her toe."[22] And so Śiva reduces the powerful battle queen to a shy maiden and eventually subservient wife.

Kālī is subdued in a dance contest. In her independent form she is described as powerful, destructive, bloodthirsty, and fearsome. When she disrupts the meditation of one of Śiva's devotees or otherwise attracts Śiva's attention, he challenges her to a contest in which he tames her by defeating her in dance. Thereafter she is said to be his wife or to take on a benign form that becomes widely worshiped. In effect, she loses her power and becomes a weak, helpless female. "Kālī acknowledged defeat; shyly . . . she worshiped the lord; she stood helplessly like a puppet, confused."[23]

It has been argued that goddesses in Hindu mythology are generally portrayed as dangerous, violent, and aggressive if they are unmarried and as docile, obedient, and calm if they are married.[24] This reinforces social norms by suggesting that it is necessary for women to marry and express their sexuality in "safe" ways and under male supervision and authority. In the human realm marriage is assumed not only to complete a woman but to tame her, channeling her dangerous sexual energy in acceptable ways. The god or the male is seen as a civilizing, calming, ordering presence. Alone, goddesses and women are perceived as powerful and dangerous.

The myths and cults of village goddesses, however, often cast males in disruptive roles and equate the village goddess with the civilized, orderly, and refined realm of the village. Outside the village is the jungle: wild, raw, and chaotic. The village goddess represents the order of the cultivated field and the security of hearth and home. She is preeminently the being who protects the village from attacks by wild, unstable, demonic spirits from the uncivilized outer world. Those demons, furthermore, are often said to be male, and Śiva himself, the deity of the Sanskrit pantheon most commonly associated with village goddesses as a consort, is well known to live on the periphery of civilization, to associate with demons, and in general to have disruptive, antisocial habits. The pattern of associating a goddess with the village, order, and civilization, on the one hand, and her male consort or counterpart with the jungle, on the other hand, is quite common in the central provinces. "The chief deity of the central provinces is Dhārni Deotā, 'earth, the deity'; her husband and companion, Bhātarsi Deotā, is a god of the hunt, related to Śiva, the archer, lord of the wild beasts and the jungle."[25]

While goddesses from the larger tradition are often assumed to be dangerous and wild when unmarried or independent from male deities, a central theme in the village-goddess cults is the association of independent female deities with the stability and order of the village. The village goddesses usually avoid both the extreme of the docile, shy, obedient married female and the extreme of the wild, frenzied, dangerous Kālī who is a threat to civilized order. The combination of the village goddesses' power and fierceness with their protectiveness of the well-being, stability, and order of their villages is beneficial. As the protector of the village the goddess *must* be powerful in view of the dangerous forces that threaten it. No shy, retiring, docile female could successfully protect the village. Although the village goddess may be dangerous because of her great power, for the most part that strength is directed against threatening forces from outside.

FESTIVALS

Although the village goddesses are typically characterized as protecting, ordering, and instituting village civilization, they also have a reputation for behaving in disruptive, violent, and dangerous ways, particularly during festivals held in their honor. This is particularly clear during festivals in honor of village goddesses during epidemics. Many village goddesses are specifically associated with diseases, and during epidemics they may play several apparently contradictory roles. They may defend the village from the disease, which may be identified with invading demons. They may be identified with the disease itself. Or they may be cast in the dual role of inflicter of the disease and protector from the disease. In whichever role, village goddesses during these festivals reveal an awesome, disruptive, violent aspect. Like the disease itself, the village goddess seems to erupt on the scene, to wake up from a state of quiescence to a state of frenzied activity. During an epidemic, or during her festival, which often coincides with an epidemic, the village goddess forces herself on the awareness of the villagers.[26]

The goddess's presence is as immediate, as real, and as disruptive and threatening as the disease that attacks the village. In fact, the two usually are inextricably related. In the case of Śītalā, the North Indian goddess associated with smallpox, the disease is said to be her "grace." Except in times of smallpox epidemics, Śītalā is quiet, withdrawn, perhaps beyond human ken.[27] Traditionally, village-goddess festivals were not undertaken regularly or routinely, although this seems to be the increasing pattern in some places today. Festivals were only held and the goddesses were only worshiped when some disaster, usually an epidemic, struck the village. Such disasters are taken to represent either the presence of demons in the village because the goddess's defenses have broken down or the anger of the awakened goddess, who is demanding worship by punishing her people for neglecting her for so long.[28] From either point of view, or from both points of view simultaneously, during the festival the village is overcome with the immediate presence of the goddess. At this time she makes herself unmistakably known, particularly in the fever of disease victims and in those she possesses.

The theme of the relationship of an epidemic or a disaster to the invasion of the village by hostile demons from outside echoes the mythic theme of the goddess's abuse by males. In the festival context the goddess confronts and overcomes the demons, and in this struggle she is helped by the villagers. While the villagers are struck down and overcome by the demons and suffer fever and sometimes death, the goddess too is said to become possessed, afflicted, or somehow invaded by the demons. Both she (in the form of her image) and the villagers afflicted by the epidemic are cooled with water and other substances, and in cooling one victim it is understood that the other is treated as well. It is as if the two are suffering the invasion of the village together. It is not necessarily a contradiction of this point of view to say that the goddess also causes the epidemic. She receives the main brunt of the onslaught, but she is unable, or unwilling, to contain it all and spreads it to the villagers, who help her deal with it. It is well known that the goddess in this situation is particularly partial to the victims of disease, perhaps because they help her bear the burden of the demonic attack.[29]

Perhaps the central dramatic event of village-goddess festivals is a blood sacrifice. This sacrifice also may be understood from two points of view. The sacrifice may be seen as a gift from the villagers with which they hope to appease the goddess so that she will withdraw her anger, which expresses itself in the form of the heat of disease. Or the sacrifice may be understood as representing the defeat of the invading demon or demons, who are also associated with the goddess's consort/husband who had afflicted or abused her in the myths. In either case, it is clear that the goddess demands the blood of a victim, that she needs that blood, either to appease her wrath or to invigorate her in her contest with the demons.

The elaborate, ritualistic way in which the sacrificial victim is treated during the sacrifice suggests his humiliation by the goddess. This in turn suggests that the victim is the goddess's enemy and thus represents an invading demon or her offending husband/consort. Traditionally, a buffalo was offered to the goddess. After it was beheaded, its leg was thrust into its mouth, fat from its stomach was smeared over its eyes, and a candle was lit on its head and then presented to the goddess. The humiliation of the victim is fairly clear here[30] and certainly suggests the defeat of an enemy, presumably the demon who caused the disaster or epidemic.

Although the themes of conflict, struggle, defeat, and death are obviously prominent in these goddess festivals, there is also the theme of the goddess's being awakened, aroused, and stimulated. Indeed, there is the suggestion that she may even have sexual intercourse with the demon or demons who invade her village.[31] A likely implication is that the goddess periodically needs this encounter with a demon/husband/consort to invigorate and enliven her. The festival also has an invigorating, enlivening effect on the village and its occupants. To a great extent, the villagers identify themselves with the goddess in her encounter with the invading demons. Like her and with her, they are aroused, invaded, and assaulted by these "outside" forces that disrupt the calm and order of their world.

During the festival the village as a whole, or at least those who are participating most actively in the worship, appear to abandon the quiet, orderly habits of everyday life. There is a stirring up of everything, a mixing up of things.[32] There is often a mixture of castes, demons are present in the village, blood is spilled in sacrificial offerings, people are awakened, aroused by both the epidemic and the festival it has occasioned. Reversal of roles often takes place, or at least social roles and rules are temporarily held in abeyance.[33] The village is awakened to the presence of sacred power, to the affirmation that a sacred power underlies and pervades the village. Morbidity is overcome, and the village organism is reactivated and reenlivened by the immediate presence of the goddess.[34]

The village-goddess festival is often the time of undertaking heroic vows, which greatly heighten the aroused state of the village. Fire walking, carrying burning pots on one's head, and swinging while suspended on hooks through one's flesh are all common during these festivals and are associated with trance and possession. These ordeals invite the presence of the goddess by expressing the devotee's willingness to fully encounter the dangerous power of the goddess, who is aroused, hot, and fierce. While there is considerable risk involved in so encountering the goddess, it is understood that the ordeal is undertaken in gratitude for her blessing in the past or her mercy in the present and that she is particularly fond of those who so approach her and will usually see that no harm will come to them. In return for villagers' taking on a part of her excess fury or heat generated by contact with demons, the goddess blesses her devotees by protecting them during their ordeal.[35] Together, as it were, the goddess and her devotees take on the dangerous but invigorating presence of the epidemic or disaster.

A striking illustration of the enlivening effects of the festival on the goddess and the village is the role played in many festivals in the South by a low-caste woman called a Mātaṅgī. The Mātaṅgīs are unmarried and hold their office for life. During a festival for the village goddess the Mātaṅgī represents the goddess. Possessed by the goddess, she will dance wildly, use obscene language, drink intoxicants, spit on spectators, and push people around with her backside. She seems to take special delight in abusing members of the high castes.

> As she rushes about spitting on those who under ordinary circumstances would almost choose death rather than to suffer such pollution from a Madiga [the low caste from which the woman comes], she breaks into wild, exulting songs, telling of the humiliation to which she is subjecting the proud caste people. She also abuses them all thoroughly, and . . . they appear to expect it and not to be satisfied without a full measure of her invective.[36]

An inversion of the usual social codes and rules takes place here.[37] The Mātaṅgī personifies social topsy-turvy. Completely unrefined, bursting with raw energy and coarse humor, and intoxicated on country liquor, she is the goddess herself: ". . . willful, impetuous, violent, irrepressible, she exults in her own aliveness and the tumult she arouses."[38]

As Victor Turner has argued, religious festivals often serve the important purpose of allowing a society, culture, or village to step out of the confines of normality so that other, often redemptive, possibilities may be glimpsed or briefly experienced or experimented with. Festivals provide a window to what Turner calls the liminal dimension of reality, the dimension that remains outside social norms and expectations but that is capable of enlivening and nourishing the realm of social order and normality.[39] Festivals provide a context for the breaking out of confining social roles, for the breaking up and mixing up of expected social relations. The Mātaṅgī dramatically acts out this liminal facet of the village-goddess festival and makes it clear that it is the goddess herself who incites and arouses her devotees to this invigorating frenzy. Having been aroused herself by the encounter with a demon/husband/consort, she in turn arouses the entire village, and together they are renewed and renourished.[40] Villagers say that in the topsy-turvy context of the festival, where reversals are dominant, the outrageous behavior of the

Mātaṅgī, ordinarily highly polluting, is purifying. Instead of avoiding her spittle and insults, people go out of their way to be subjected to her abuse.[41]

DEATH, DISEASE, AND AMBIVALENCE

The close association of village, local, and regional goddesses with disease, epidemic, disaster, and sudden death deserves further comment. Because the village goddesses institute, nourish, and protect villages, it would make sense to interpret their myth, cult, and worship as primarily revolving around their periodic struggles with invading demons who bring sickness, death, and disruption to the villages. Yet given the overwhelming association of these goddesses with the diseases themselves, given the common identification of epidemics with the goddesses' "grace," it would make sense to interpret their worship as primarily the attempt to propitiate them so that they will withhold their wrath from their people. Unfortunately, neither point of view alone does justice to the facts, namely, that the goddesses are cast in two contrasting roles: (1) guardians of the village and (2) the cause and source of disease and sudden death that threaten the existence of the village. Richard Brubaker sums up the ambivalent nature of the village goddesses this way:

> Thus the goddess is the one who manifests herself in epidemic disease, who guards against it and keeps it at bay, who inflicts it upon her people in wrath, who joins her people in fighting and conquering it, who suffers it herself; she it is who invites its appearance and then struggles against it; she enters people's bodies by means of it, but sometimes heals them by taking it upon herself; she uses it as a means to enhance her own worship; she is enflamed by its heat and needs to be cooled, and may be cooled by the fanning of disease-heated humans, while the latter may also be cooled by pouring water on her image; she is both the scourge and the mistress of disease demons, and perhaps even their mistress in both senses of the term; she mercilessly chastizes her people with the disease, but holds its victims especially dear; she delights in the disease, is aroused by it, goes mad with it; she kills with it and uses it to give new life.[42]

The ultimate mystery and potency of these village/disease goddesses may well lie precisely in the fact that their ambivalent natures are not capable of being comprehended rationally. That the patron deity of a village who is its founder and protector should also assault that village with devastating epidemics seems to suggest a depth of irrationality beyond logical analysis. Nonetheless, some scholars such as Victor Turner have argued that the ongoing well-being of a society and culture depends on its being able to participate periodically in chaos, disorder, and tumult. Religious ritual and festival are the traditional means by which this is done.[43] Another scholar puts the case in similar terms: "The festival rite utilizes the potency of disorder. It harnesses the disorder of the 'other mind,' possession, trance, dreams, ecstasy . . . ; if these powers are harnessed properly, the society recovers a special potency from chaos beyond the limits of order."[44]

Speaking of shamanic initiation, another scholar applies this logic to the individual level:

> Thus the shaman's initiatory experience is represented as an involuntary surrender to disorder, as he is thrust protesting into the chaos which the ordered and controlled life of society strives so hard to deny, or at least to keep at bay. No matter how valiantly he struggles, disorder eventually claims him and marks him with the brand of a transcendental encounter. At its worst, in peripheral cults, this is seen as a baneful intrusion of malign power. At its best, in central possession religions it represents a danger-laden exposure to the powers of the cosmos. In both cases the initial experience withdraws the victim from the secure world of society and of ordered existence, and exposes him directly to those forces which, though they may be held to uphold the social order, also ultimately threaten it.
>
> . . . The shaman is not the slave, but the master of anomaly and chaos. . . . Out of the agony of affliction and the dark night of the soul comes literally the ecstasy of spiritual victory. In rising to the challenge of the powers which rule his life and by valiantly overcoming them in this crucial initiatory rite which reimposes order on chaos and despair, man reasserts his mastery of the universe and affirms his control of destiny and fate.[45]

Village goddesses, in their association with disease, sudden death, and other realities that threaten the stability or even the existence of the village system, might be understood as instigating society's confrontation with the chaotic, demonic, disruptive dimensions of life, particularly in the context of festivals, when the village goddesses are fully aroused. From this confrontation a new, more vigorous, more durable order might be won. The very ambivalence of these goddesses heightens their effectiveness in this role. They, like the diseases so often associated with

Manasā, goddess of snakes. A painted pottery image. Contemporary, Bengal. Sudhansu Kumar Ray, *The Ritual Art of the Bratas of Bengal* (Calcutta: Firma K. L. Mukhoipadhyay, 1961), plate xiv.

them, are unpredictable in their moods. They erupt onto the scene suddenly, always powerfully and undeniably, and usually dangerously. Manasā, the North Indian goddess associated with snakes,[46] strikes suddenly and usually fatally and in so doing violently introduces terrifying chaos into the lives of those who are affected. Suddenly, unmistakably, the fragility of existence is underlined, and the normality of ordered, civilized village life is called into question. Similarly, Śītalā and Māriyamman, both of whom are associated with smallpox, remind people that their tightly ordered worlds may be reduced to chaos at any moment. To pay attention to such goddesses, however, is to make one's view of reality less fragile, less prone to being shattered by sudden death.[47]

The Bengali goddess Śītalā's presence in the form of smallpox[48] is referred to as her "grace" or play. Edward Dimock suggests that this grace might be understood as her ability to permit people a wider vision of reality. Normal human consciousness tends to impose a diachronic scheme on events whereby a limited, controlled, sequential angle of vision dominates the individual's perception of reality. Sickness, death, disease, and suffering generally seem to come and go, according to this way of viewing things. There are good times, and there are bad times, and the bad times are for the most part forgotten or repressed. A synchronic view of reality, however, in which past, present, and future are collapsed, in which sequential time is seen to be a mere construct, superimposes the whole range of human events—blessings, tragedies, good times, and bad times—on one another so that they may be viewed simultaneously. In this view the bad times are always with us. Disease, death, and disaster are endemic in good times, and vice versa. The goddess Śītalā, in her periodic visitations in which the bad times become epidemic, reminds people that only a synchronic vision of life comes close to reality.[49] "By hearing of suffering, by realising the extent of human frailty, one with the eyes to see may be spared the necessity of more particular pain. Śītalā allows us cognition of our position in the universe. . . . Her grace is that she allows us restitution in return for the understanding of her constant presence."[50] To worship Śītalā, to pay attention to what she represents, is to provide oneself with a more realistic, less fragile view of life, which in turn makes the inevitable outbursts of disease or tragic occurrences less devastating.

APPENDIX

THE INDUS VALLEY CIVILIZATION

The historian of Hindu religion must resist two temptations when faced with interpreting the data of the Indus Valley civilization. The first temptation is to say very little. The second temptation, the one that most scholars have chosen, is to say too much. The proper approach to the materials, I think, is to try to interpret them in their own context and not to seek interpretive keys from other cultures, such as those of the ancient Near East or the subsequent Indian tradition, unless overwhelming parallels can be demonstrated.

In reflecting on the history of goddess worship in the Hindu tradition, one has to acknowledge that the impressive data available in the Indus Valley civilization and in neighboring Baluchistan cultures may bear on such a history. While it is speculation to call these cultures Hindu, the presence of such evidence of goddess worship in the Indian subcontinent at such an early period surely deserves some comment. It also deserves comment because other scholars, a bit uncritically, I think, have traced the source of goddess worship in the Hindu tradition to the Indus Valley civilization.

What is the evidence, and what are we to make of it? We have evidence of three peasant cultures, centered in villages west of the Indus Valley in Baluchistan, which probably predate the Indus Valley culture itself. Two of these cultures, the Zhob Valley and the Kulli cultures, dating back to the third millennium B.C.E., have yielded female figurines. The Kulli figurines, which are earlier than the Zhob, are only shown from the waist up. They are heavily adorned with jewelry, and their heads and faces are pinched and somewhat resemble a hen's head. The faces are not clearly depicted, and the figurines thus have a somewhat anonymous look to them. Unlike the Indus Valley figures, their hair is not elaborate, and their breasts are not accented or exaggerated. The female figurines from the Zhob Valley in northern Baluchistan are also only shown from the waist up. They do not wear as much jewelry as the Kulli figures, but their hair is more elaborately depicted and arranged. The most dramatic feature of the Zhob figures is the face. The faces all have large eyes that are hollow or bulbous, slit mouths, and fairly prominent noses. The breasts of the Zhob figures, though more clearly emphasized than those of the Kulli figurines, are not exaggerated either.[1]

Although there are similarities between these figures and the figurines from the Indus Valley civilization (for example, the emphasis on jewelry and the elaborate coiffures of the Zhob specimens), the peasant-culture figures are distinctively different from the Indus Valley examples and should be discussed in their own right. While cultural contact between these cultures and the Indus Valley culture is quite likely, it cannot be shown to have been overwhelming, and the figurines of the peasant cultures may have meant something quite different from what the figurines in the city culture of the plains meant. Because of the dissimilarities in appearance, then, I will treat the Kulli and Zhob figurines independently from the remains of the greater culture of the plains.

Little, indeed, can be said about what these female figures might have represented. It is even something of a conjecture to suggest that they were images of goddesses. The flat bases might imply that the figures were meant to be set up, perhaps for worship. The nudity of the figures calls attention to their female physiology, but this physiology is not unduly accented. If these figures did represent goddesses, it is difficult to say what these goddesses might have been like and what functions they fulfilled or what truths they revealed on the basis of their sex. The elaborate jewelry might suggest that they were adored with gifts; it also might imply high rank or simply suggest the usual costume of the peasant women. It is impossible to say. The unusual faces, although striking, also present us with no clear indication of who these figures might have been. On the one hand, the anonymity might call our attention to the sex of the figures rather than to their "personalities." On the other hand, the faces might simply be the result of crude craftmanship or artistic stylization. Most interpreters of the Zhob Valley figurines have said that the faces portray negative qualities. One of the heads somewhat resembles a skull. One scholar, for example, says the type of figurine found in the Zhob Valley "is clearly intended to inspire horror and can hardly fail to remind us of the terrible and loathly images of the malignant Kali of which these figurines may be taken to be an early prototype."[2]

While I agree that the faces perhaps have grotesque overtones, I am not sure that they were intended to inspire horror or any other negative emotion. Again, the large eyes and small mouths simply may have been stylized and may have had no malign significance for the artists. In any case, I consider it unjustified to conclude that we have here a prototype of the Hindu goddess Kālī. None of the Zhob figurines has any particular similarities to images of Kālī, and no association with burial or cremation has been established by scholars seeking to interpret these early figures. If these Zhob "goddesses" were clearly associated with funeral ceremonies or burial or cremation grounds, then perhaps one might postulate an association with the much later goddess Kālī. But even then it would be a weak association insofar as Kālī's function and meaning are not nearly exhausted in terms of her role as mistress of the cremation ground.

I am forced to yield to the first temptation mentioned above and say next to nothing about what these figurines might imply in relation to the later Hindu tradition. All one can justifiably conclude is that there is evidence of goddess figurines in two peasant cultures in the hills of Baluchistan in the second or perhaps late third millennium B.C.E. Insofar as male figures are lacking, one might go further and suggest that if these figurines represent goddesses, their religion, whatever it might have been, was more open to the divine or the sacred as revealed through women than through men and that this might have had something to do with the fertility of the crops. Again, the figurines do not seem to accentuate or exaggerate feminine physiology or the biologically creative role of females.

In moving from the Zhob Valley and Kulli cultures to the Indus Valley civilization we move from the mountains to the plains, from highly localized peasant cultures situated in small villages to an extensive, highly organized culture that was centralized in two large cities. The data relevant to goddess worship are also more extensive and complex when we turn to the culture of the plains.

Hundreds of female figurines have been found in the Indus Valley civilization. The very number of figurines has prompted one scholar to proclaim that there must have been a female figurine in every household.[3] The figurines themselves vary quite widely. Most are made quite crudely and are of terra-cotta. Others, notably the famous "dancing girl," are skillfully crafted and made of bronze.[4] A few male figures have been found, but in comparison to the female figurines their numbers are fairly insignificant (although several of them are striking and among the most dramatic figures found).[5] Some of the figures are virtually indistinguishable according to sex, whereas others appear to be androgynous, having breasts and what appear to be male genitals.[6]

Generally, the female figurines are not like the so-called Venus figurines that have been found in prehistoric Europe.[7] Very few of the Indus Valley statues accentuate the breasts, hips, or genital areas. Although there are some examples of this type,[8] most of the Indus Valley figures are on the slim side, often small breasted or sharp breasted. Many of the figures are of almost boyish build.[9] A few of the figurines have very narrow waists, sharp breasts, and flared hips reminiscent of the way in which female figures are often portrayed in later Hinduism.[10] A striking characteristic of most of the figurines is the well-articulated head. The coiffures of the figurines are usually highly elaborate.[11] Head ornaments, or even horns, might be shown instead of or in addition to hair. In most cases one's attention is drawn to the figure's head because of these characteristics.[12] This stands in sharp contrast to the Venus type of figure, in which the head is usually tiny and nondescript, the viewer's attention being struck by the breasts, rump, and thighs. A few of the Indus Valley images do seem to assume poses that expose the genitals,[13] but this is not typical, and none of these figures is a particularly good example of the splayed-thighs posture that clearly attracts attention to the female womb or genital area.[14] Finally, none of the figurines can positively be said to be pregnant.

Another feature of most of the figurines is the crudeness with which they were made. The faces seem to have been stuck together in a hurry (the features often being represented by lumps of clay stuck onto the face). In contrast to this is the figures' elaborate decoration with jewelry. Rarely is a figure shown with much clothing, although many of the figures wear a girdle.[15] Finally, a few of the figures seem to have horns.[16]

There are a few additional female figures on small clay seals, most of whom are more dramatically suggestive than the figurines themselves. One tableau shows what appears to be a nude figure, probably a woman, but it is not entirely clear, with her legs spread and a tree emerging from her womb. The reverse of the seal shows a female figure seated or kneeling with a male figure standing beside her with what looks like a sickle.[17] Another seal shows a "goddess" emerging from or standing in a bush or tree with a kneeling figure beside it and an animal facing her.[18] A third scene depicts a nude female figure with an animal head (or mask) and perhaps animal feet (hooves) who leans over a rearing animal, a horned tiger perhaps. Her hand is placed on (or perhaps stabs) his shoulder, and a tree stands to the side of the animal-headed female figure.[19] A fourth scene shows a clothed figure, whose sex is difficult to determine, standing between two animals with which he or she seems to be holding hands.[20]

To complete our survey of the data that seem most relevant to possible goddess worship or exaltation of the feminine in the Indus Valley culture, mention should be made of several small circular stone objects or discs with holes in the center. Some commentators have concluded that in conjunction with other objects that have been interpreted as phalluses the circular, pierced discs are meant to represent the vagina and that what we have in the Indus Valley civilization is an example of a religion that emphasized the sacred power of human sexuality. These objects are held to be prototypes of the yoni and liṅga of later Hinduism.[21]

The majority of scholars who have sought to interpret this data have concluded that goddesses of one sort or another were a central part of the religion of the Indus Valley civilization. The evidence does seem to point to this conclusion. The nature of the goddesses worshiped, however, and the truths these beings have revealed are much more difficult questions. Some scholars have concluded that the Indus Valley culture was dominated by a cult of the Great Mother similar to cults in Asia Minor and the Mediterranean.[22] Some scholars have also hypothesized that the religion of the Indus Valley culture represents an early form of Śāktism or an early form of the kind of goddess worship we find in medieval Hinduism.[23] Both of these conclusions are tempting. To exegete the relatively mute evidence of the Indus Valley on the basis of materials from other cultures is attractive because the Indus script has not yet been deciphered and therefore we have no textual descriptions or myths concerning the figurines discovered there. To suggest that the Indus Valley figurines are prototypes of later Hindu goddesses is also tempting insofar as it helps explain what appears to be a drastic change in emphasis in the history of the Hindu tradition, a change, that is, from the Vedic tradition, which is dominated by male deities, to a mythology in which goddesses become far more common and dominant. It seems logical to suppose that the emphasis on the feminine in later Hinduism is a survival or persistence of an indigenous, non-Āryan religiosity that has finally "surfaced" in the Hindu tradition.

What are the facts that enable us to resort to either of these solutions in interpreting the Indus Valley data? It is true that there was trade between the Indus Valley and the ancient Near East,[24] and it is also true that in both the Indus Valley and the ancient Near East we have roughly contemporary city cultures located on rivers. There is little evidence, however, that the Indus Valley civilization was culturally dependent on ancient Near Eastern cultures or vice versa. Specifically, in the cultures of the ancient Near East which were roughly contemporary with the Indus Valley culture there seem to be no clear examples of figurines or scenes that suggest similarities to the Indus Valley data. The only striking examples, which are extremely few, are found in historically later cultures of the ancient Near East. Quite simply, one is struck by the dissimilarities in appearance between the feminine images of the Indus Valley and the feminine images in the ancient Near East. The evidence of cultural dependence is not overwhelming. This does not mean that the Indus Valley "goddess cults" might not have been very similar to those of the ancient Near East. The differences in appearance between the figurines in the two areas may be merely artistic and stylistic. If one does presume cultural dependence, however, one does so on the basis of no clear evidence to that effect.

Turning to the goddess cults in later Hinduism for possible interpretive direction, we are in a similar dilemma. There are similarities between the Indus Valley data and the Hindu goddess cults, but these similarities, it seems to me, are more superficial than essential or may suggest only superficial continuities rather than essential continuities. It seems typical of both Indus Valley iconography and medieval Hindu iconography to emphasize elaborate adornment when portraying goddesses. In both cases, too, there is a tendency to portray goddesses with elaborate coiffures or lavishly adorned hair. There are also a few examples of images in the Indus Valley which are reminiscent of the slim-waisted, large-breasted images of goddesses in later Hinduism. Beyond these similarities in appearance, which are not overwhelming, there is really nothing else to suggest continuity between the Indus Valley images and later Hindu goddess cults. Marshall's interpretation of circular stones with holes in the middle as proto-yonis and of other oblong objects as proto-liṅgas is highly speculative. To my knowledge, the two types of objects have not been found conjoined, which would suggest a liṅga set in a yoni, the central image in most Śiva temples. The dramatic scenes depicted on seals mentioned above do not help us much either. None of the scenes reminds us in any striking way of later Hindu myths that feature goddesses, nor do they suggest central themes in later Hindu goddess cults.

Finally, other evidence not bearing directly on goddesses from the Indus Valley does not allow us to presume any essential continuity with later Hinduism. While some scholars have been impressed with the so-called proto-Śiva[25] and the highly ordered and probably hierarchical social system of the Indus Valley culture as being similar to aspects of later Hinduism, these similarities are not sufficient to allow us to presume an essential continuity between a highly developed city civilization with a strong centralized authority and later Hinduism, which is clearly village centered, lacks a strong central authority, and has a literary tradition greatly influenced by Āryan religion.[26] The evidence for continuity is not so overwhelming that we can read back into the Indus Valley religion elaborate metaphysical truths and complex mythologies that emerge in later Hinduism a thousand years or more after the collapse of the Indus Valley civilization. Clearly, the proper procedure to follow in interpreting the Indus Valley culture is to isolate the evidence and seek to discern meanings on the basis of the evidence itself without reference to contemporary foreign cultures or to a complex religion that postdates the Indus Valley civilization by a millennium.

Data relevant to goddess worship in the Indus Valley civilization show that very few images clearly accentuate feminine physiology. The majority of images stand in sharp contrast to the Venus type of image, in which the breasts, hips, rump, and genital area are exaggerated. In the Indus Valley images the focus of attention is directed not to their bodies but to their heads, which are unusually well formed and accentuated by elaborate coiffures or headdresses. Many of the figurines thus give the impression of being top heavy. Insofar as this is the case, it seems likely that whatever truths these images sought to convey had less to do with feminine physiology than with feminine psychology. Unless we limit our commentary to a few figures (clearly in the minority) that approximate the Venus type, we are not justified in speaking of a religion or a vision of reality that exalted the productive, nourishing, creative roles of the feminine. While these aspects are suggested in some images, these emphases cannot be said to be dominant themes on the basis of the data alone, which in general appear to deemphasize those features of feminine physiology that emphasize fertility and nourishment. Among the hundreds of figurines and in the few scenes depicted on seals there are hardly any examples of pregnant women, figures giving birth, figures displaying their genital organs, or figures suckling children.

The most promising data for purposes of interpretation are the female figures portrayed on the seals. Several general ideas seem to be conveyed here. The seal depicting a tree issuing from the womb of a nude woman may emphasize the relation between vegetative life and some (probably) divine feminine being.[27] It seems, on the basis of this figure, that this ancient culture knew a goddess who was associated with or manifested herself through vegetation, or perhaps was identified with the sap and vigor of plants or perhaps life in general, insofar as the tree issuing from her womb might be a symbol of all life. The reverse of the seal, showing a kneeling or seated female figure with a male figure standing over her holding a sickle, might suggest both an association of this female being with the crops (the sickle being an agricultural tool) and a ritual sacrifice of some sort.[28] If a sacrifice, or a sacrificial victim, is depicted here, we might hypothesize that a blood offering was made to a goddess to reinvigorate her productive energy, thus ensuring abundant and continued crops. But no sacrifice at all may be implied. The kneeling female figure may simply be receiving a blessing from or showing obeisance to a male deity associated with the harvest. In any case, the combination of these two very suggestive scenes on the same seal (implying some clear relation) does lead us to conclude that a female being or goddess was known who gave birth to vegetation and had some association with crops. Insofar as the Indus Valley civilization was economically grounded in agriculture, this is not at all surprising. What is surprising is that there is so little further evidence of such a goddess.

Another seal stresses the association of a female being with vegetation. This seal shows a naked female figure standing in or emerging from a bush.[29] That this being is a goddess seems likely because a row of kneeling figures is pictured beneath her, apparently adoring or worshiping her. What is odd about this scene is that an animal faces her, and apparently not a domestic animal but a wild animal. That seal in conjunction with the third seal portraying a dramatic scene featuring a female figure leads us to hypothesize another type of goddess, or female being, who is not so much associated with the fertility of the crops as with wild animals and vegetative life in general. This third seal shows a masked or animal-headed naked female apparently slaying (or leaning on) a horned tiger.[30] A tree also appears on the right of the seal. While this scene may depict a goddess defeating a demon in combat, what is more clearly suggested is some type of mistress of animals, a being who rules over the various animal species and is responsible both for the well-being of those species and for making them available for the welfare of human beings in the hunt. This type of figure admittedly seems to have very little place in an agriculturally based culture in which the economy must have been only peripherally associated with hunting. Nevertheless, the frequency with which wild animals are shown in the Indus Valley data is remarkable and forces one to use caution before concluding that the religion of the Indus Valley culture revolved around agriculture, the fertility of the crops, and ritual blood sacrifices aimed at ensuring the continued vitality of the crops.

In conclusion, then, what can be said about the meaning and importance of goddess worship in the Indus Valley civilization? First, we can surmise simply on the basis of the great number of female images found that goddesses were known and probably widely worshiped or exalted in this culture. Second, primarily on the basis of three scenes depicted on seals, we can surmise that a goddess was known who was associated with vegetation and most likely with the fertility of the crops. Also on the basis of the three seals and the frequency with which wild animals were shown, we can conclude that a female being was also known who had some connection with animals, perhaps the fertility of animals. If these two types of goddesses were in fact the same goddess, we might further conclude that a goddess was known who presided over all life, plant and animal, and was adored for her life-giving and life-sustaining powers. Whether such a being was also associated with or dependent on a male consort, was the recipient of ritual sacrifice, was mistress of the dead, or was fierce or benign in nature are almost impossible questions to answer.

If the majority of figurines are in fact additional representations of this being, then we might say that she was generally benign in character, for hardly any of the figurines successfully convey frightening aspects. We might say further, if the majority of the figurines are related to the scenes depicted on the seals, that this being was extraordinarily popular, not simply goddess of the elite. It seems likely from the very number of the figurines found that almost every household had such a figure.

There is one drawback to relating the vast number of terra-cotta figures to the female beings shown on the seals, however, and that is that the figures shown on the seals are not dressed like the majority of figurines. The ones on the seals are nude and do not wear elaborate jewelry or have elaborate coiffures. Insofar as the seals must aim at economy of line, however, as they are quite small, these details may simply have been left out. It is also the case, though, that none of the terra-cotta figurines has an animal head or is masked like the figure "slaying" the horned tiger. In conclusion, it is not clear that the terra-cotta figurines were representations of the female figures on the seals, so any conclusions that depend on this association must be tentative.

NOTES

INTRODUCTION

1. For example, Narendra Nath Bhattacharyya, *History of the Śākta Religion* (New Delhi: Munshiram Manoharlal Publishers, 1974), and *Indian Mother Goddess* (Calcutta: Indian Studies Past and Present, 1971); Sadanand K. Dikshit, *The Mother Goddess* (New Delhi: Published by the author, 1957); Pushpendra Kumar, *Śakti Cult in Ancient India* (Banaras: Bhartiya Publishing House, 1974); Ernest Alexander Payne, *The Śāktas* (Calcutta: YMCA Publishing House, 1933); and M. C. P. Srivastava, *Mother Goddess in Indian Art, Archaeology and Literature* (Delhi: Agam Kala Prakashan, 1979).

2. For example, Raghunath Airi, *Concept of Sarasvatī (in Vedic Literature)* (Delhi: Munshiram Manoharlal Publishers, 1977; Upendra Nath Dhal, *Goddess Laksmi: Origin and Development* (New Delhi: Oriental Publishers, 1978); Mohammad Israil Khan, *Sarasvati in Sanskrit Literature* (Ghaziabad: Crescent Publishing House, 1978); Bandana Saraswati, "The History of the Worship of Śrī in North India to cir. A.D. 550" (Ph.D. diss., University of London, 1971); C. Sivaramamurti, *Gaṅgā* (New Delhi: Orient Longman, 1976); Jagdish Narain Tiwari, "Studies in Goddess Cults in Northern India, with Reference to the First Seven Centuries A.D." (Ph.D. diss., Australian National University, n.d.).

3. For example, Rita Gross, "Hindu Female Deities as a Resource for the Contemporary Rediscovery of the Goddess," *Journal of the American Academy of Religion* 46, no. 3 (September 1978): 269–292.

4. David Kinsley, *The Sword and the Flute—Kṛṣṇa and Kālī* (Berkeley, Los Angeles, London: University of California Press, 1975).

5. See my chapter 9, "The Mahādevī."

1: GODDESSES IN VEDIC LITERATURE

1. Sometimes the idea of *śruti* is narrowed to mean primarily the *Upaniṣads*. The idea of *śruti* often also includes the *Bhāgavad-gītā*, which is much later than most Vedic literature.

2. For example, Sukumari Bhattacharji, *The Indian Theogony* (Cambridge: Cambridge University Press, 1970), pp. 160–161; Stella Kramrisch, "The Indian Great Goddess," *History of Religions* 14, no. 4 (May 1975): 235–265.

3. For example, *Śatapatha-brāhmaṇa* 2.2.1.19; 3.2.3.6, 19; 4.5.1.2; *Aitareya-brāhmaṇa* 1.8.

4. For example, *Śatapatha-brāhmaṇa* 14.2.1.12; *Aitareya-brāmaṇa* 6.7; *Kauṣitaki-brāhmaṇa* 5.1; 10.6; 12.2, 8; 14.5.

5. *Śatapatha-brāhmaṇa* 3.2.1.18–3.2.3.30.

6. Ibid. 5.5.5.12.

7. Ibid. 4.6.7.1–3.

8. Ibid. 4.6.9.16.

9. Ibid. 6.1.2.5–11.

10. Ibid. 10.5.3.4–12.

11. *Taittirīya-brāhmaṇa* 1.6.1.4.

12. *Atharva-veda* 5.7.9.

13. *Śatapatha-brāhmaṇa* 5.2.3.3.

14. Ibid. 9.1.2.9.

15. *Ṛg-veda* 1.34.1; *Atharva-veda* 19.47.2.

16. *Atharva-veda* 19.48.6.

17. *Ṛg-veda* 5.5.6.

18. Ibid. 10.127.6.

19. *Atharva-veda* 19.48.3.

20. Ibid. 19.49.4

21. Kramrisch, "The Indian Great Goddess," pp. 236–239.

22. See my chapater 4, "Sarasvatī."

23. J. Przyluski, "The Great Goddess of India and Iran," *Indian Historical Quarterly* 10 (1934): 405–430; Kramrisch, "The Indian Great Goddess," pp. 235–265.

24. In Vedic literature some gods are frequently identified or associated with each other. We have noted above, for example, that Pṛthivi and Dyaus, Vāc and Sarasvatī, and Pṛthivi and Aditi are often identified or associated with each other. These identifications, however, are selective and consistent and should not lead us to suppose that the authors of Vedic literature presupposed that all deities were manifestations of one great god or one great goddess. While a very strong and articulate monistic position arises in Upaniṣadic literature, there are only hints of this position in earlier Vedic texts.

25. See my chapter 9, "The Mahādevī."

26. In the *Brāhmaṇas* Pṛthivi is identified with Aditi, and Sarasvatī is sometimes identified with Vāc.

2: ŚRĪ-LAKṢMĪ

1. Throughout this chapter I have assumed that Śrī and Lakṣmī are the same. It seems clear that in almost every case the names refer to the same goddess. For a discussion of the evidence suggesting their independent identity, see

Bandana Saraswati, "The History of the Worship of Srī in North India to cir. A.D. 550" (Ph.D. diss., University of London, 1971), pp. 291-296.

2. Jan Gonda, *Aspects of Early Viṣṇuism*, 2d ed. (Delhi: Motilal Banarsidass, 1969), p. 188.

3. Although a process of personification seems evident in the origin of the goddess Śrī in Vedic literature, it may be that her origins lie in pre-Vedic Indo-European traditions in which goddesses of royal power are common. It has long been known that the authors of the *Vedas* are Indo-Aryans and therefore related to other Indo-European peoples. As regards the goddess Śrī, it is significant to note that goddesses like her, goddesses associated with royal power and authority, are found in several Indo-European traditions. The Irish goddess Flaith or Flaith Erenn is a good example. See Alf Hiltebeitel, *The Ritual of Battle* (Ithaca, N.Y.: Cornell University Press, 1976), p. 176.

4. *Śatapatha-brāhmaṇa* 11.4.3.1 ff.

5. For the text and translation of this hymn, see Saraswati, "The Worship of Srī," pp. 22-31.

6. Upendra Nath Dhal, *Goddess Laksmi: Origin and Development* (New Delhi: Oriental Publishers, 1978), p. 178; see also the worship of Śrī later in this chapter.

7. F. D. K. Bosch, *The Golden Germ* ('s Gravenhage: Mouton, 1960), pp. 81-82.

8. Curt Maury, *Folk Origins of Indian Art* (New York: Columbia University Press, 1969), p. 114. Maury interprets the lotus as a symbol of the female sexual organ, which also emphasizes the meaning of the lotus as the source of all life or a symbol of all life (pp. 110-111).

9. Niranjan Ghosh, *Concept and Iconography of the Goddess of Abundance and Fortune in Three Religions of India* (Burdwan: University of Burdwan, 1979), p. 54; Bosch, *The Golden Germ*, p. 80; Ananda Coomaraswamy, *Yaksas*, 2 parts (Delhi: Munshiram Manoharlal, 1971), pt. 2, pp. 56-60.

10. For a discussion of these images, see Ghosh, *Concept and Iconography*, pp. 75-87; Saraswati, "The Worship of Srī," pp. 159-161; Kiran Thaplyal, "Gajalakṣmī on Seals," in D. C. Sircar, ed., *Foreigners in Ancient India and Lakṣmī and Sarasvatī in Art and Literature* (Calcutta: University of Calcutta, 1970), pp. 112-125.

11. Heinrich Zimmer, *The Art of Indian Asia*, 2 vols. (New York: Pantheon Books, 1955), 1:160-161.

12. Jan Gonda, *Ancient Indian Kingship from the Religious Point of View* (Leiden: E. J. Brill, 1969), pp. 7-8.

13. J. C. Heesterman, *The Ancient Indian Royal Consecration* (The Hague: Mouton, 1957), pp. 114-122.

14. Gonda, *Ancient Indian Kingship*, p. 37, notes that Lakṣmī is equated with *abhiśekha* in some texts and is said to dwell in the royal umbrella.

15. Saraswati, "The Worship of Srī," p. 187.

16. Ibid., pp. 157-159.

17. Dhal, *Goddess Laksmi*, pp. 65-66; Saraswati, "The Worship of Srī," pp. 150-153.

18. Dhal, *Goddess Laksmi*, pp. 68-69.

19. Saraswati, "The Worship of Srī," pp. 138-147.

20. *Mahābhārata* 12.124.45-47.

21. *Vāmana-purāna* 49.14-50; *Māhābhārata* 12.216.16; *Devī-bhāgavata-purāṇa* 8.19.15. See Dhal, *Goddess Laksmi*, pp. 94-95.

22. *Mahābhārata* 12.221.14 ff.; Dhal, *Goddess Laksmi*, pp. 88-89.

23. For Indra's association with the plough, see *Ṛg-veda* 2.21.1 and 6.20.1. For Indra as a phallic god of fertility, see Wendy O'Flaherty, *Asceticism and Eroticism in the Mythology of Śiva* (London: Oxford University Press, 1973), pp. 85-86.

24. Maury, *Folk Origins*, p. 105, thinks that Śrī-Lakṣmī's association with wealth is secondary and subsidiary to her association with vegetation and calls her association with wealth the result of a crass preoccupation with "mundane vanities." Śrī-Lakṣmī's association with wealth, however, seems both ancient and consistent with her other qualities.

25. Dhal, *Goddess Laksmi*, pp. 91-93.

26. Saraswati, "The Worship of Srī," pp. 173-177.

27. See Ananda Coomaraswamy, *Yaksas*, 2 parts (Delhi: Munshiram Manoharlal, 1971), pt. 1, pp. 32 ff., for the woman-and-tree motif.

28. See ibid., pt. 2, pls. 34 and 35.

29. For example, *Mahābhārata* 12.220.44-46.

30. Banabhaṭṭa, *Kādambarī* (Bombay: Mathurānāth Śastrī, 1940), pp. 210 ff.; Saraswati, "The Worship of Srī," pp. 287-288.

31. For the early history of Śrī's association with Viṣṇu, see Saraswati, "The Worship of Srī," pp. 113-121.

32. Dhal, *Goddess Laksmi*, pp. 78-80.

33. The story of the churning of the ocean is found in the following texts: *Mahābhārata* 5.102.12 ff.; *Rāmāyaṇa* 4.58.13; *Viṣṇu-purāṇa* 1.9.105; *Padma-purāṇa* 5.4.1 ff.; *Bhāgavata-purāṇa* 8.8.7-28; Saraswati, "The Worship of Srī," pp. 299 ff.

34. For a discussion of the water cosmology, see Coomaraswamy, *Yaksas*, pt. 2, pp. 19-26.

35. Heinrich Zimmer, *The Art of Indian Asia*, 2 vols. (New York: Pantheon Books, 1955), 1:165-166.

36. *Viṣṇu-purāṇa* 1.9 ff.; *Padma-purāṇa* 1.5.4 ff.; Dhal, *Goddess Laksmi*, pp. 84-85.

37. Gonda, *Aspects of Early Viṣṇuism*, pp. 164-167.

38. See Zimmer, *Art of Indian Asia*, vol. 2, pl. 111; Saraswati, "The Worship of Srī," pp. 234-238.

39. For Śrī-Lakṣmī accompanying Viṣṇu in his different *avatāras*, see Saraswati, "The Worship of Srī," pp. 133, 267-273; *Lakṣmī-tantra* 8.31-50; K. S. Behera, "Lakṣmī in Orissan Literature and Art," in Sircar, ed., *Foreigners in Ancient India*, pp. 96-97.

40. Behera, *Lakṣmī in Orissan Literature and Art*, p. 101.

41. Saraswati, "The Worship of Srī," p. 242.

42. *Brahma-vaivarta-purāṇa* 3.23.19 ff.; Dhal, *Goddess Laksmi*, p. 117.

43. *Garuḍa-purāṇa* 5.37; Dhal, *Goddess Laksmi*, p. 118.
44. Ibid., p. 118.
45. Saraswati, "The Worship of Srī," p. 239.
46. Ibid., p. 244.
47. D. C. Sircar, "Ardhanārī-Nārayaṇa," in Sircar, ed., *Foreigners in Ancient India*, pp. 132-141; Ghosh, *Concept and Iconography*, pp. 92-96.
48. Saraswati, "The Worship of Srī," pp. 133-135.
49. F. Otto Schrader, *Introduction to the Pāncarātra and the Ahirbudhnya Saṃhitā* (Madras: Adyar Library, 1916), pp. 34-35.
50. Translations are from the *Lakṣmī Tantra, a Pāñcarātra Text*, trans. Sanjukta Gupta (Leiden: E. J. Brill, 1972).
51. For example, *Lakṣmī-tantra* 45.16-21.
52. Ghosh, *Concept and Iconography*, p. 28.
53. It is interesting to note that Śrī does *not* play a significant role in this respect in the thought of Rāmānuja, the most famous philosopher of the Śrī Vaiṣṇava movement; John Carman, *The Theology of Rāmānuja* (New Haven, Conn.: Yale University Press, 1974), pp. 238-244.
54. Vasuda Narayanan, "The Goddess Śrī: The Blossoming Lotus and Breast Jewel of Viṣṇu," in John Stratton Hawley and Donna Marie Wulff, eds., *The Divine Consort: Rādhā and the Goddesses of India* (Berkeley, Calif.: Religious Studies Series, 1982), p. 225.
55. Ibid., p. 226.
56. Vasudhā Nārāyaṇaṉ, "*Karma* and *Kṛpā*. Human Bondage and Divine Grace: The Teṅkalai Śrī Vaiṣṇava Position" (DePaul University, n.d.), p. 4.
57. Ibid., p. 5.
58. Nārāyaṇan, "The Goddess Śrī," pp. 228-230.
59. Maury, *Folk Origins*, pp. 101-102.
60. Dhal, *Goddess Laksmi*, pp. 164-184.
61. M. Srivastava, *Mother Goddess*, p. 189.
62. Dhal, *Goddess Laksmi*, p. 176.
63. Behera, *Lakṣmī in Orissan Literature and Art*, pp. 104-105.
64. See my chapter 7, "Durgā."
65. Dhal, *Goddess Laksmi*, p. 179.
66. Ibid., p. 178.
67. Ibid, pp. 150-156, 177-178.
68. M. Srivastava, *Mother Goddess*, p. 190.
69. Dhal, *Goddess Laksmi*, pp. 166-167.
70. Behera, *Lakṣmī in Orissan Literature and Art*, pp. 100-102, speaking of the festival tradition at the Jagannātha temple in Puri.

3: PĀRVATĪ

1. *Vājasaneyī-saṁhitā* 3.57.
2. *Taittirīya-brāhmāṇa* 1.6.10.4-5.
3. For example, *Śiva-purāṇa*, Vāyavīya-saṁhitā 2.2.46-60.

4. M. C. P. Srivastava, *Mother Goddess in Indian Art, Archaeology and Literature* (Delhi: Agam Kala Prakashan, 1979), p. 81.

5. The following account of the myth of Satī primarily follows the *Śiva-purāṇa*'s account of the story.

6. For example, *Kālikā-purāṇa* 2–4.

7. See my chapter 12, "Goddesses and Sacred Geography."

8. Kāmarūpa is one of the most famous centers of goddess worship in India today. At the goddess's temple in Kāmarūpa the sacred image is in the form of a yoni.

9. *Bṛhaddharma-purāṇa* 2.6–10; *Kālikā-purāṇa* 15–18; *Māhabhāgavata-purāṇa* 8–11.

10. Wendy Doniger O'Flaherty, *Asceticism and Eroticism in the Mythology of Śiva* (London: Oxford University Press, 1973), passim.

11. Ibid., p. 83; see particularly the Śatarudrīya hymn, which has many names for Śiva that suggest his dangerous nature (*Taittīriya-saṁhitā* 4.5.1–10), and the account of the Śulagava ritual as described in the *Aśvalāyana-gṛhya-sutra* 4.8.1–40.

12. See my chapter 12, "Goddesses and Sacred Geography."

13. For a discussion of the relation between Satī and suttee, see Paul Courtright, "Satī and Suttee: Widow Immolation in Hinduism and Its Western Interpretations" (University of North Carolina at Greensboro, 1982).

14. A long list of goddesses called Mātṛkās (mothers) is mentioned in the *Mahābhārata* 9.45, and they are said to dwell in inaccessible places, including mountains. One of Durgā's popular epithets is Vindhyavāsinī, "she who dwells in the Vindhya Mountains."

15. For example, *Devī-bhāgavata-purāṇa* 7.29.26–30; 3.4.1–37.

16. See my chapter 9, "The Mahādevī."

17. The following account of Pārvatī's mythology primarily follows the *Śiva-purāṇa*.

18. *Śiva-purāṇa*, Rudra-saṁhitā 3.4.26; 3.8.45–48.

19. *Devī-bhāgavata-purāṇa* 7.31.55–57; *Śiva-purāṇa*, Rudra-saṁhitā 3.5.29.

20. *Śiva-purāṇa*, Rudra-saṁhitā 3.5.31.

21. For example, *Vāmana-purāṇa* 25–27; *Śiva-purāṇa*, Rudra-saṁhitā 3.6.24.

22. *Śiva-purāṇa*, Rudra-saṁhita 3.8.8–11.

23. Ibid. 3.17–19; the resuscitation of Kāma: 3:51.10–17.

24. Ibid. 3.32.

25. The idea that heat is accumulated by doing austerities may have to do with the obvious phenomenon that heat is expended with vigorous exercise. One loses heat when acting in the world, one sweats when exerting oneself. Asceticism generally involves withdrawal from the world and the severe restricting of most normal bodily functions, particularly sex. By thus stopping or hindering the normal outflow or leakage of heat one accumulates great amounts of heat, which may then be used to burn away impurities, to threaten or harm an opponent, or to force the gods to grant a boon.

26. *Śiva-purāṇa*, Rudra-saṁhita 3.23.19–34.
27. Ibid. 3.25.45–51; 3.27.10–38, where Śiva himself speaks to Pārvatī.
28. Ibid. 3.43.5–65.
29. Ibid. 4.1.44–46.
30. Ibid. 4.2.9–70.
31. Ibid. 4.13–18.
32. T. A. Gopinatha Rao, *Elements of Hindu Iconography*, 2d ed., 2 vols. (New York: Paragon, 1968), vol. 2, pt. 1, pls. 23, 24, 26.
33. For example, ibid., pl. 25.
34. Wendy O'Flaherty, *Hindu Myths* (Baltimore: Penguin, 1975), cover picture; see also O'Flaherty, *Asceticism and Eroticism*, pl. 10 facing p. 224.
35. O'Flaherty, *Asceticism and Eroticism*, p. 252.
36. For example, Edward J. Thompson and Arthur Marshman Spencer, trans., *Bengali Religious Lyrics, Śākta* (Calcutta: Association Press, 1923), no. 98, p. 98.
37. *Mahābhārata* 13.140.
38. *Śiva-purāṇa*, Vāyavīya-saṁhitā 25.1–48.
39. *Vāmana-purāṇa* 29–30.
40. For example, *Liṅga-purāṇa* 1.106; 1.72.66–68.
41. Glenn Yocum, *Hymns to the Dancing Śiva: A Study of Maṇikkavācakar's "Tiruvācakam"* (Columbia, Mo.: South Asia Books, 1982), p. 119.
42. *Mahābhārata* 3.81.105–110.
43. O'Flaherty, *Asceticism and Eroticism*, p. 158.
44. Ibid., p. 157.
45. Ibid.
46. C. Sivaramamurti, *Nataraja in Art, Thought and Literature* (New Delhi: National Museum, 1974), p. 144.
47. Ibid., p. 138.
48. Kumaraguruparar, *Mīnākṣi-ammam Pillaittamiḻ*, translated from Tamil for me by K. Sivaraman, Department of Religious Studies, McMaster University.
49. Sivaramamurti, *Nataraja in Art*, p. 138.
50. For the madness of Śiva, see David Kinsley, "'Through the Looking Glass': Divine Madness in the Hindu Religious Tradition," *History of Religions* 13, no. 4 (May 1974): 274–278; Glen Yocum, "Māṇikkavācakar's Image of Śiva," *History of Religions* 16, no. 1 (August 1976): 27–31; Glen Yocum, "The Goddess in a Tamil Śaiva Devotional Text, Māṇikkavācakar's *Tiruvācakam*," *Journal of the American Academy of Religion* 45, no. 1, supplement (March 1977): K, 372–373.
51. *Śiva-purāṇa*, Rudra-saṁhitā 3.12.28–33.
52. Śiva sometimes plays the role of subduing or taming a goddess. This goddess is usually the fierce, wild Kālī or a goddess who plays the role of a warrior, such as Mīnākṣi. Prior to her taming or her marriage to Śiva, the goddess in these stories is described as dangerous. See David Shulman, *Tamil Temple Myths* (Princeton, N.J.: Princeton University Press, 1980), pp. 176–211. It has also been argued that outside of marriage, or prior to marriage, goddesses are generally fierce and dangerous, but they are tamed when married. The implication of this is

that the male deity somehow tames the goddess to whom he becomes married. See Lawrence A. Babb, *The Divine Hierarchy: Popular Hinduism in Central India* (New York: Columbia University Press, 1975), pp. 217–226. In the case of Pārvatī and Śiva, though, it is Śiva who needs taming, and he is tamed by Pārvatī; she is never described as dangerous or wild prior to her marriage to Śiva.

53. O'Flaherty, *Asceticism and Eroticism*, p. 225.
54. Ibid., p. 220.
55. Ibid.
56. Ibid., p. 151.
57. Ibid., p. 257.
58. *Śiva-purāṇa*, Vāyavīya-saṁhitā 2.4.18, 29–30.
59. *Liṅga-purāṇa* 2.11.4.
60. *Śiva-purāṇa*, Vāyavīya-saṁhitā 2.4.38, 54, 75; *Liṅga-purāṇa* 2.11.19–32.
61. *Liṅga-purāṇa* 2.11.5.
62. *Śiva-purāṇa*, Vāyavīya-saṃhitā 2.4.55.
63. *Liṅga-purāṇa* 2.11.6.
64. *Śiva-purāṇa*, Vāyavīya-saṁhitā 2.4.42.
65. *Liṅga-purāṇa* 2.11.28.
66. *Śiva-purāṇa*, Vāyavīya-saṁhitā 2.4.62.
67. *Liṅga-purāṇa* 2.11.29.
68. Ibid. 2.11.4.
69. Ibid. 2.11.26.
70. Ibid. 2.11.4.
71. For example, Jitendra Nath Banerjea, *The Development of Hindu Iconography*, 2d ed. (Calcutta: University of Calcutta, 1956), pl. 38, no. 4.
72. *Śiva-purāṇa*, Śatarudra-saṁhitā 1.4–24; Vāyavīya-saṁhitā 1.15.1–33.
73. Śiva is actually referred to as mother in some of the hymns of Maṇikkavācakar; Yocum, *Hymns to the Dancing Śiva*, pp. 126–127.
74. For example, Philip Rawson, *The Art of Tantra* (London: Thames and Hudson, 1973), fig. 30, p. 51; fig. 166, p. 200.
75. O'Flaherty, *Asceticism and Eroticism*, pp. 1–38.
76. *Śiva-purāṇa*, Rudra-saṁhitā 3.27.10–38.
77. Ibid. 3.22.28–62.
78. Yocum, *Hymns to the Dancing Śiva*, p. 120.
79. Ibid., p. 120.
80. Ibid., pp. 124–125.
81. Ibid., p. 117.
82. Pārvatī plays a similar role in Maṇikkavācakar's poems; Yocum, *Hymns to the Dancing Śiva*, p. 127.
83. Mariasusai Dhavamony, *Love of God according to Śaiva Siddhānta* (Oxford: Clarendon Press, 1971), p. 186.
84. Ibid., pp. 188, 190.
85. For example, *Śiva-purāṇa*, Kailāsa-saṁhitā 2–9.
86. For example, *Mahānirvāna-tantra*, which consists entirely of a dialogue between Śiva as teacher and Pārvatī as student.

4: SARASVATĪ

1. See my chapter 1, "Goddesses in Vedic Literature."
2. See my chapter 12, "Goddesses and Sacred Geography."
3. See Mircea Eliade, *Patterns in Comparative Religion* (Cleveland: World Publishing Co., 1963), chapter 5, "The Waters and Water Symbolism," pp. 188-215.
4. A. K. Chaterjee, "Some Aspects of Sarasvatī," in D. C. Sircar, ed., *Foreigners in Ancient India and Laksmi and Sarasvati in Art and Literature* (Calcutta: University of Calcutta, 1970), p. 150.
5. Raghunath Airi, *Concept of Sarasvati in Vedic Literature* (Delhi: Munshiram Manoharlal Publishers, 1977), pp. 3 ff.
6. *Vāmana-purāṇa* 40.140; *Skanda-purāṇa* 6.46.28; M. C. P. Srivastava, *Mother Goddess in Indian Art, Archaelogy and Literature* (Deli: Agam Kala Prakashan, 1979), p. 190.
7. *Matsya-purāṇa* 3.30-47.
8. *Brahma-vaivarta-purāṇa* 2.1.1 ff.; *Devī-bhāgavata-purāṇa* 9.1.1 ff.
9. *Devī-bhāgavata-purāṇa* 9.1.30-33.
10. Ibid. 9.1.34.
11. *Brahama-vaivarta-purāṇa* 2.2.54 ff.; *Devī-bhāgavata-purāṇa* 9.1.34.
12. Anand Swarup Gupta, "Conception of Sarasvatī in the Purāṇas," *Purāṇa* 4, no. 1 (1962): 71.
13. *Skanda-purāṇa* 7.33.96; Gupta, "Conception of Sarasvatī," p. 72.
14. Chaterjee, "Some Aspects of Sarasvatī," p. 151.
15. See my chapter 4, note 6.
16. Gupta, "Conception of Sarasvatī," p. 60.
17. See also *Skanda-purāṇa* 6.46.28; Gupta, "Conception of Sarasvatī," p. 60.
18. Gupta, "Conception of Sarasvatī," pp. 76-77.
19. Ibid., p. 69.
20. Ibid. Sarasvatī often acts as the arbiter in philosophical debates and "is also widely known as bestowing upon mortals the ability to solve philosophical problems," for example, in *Brahma-vaivarta-purāṇa*, Prakṛti-khanda 5.21-27; Phyllis Granoff, "Scholars and Wonder-Workers: Some Remarks on the Role of the Supernatural in Philosophical Contests in Vedānta Hagiographies" (McMaster University, 1984), p. 22.
21. Ibid.
22. Ibid., p. 76.
23. Ibid., p. 69.
24. *Agni-purāṇa* 50.16; Mohammad Israil Khan, *Sarasvati in Sanskrit Literature* (Ghaziabad: Crescent Publishing House, 1978), pls. 3, 9, 11.
25. M. Srivastava, *Mother Goddess*, p. 133; Gupta, "Conception of Sarasvatī," pp. 80-81.
26. Gupta, "Conception of Sarasvatī," p. 80.
27. Ibid.

28. Ibid., p. 81.
29. Ibid.
30. *Devī-bhāgavata-purāṇa* 9.1.34.
31. Gupta, "Conception of Sarasvatī," pp. 78–79, gives a few examples.
32. Kahn, *Sarasvati in Sanskrit Literature*, pls. 6, 7.
33. Gupta, *Conception of Sarasvati*, p. 87.
34. Ibid., pp. 87–88.

5: SĪTĀ

1. Edmour Babineau, "The Interaction of Love of God and Social Duty in the Rāmcaritmānas" (Ph.D. diss., McMaster University, 1975), pp. 46–48; R. G. Bhandarkar, *Vaiṣṇavism, Śaivism and Minor Religious Systems* (Strassburg: K. J. Trübner, 1913), pp. 75–76.
2. *Ṛg-veda* 4.57.6–7; *The Hymns of the Ṛgveda*, trans. Ralph Griffith, 4th ed., 2 vols. (Banaras: Chowkhamba Sanskrit Series Office, 1963), 1:461.
3. Cornelia Dimmitt, "Sītā: Mother Goddess and *Śakti*," in John Stratton Hawley and Donna Marie Wulff, eds., *The Divine Consort: Rādhā and the Goddesses of India* (Berkeley, Calif.: Berkeley Religious Studies Series, 1982), p. 211.
4. Ibid., p. 212.
5. Ibid.
6. *Śatapatha-brāhmaṇa* 7.2.2.2–21.
7. Dimmitt, "Sītā," p. 212.
8. Jan Gonda, *Ancient Indian Kingship from the Religious Point of View* (Leiden: E. J. Brill, 1969), pp. 6–8, 129.
9. For example, *Ṛg-veda* 1.22.
10. Gonda, *Ancient Indian Kingship*, p. 130; Phyllis Kaplan Herman, "Ideal Kingship and the Feminine Power: A Study of the Depiction of 'Rāmrājya' in the Vālmīki Rāmāyaṇa" (Ph.D. diss., University of California, Los Angeles, 1979), pp. 65–75.
11. *Mahābhārata* 5.102 ff.; *Rāmāyaṇa* 4.58; *Viṣṇu-purāṇa* 1.9.105; *Padma-purāṇa* 5.4.1 ff.; *Bhāgavata-purāṇa* 8.8.7–28.
12. Herman, "Ideal Kingship and the Feminine Power," p. 56.
13. *Viṣṇu-purāṇa* 4.5.28; Herman, "Ideal Kingship and the Feminine Power," p. 114.
14. Mircea Eliade, *Patterns in Comparative Religion* (Cleveland: World Publishing Co., 1963), pp. 259–260.
15. *Rāmāyaṇa* 2.114.
16. Ibid. 3.63.
17. Ananda Coomaraswamy, "On the Loathly Bride," *Speculum: A Journal of Medieval Studies* 20, no. 4 (1945): 396.
18. *The Laws of Manu*, trans. G. Bühler (Delhi: Motilal Banarsidass, 1975), p. 196.
19. Ibid., p. 328.
20. *Rāmāyaṇa* 5.22.

21. *The Ramayaṇa of Valmiki*, trans. Hari Prasad Shastri, 3 vols. (London: Shantisadan, 1957–62), 1:233.

22. Ibid., 1:236–237.

23. Ibid., 1:238.

24. Ibid., 2:373–374.

25. Ibid., 2:377.

26. Ibid., 2:379.

27. Ibid., 3:336.

28. Ibid., 3:338.

29. Ibid., 3:529.

30. Ibid., 3:617.

31. M. N. Srinivas, *Marriage and Family in Mysore* (Bombay: New Book Co., 1942), p. 195.

32. Sudhir Kakar, *The Inner World: A Psycho-analytic Study of Childhood and Society in India* (Oxford: Oxford University Press, 1978), p. 62.

33. Akshaykumar Kayal, "Women in Folk-Sayings of West Bengal," in Sankar Sen Gupta, ed., *A Study of Women in Bengal* (Calcutta: Indian Publications, 1970), p. xxiii.

34. Kakar, *The Inner World*, p. 64.

35. Babineau, "Love of God and Social Duty," pp. 161–238.

36. Tulsī Dās, *Kavitāvalī*, trans. F. R. Allchin (London: George Allen and Unwin, 1964), p. 76.

37. *Vinaya-patrikā* 104.1; Tulsī Dās, *The Petition to Rām: Hindu Devotional Hymns of the Seventeenth Century (Vinaya-patrikā)*, trans. Raymond Allchin (London: George Allen and Unwin, 1966), p. 155.

38. Tulsī Dās, *The Ramayana of Tulsidas*, trans. A. C. Atkins, 2 vols. (New Delhi: Hindustan Times, n.d.), 1:1.

39. Norvin Hein, "The Rām Līlā," in Milton Singer, ed., *Traditional India: Structure and Change* (Philadelphia: American Folklore Society, 1959), p. 87.

40. For example, *Vinaya-patrikā* 53.4; 55.2, 58.1; 63.8; 77.1.

41. Introductory hymn to *Rāmcarit-mānas*; hymns introducing *Vinaya-patrikā* 15 and 16 to Pārvatī, Durgā, and Kālikā; 17–20 to Gaṅgā; and 21 to Yamunā.

42. *Vinaya-patrikā* 41–42.

43. Babineau, "Love of God and Social Duty," p. 287.

6: RĀDHĀ

1. See David Kinsley, *The Divine Player—A Study of Kṛṣṇa Līlā* (Delhi: Motilal Banarsidass, 1979), pp. 112–118.

2. For the early history of Rādhā, see Jayadeva, *Love Song of the Dark Lord: Jayadeva's "Gitagovinda,"* ed. and trans. Barbara Miller (New York: Columbia University Press, 1977), pp. 26–37; S. C. Mukherji, *A Study of Vaiṣṇavism in Ancient and Medieval Bengal* (Calcutta: Punthi Pustak, 1966), pp. 183–195.

3. Jayadeva, *Love Song of the Dark Lord*, p. 29.
4. Ibid., p. 30.
5. Ibid., p. 34.
6. Ibid., p. 33.
7. Ibid., p. 35.
8. For the date and setting of the *Bhāgavata-purāṇa*, see Thomas J. Hopkins, "The Social Teachings of the *Bhāgavata Purāṇa*," and J. A. B. van Buitenen, "On the Archaism of the *Bhāgavata Purāṇa*," in Milton Singer, ed., *Krishna: Myths, Rites, and Attitudes* (Honolulu: East-West Center Press, 1966), pp. 3–22 and 23–40.
9. Jayadeva, *Love Song of the Dark Lord*, p. 74.
10. Craig Jones, "Rādhā: The Paroḍhā Nāyikā" (M.A. thesis, McMaster University, 1980), pp. 19–20.
11. Edward C. Dimock, Jr., and Denise Levertov, trans., *In Praise of Krishna: Songs from the Bengali* (Garden City, N.Y.: Doubleday, 1967), p. 51; excerpt from "I who body and soul," copyright © 1965 by Modern Poetry Association from the book *In Praise of Krishna* by Edward C. Dimock and Denise Levertov; reprinted by permission of Doubleday & Company, Inc.
12. Vidyāpati, *Love Songs of Vidyāpati*, trans. Deben Bhattacharya (London: George Allen and Unwin, 1963), p. 65.
13. Caṇḍīdās, *Love Songs of Candidās*, trans. Deben Bhattacharya (London: George Allen and Unwin, 1967), p. 135.
14. Ibid., p. 67.
15. Richard Barz, *The Bhakti Cult of Vallabhācārya* (Faridabad, Haryana: Thomson Press, 1976), p. 90.
16. S. K. De, *Early History of the Vaisnava Faith and Movement in Bengal* (Calcutta: Firma K. L. Mukhopadhyay, 1961), pp. 409–410; Edward C. Dimock, *The Place of the Hidden Moon* (Chicago: University of Chicago Press, 1966), pp. 17, 162, 211–213.
17. Dimock, *The Place of the Hidden Moon*, pp. 208–210.
18. Rūpa Gosvāmin, *Vidagdhamādhava* 2.17; Donna Marie Wulff, "A Sanskrit Portrait: Rādhā in the Plays of Rūpa Gosvāmī," in John Stratton Hawley and Donna Marie Wulff, eds., *The Divine Consort: Rādhā and the Goddesses of India* (Berkeley, Calif.: Berkeley Religious Studies Series, 1982), p. 29.
19. Wulff, "A Sanskrit Portrait," p. 31.
20. *Vidagdhamādhava* 5.18; Wulff, "A Sanskrit Portrait," p. 31.
21. Wulff, "A Sanskrit Portrait," pp. 32–35.
22. Ibid., p. 36. For Rādhā's adoration, see also John Stratton Hawley, *At Play with Krishna: Pilgrimage Dramas from Brindavan* (Princeton, N.J.: Princeton University Press, 1981), pp. 168 ff. It should also be noted in reference to Rādhā's lofty status that in most North Indian Kṛṣṇa temples and shrines the central image is of Kṛṣṇa *and* Rādhā.
23. Kinsley, *The Divine Player*, pp. 109–110. The contemporary expression of this idea is seen in the invocation addressed to Rādhā and Kṛṣṇa at the beginning of a religious drama in Brindavan: "Homage to Radha, Krishna's essence, and Krishna, the essence of Radha" (Hawley, *At Play with Krishna*, p. 168).
24. Jones, "Rādhā," pp. 48–60.

25. The *Devī-bhāgavata-purāṇa* contains several parallel passages in which Rādhā figures prominently. See Cheever Mackenzie Brown, *God as Mother: A Feminine Theology in India* (Hartford, Vt.: Claude Stark, 1974), pp. 207-215.
26. Prakṛti-khaṇḍa 55.86-87; Brown, *God as Mother*, p. 124.
27. Kṛṣṇajanma-khaṇḍa 15.59-60; Brown, *God as Mother*, p. 128.
28. Kṛṣṇajanma-khaṇḍa 6.202-203; Brown, *God as Mother*, p. 138.
29. Kṛṣṇajanma-khaṇḍa 6.208-212; Brown, *God as Mother*, pp. 130-131.
30. Kṛṣṇajanma-khaṇḍa 67.13-14; Brown, *God as Mother*, p. 132.
31. Kṛṣṇajanma-khaṇḍa 124.9-11; Brown, *God as Mother*, p. 198.
32. Prakṛti-khaṇḍa 2-3; Brown, *God as Mother*, pp. 168-169.
33. Brown, *God as Mother*, p. 179.
34. Prakṛti-khaṇḍa 15.16-29.
35. Kṛṣṇajanma-khaṇḍa 130.48-88.
36. J. N. Farquhar, *An Outline of the Religious Literature of India* (Delhi: Motilal Banarsidass, 1967), p. 318.

7: DURGĀ

1. *Taittirīya-āranyaka* 10.1.7.
2. M. C. P. Srivastava, *Mother Goddess in Indian Art, Archaeology and Literature* (Delhi: Agam Kala Prakashan, 1979), pp. 111-113; Jitendra Nath Banerjea, *The Development of Hindu Iconography*, 2d ed. (Calcutta: University of Calcutta, 1956), pp. 495-500.
3. The most celebrated text describing Durgā's mythological exploits is the *Devī-māhātmya*, which constitutes chapters 81-93 of the *Mārkandeya-purāṇa*. The myth of Durgā defeating Mahiṣa is also found in the *Vāmana-purāṇa* 19.1-21.52; *Varāha-purāṇa* 62.1-95.65; *Śiva-purāṇa* 5.46.1-63; *Devī-bhāgavata-purāṇa* 5.2-20; *Skanda-purāṇa*; and several *Upa-purāṇas*. The myth concerning Durgā's slaying of Śumbha and Niśumbha is also found in the *Vāmana-purāṇa* 29.1-30.73; *Śiva-purāṇa* 5.47.1-48.50; *Skanda-purāṇa* 7.3.24.1-22; and several *Upa-purāṇas*. The worship of Durgā is enjoined and described in the *Kālikā-purāna* 61; *Mahābhāgavata-purāṇa* 45-48; and *Devī-purāṇa* 21-23.
4. For example, the hymn to Āryā in *Harivaṁśa* 3.3; *Viṣṇu-purāṇa* 5.1.95; and *Mahābhārata*, Virāṭa-parva 6.
5. M. Srivastava, *Mother Goddess*, p. 110.
6. *Devī-māhātmya* 5.38; *Vāmana-purāṇa* 28.6-25.
7. Heinrich Zimmer, *Myths and Symbols of Indian Art and Civilization*, ed. Joseph Campbell (New York: Harper and Row, 1962), pl. 56.
8. See my chapter 8, "Kālī," and chapter 10, "The Mātṛkās."
9. *Devī-māhātmya* 8.62.
10. The term *liminal* has been used by Victor Turner to designate boundary situations, characteristics, and so on. He notes that many rituals purposely seek to involve participants in such situations to allow them to step outside their normal social roles and restraints. See his *Dramas, Fields, and Metaphors: Symbolic Action in Human Society* (Ithaca, N.Y.: Cornell University Press, 1974), pp. 231-270.

11. David Dean Shulman, *Tamil Temple Myths: Sacrifice and Divine Marriage in the South Indian Saiva Tradition* (Princeton, N.J.: Princeton University Press, 1980), pp. 186-187.

12. *Devī-māhātmya* 5.56-65; *Devī-bhāgavata-purāṇa* 5.2-20.

13. *Devī-bhāgavata-purāṇa* 5.11.17-30.

14. For example, *Manu-dharma-śāstra* 9.14-17; 5.147-149.

15. See Victor Turner, *The Ritual Process: Structure and Anti-structure* (Ithaca, N.Y.: Cornell University Press, 1977).

16. Pearl Ostroff, "The Demon-slaying Devī: A Study of Her Purāṇic Myths" (M.A. thesis, McMaster University, 1978), pp. 56-57.

17. David Kinsley, "The Portrait of the Goddess in the *Devī-māhātmya*," *Journal of the American Academy of Religion* 46, no. 4 (December 1978): 497-498.

18. *Devī-māhātmya* 2.9-10.

19. David Kinsley, *The Divine Player—A Study of Kṛṣṇa Līlā* (Delhi: Motilal Banarsidass, 1979), pp. 1-55.

20. Balram Srivastava, *Iconography of Śakti: A Study Based on Śrītattvanidhi* (Delhi: Chaukhambha Orientalia, 1978), plate facing p. 67.

21. Pandurang V. Kane, *History of Dharmaśāstra*, 5 vols. (Poona: Bhandarkar Oriental Institute, 1930-62), 5:171; Pratāpachandra Ghosha, *Durga Puja: With Notes and Illustrations* (Calcutta: Hindoo Patriot Press, 1871), p. 39.

22. Abbé J. A. Dubois, *Hindu Manners, Customs and Ceremonies*, trans. Henry K. Beauchamp, 3d ed. (Oxford: Clarendon Press, 1906), pp. 569-570; see also Paul Thomas, *Hindu Religion, Customs and Manners* (Bombay: Taraporevala, n.d.), p. 147. I am indebted to Pearl Ostroff for showing the connection between Durgā and military themes in Hinduism.

23. Alexander Kinloch Forbes, *Rās-Mālā: Hindu Annals of Western India* (New Delhi: Heritage Publishers, 1973), p. 614.

24. Kane, *History of Dharmaśāstra*, 5:190.

25. Ibid., p. 193.

26. Krishna Kanta Handiqui, *Yaśastilaka and Indian Culture* (Sholapur: Jaina Saṁskṛiti Saṁrakshaka Sangha, 1949), p. 398.

27. *Garuḍa-purāṇa* 135.5; *Viṣṇudharmottara-purāṇa* 2.158; *Devī-purāṇa* 21.22.

28. *Vākpatirāja's Gauḍavaho*, trans. N. G. Suru (Ahmedabad: Prakrit Text Society, 1975), verses 285-337.

29. For a discussion of the relationship between the *śami* tree and weapons in both the *Mahābhārata* and the present day during Durgā Pūjā, see Madeleine Biardeau, "L'arbre *śami* et le buffle sacrificiel," in Madeleine Biardeau, ed., *Autour de la déesse hindoue* (Paris: Centre d'Études de l'Inde et de l'Asie du Sud, 1981.

30. *Worship of the Goddess according to the Kālikāpurāṇa*, trans. K. R. Van Kooij (Leiden: E. J. Brill, 1972) 62.24-27, 30-32, 41-43, 49; see also *Mahābhāgavata-purāṇa* 36-48; *Bṛhaddharma-purāṇa* 1.18-22.

31. Narendra Nath Bhattacharyya, *History of the Śākta Religion* (New Delhi: Munshiram Manoharlal Publishers, 1964), pp. 133, 149.

32. Ákos Öster, *The Play of the Gods: Locality, Ideology, Structure, and Time in the Festivals of a Bengali Town* (Chicago: University of Chicago Press, 1980), p. 18.

33. P. K. Gode, "Hari Kavi's Contribution to the Problem of the Bhavāni Sword of Shivaji the Great," *New Indian Antiquary* 3 (1940–41): 82–83.

34. Ibid., pp. 84–85, 92.

35. Ibid., p. 98.

36. James Tod, *Annals and Antiquities of Rajast'han*, 2 vols. (New Delhi: M. N. Publishers, 1978), 1:465.

37. Ibid., p. 184.

38. Kane, *History of Dharmaśāstra*, 5:163; Ghosha, *Durga Puja*, pp. 41–51.

39. Ghosha, *Durga Puja*, p. 41.

40. Ibid., p. 47.

41. Ibid., p. 49.

42. Ibid., p. 50.

43. Ibid., p. 22.

44. Ibid., pp. 14, 23.

45. Ibid., p. 23.

46. Kane, *History of Dharmaśāstra*, 5:156.

47. Ghosha, *Durga Puja*, p. 46.

48. Ibid., p. 14.

49. Ibid., pp. 76, lxvii.

50. See especially the Rudhirādhyāya (chapter on blood) of the *Kālikā-purāṇa* 71.

51. *Devī-māhātmya* 13.8.

52. *Harivaṁśa* 3.3.

53. Joseph Campbell, *The Masks of God: Primitive Mythology* (New York: Viking Press, 1959), pp. 216–224; Mircea Eliade, *Patterns in Comparative Religion* (Cleveland: World Publishing Co., 1963), pp. 341–347.

54. Kane, *History of Dharmaśāstra*, 5:177; *Bṛhaddharma-purāṇa* 1.21–22; *Kālikā-purāṇa* 61.

55. Ghosha, *Durga Puja*, p. 82; Abhay Charan Mukerji, *Hindu Feasts and Fasts* (Allahabad: Indian Press, 1916), pp. 156, 162; *Kālikā-purāṇa* 61–63.

56. Eliade, *Patterns in Comparative Religion*, pp. 314–316, 332–334.

57. Edward J. Thompson and Arthur Marshman Spencer, trans., *Bengali Religious Lyrics, Śākta* (Calcutta: Association Press, 1923), p. 98.

58. Laurence A. Babb, *The Divine Hierarchy: Popular Hinduism in Central India* (New York: Columbia University Press, 1975), pp. 216–224, argues that a typical theme in Hindu mythology is the danger presented by unmarried goddesses and females and that unmarried goddesses are generally aggressive and dangerous in their actions. This danger might be presumed to arise from such goddesses' pent-up sexual energy.

59. This may reflect the male fear of sexual intercourse which sees in the loss of semen something spiritually harmful. An important notion in Indian asceticism is that by retaining this semen a male may build up great spiritual vigor.

60. Shulman, *Tamil Temple Myths*, pp. 176–191, 211–223.

8: KĀLĪ

1. *Agni-purāṇa* 133, 134, 136; *Garuḍa-purāṇa* 38.

2. Śaśibhūsan Dāsgupta, *Bhārater Śakti-sādhana o Śākta Sāhitya* (Calcutta: Sāhitya Saṅgsad, 1367 B.S. [1961]), pp. 66–67.

3. D. C. Sircar, *The Śākta Pīṭhas* (Delhi: Motilal Banarsidass, 1973), p. 20.

4. *Bhavabhūti's Mālatīmādhava with the Commentary of Jagaddhara*, ed. and trans. M. R. Kale (Delhi: Motilal Banarsidass, 1967), pp. 44–48.

5. Krishna Kanta Handiqui, *Yaśastilaka and Indian Culture* (Sholapur: Jaina Saṁskṛiti Saṁrakshaka Sangha, 1949), p. 56.

6. Ibid., p. 22.

7. See my chapter 10, "The Mātṛkās."

8. *Skanda-purāṇa* 5.82.1–21.

9. Summarized in *Principles of Tantra: The Tantratattva of Śrīyukta Śiva Candra Vidyārnava Bhattācārya Mahodaya*, ed. Arthur Avalon (Madras: Ganesh, 1960), pp. 208–213.

10. *Adbhūta Rāmāyaṇa*, Sāralā Dāsa's Oriyan *Rāmāyaṇa*, and the Bengali *Jaiminibhārata Rāmāyaṇa*; Narendra Nath Bhattacharyya, *History of the Śākta Religion* (New Delhi: Munshiram Manoharlal Publishers, 1974), p. 149.

11. C. Sivaramamurti, *Nataraja in Art, Thought and Literature* (New Delhi: National Museum, 1974), pp. 378–379, 384; M. A. Dorai Rangaswamy, *The Religion and Philosophy of Tēvāram*, 2 books (Madras: University of Madras, 1958), 1:442, 444–445; R. K. Das, *Temples of Tamilnad* (Bombay: Bharatiya Vidya Bhavan, 1964), p. 195.

12. Some renditions of Śiva's dance, in which the entire Hindu pantheon is shown as spectators or musicians, do include Kālī standing passively by: for example, the painting at the sixteenth-century Śiva temple at Ettumanur (Sivaramamurti, *Nataraja in Art*, fig. 150, p. 282) and the scene from a seventeenth-century temple at Tripprayār, Kerala (ibid., fig. 152, p. 284). In both scenes Kālī rides a *preta* (ghost), and her appearance is unchanged.

13. That Śiva should have to resort to his *tāṇḍava* dance to defeat Kālī suggests the theme of Kālī's inciting Śiva to destructive activity. Śiva's *tāṇḍava* dance is typically performed at the end of the cosmic age and destroys the universe. Descriptions of it often dwell on its destructive aspects. The chaotic dancing of Śiva, who wields a broken battle-ax, must be tempered by the soft glances of Pārvatī (Sivaramamurti, *Nataraja in Art*, p. 138). Śiva tends to get out of control in his *tāṇḍava* dance, and in the legend of the dance contest with Kālī, it is she who provokes him to it.

14. *Bhavabhūti's Mālatīmādhava*, pp. 44–48.

15. M., *The Gospel of Sri Ramakrishna*, trans. Swami Nikhilananda (New York: Ramakrishna-Vivekananda Center, 1942), p. 961.

16. The theme of Pārvatī's acting as a restraining influence on Śiva is mentioned by Glen Yocum, "The Goddess in a Tamil Śaiva Devotional Text, Māṇikkavācakar's *Tiruvācakam*," *Journal of the American Academy of Religion* 45, no. 1, supplement (March 1977): K, 372.

17. *Principles of Tantra: The Tantratattva of Śrīyukta Śiva Candra Vidyār-*

nava Bhattācārya Mahodaya, ed. Arthur Avalon (Madras: Ganesh, 1960), pp. 327–328.

18. *Hymn to Kālī (Karpūrādi-stotra)*, ed. and trans. Arthur Avalon (Madras: Ganesh, 1965), p. 34.

19. Ibid.

20. Ibid.

21. For example, *Mahānirvāṇa-tantra* 5.140–141; 6.68–76; 10.102.

22. *Tantra of the Great Liberation (Mahānirvāna Tantra)*, trans. Arthur Avalon (Madras: Ganesh, 1972), pp. 49–50.

23. For the *pañcatattva* ritual see *Mahānirvāṇa-tantra* 5–6; Agehananda Bharati, *The Tantric Tradition* (London: Rider, 1965), pp. 228–278; Mircea Eliade, *Yoga: Immortality and Freedom* (New York: Pantheon Books, 1958), pp. 254–262; Heinrich Zimmer, *Philosophies of India* (Cleveland: World Publishing Co., 1956), pp. 572–580.

24. *Hymn to Kālī*, pp. 84, 86.

25. In at least one Tantric text Kālī is identified with Lakṣmī and by implication Viṣṇu (*Lakṣmī-tantra* 8.13).

26. Throughout North India Kālī is associated with Bengal, where she is most popular. Outside Bengal, for example, her temples will be established by Bengalis, Bengalis will often act as her temple priests, or the image of Kālī in the temple will be said to have some connection with Bengal.

27. *Rama Prasada's Devotional Songs: The Cult of Shakti*, trans. Jadunath Sinha (Calcutta: Sinha Publishing House, 1966), no. 181, p. 97.

28. Edward J. Thompson and Arthur Marshman Spencer, trans., *Bengali Religious Lyrics, Śākta* (Calcutta: Association Press, 1923), p. 22.

29. For Annapūrṇā, Jagaddhātrī, and Satākṣī, see my chapter 9, "The Mahādevī."

30. David Kinsley, *The Sword and the Flute—Kṛṣṇa and Kālī* (Berkeley, Los Angeles, London: University of California Press, 1975), pp. 133–145.

31. *Rama Prasada's Devotional Songs*, no. 221, pp. 118–119.

32. Thompson and Spencer, trans., *Bengali Religious Lyrics*, pp. 85–86.

33. Ibid., p. 84.

34. *Rama Prasada's Devotional Songs*, p. 106.

35. In *Purity and Danger: An Analysis of Concepts of Pollution and Taboo* (Harmondsworth: Penguin Books, 1970), Mary Douglas locates taboo in the idea of dirt out of place. In a sense Kālī may be regarded as taboo, a dangerous being out of place in the civilized sphere.

36. Ibid., p. 193.

37. "The unusual, the paradoxical, the illogical, even the perverse, stimulate thought and pose problems, 'cleanse the Doors of Perception,' as Blake put it"; Victor Turner, *Dramas, Fields, and Metaphors: Symbolic Action in Human Society* (Ithaca, N.Y.: Cornell University Press, 1974), p. 256.

38. The term *antistructure* is used here in the way Turner uses it, as a positive phenomenon that enables a culture to step outside itself in order to perceive itself more clearly. Antistructure is not necessarily chaotic or destructive.

39. The story is told in the *Adbhūta Rāmāyaṇa*, the Oriyan *Rāmāyaṇa* of

Sāralā Dāsa, and the Bengali *Jaiminibharata Rāmāyaṇa*; Narendra Nath Bhattacharyya, *History of the Śākta Religion* (New Delhi: Munshiram Manoharlal Publishers, 1974), p. 149.

40. *Liṅga-purāṇa* 1.106.20–28.

9: THE MAHĀDEVĪ

1. Some scholars have assumed that an underlying goddess theology asserting the essential unity of all goddesses has existed in Hinduism since the Vedic period. See, for example, Stella Kramrisch, "The Indian Great Goddess," *History of Religions* 14, no. 4 (May 1975): 235–265; J. Przyluski, "The Great Goddess of India and Iran," *Indian Historical Quarterly* 10 (1934): 405–430; and Sadanand K. Dikshit, *The Mother Goddess* (New Delhi: Published by the author, 1957). There is little or no evidence for this position, however, and none is adduced by these authors.

2. Thomas B. Coburn, "Consort of None, *Śakti* of All: The Vision of the *Devī-māhātmya*," in John Stratton Hawley and Donna Marie Wulff, eds., *The Divine Consort: Rādhā and the Goddesses of India* (Berkeley, Calif.: Berkeley Religious Studies Series, 1982), pp. 153 ff.

3. For example, the Pāñcarātra school (Surendranath Dasgupta, *A History of Indian Philosophy*, 5 vols. [Cambridge: Cambridge University Press, 1968], 3:35); the philosophy of Yāmunācārya (latter part of the tenth century), the founder of the Viśiṣṭā-dvaita school (ibid., 3:155); Bengal Vaiṣṇavism (S. K. De, *Early History of the Vaisnava Faith and Movement in Bengal* [Calcutta: Firma K. L. Mukhopadhyay, 1961], pp. 276 ff.); and Kashmir Śaivism (Sudhendukumar Das, *Sakti or Divine Power* [Calcutta: University of Calcutta, 1934], p. 61).

4. For example, Kashmir Śaivism; see S. Das, *Sakti*, p. 61.

5. For example, the *Devī-bhāgavata-purāṇa*, where she sits on a couch composed of the great male deities (7.29.7; 12.12.12), and the *Saundaryalaharī*, where the same image is described (verse 94).

6. This point is dramatically made in the stories about Viṣṇu's teaching the sage Narada about the nature of his *māyā* when the sage experiences rebirth as a woman. Forgetfulness of one's past lives, total identification with one's present life, is exactly what *māyā* is said to be in these tales. See Heinrich Zimmer, *Myths and Symbols of Indian Art and Civilization*, ed. Joseph Campbell (New York: Harper and Row, 1962), pp. 30–35.

7. For example, the first episode of the *Devī-māhātmya*, where the Devī is equated with Viṣṇu's sleep and the deluding power of the world (1.68–69; 1.40).

8. For example, *Devī-bhāgavata-purāṇa* 7.33.21–41.

9. For example, ibid. 1.8.40; 3.4.38–39; 3.24.38.

10. Ibid. 3.3.35–67; 12.10–12.

11. For example, *Lalitā-sahasranāma* 281; *Saundaryalaharī* 56; *Sītā-upanisad* 34.

12. For example, *Devī-bhāgavata-purāṇa* 3.5.4; 7.33.13; 12.8.77; *Saundaryalaharī* 53.

13. For example, *Devī-bhāgavata-purāṇa* 7.29.26-30.

14. *Devī-bhāgavata-purāṇa* 7.29.7.

15. Ibid. 5.7.57-60.

16. The Daśamahāvidyās will be discussed in my chapter 11.

17. The Devī's manifestations are sometimes grouped according to the three *guṇas,* for example, *Devī-purāṇa* 50.5-17. In this case the Devī's auspicious forms are grouped under the *sattva* (and to some extent the *rajas*) *guṇa,* and the terrible forms are grouped primarily under the *tamas guṇa.*

18. Arthur Avalon and Ellen Avalon, trans., *Hymns to the Goddess,* 3d ed. (Madras: Ganesh, 1964), pp. 146-152.

19. Ibid., pp. 146, 149, 151.

20. Bhīṣma-parva 23; Avalon and Avalon, trans., *Hymns to the Goddess,* pp. 155-156.

21. Virāṭa-parva 6; Avalon and Avalon, trans., *Hymns to the Goddess,* p. 144.

22. *The Saundaryalaharī or Flood of Beauty,* ed. and trans. W. Norman Brown (Cambridge, Mass.: Harvard University Press, 1958), p. 52, verse 13.

23. For example, *Saundaryalaharī* 6. The Devī is said in some texts to appear in the form of a great bee or in a form that is surrounded by bees. In this form she is called Bhrāmarīdevī. In Sanskrit erotic literature the bee symbolizes erotic desire, and the Devī's form as Bhrāmarīdevī may convey this dimension of her character. *Devī-bhāgavata-purāṇa* 10.13; *Devī-māhātmya* 11.50.

24. *Devī-bhāgavata-purāṇa* 7.28; *Devī-māhātmya* 11.45.

25. *Devī-bhāgavata-purāṇa* 7.28.1-68.

26. Ibid. 7.28.30-45.

27. Diana L. Eck, *Banaras, City of Light* (New York: Alfred A. Knopf, 1982), p. 161.

28. Ibid., pp. 163-164.

29. Ibid., p. 164.

30. *Lalitā-sahasranāma* 935.

31. See my chapter 8, "Kālī."

32. For example, the *Saundaryalaharī.*

33. David Kinsley, "Blood and Death Out of Place: Reflections on the Goddess Kālī," in Hawley and Wulff, eds., *The Divine Consort,* pp. 145-146.

34. *Liṅga-purāṇa* 1.106, where Pārvatī transforms herself into Kālī.

35. *Devī-māhātmya* 7.5, where Durgā produces Kālī in her rage.

36. *Vāmana-purāṇa* 30, where the seven Mātṛkās (mothers) are born from different parts of the Devī's body.

37. For a discussion of the significance of the Devī splitting herself into many goddesses, see Pearl Ostroff, "The Demon-slaying Devī: A Study of Her Purāṇic Myths" (M.A. thesis, McMaster University, 1978), pp. 33-47.

38. For example, *Devī-māhātmya* 8.62; *Matsya-purāṇa* 179.8-90; *Garuḍa-purāṇa* 241; *Devī-bhāgavata-purāṇa* 5.28.45-63.

39. Narendra Nath Bhattacharyya, *Indian Mother Goddess* (Calcutta: Indian Studies Past and Present, 1971), pp. 54–56.

40. U. N. Ghoshal, *Studies in Indian History and Culture* (Bombay: Orient Longmans, 1965), "The Rite of Head-offering to the Deity in Ancient Indian Literature and Art," pp. 333–340.

41. N. Bhattacharyya, *Indian Mother Goddess*, p. 54.

42. T. V. Mahalingam, "The Cult of Śakti in Tamiland," in D. C. Sircar, ed., *The Śakti Cult and Tārā* (Calcutta: University of Calcutta, 1967), p. 28.

43. *Bhavabhūti's Mālatīmadhava with the Commentary of Jagaddhara*, ed. and trans. M. R. Kale (Delhi: Motilal Banarsidass, 1967), pp. 44–48.

44. Ramendra Nath Nandi, *Religious Institutions and Cults in the Deccan* (Delhi: Motilal Banarsidass, 1973), p. 143.

45. N. Bhattacharyya, *Indian Mother Goddess*, p. 54; for other examples of blood offerings to goddesses, see Philip Spratt, *Hindu Culture and Personality* (Bombay: Manaktalas, 1966), pp. 236, 238, 245, 282, 284.

46. J. P. Vogel, "The Head-offering to the Goddess in Pallava Sculpture," *Bulletin of the School of Oriental Studies* (London) 6:539–543.

47. Ghoshal, *Studies in Indian History and Culture*, p. 333.

48. Ibid.

49. Ibid., pp. 335–336; Nandi, *Religious Institutions*, pp. 145–146.

50. Vogel, "The Head-offering to the Goddess," pp. 539–543.

51. Prince Ilango Adigal, *Shilappadikaram*, trans. Alain Danielou (New York: New Directions Book, 1965), canto 12, pp. 76–85.

52. Nandi, *Religious Institutions*, p. 136.

53. Brenda Beck, "The Goddess and the Demon: A Local South Indian Festival and Its Wider Context" (University of British Columbia, 1979), passim; Henry Whitehead, *The Village Gods of South India*, 2d ed. (Delhi: Sumit Publications, 1976), passim.

54. Whitehead, *Village Gods of South India*, p. 18, his emphasis.

55. See, for example, the play *Sacrifice*, by Rabindranath Tagore, which is a sustained criticism of animal sacrifice.

56. Eck, *Banaras*, p. 52, traces blood offerings all the way back to Yakṣa worship, perhaps the oldest surviving stratum of Hindu religion. She also notes the increasing use of red powder instead of blood in the propitiation of Yakṣa images in recent times.

57. Krishna Kanta Handiqui, *Yaśastilaka and Indian Culture* (Sholapur: Jaina Saṁskṛiti Saṁrakskaka Sangha, 1949), p. 168.

58. *Bhavabhūti's Mālatīmādhava*, pp. 44–48.

59. C. Sivaramamurti, *Nataraja in Art, Thought and Literature* (New Delhi: National Museum, 1974), p. 72.

60. The *Karpūrādi-stotra* 15–16 and Kṛṣṇānanda Āgamavāgīśa's *Bṛhat Tantrasāra* (2 vols. [Calcutta: Basumatī Sāhitya Mandir, 1934], 1:374) give the *dhyāna-mantra* of Śmaśāna-kālī (Kālī of the cremation grounds), in which the adept is advised to worship Kālī at dead of night, naked, in the cremation grounds.

61. *Bhavabhūti's Mālatīmādhava*, pp. 44–48.

62. Nandi, *Religious Institutions*, p. 135; see also Nalina Bhattasali, *Iconography of Buddhist and Brahmanical Sculptures in the Dacca Museum* (Dacca: Rai S. N. Bhadra Bahadur, 1929), pl. 71(b) facing p. 206.

63. See also the description of Dikkarvāsinī in the *Kālikā-purāṇa* 83.64–65.

64. Pushpendra Kumar, *Śakti Cult in Ancient India* (Banaras: Bhartiya Publishing House, 1974), p. 265; see also the description of Bhīmādevī, who is described as holding a bowl of blood and flesh in her hands, in the *Viṣṇudharmottara-purāṇa* 3.73.40 ff.

65. Handiqui, *Yaśastilaka*, p. 56.

66. R. C. Majumdar, ed., *History of Bengal*, 2 vols. (Dacca: Dacca University, 1943), 1:455, pl. 14; cited in Vibhuti Bhushan Mishra, *Religious Beliefs and Practices of North India during the Early Medieval Period* (Leiden: E. J. Brill, 1973), p. 25; see also Bhattasali, *Iconography of Buddhist and Brahmanical Sculptures*, pl. 72(a) facing p. 219.

67. Kanwar Lal, *Temples and Sculptures of Bhubaneswar* (Delhi: Arts and Letters, 1970), pl. 28.

68. Jitendra Nath Banerjea, *The Development of Hindu Iconography*, 2d ed. (Calcutta: University of Calcutta), p. 507, pl. 44, fig. 5; see also pl. 45, fig. 1, for an image of Danturā.

69. Richard Brubaker, "The Uses of Decapitation" (paper presented at the annual meeting of the American Academy of Religion, New York, November 17, 1979), p. 4.

10: THE MĀTṚKĀS

1. Jagdish Narain Tiwari, "Studies in Goddess Cults in Northern India, with Reference to the First Seven Centuries A.D." (Ph.D. diss., Australian National University, n.d.), pp. 215–244.

2. *Mahābhārata*, Vana-parva 217.

3. Ibid. 219.22–23.

4. Ibid. 219.20–45.

5. Jitendra Nath Banerjea, *The Development of Hindu Iconography*, 2d ed. (Calcutta: University of Calcutta, 1956), pp. 380–381; see also Nalini Kanta Bhattasali, *Iconography of Buddhist and Brahmanical Sculptures in the Dacca Museum* (Dacca: Rai S. N. Bhadra Bahadur, 1929), pp. 63–67.

6. *Mahābhārata*, Vana-parva 219.27.

7. *Bhāgavata-purāṇa* 10.6.4–18.

8. T. A. Gopinatha Rao, *Elements of Hindu Iconography*, 2d ed., 2 vols. (New York: Paragon), vol. 1, pt. 2, p. 393.

9. For example, Brenda E. F. Beck, "The Goddess and the Demon: A Local South Indian Festival and Its Wider Context" (University of British Columbia, 1979), p. 25; Richard L. Brubaker, "The Ambivalent Mistress: A Study of South Indian Village Goddesses and Their Religious Meaning" (Ph.D. diss., University of Chicago, 1978), pp. 30–31.

10. *Mahābhārata*, Śalya-parva 45.

11. The non-Brahmanic, Śaivite associations of the Mātṛkās are also seen in their association with Gaṇeśa and Vīrabhadra, two other members of the Śaivite "family," with whom the Mātṛkās are often pictured iconographically; Tiwari, "Goddess Cults in Northern India," pp. 194–198.

12. See my chapter 13, "Village Goddesses."

13. Tiwari, "Goddess Cults in Northern India," p. 139.

14. Ibid., p. 140.

15. Ibid., p. 142.

16. Ibid., p. 143.

17. Ibid., pp. 144–155.

18. Andhaka in this myth has the same ability to reduplicate himself that Raktabīja has in the *Devī-māhātmya* and *Vāmana-purāṇa* accounts of the Mātṛkās.

19. *Matsya-purāṇa* 179.9–32.

20. The *Devī-bhāgavata-purāṇa* account of the Mātṛkās (5.28.13–33) names ten goddesses and then says that the *śaktis* of some gods also appeared to do battle.

21. Rao, *Elements of Hindu Iconography*, vol. 1, pt. 2, pp. 348–349. This observation is made by Pearl Ostroff, "The Demon-slaying Devī: A Study of Her Purāṇic Myths" (M.A. thesis, McMaster University, 1978), pp. 37–38.

22. Tiwari, "Goddess Cults in Northern India," p. 180.

23. Ibid., p. 181.

24. Ibid.

25. Ibid.

26. Narendra Nath Bhattacharyya, *History of the Śākta Religion* (New Delhi: Munshiram Manoharlal Publishers, 1974), p. 102.

27. An exception to this is Cāmuṇḍā, who is sometimes listed among the Mātṛkās. Cāmuṇḍā, who is very often identified with Kālī and is very much like her in appearance and habit, is an important goddess in her own right.

28. See my chapter 13, "Village Goddesses."

11: TĀRĀ, CHINNAMASTĀ, AND THE MAHĀVIDYĀS

1. See my chapter 9, "The Mahādevī."

2. For example, *Vāmana-purāṇa* 30.3–9.

3. For example, *Devī-māhātmya* 11.38–50.

4. D. C. Sircar, *The Śākta Pīṭhas* (Delhi: Motilal Banarsidass, 1973), p. 48.

5. David Kinsley, "The Portrait of the Goddess in the *Devī-māhātmya*," *Journal of the American Academy of Religion* 46, no. 4 (December 1978): 498.

6. *Mahābhāgavata-purāṇa* 8.50–52.

7. Ibid. 8.57–71. The list of ten Mahāvidyās is the same in the *Bṛhaddharma-purāṇa*, except that the goddesses are given in a different order (Madhya-khanda 6). Other lists of Mahāvidyās, some containing more than ten goddesses, and including different goddesses from the ten given above, may be found in the

Śāradātilaka, the *Mālinīvijaya*, the *Muṇḍamālā*, and Kṛṣṇānanda Āgamavāgīśa's *Tantrasāra*; Chintaharan Chakravarti, *Tantras: Studies on Their Religion and Literature* (Calcutta: Punthi Pustak, 1963), pp. 85–86.

8. Kṛṣṇānanda Āgamavāgīśa, *Bṛhat Tantrasāra*, 2 vols. (Calcutta: Basumatī Sāhitya Mandir, 1934), 1:310–311.

9. Alain Danielou, *Hindu Polytheism* (New York: Pantheon Books, 1964), p. 277; Pushpendra Kumar, *Śakti Cult in Ancient India* (Banaras: Bhartiya Publishing House, 1974), p. 156; Philip Rawson, *The Art of Tantra* (London: Thames and Hudson, 1973), p. 125.

10. Danielou, *Hindu Polytheism*, pp. 280–281; Kumar, *Śakti Cult*, pp. 157–158; Ajit Mookerjee, *Tantra Asana: A Way to Self-Realization* (New Delhi: Ravi Kumar, 1971), pl. 47, p. 77.

11. Kumar, *Śakti Cult*, p. 157; Rawson, *The Art of Tantra*, p. 126.

12. Danielou, *Hindu Polytheism*, p. 283; Kumar, *Śakti Cult*, p. 159; Rawson, *The Art of Tantra*, p. 130.

13. Kumar, *Śakti Cult*, pp. 158–159; Rawson, *The Art of Tantra*, p. 130; Mookerjee, *Tantra Asana*, pl. 81, p. 118.

14. Danielou, *Hindu Polytheism*, p. 284; Kumar, *Śakti Cult*, pp. 159–60; Rawson, *The Art of Tantra*, p. 130.

15. Danielou, *Hindu Polytheism*, pp. 283–284; Kumar, *Śakti Cult*, p. 159; Rawson, *The Art of Tantra*, p. 130.

16. Kumar, *Śakti Cult*, p. 156; Rawson, *The Art of Tantra*, pp. 125–126.

17. Danielou, *Hindu Polytheism*, pp. 281–282; Kumar, *Śakti Cult*, p. 157.

18. An exception to this is found in the *Devī-bhāgavata-purāṇa* 7.28.46–68, where the Mahāvidyās arise from the Devī's body in order to help her defeat the demon Durgama.

19. *Bṛhaddharma-purāṇa*, Madhya-khaṇḍa 6.

20. *Mahābhāgavata-purāṇa* 8; *Bṛhaddharma-purāṇa*, Madhya-khaṇḍa 6.

21. See my chapter 8, "Kālī."

22. Caitanya (1485–1531) is mentioned converting Buddhists in Bengal; A. K. Majumdar, *Caitanya, His Life and Doctrine: A Study of Vaiṣṇavism* (Bombay: Bharatiya Vidya Bhavan, 1969), p. 187.

23. Stephen Beyer, *The Cult of Tārā: Magic and Ritual in Tibet* (Berkeley, Los Angeles, London: University of California Press, 1973), p. 7.

24. John Blofeld, *Bodhisattva of Compassion: The Mystical Tradition of Kuan Yin* (Boulder, Colo.: Shambhala Publications, 1978), p. 53; Heinrich Zimmer, *Philosophies of India* (Cleveland: World Publishing Co., 1956), p. 534.

25. Beyer, *The Cult of Tārā*, pp. 8–10.

26. Ibid., p. 4.

27. Ibid., p. 469, for references on the history of Tārā.

28. Ibid., p. 12.

29. Ibid., p. 13.

30. See my chapter 7, "Durgā," and D. C. Bhattacharya, "An Unknown Form of Tārā," in D. C. Sircar, ed., *The Śakti Cult and Tārā* (Calcutta: University of Calcutta, 1967), pp. 138–139.

31. For a depiction of the "eight terrors" from which Tārā is said to save, see Giuseppe Tucci, *Tibetan Painted Scrolls*, 2 vols. (Rome: Libraria dello Stato, 1949), *tanka* 44, pl. 78, discussed in vol. 2, pp. 403 ff.

32. For examples, see Beyer, *The Cult of Tārā*, pp. 233–240; Blofeld, *Bodhisattva of Compassion*, pp. 55–71.

33. For example, Beyer, *The Cult of Tārā*, pp. 386–388.

34. Ibid., p. 386.

35. Blofeld, *Bodhisattva of Compassion*, p. 59, where she blesses a young couple with a child after rescuing them from calamity.

36. Beyer, *The Cult of Tārā*, pp. 61–62.

37. Blofeld, *Bodhisattva of Compassion*, pp. 57–58.

38. Beyer, *The Cult of Tārā*, pp. 212–213.

39. Beyer, *The Cult of Tārā*, p. 302, shows quite clearly that Kurukullā was originally an Indian tribal deity.

40. Ibid., p. 303; see also Benoytosh Bhattacharyya, *The Indian Buddhist Iconography: Mainly Based on the Sādhanamālā and the Cognate Tāntric Texts of Rituals* (Calcutta: Firma K. L. Mukhopadhyay, 1968), pp. 147–152.

41. Beyer, *The Cult of Tārā*, p. 302.

42. Ibid., p. 306.

43. B. Bhattacharyya, *Indian Buddhist Iconography*, pp. 134–146.

44. Beyer, *The Cult of Tārā*, p. 292.

45. B. Bhattacharyya, *Indian Buddhist Iconography*, p. 190; see also Nalini Kanta Bhattasali, *Iconography of Buddhist and Brahmanical Sculptures in the Dacca Museum* (Dacca: Rai S. N. Bhadra Bahadur, 1929), pl. 71(a) facing p. 206.

46. B. Bhattacharyya, *Indian Buddhist Iconography*, pp. 190–191; Danielou, *Hindu Polytheism*, p. 277, cites a Hindu text that says that Tārā should be worshiped according to the Buddhist way.

47. *Tārā-tantraṁ*, ed. A. K. Maitra (Ghorāmārā, Rājshāhi: Pandit Purandara Kāvyatirtha, 1913), pp. 18–19.

48. *Mahābhāgavata-purāṇa* 8; *Bṛhaddharma-purāṇa*, Madhya-khaṇḍa 6; Chakravarti, *Tantras*, p. 88.

49. B. Bhattacharyya, *Indian Buddhist Iconography*, pp. 247–248; see also Benoytosh Bhattacharyya, *An Introduction to Buddhist Esoterism* (Banaras: Chowkhamba Sanskrit Series Office, 1964), pp. 159–160.

50. For pictorial representations of Chinnamastā see Ajit Mookerjee, *Tantra Art: Its Philosophy and Physics* (New Delhi: Ravi Kumar, 1966), pl. 65; A. Mookerjee and Madhu Khanna, *The Tantric Way: Art, Science, Ritual* (London: Thames and Hudson, 1977), p. 84.

51. The only myth about Chinnamastā that I have been able to locate says that once upon a time her two devotees Jaya and Vijaya complained to her that they were hungry. After twice telling them to be patient, she responded to their third complaint by cutting off her head to feed them with her own blood. Śrī Svāmī Mahārāja Datiyā, *Śrī Chinnamastā Nityārchana* (Prayag: Kalyāṇ Mandir Prakaśan, 1978), p. 5.

52. See U. N. Ghoshal, *Studies in Indian History and Culture* (Bombay: Orient Longman, 1965), pp. 333–340.

53. B. Bhattacharyya, *An Introduction to Buddhist Esoterism,* p. 159.

54. Jagdish Narain Tiwari, "Studies in Goddess Cults in Northern India, with Reference to the First Seven Centuries A.D." (Ph.D. diss., Australian National University, n.d.), pp. 312–337.

55. Ibid., pp. 313–315.

56. Ibid., p. 317.

57. Ibid., pp. 328–333.

58. Ibid., p. 334.

12: GODDESSES AND SACRED GEOGRAPHY

1. See the section on Pṛthivī in my chapter 1.

2. An even earlier example of this idea is found in *Ṛg-veda* 10.90, where the creation of the world is described as the result of the sacrifice of a giant being who is dismembered. The parts of the world are composed of the parts of his body.

3. Wendy O'Flaherty, *Asceticism and Eroticism in the Mythology of Śiva* (London: Oxford University Press, 1973), passim, has shown that a similar idea underlies much of Śaivite mythology. Śiva alternates between two poles, the ascetic and the erotic, the former creating great reserves of energy that are released when Śiva enters his erotic phase.

4. The idea pervades the entire section of the *Śatapatha-brāhmaṇa,* which deals with the elaborate rituals involved in building the fire altar. The idea that the world is periodically evolved out of a cosmic being is also seen in the mythology of Viṣṇu, who inhales the world after it has worn down at the end of the Kali Yuga and then gives it rebirth when it emerges from a great lotus that grows from his navel. The origin of the world from a giant being is also seen in the opening passage of the *Bṛhadāraṇyaka-upaniṣad,* where the world is said to have been created from a great sacrificial horse.

5. For example, *Bhāgavata-purāṇa* 10.1.17–22, where Viṣṇu decides to take the form of Kṛṣṇa because of the earth's complaint about Kaṁsa.

6. For example, T. A. Gopinatha Rao, *Elements of Hindu Iconography,* 2d ed., 2 vols. (New York: Paragon, 1968), vol. 1, pt. 1, pls. 22, 23, 25, 26, 27.

7. See my chapters 2, "Śrī-Lakṣmī," and 9, "The Mahādevī."

8. For example, *Devī-bhāgavata-purāṇa* 4.19.23–24.

9. For example, *Devī-māhātmya* 1.59; 5.7; *Lalitā-sahasranāma* 397; *Saundaryalaharī* 11; *Devī-bhāgavata-purāṇa,* passim.

10. Jainism contains a similar vision of the universe as a cosmic giant, whose lower limbs are identified with the nether worlds.

11. Vibhuti Bhushan Mishra, *Religious Beliefs and Practices of North India during the Early Medieval Period* (Leiden: E. J. Brill, 1973), p. 25.

12. John F. Fleet, *Inscriptions of the Early Gupta Kings and Their Successors* (Banaras: Indological Book House, 1970), p. 86.

13. For images of this, see Veronica Ions, *Indian Mythology* (London: Paul

Hamlyn, n.d.), p. 35; Jitendra Nath Banerjea, *The Development of Hindu Iconography*, 2d ed. (Calcutta: University of Calcutta, 1956), pl. 25.

14. Michael McKnight, "Kingship and Religion in the Gupta Age" (Ph.D. diss., McMaster University, 1976), p. 215.

15. Bankim Chandra Chatterjee, *The Abbey of Bliss*, trans. Nares Chandra Sengupta (Calcutta: Padmini Mohan Neogi, n.d.), pp. 39–41.

16. Ibid., p. 41.

17. Ibid., p. 99.

18. Ibid., p. 32.

19. Ibid., pp. 32–33.

20. *India: A Reference Manual, 1980* (New Delhi: Publication Division, Ministry of Education and Broadcasting, Government of India, 1980), p. 16.

21. Diana L. Eck, *Banaras: City of Light* (New York: Alfred A. Knopf, 1982), pp. 38–39.

22. Diana Eck, "India's *Tīrthas:* 'Crossings' in Sacred Geography," *History of Religions* 20, no. 4 (May 1981): 323–344.

23. In some cases the two—the geographical place and the deity—are hardly distinguishable. See below (pp. 187–196) on the sacrality of rivers and the Ganges.

24. Eck, *Banaras*, p. 157, has shown that in myths concerning the origins of Banaras it was the beauty and holiness of the city that attracted Śiva to it in the first place. The sacrality of Banaras, then, does not stem primarily from the fact that it is Śiva's city, although Śiva's residing there enhances its sacrality.

25. For example, Agehananda Bharati, "Pilgrimage Sites and Indian Civilization," in Joseph W. Elder, ed., *Chapters in Indian Civilization* (Dubuque, Iowa: Kendall/Hunt Publishing Co., 1970), p. 102; Surinder Mohan Bhardwaj, *Hindu Places of Pilgrimage in India* (Berkeley, Los Angeles, London: University of California Press, 1973), passim.

26. Eck, "India's *Tīrthas*," p. 336.

27. Narendra Nath Bhattacharyya, *History of the Śākta Religion* (New Delhi: Munshiram Manoharlal Publishers, 1974), pp. 139–140.

28. Diana Eck, paper on *pīṭhas* delivered at the annual meeting of the New England Region, American Academy of Religion, Dartmouth, N.H., 1979.

29. D. C. Sircar, *The Śākta Pīṭhas* (Delhi: Motilal Banarsidass, 1973), pp. 1–34.

30. This is reminiscent of the sacrifice of the giant in *Ṛg-veda* 10.90 from whose body the world was created.

31. *Matsya-purāṇa* 13; *Devī-bhāgavata-purāṇa* 7.30; *Kālikā-purāṇa* 18; *Mahābhāgavata-purāṇa* 11; *Bṛhaddharma-purāṇa*, Madhya-khaṇḍa 10.

32. Edward Gait, *A History of Assam* (Calcutta: Thacker Spink, 1963), pp. 11–13.

33. N. Bhattacharyya, *History of the Śākta Religion*, p. 142.

34. In much the same way when the remains of the Buddha were enshrined in stupas they sacralized India and other countries to which Buddhism spread.

35. Although the myth tries to be universal in the sense of applying to all areas of India, it is most applicable to northern areas of India and to goddesses

worshiped at northern shrines. In most versions of the myth it is clear that southern geography is not well known, while the regions of Bengal, Assam, and the Northwest are often known in great detail. Bengal, Assam, and the Northwest were and still are centers of Tantric worship, and the cult of the *pīṭhas* may be related to Tantric masters and the sites at which they performed their *sādhana*. Some texts instruct the Tantric adept to "place" the goddesses enshrined at the *pīṭhas* into various parts of his body by means of the *nyāsa* ritual. In this way the adept identifies himself, piece by piece, with the goddess he worships. Sircar, *The Śākta Pīṭhas*, pp. 3, 15–17; N. Bhattacharyya, *History of the Śākta Religion*, pp. 119–122.

36. Sircar, *The Śākta Pīṭhas*, pp. 35–41.

37. See my chapter 4, "Sarasvatī."

38. See especially *Ṛg-veda* 7.49 for the divinity of waters and rivers; see also Pandurang Vaman Kane, *History of Dharmaśāstra*, 5 vols. (Poona: Bhandarkar Oriental Institute, 1930–62), 4:555–556.

39. *Mahābhārata*, Vana-parva 104–108; *Rāmāyaṇa* 1.38–44; *Bhāgavata-purāṇa* 9.8–9; *Brahma-vaivarta-purāṇa*, Prakṛti-khaṇḍa 10; *Devī-bhāgavata-purāṇa* 9.11.

40. *Kurma-purāṇa* 1.44; *Brahama-vaivarta-purāṇa*, Kṛṣṇajanma-khaṇḍa 34; *Bhāgavata-purāṇa* 5.17; *Devī-bhāgavata-purāṇa* 8.7; Viṣṇu-purāṇa 2.2, 8.

41. *Mahābhāgavata-purāṇa* 65; *Bṛhaddharma-purāṇa*, Madhya-khaṇḍa 17.

42. *Bṛhaddharma-purāṇa*, Madhya-khaṇḍa 14.

43. Conversely, the Ganges is understood as purifying the deities she comes in contact with; C. Sivaramamurti, *Gaṅgā* (New Delhi: Orient Longman, 1976), p. 45.

44. For a detailed and clear exposition of how purity and pollution are understood and ritually dealt with, see Edward B. Harper, "Ritual Pollution as an Integrator of Caste and Religion," *Journal of Asian Studies* 23 (June 1964): 151–197.

45. The generation of *tapas* (heat or fire) as a result of ascetic practices is a good example of the purifying role of fire, as is the understanding of the cremation fire as a final purifying act.

46. *Agni-purāṇa* 110; see also *Padma-purāṇa* 5.60.1–127 and Kane, *History of Dharmaśāstra*, 4:585.

47. Diana Eck, "Gaṅgā: The Goddess in Hindu Sacred Geography," in John Stratton Hawley and Donna Marie Wulff, eds., *The Divine Consort: Rādhā and the Goddesses of India* (Berkeley, Calif.: Berkeley Religious Studies Series, 1982), p. 174.

48. *Bṛhaddharma-purāṇa*, Madhya-khaṇḍa 26.

49. Jitendra Nath Banerjea, *The Development of Hindu Iconography*, 2d ed. (Calcutta: University of Calcutta, 1956), pp. 353–354; Sivaramamurti, *Gaṅgā*, figs. 22–27; in Odette Viennot's *Les divinités fluviales Gaṅgā et Yamunā* (Paris: Presses Universitaires de France, 1964) nearly every plate depicts either Gaṅgā or Yamunā on a temple or at the doorway of a temple.

50. Eck, "Gaṅgā," p. 176.

51. Ibid.

52. Ibid.
53. Sivaramamurti, *Gaṅgā,* p. 81.
54. Eck, *Banaras,* pp. 324-344.
55. Eck, "Gaṅgā," p. 176.
56. Jonathan Parry, "Death and Cosmogony in Kāshī," *Contributions to Indian Sociology* 15 (1981): 337-365.
57. Eck, "Gaṅgā," p. 181.
58. Eck, *Banaras,* p. 218.
59. Eck, "India's *Tīrthas,*" p. 327.
60. Sivaramamurti, *Gaṅgā,* p. 49.
61. Ibid., fig. 42.
62. Ibid., figs. 19-21.
63. Steven G. Darian, *The Ganges in Myth and History* (Honolulu: University of Hawaii Press, 1978), p. 37; see also his p. 61.
64. Ibid., p. 152.
65. *Mahāsuka Jātaka,* no. 429; Darian, *The Ganges,* pp. 36-37.
66. See my chapter 3, "Pārvatī."
67. For a discussion of this theme in Śaivite mythology, see O'Flaherty, *Asceticism and Eroticism,* pp. 95-110.
68. Darian, *The Ganges,* p. 111.
69. Eck, "Gaṅgā," pp. 178-179.
70. Ibid., pp. 166-167.
71. Ibid., p. 182.

13: VILLAGE GODDESSES

1. For example, S. C. Dube, *Indian Village* (New York: Harper and Row, 1967), p. 96. Dube mentions four goddesses in a village of under 2,500; these goddesses are associated with different castes.
2. Henry Whitehead, *The Village Gods of South India,* 2d ed. (Delhi: Sumit Publications, 1976), p. 23.
3. Richard L. Brubaker, "The Ambivalent Mistress: A Study of South Indian Village Goddesses and Their Religious Meaning" (Ph.D. diss., University of Chicago, 1978), p. 61.
4. Śiva is often pictured as a harassed farmer in folk tales in Bengal, for example, and bears little resemblance to the Śiva of the *Purāṇas.*
5. Whitehead, *Village Gods of South India,* pp. 17-18.
6. Brubaker, "The Ambivalent Mistress," p. 69.
7. Ibid., p. 194.
8. Ibid., p. 57.
9. Ibid., pp. 297-298.
10. Ibid., p. 79.
11. Ibid., p. 298.
12. In South India a common distinction is made between right-division castes and left-division castes. The former are agriculturally based and tied to the

land, whereas the latter are urban based and pursue artisan-related skills in their traditional occupations. In festivals in honor of village goddesses, the right-division castes tend to play a more central role. For example, the *pūjāris*, ritual priests at the village-goddess festivals, come from the right-division castes. This may be because the right-division castes are closer to the soil and have more at stake in terms of the well-being of the village. Traditionally the left-division castes have been more mobile and less tied to one specific locale. See Brenda E. F. Beck, *Peasant Society in Koṅku: A Study of Right and Left Subcastes in South India* (Vancouver: University of British Columbia Press, 1972), p. 118; and Brubaker, "The Ambivalent Mistress," pp. 182, 191.

13. Brubaker, "The Ambivalent Mistress," p. 172.

14. Ibid., p. 170.

15. Ibid., p. 92; Brenda E. F. Beck, "The Goddess and the Demon: A Local South Indian Festival and Its Wider Context" (University of British Columbia, 1979), p. 15.

16. Brubaker, "The Ambivalent Mistress," pp. 99–101.

17. Ibid., p. 110.

18. Ibid., pp. 127–134; Whitehead, *Village Gods of South India*, pp. 126–137; Wilber Theodore Elmore, *Dravidian Gods in Modern Hinduism: A Study of the Local and Village Deities of Southern India* (Hamilton, N.Y.: Published by the author, 1915), pp. 89–90.

19. For example, *Manu-dharma-śāstra* 5.147–149.

20. Brubaker, "The Ambivalent Mistress," pp. 140–141.

21. David Dean Shulman, *Tamil Temple Myths: Sacrifice and Divine Marriage in the South Indian Saiva Tradition* (Princeton, N.J.: Princeton University Press, 1980), pp. 147–148.

22. Ibid., p. 202.

23. Ibid., p. 216; David Kinsley, *The Sword and the Flute—Kṛṣṇa and Kālī* (Berkeley, Los Angeles, London: University of California Press, 1975), pp. 105–106.

24. Lawrence A. Babb, *The Divine Hierarchy: Popular Hinduism in Central India* (New York: Columbia University Press, 1975), pp. 215–237.

25. Heinrich Zimmer, "The Indian World Mother," in Joseph Campbell, ed., *The Mystic Vision* (Princeton, N.J.: Princeton University Press, 1976), p. 76.

26. Brubaker, "The Ambivalent Mistress," p. 166.

27. Edward C. Dimock, Jr., "A Theology of the Repulsive: The Myth of the Goddess Śitalā," in John Stratton Hawley and Donna Marie Wulff, eds., *The Divine Consort: Rādhā and the Goddesses of India* (Berkeley, Calif.: Berkeley Religious Studies Series, 1982), pp. 184–186.

28. Brubaker, "The Ambivalent Mistress," p. 162.

29. Babb, *The Divine Hierarchy*, p. 227; Brubaker, "The Ambivalent Mistress," p. 319.

30. Brubaker, "The Ambivalent Mistress," p. 338.

31. Ibid., pp. 347–352.

32. Ibid., p. 291.

33. Ibid.; Beck, "The Goddess and the Demon," p. 36.

34. Brubaker, "The Ambivalent Mistress," pp. 295-296.

35. Ibid., pp. 277-283.

36. Elmore, *Dravidian Gods*, p. 31; see also Edgar Thurston, *Castes and Tribes of Southern India*, 7 vols. (Madras: Madras Government Press, 1909), 4:295-307, 316-317.

37. Beck, "The Goddess and the Demon," p. 36.

38. Brubaker, "The Ambivalent Mistress," pp. 273-274.

39. Victor Turner, *Dramas, Fields, and Metaphors: Symbolic Action in Human Society* (Ithaca, N.Y.: Cornell University Press, 1974), pp. 231-270.

40. Brubaker, "The Ambivalent Mistress," p. 291.

41. Ibid., p. 269.

42. Ibid., p. 382.

43. Victor Turner, *Process, Performance and Pilgrimage* (New Delhi: Concept Publishing Co., 1979), pp. 11-59.

44. Richard Lannoy, *The Speaking Tree: A Study of Indian Culture and Society* (London: Oxford University Press, 1971), p. 201.

45. I. M. Lewis, *Ecstatic Religion: An Anthropological Study of Spirit Possession and Shamanism* (Harmondsworth: Penguin Books, 1978), pp. 188-189.

46. For Manasā see Edward C. Dimock, Jr., "The Goddess of Snakes in Medieval Bengali Literature," *History of Religions* 1, no. 2 (Winter 1962): 307-321; Edward C. Dimock, Jr., and A. K. Ramanujan, "The Goddess of Snakes in Medieval Bengali Literature, Part II," *History of Religions* 3, no. 2 (Winter 1964): 300-322; and Pradyot Kumar Maity, *Historical Studies in the Cult of the Goddess Manasā* (Calcutta: Punthi Pustak, 1966).

47. Brubaker, "The Ambivalent Mistress," p. 384.

48. Śītālā is popular across North India and is worshiped particularly during the height of the dry season, when smallpox was most easily spread. Although smallpox has been eradicated, Śītālā is still widely worshiped to help alleviate or prevent skin diseases and to help solve personal problems. One of the largest and busiest temples in Banaras is a Śītālā temple. Most of her shrines, though, are small and primarily attract local residents during the dry season.

49. Dimock, "A Theology of the Repulsive," p. 187.

50. Ibid., p. 196.

APPENDIX: THE INDUS VALLEY CIVILIZATION

1. Sir John Marshall, ed., *Mohenjo-daro and the Indus Civilization*, 3 vols. (London: Arthur Probshtan, 1931), vol. 1, pl. 12, Kulli figures, nos. 3-5, Zhob figures, nos. 6-10; Stuart Piggott, *Prehistoric India* (Harmondsworth: Penguin Books, 1950), fig. 16, p. 129.

2. Marshall, *Mohenjo-daro*, 1:50; Piggott, *Prehistoric India*, p. 129, agrees that the figures are "terrifying."

3. Marshall, *Mohenjo-daro*, 1:339.

4. Ibid., vol. 3, pl. 94, nos. 6-8.

5. Ibid., vol. 3, pl. 98.

6. E. J. H. MacKay, *Further Excavations at Mohenjo-daro*, 2 vols. (Delhi: Government of India Press, 1938), vol. 1, pl. 72, nos. 8–10; pl. 73, no. 8; pl. 74, nos. 23–24.

7. See, for example, André Leroi-Gourhan, *Treasures of Prehistoric Art* (New York: Harry Abrams Publishers, n.d.), pls. 53, 55; p. 520.

8. MacKay, *Excavations at Mohenjo-daro*, vol. 1, pl. 75, nos. 9, 19; pl. 76, no. 10.

9. Ibid., pl. 72, nos. 8–9; pl. 73, nos. 9–11.

10. Ibid., pl. 75, no. 5; Marshall, *Mohenjo-daro*, vol. 1, pl. 94, no. 14.

11. It is not always clear if hair is being depicted.

12. See MacKay, *Excavations at Mohenjo-daro*, vol. 1, pl. 73, nos. 3, 4, 6; pl. 75, nearly every example.

13. Ibid., pl. 76, nos. 6, 14.

14. For example, Philip Rawson, *The Art of Tantra* (London: Thames and Hudson, 1973), pls. 32, 33.

15. MacKay, *Excavations at Mohenjo-daro*, vol. 1, pl. 75, nos. 10, 17.

16. Ibid., pl. 76, nos. 1–5.

17. Marshall, *Mohenjo-daro*, vol. 1, pl. 12, no. 12.

18. Ibid., pl. 12, no. 18.

19. Ibid., pl. 13, no. 17.

20. MacKay, *Excavations at Mohenjo-daro*, vol. 1, pl. 84, nos. 75, 86.

21. Marshall, *Mohenjo-daro*, 1:58–63. Examples of the objects are found in ibid., pl. 13; vol. 3, pl. 156.

22. Narendra Nath Bhattacharyya, *History of the Śākta Religion* (New Delhi: Munshiram Manoharlal Publishers, 1974), p. 14; J. Przyluski, "The Great Goddess of India and Iran," *Indian Historical Quarterly* 10 (1934): 405–430; Sadanand K. Dikshit, *The Mother Goddess* (New Delhi: Published by the author, 1957).

23. N. Bhattacharyya, *History of the Śākta Religion*, pp. 13–15; Marshall, *Mohenjo-daro*, 1:51, 57–58.

24. N. Bhattacharyya, *History of the Śākta Religion*, pp. 13–14; Marshall, *Mohenjo-daro*, 1:76–78; Piggott, *Prehistoric India*, pp. 211–213.

25. Marshall, *Mohenjo-daro*, vol. 1, pl. 12, no. 17.

26. For a balanced reappraisal of the religion of the Indus civilization, see Herbert P. Sullivan, "A Re-examination of the Religion of the Indus Civilization," *History of Religions* 4, no. 1 (Summer 1964): 115–125.

27. Marshall, *Mohenjo-daro*, vol. 1, pl. 12, no. 12.

28. Ibid., p. 64; Sullivan, "The Religion of the Indus Civilization, " p. 117.

29. Marshall, *Mohenjo-daro*, vol. 1, pl. 12, no. 18.

30. Ibid., pl. 13, no. 17.

BIBLIOGRAPHY

Agni-purāṇa. Poona: Ānandāśrama Sanskrit Series, 1957.

Agni Purāṇam. Translated by Manmatha Nath Dutt Shastri. 2 vols. Banaras: Chowkhamba Sanskrit Series Office, 1967.

Airi, Raghunath. *Concept of Sarasvati (in Vedic Literature)*. Delhi: Munshiram Manoharlal Publishers, 1977.

[*Aitareya-brāhmaṇa*]. *Rigveda Brāhmaṇas: The Aitareya and Kauṣītaki Brāhmaṇas of the Rigveda*. Translated by Arthur B. Keith. Delhi: Motilal Banarsidass, 1971.

[*Āsvalayana-gṛhya-sūtra*]. *The Gṛihya-sutras, Rules of Vedic Domestic Ceremonies*. Translated by Hermann Oldenberg. 2 vols. Delhi: Motilal Banarsidass, 1967.

Atharva-veda. With the Commentary of Sāyaṇa. Edited by Vishva Bandhu and others. 4 parts. Hoshiarpur: Visveshvaranand Indological Series, 1960–64.

[*Atharva-veda*]. *The Hymns of the Atharvaveda*. Translated by Ralph T. H. Griffith. 2 vols. Banaras: Chowkhamba Sanskrit Series Office, 1968.

Avalon, Arthur, and Ellen Avalon, trans. *Hymns to the Goddess*. 3d ed. Madras: Ganesh, 1964.

Babb, Lawrence A. *The Divine Hierarchy: Popular Hinduism in Central India*. New York: Columbia University Press, 1975.

Babineau, Edmour. "The Interaction of Love of God and Social Duty in the Rāmcaritmānas." Ph.D. diss., McMaster University, 1975.

Bāṇabhaṭṭa. *Kādambarī*. Bombay: Mathurānāth Śastrī, 1940.

Banerjea, Jitendra Nath. *The Development of Hindu Iconography*. 2d ed. Calcutta: University of Calcutta, 1956.

Barz, Richard. *The Bhakti Cult of Vallabhācārya*. Faridabad, Haryana: Thomson Press, 1976.

Beck, Brenda E. F. "The Goddess and the Demon: A Local South Indian Festival and Its Wider Context." University of British Columbia, 1979.

______. *Peasant Society in Koṅku: A Study of Right and Left Subcastes in South India*. Vancouver: University of British Columbia Press, 1972.

Behera, K. S. "Lakṣmī in Orissan Literature and Art." In D. C. Sircar, ed. *Foreigners in Ancient India and Laksmī and Sarasvatī in Art and Literature*, pp. 91-105. Calcutta: University of Calcutta, 1970.

Beyer, Stephen. *The Cult of Tārā: Magic and Ritual in Tibet*. Berkeley, Los Angeles, London: University of California Press, 1973.

Bhāgavata-purāṇa. Gorakhpur: Gītā Press, Saṁvat 2021.

The Bhāgavata Purāṇa. Translated and annotated by Ganesh Vasudeo Tagare. 4 vols. Delhi: Motilal Banarsidass, 1976.

Bhandarker, R G. *Vaiṣṇavism, Śaivism and Minor Religious Systems*. Strassburg: K. J. Trübner, 1913.

Bharati, Agehananda. "Pilgrimage Sites and Indian Civilization." In Joseph W. Elder, ed. *Chapter in Indian Civilization*, pp. 83-126. Dubuque, Iowa: Kendall/Hunt Publishing Co., 1970.

______. *The Tantric Tradition*. London: Rider, 1965.

Bhardwaj, Surinder Mohan. *Hindu Places of Pilgrimage in India*. Berkeley, Los Angeles, London: University of California Press, 1973.

Bhattacharji, Sukumari. *The Indian Theogony*. Cambridge: Cambridge University Press, 1970.

Bhattacharya, D. C. "An Unknown Form of Tārā." In D. C. Sircar, ed., *The Śakti Cult and Tara*, pp. 134-142. Calcutta: University of Calcutta, 1967.

Bhattacharyya, Benoytosh. *The Indian Buddhist Iconography: Mainly Based on the Sādhanamālā and Cognate Tāntric Texts of Rituals*. Calcutta: Firma K. L. Mukhopadhyay, 1968.

______. *An Introduction to Buddhist Esoterism*. Banaras: Chowkhamba Sanskrit Series Office, 1964.

Bhattacharyya, Narendra Nath. *History of the Śākta Religion*. New Delhi: Munshiram Manoharlal Publishers, 1974.

______. *Indian Mother Goddess*. Calcutta: Indian Studies Past and Present, 1971.

Bhattasali, Nalini Kanta. *Iconography of Buddhist and Brahmanical Sculptures in the Dacca Museum*. Dacca: Rai S. N. Bhadra Bahadur, 1929.

Bhavabhūti's Mālatīmādhava with the Commentary of Jagaddhara. Edited and translated by M. R. Kale. Delhi: Motilal Banarsidass, 1967.

Biardeau, Madeleine. "L'arbre *śami* et le buffle sacrificiel." In Madeleine Biardeau, ed. *Autour de la déesse hindoue. Purusartha: sciences sociales en Asie du Sud*. Collection no. 5. Paris: Centre d'Études de l'Inde et de l'Asie du Sud, 1981.

Blofeld, John. *Bodhisattva of Compassion: The Mystical Tradition of Kuan Yin*. Boulder, Colo.: Shambhala Publications, 1978.

Bosch, F. D. K. *The Golden Germ*. 's Gravenhage: Mouton, 1960.

Brahma-vaivarta-purāṇa. Poona: Ānandāśrama Sanskrit Series, 1935.

Brahma-Vaivarta Puranam. Translated by Rajendra Nath Sen. 2 parts. Allahabad: Sudhindra Nath Vasu, 1920, 1922.

Bṛhaddharma-purāṇa. Banaras: Chaukhamba Amarabharati Prakashan, 1897.

Brown, Cheever Mackenzie. *God as Mother: A Feminine Theology in India*. Hartford, Vt.: Claude Stark, 1974.

Brubaker, Richard L. "The Ambivalent Mistress: A Study of South Indian Village Goddesses and Their Religious Meaning." Ph.D. diss., University of Chicago, 1978.

______. "The Uses of Decapitation." Paper presented at the annual meeting of the American Academy of Religion, New York, November 17, 1979.

Campbell, Joseph. *The Masks of God: Primitive Mythology*. New York: Viking Press, 1959.

[Caṇḍīdās.] *Love Songs of Chandidās*. Translated by Deben Bhattacharya. London: George Allen and Unwin, 1967.

Carman, John. *The Theology of Rāmānuja*. New Haven, Conn.: Yale University Press, 1974.

Chakravarti, Chintaharan. *Tantras: Studies on Their Religion and Literature*. Calcutta: Punthi Pustak, 1963.

Chaterjee, A. K. "Some Aspects of Sarasvatī." In D. C. Sircar, ed. *Foreigners in Ancient India and Lakṣmī and Sarasvatī in Art and Literature*, pp. 148–153. Calcutta: University of Calcutta, 1970.

Chatterjee, Bankim Chandra. *The Abbey of Bliss*. Translated by Nares Chandra Sengupta. Calcutta: Padmini Mohan Neogi, n.d.

Coburn, Thomas B. "Consort of None, *Śakti* of All: The Vision of the *Devī-Māhātmya*." In John Stratton Hawley and Donna Marie Wulff, eds. *The Divine Consort: Rādhā and the Goddesses of India*, pp. 153–165. Berkeley, Calif.: Berkeley Religious Studies Series, 1982.

Coomaraswamy, Ananda. "On the Loathly Bride." *Speculum: A Journal of Medieval Studies* 20, no. 4 (1945): 391–404.

______. *Yaksas*. 2 parts. Delhi: Munshiram Manoharlal, 1971.

Courtright, Paul. "Satī and Suttee: Widow Immolation in Hinduism and Its Western Interpretations." University of North Carolina at Greensboro, 1982.

Danielou, Alain. *Hindu Polytheism*. New York: Pantheon Books, 1964.

Darian, Steven G. *The Ganges in Myth and History*. Honolulu: University of Hawaii Press, 1978.

Das, R. K. *Temples of Tamilnad*. Bombay: Bharatiya Vidya Bhavan, 1964.

Das, Sudhendukumar. *Sakti or Divine Power*. Calcutta: University of Calcutta, 1934.

Dāsgupta, Śaśibhūsan. *Bhārater Śakti-sādhana o Śākta Sāhitya*. Calcutta: Sāhitya Saṅgsad, 1367 B.S. [1961].

Dasgupta, Surendranath. *A History of Indian Philosophy*. Vol. 3. 5 vols. Cambridge: Cambridge University Press, 1968.

Datiyā, Śrī Svāmī Mahārāja. *Śrī Chinnamastā Nityārchana*. Prayag: Kalyāṇ Mandir Prakaśan, 1978.

De, S. K. *Early History of the Vaisnava Faith and Movement in Bengal*. Calcutta: Firma K. L. Mukhopadhyay, 1961.

Devī-bhāgavata-purāṇa. Banaras: Paṇḍita Pustakālaya, 1969.

[*Devī-bhāgavata-purāṇa*]. *The Sri Mad Devi Bhagavatam*. Translated by Swami Vijnanananda. Allahabad: Sudhindra Nath Vasu, 1921–23.

[*Devī-māhātmya*]. *The Glorification of the Great Goddess.* Edited and translated by Vasudeva S. Agrawala. Banaras: All-India Kashiraj Trust, 1963.

Devī-purāṇa. Edited by Pushpendra Kumar Sharma. New Delhi: Kendriya Sanskrit Vidyapeeth, 1973.

Dhal, Upendra Nath. *Goddess Laksmi: Origin and Development.* New Delhi: Oriental Publishers, 1978.

Dhavamony, Mariasusai. *Love of God according to Śaiva Siddhānta.* Oxford: Clarendon Press, 1971.

Dikshit, Sadanand K. *The Mother Goddess.* New Delhi: Published by the author, 1957.

Dimmitt, Cornelia. "Sītā: Mother Goddess and *Śakti.*" In John Stratton Hawley and Donna Marie Wulff, eds. *The Divine Consort: Rādhā and the Goddesses of India,* pp. 210–223. Berkeley, Calif.: Berkeley Religious Studies Series, 1982.

Dimock, Edward C., Jr. "The Goddess of Snakes in Medieval Bengali Literature." *History of Religions* 1, no. 2 (Winter 1962): 307–321.

______. *The Place of the Hidden Moon.* Chicago: University of Chicago Press, 1966.

______. "A Theology of the Repulsive: The Myth of the Goddess Śītalā." In John Stratton Hawley and Donna Marie Wulff, eds. *The Divine Consort: Rādhā and the Goddesses of India,* pp. 184–203. Berkeley, Calif.: Berkeley Religious Studies Series, 1982.

Dimock, Edward C., Jr., and Denise Levetov, trans. *In Praise of Krishna: Songs from the Bengali.* Garden City, N.Y.: Doubleday, 1967.

Dimock, Edward C., Jr., and A. K. Ramanujan. "The Goddess of Snakes in Medieval Bengali Literature, Part II." *History of Religions* 3, no. 2 (Winter 1964): 300–322.

Douglas, Mary. *Purity and Danger: An Analysis of Concepts of Pollution and Taboo.* Harmondsworth: Penguin Books, 1970.

Dube, S. C. *Indian Village.* New York: Harper and Row, 1967.

Dubois, Abbé J. A. *Hindu Manners, Customs and Ceremonies.* Translated by Henry K. Beauchamp. 3d ed. Oxford: Clarendon Press, 1906.

Eck, Diana L. *Banaras, City of Light.* New York: Alfred A. Knopf, 1982.

______. "Gaṅgā: The Goddess in Hindu Sacred Geography." In John Stratton Hawley and Donna Marie Wulff, eds., *The Divine Consort: Rādhā and the Goddesses of India,* pp. 166–183. Berkeley, Calif.: Berkeley Religious Studies Series, 1982.

______. "India's *Tīrthas*: 'Crossings' in Sacred Geography." *History of Religions* 20, no. 4 (May 1981): 323–344.

______. Paper on *pīṭhas* presented at the annual meeting of the New England Region, American Academy of Religion, Dartmouth, N.H., 1979.

Eliade, Mircea. *Patterns in Comparative Religion.* Cleveland: World Publishing Co., 1963.

______. *Yoga: Immortality and Freedom.* New York: Pantheon Books, 1958.

Elmore, Wilber Theodore. *Dravidian Gods in Modern Hinduism: A Study of the Local and Village Deities of Southern India.* Hamilton, N.Y.: Published by the author, 1915. Reprinted from *University Studies of the University of Nebraska* 15, no. 1 (1915).

Farquhar, J. N. *An Outline of the Religious Literature of India.* Delhi: Motilal Banarsidass, 1967.

Fleet, John F. *Inscriptions of the Early Gupta Kings and Their Successors.* Banaras: Indological Book House, 1970.

Forbes, Alexander Kinloch. *Rās-Mālā: Hindu Annals of Western India.* New Delhi: Heritage Publishers, 1973.

Gait, Edward. *A History of Assam.* Calcutta: Thacker Spink, 1963.

Garuḍa-purāṇa. Edited by Ramshankar Bhattacarya. Banaras: Kashi Sanskrit Series, 1964.

The Garuḍa-purāṇam. Translated by Manmatha Nath Dutt Śastrī. Banaras: Chowkhamba Sanskrit Series Office, 1968.

Ghosh, Niranjan. *Concept and Iconography of the Goddess of Abundance and Fortune in Three Religions of India.* Burdwan: University of Burdwan, 1979.

Ghosha, Pratāpachandra. *Durga Puja: With Notes and Illustrations.* Calcutta: Hindoo Patriot Press, 1871.

Ghoshal, U. N. *Studies in Indian History and Culture.* Bombay: Orient Longman, 1965.

Gode, P. K. "Hari Kavi's Contribution to the Problem of the Bhavāni Sword of Shivaji the Great." *New Indian Antiquary* 3 (1940–41).

Gonda, Jan. *Ancient Indian Kingship from the Religious Point of View.* Leiden: E. J. Brill, 1969.

______. *Aspects of Early Viṣṇuism.* 2d ed. Delhi: Motilal Banarsidass, 1969.

Granoff, Phyllis. "Scholars and Wonder-Workers: Some Remarks on the Role of the Supernatural in Philsophical Contests in Vedānta Hagiographies." McMaster University, 1984.

Gross, Rita. "Hindu Female Deities as a Resource for the Contemporary Rediscovery of the Goddess." *Journal of the American Academy of Religion* 46, no. 3 (September 1978): 269–292.

Gupta, Anand Swarup. "Conception of Sarasvatī in the Purānas," *Purāṇa* 4, no. 1 (1962): 55–95.

Handiqui, Krishna Kanta. *Yaśastilaka and Indian Culture.* Sholapur: Jaina Saṁskṛiti Saṁrakshaka Sangha, 1949.

Harivaṁśa. Edited by Ramachandra Shastri. Poona: Oriental Research Institute, 1936.

Harivamsha. Translated by Manmatha Nath Dutt. Calcutta: Elysium Press, 1897.

Harper, Edward B. "Ritual Pollution as an Integrator of Caste and Religion." *Journal of Asian Studies* 23 (June 1964): 151–197.

Hawley, John Stratton. *At Play with Krishna: Pilgrimage Dramas from Brindavan.* Princeton, N.J.: Princeton University Press, 1981.

Hazra, R. C. *Studies in the Upapurāṇas.* Vol. 2: *Śākta and Non-sectarian Upapurānas.* Calcutta: Calcutta Sanskrit College Research Series, 1963.

Heesterman, J. C. *The Ancient Indian Royal Consecration*. The Hague: Mouton, 1957.

Hein, Norvin. "The Rām Līlā." In Milton Singer, ed. *Traditional India: Structure and Change*, pp. 73–98. Philadelphia: American Folklore Society, 1959.

Herman, Phyllis Kaplan. "Ideal Kingship and the Feminine Power: A Study of the Depiction of 'Rāmrājya' in the Vālmīki Rāmāyaṇa." Ph.D. diss., University of California, Los Angeles, 1979.

Hiltebeitel, Alf. *The Ritual of Battle*. Ithaca, N.Y.: Cornell University Press, 1976.

Hopkins, Thomas J. "The Social Teachings of the *Bhāgavata Purāṇa*." In Milton Singer, ed. *Krishna: Myths, Rites, and Attitudes*, pp. 3–22. Honolulu: East-West Center Press, 1966.

Hymn to Kālī (Karpūrādi-stotra). Edited and translated by Arthur Avalon. Madras: Ganesh, 1965.

The Hymns of the Ṛgveda. Translated by Ralph T. H. Griffith. 4th ed. 2 vols. Banaras: Chowkhamba Sanskrit Series Office, 1963.

India: A Reference Manual, 1980. New Delhi: Publication Division, Ministry of Education and Broadcasting, Government of India, 1980.

Ions, Veronica. *Indian Mythology*. London: Paul Hamlyn, n.d.

Jayadeva. *Love Song of the Dark Lord: Jayadeva's "Gītagovinda."* Edited and translated by Barbara Stoler Miller. New York: Columbia University Press, 1977.

Jones, Craig. "Rādhā: The Paroḍhā Nāyikā." M.A. thesis, McMaster University, 1980.

Kakar, Sudhir. *The Inner World: A Psycho-analytic Study of Childhood and Society in India*. Oxford: Oxford University Press, 1978.

Kālikā-purāṇa. Bombay: Veṅkaṭeśvara Press, 1891.

Kālikā-purāṇa. See *Worship of the Goddess according to the Kālikā-purāṇa*.

Kane, Pandurang Vaman. *History of Dharmaśāstra*. 5 vols. Poona: Bhandarkar Oriental Insititute, 1930–62.

Karpūrādi-stotra. See *Hymn to Kālī*.

[*Kauṣītaki-brāhmaṇa*]. *Rigveda Brāhmaṇas: The Aitareya and Kauṣītaki Brāhmaṇas of the Rigveda*. Translated by Arthur B. Keith. Delhi: Motilal Banarsidass, 1971.

Kayal, Akshaykumar. "Women in Folk-Sayings of West Bengal." In Sankar Sen Gupta, ed. *A Study of Women in Bengal*, pp. ix–xxxii. Calcutta: Indian Publications, 1970.

Khan, Mohammad Israil. *Sarasvati in Sanskrit Literature*. Ghaziabad: Crescent Publishing House, 1978.

Kinsley, David. "Blood and Death Out of Place: Reflections on the Goddess Kālī." In John Stratton Hawley and Donna Marie Wulff, eds., *The Divine Consort: Rādhā and the Goddesses of India*, pp. 144–152. Berkeley, Calif.: Berkeley Religious Studies Series, 1982.

———. *The Divine Player—A Study of Kṛṣṇa Līlā*. Delhi: Motilal Banarsidass, 1979.

______. "The Portrait of the Goddess in the *Devī-māhātmya*." *Journal of the American Academy of Religion* 46, no. 4 (December 1978): 489-506.

______. *The Sword and the Flute—Kṛṣṇa and Kālī*. Berkeley, Los Angeles, London: University of California Press, 1975.

______. " 'Through the Looking Glass': Divine Madness in the Hindu Religious Tradition." *History of Religions* 13, no. 4 (May 1974): 270-305.

Kramrisch, Stella. "The Indian Great Goddess." *History of Religions* 14, no. 4 (May 1975): 235-265.

Kṛṣṇānanda Āgamavāgīśa. *Bṛhat Tantrasāra*. 2 vols. Calcutta: Basumatī Sāhitya Mandir, 1934.

Kumar, Pushpendra. *Śakti Cult in Ancient India*. Banaras: Bhartiya Publishing House, 1974.

Kūrma-purāṇa. Edited by Anand Swarup Gupta. Translated by Ahibhushan Bhattacharya and others. Banaras: All-India Kashi Raj Trust, 1972.

Lakṣmī Tantra, a Pāñcarātra Text. Translated by Sanjukta Gupta. Leiden: E. J. Brill, 1972.

Lal, Kanwar. *Temples and Sculptures of Bhubaneswar*. Delhi: Arts and Letters, 1970.

[*Lalitā-sahasranāma*]. *Sri Lalita Sahasranamam*. Translated by Chaganty Suryanarayanamurthy. Madras: Ganesh, 1962.

Lalitā-sahasranāman with Bhāskararāya's Commentary. Translated by R. Ananthakrishna Sastry. Madras: Theosophical Publishing House, 1951.

Lannoy, Richard. *The Speaking Tree: A Study of Indian Culture and Society*. London: Oxford University Press, 1971.

The Laws of Manu. Translated by G. Bühler. Delhi: Motilal Banarsidass, 1975.

Leroi-Gourhan, André. *Treasures of Prehistoric Art*. New York: Harry N. Abrams Publishers, n.d.

Lewis, I. M. *Ecstatic Religion: An Anthropological Study of Spirit Possession and Shamanism*. Harmondsworth: Penguin Books, 1978.

Liṅga-purāṇa. Edited by J. V. Bhattacharya. Calcutta: J. V. Bhattacharya, 1885.

The Liṅga-Purāṇa. Translated by a Board of Scholars. 2 parts. Delhi: Motilal Banarsidass, 1973.

MacKay, E. J. H. *Further Excavations at Mohenjo-daro*. 2 vols. Delhi: Government of India Press, 1938.

Mahābhāgavata-purāṇa. Bombay: Manilal Itcharam Desai, 1913.

Mahābhārata. Edited by Vishnu S. Sukthankar et al. Poona: Bhandarkar Oriental Research Institute, 1933.

The Mahābhārata. Translated and edited by J. A. B. van Buitenen. Vol. 1: *The Book of the Beginning*. Vol. 2: *The Book of the Assembly Hall and the Book of the Forest*. Vol. 3: *The Book of Virāṭa and the Book of the Effort*. Chicago: University of Chicago Press, 1973, 1975, 1978. (Incomplete.)

The Mahabharata of Krishna-Dwaipayana. Translated by K. M. Ganguly. 12 vols. Calcutta: Oriental Publishing Co., n.d.

Mahalingam, T. V. "The Cult of Śakti in Tamilnad." In D. C. Sircar, ed. *The Śakti Cult and Tārā*, pp. 17-33. Calcutta: University of Calcutta, 1967.

Mahānirvāna-tantra. See *Tantra of the Great Liberation*.

M. [Mahendranath Gupta]. *The Gospel of Sri Ramakrishna*. Translated by Swami Nikhilananda. New York: Ramakrishna-Vivekananda Center, 1942.

Maity, Pradyot Kumar. *Historical Studies in the Cult of the Goddess Manasā*. Calcutta: Punthi Pustak, 1966.

Majumdar, A. K. *Caitanya, His Life and Doctrine: A Study of Vaiṣṇavism*. Bombay: Bharatiya Vidya Bhavan, 1969.

Majumdar, R. C., ed. *History of Bengal*. 2 vols. Dacca: Dacca University, 1943.

Majumdar, R. C., H. C. Rachaudhuri, and Kalikinkar Datta. *An Advanced History of India*. New York: St. Martin's Press, 1967.

Manu-dharma-śāstra. See *The Laws of Manu*.

Marshall, Sir John, ed. *Mohenjo-daro and the Indus Civilization*. 3 vols. London: Arthur Probshtan, 1931.

Matsya-purāṇa. Bombay: Veṅkaṭesvara Press, 1938.

Matsya Purāṇam. Translated by a Taluqdar of Oudh. Allahabad: Sudhindra Nath Vasu, 1916.

Maury, Curt. *Folk Origins of Indian Art*. New York: Columbia University Press, 1969.

McKnight, Michael. "Kingship and Religion in the Gupta Age." Ph.D. diss., McMaster University, 1976.

Mishra, Vibhuti Bhushan. *Religious Beliefs and Practices of North India during the Early Medieval Period*. Leiden: E. J. Brill, 1973.

Mookerjee, Ajit. *Tantra Art: Its Philosophy and Physics*. New Delhi: Ravi Kumar, 1966.

———. *Tantra Asana: A Way to Self-Realization*. New Delhi: Ravi Kumar, 1971.

Mookerjee, A., and Madhu Khanna. *The Tantric Way: Art, Science, Ritual*. London: Thames and Hudson, 1977.

Mukerji, Abhay Charan. *Hindu Feasts and Fasts*. Allahabad: Indian Press, 1916.

Mukherji, S. C. *A Study of Vaiṣṇavism in Ancient and Medieval Bengal*. Calcutta: Punthi Pustak, 1966.

Nandi, Ramendra Nath. *Religious Institutions and Cults in the Decan*. Delhi: Motilal Banarsidass, 1973.

Narayanan, Vasudha. "The Goddess Śrī: The Blossoming Lotus and Breast Jewel of Viṣṇu." In John Stratton Hawley and Donna Marie Wulff, eds., *The Divine Consort: Rādhā and the Goddesses of India*, pp. 224–237. Berkeley, Calif.: Berkeley Religious Studies Series, 1982.

———. "*Karma* and *Kṛpā*. Human Bondage and Divine Grace: The Teṅkalai Śrī Vaiṣṇava Position." DePaul University, n.d.

O'Flaherty, Wendy Doniger. *Asceticism and Eroticism in the Mythology of Śiva*. London: Oxford University Press, 1973.

———. *Hindu Myths*. Baltimore: Penguin Books, 1975.

Öster, Ákos. *The Play of the Gods: Locality, Ideology, Structure, and Time in the Festivals of a Bengali Town*. Chicago: University of Chicago Press, 1980.

Ostroff, Pearl. "The Demon-slaying Devī: A Study of Her Purāṇic Myths." M.A. thesis, McMaster University, 1978.

Padma-purāṇa. Edited by Khemaraj Srikrishnadas. Bombay: Venkatesvara Press, n.d.

Parry, Jonathan. "Death and Cosmogony in Kāshī." *Contributions to Indian Sociology* 15 (1981): 337–365.

Payne, Ernest Alexander. *The Śāktas*. Calcutta: YMCA Publishing House, 1933.

Piggott, Stuart. *Prehistoric India*. Harmondsworth: Penguin Books, 1950.

Prince Ilango Adigal. *Shilappadikaram*. Translated by Alain Danielou. New York: New Directions Book, 1965.

Principles of Tantra: The Tantratattva of Śrīyukta Śiva Candra Vidyārnava Bhattācārya Mahodaya. Edited by Arthur Avalon. Madras: Ganesh, 1960.

Przyluski, J. "The Great Goddess of India and Iran." *Indian Historical Quarterly* 10 (1934): 405–430.

Rama Prasada's Devotional Songs: The Cult of Shakti. Translated by Jadunath Sinha. Calcutta: Sinha Publishing House, 1966.

Rāmāyaṇa. Edited by J. M. Mehta and others. Baroda: Oriental Institute, 1960.

The Ramayana of Valmiki. Translated by Hari Prasad Shastri. 3 vols. London: Shantisadan, 1957–62.

Rangaswamy, M. A. Dorai. *The Religion and Philosophy of Tēvāram*. 2 books. Madras: University of Madras, 1958.

Rao, T. A. Gopinatha. *Elements of Hindu Iconography*. 2d ed. 2 vols. New York: Paragon, 1968.

Rawson, Philip. *The Art of Tantra*. London: Thames and Hudson, 1973.

Ṛg-veda. With the commentary of Sāyaṇa. Edited by N. S. Sontakke and C. G. Kashikar. 5 vols. Poona: Vaidika Saṁsodhana Maṇḍala, 1933–51.

Ṛg-veda. See *Hymns of the Ṛgveda*.

The Śākta Upaniṣads. Translated by A. G. Krisna Warrier. Madras: Adyar Library and Research Center, 1967.

Saraswati, Bandana. "The History of the Worship of Srī in North India to cir. A.D. 550." Ph.D. diss., University of London, 1971.

Śatapatha-brāhmaṇa. Edited by Albrecht Weber. Banaras: Chowkhamba Sanskrit Series, 1964.

The Śatapatha-brāhmaṇa. Translated by Julius Eggeling. 5 vols. Delhi: Motilal Banarsidass, 1966.

The Saundaryalaharī or *Flood of Beauty*. Edited and translated by W. Norman Brown. Cambridge, Mass.: Harvard University Press, 1958.

Schrader, F. Otto. *Introduction to the Pāncarātra and the Ahirbudhnya Saṃhitā*. Madras: Adyar Library, 1916.

Shulman, David Dean. *Tamil Temple Myths: Sacrifice and Divine Marriage in the South Indian Saiva Tradition*. Princeton, N.J.: Princeton University Press, 1980.

Śilappadihāram. See Prince Ilango Adigal.

Sircar, D. C. "Ardhanārī-Nārāyaṇa." In D. C. Sircar, ed. *Foreigners in Ancient India and Lakṣmī and Sarasvatī in Art and Literature*, pp. 132–141. Calcutta: University of Calcutta, 1970.

______. *The Śākta Pīṭhas*. Delhi: Motilal Banarsidass, 1973.

Sītā-upaniṣad. See *The Śākta Upaniṣads*.

The Śiva-Purāṇa. Translated by a Board of Scholars. 4 vols. Delhi: Motilal Banarsidass, 1970.

Sivaramamurti, C. *Gaṅgā*. New Delhi: Orient Longman, 1976.

———. *Nataraja in Art, Thought and Literature*. New Delhi: National Museum, 1974.

Skanda-purāṇa. 5 vols. Calcutta: Mansukharaja Mora, 1959–62.

Somadeva. *Yaśastilaka*. See Handiqui.

Spratt, Philip. *Hindu Culture and Personality*. Bombay: Manaktalas, 1966.

Srinivas, M. N. *Marriage and Family in Mysore*. Bombay: New Book Co., 1942.

Srivastava, Balram. *Iconography of Śakti: A Study Based on Śrītattvanidhi*. Delhi: Chaukhambha Orientalia, 1978.

Srivastava, M. C. P. *Mother Goddess in Indian Art, Archaeology and Literature*. Delhi: Agam Kala Prakashan, 1979.

Sullivan, Herbert P. "A Re-examination of the Religion of the Indus Civilization." *History of Religions* 4, no. 1 (Summer 1964): 115–125.

Taittirīya-āraṇyaka. 3d ed. 2 vols. Poona: Ānandāśrama Sanskrit Series, 1967–69.

Taittirīya-brāhmaṇa. 2 vols. Poona: Ānandāśrama Sanskrit Series, 1934, 1938.

Tantra of the Great Liberation (Mahānirvāna Tantra). Translated by Arthur Avalon. New York: Dover Publications, 1972.

Tantrasāra. See Kṛṣṇānanda Āgamavāgīśa.

Tārā-tantraṁ. Edited by A. K. Maitra. Ghorāmārā, Rājshāhi: Pandit Purandara Kāvyatirtha, 1913.

Thaplyal, Kiran. "Gajalakṣmī on Seals." In D. C. Sircar, ed. *Foreigners in Ancient India and Lakṣmī and Sarasvatī in Art and Literature*, pp. 112–125. Calcutta: University of Calcutta, 1970.

Thomas, Paul. *Hindu Religion, Customs and Manners*. Bombay: Taraporevala, n.d.

Thompson, Edward J., and Arthur Marshman Spencer, trans. *Bengali Religious Lyrics, Śākta*. Calcutta: Association Press, 1923.

Thurston, Edgar. *Castes and Tribes of Southern India*. 7 vols. Madras: Government Press, 1909.

Tiwari, Jagdish Narain. "Studies in Goddess Cults in Northern India, with Reference to the First Seven Centuries A.D." Ph.D. diss., Australian National University, n.d.

Tod, James. *Annals and Antiquities of Rajast'han*. 2 vols. New Delhi: M. N. Publishers, 1978.

Tucci, Giuseppe. *Tibetan Painted Scrolls*. 2 vols. Rome: Libraria dello Stato, 1949.

Tulsī Dās. *Kavitāvalī*. Translated by F. R. Allchin. London: George Allen and Unwin, 1964.

———. *The Petition to Rām: Hindi Devotional Hymns of the Seventeenth Century (Vinaya-patrikā)*. Translated by F. R. Allchin. London: George Allen and Unwin, 1966.

———. *The Ramayana of Tulsidas*. [*Rāmcarit-mānas*.] Translated by A. G. Atkins. 2 vols. New Delhi: Hindustan Times, n.d.

Turner, Victor. *Dramas, Fields, and Metaphors: Symbolic Action in Human Society*. Ithaca, N.Y.: Cornell University Press, 1974.

______. *Process, Performance and Pilgrimage.* New Delhi: Concept Publishing Co., 1979.

______. *The Ritual Process: Structure and Anti-structure.* Ithaca, N.Y.: Cornell University Press, 1977.

[*Ūpaniṣads*]. *The Thirteen Principal Upanishads.* Translated by Robert Ernest Hume. London: Oxford University Press, 1931.

Vājasaneyī-saṁhitā. Bombay: V. L. Shastri Panikhar, 1912.

Vākpatirāja's Gauḍavaho. Edited and translated by N. G. Suru. Ahmedabad: Prakrit Text Society, 1975.

Vāmana-purāṇa. Edited by Anand Swarup Gupta. Translated into English by S. M. Mukhopadhyaya and others. Banaras: All-India Kashiraj Trust, 1968.

van Buitenen, J. A. B. "On the Archaism of the *Bhāgavata Purāṇa.*" In Milton Singer, ed. *Krishna: Myths, Rites, and Attitudes,* pp. 23–40. Honolulu: East-West Center Press, 1966.

Varāha-purāṇa. Mathura: Gītā Press, n.d.

Vidyāpati. *Love Songs of Vidyāpati.* Translated by Deben Bhattacharya. London: George Allen and Unwin, 1963.

Viennot, Odette. *Les divinités fluviales Gaṅgā et Yamunā.* Paris: Presses Universitaires de France, 1964.

Viṣṇu-dharmottara-purāṇa. Bombay: Venkateśvara Steam Press, 1938.

Viṣṇu-purāṇa. Gorakhpur: Gītā Press, Saṁvat 2024.

[*Viṣṇu-purāṇa*]. *The Vishnu Purana, a System of Hindu Mythology and Tradition.* Translated by H. H. Wilson. 3d ed. Calcutta: Punthi Pustak, 1961.

Vogel, J. P. "The Head-offering to the Goddess in Pallava Sculpture." *Bulletin of the School of Oriental Studies* (London) 6:539–543.

Whitehead, Henry. *The Village Gods of South India.* 2d ed. Delhi: Sumit Publications, 1976.

Worship of the Goddess according to the Kālikāpurāṇa. Translated by K. R. Van Kooij. Leiden: E. J. Brill, 1972.

Wulff, Donna Marie. "A Sanskrit Portrait: Rādhā in the Plays of Rūpa Gosvāmī." In John Stratton Hawley and Donna Marie Wulff, eds., *The Divine Consort: Rādhā and the Goddesses of India,* pp. 27–41. Berkeley, Calif.: Berkeley Religious Studies Series, 1982.

Yocum, Glen. "The Goddess in a Tamil Śaiva Devotional Text, Māṇikkavācakar's *Tiruvācakam.*" *Journal of the American Academy of Religion* 45, no. 1, supplement (March 1977): K, 369–388.

______. *Hymns to the Dancing Śiva: A Study of Māṇikkavācakar's "Tiruvācakam."* Columbia, Mo.: South Asia Books, 1982.

______. "Māṇikkavācakar's Image of Śiva." *History of Religions* 16, No. 1 (August 1976): 20–41.

Zimmer, Heinrich. *The Art of Indian Asia.* 2 vols. New York: Pantheon Books, 1955.

______. "The Indian World Mother." In Joseph Campbell, ed. *The Mystic Vision.* Princeton, N.J.: Princeton University Press, 1976.

______. *Myths and Symbols of Indian Art and Civilization.* Edited by Joseph Campbell. New York: Harper and Row, 1962.

______. *Philosophies of India.* Cleveland: World Publishing Co., 1956.

INDEX